The Best AMERICAN ESSAYS College Edition

The *Best*
AMERICAN
ESSAYS
College Edition

Edited and with an Introduction
by ROBERT ATWAN

Houghton Mifflin Company   Boston   Toronto
Geneva, Illinois   Palo Alto   Princeton, New Jersey

Sponsoring Editor: Kristin Watts Peri
Associate Editor: Nandana Dev Sen
Editorial Assistant: Stefanie Jacobs
Senior Project Editor: Carol Newman
Senior Production/Design Coordinator: Sarah Ambrose
Senior Manufacturing Coordinator: Marie Barnes
Marketing Manager: George Kane

Cover design: Carin Goldberg

Printed in the U.S.A.

Text ISBN: 0-395-69467-1
Examination Copy ISBN 0-395-71666-7

Library of Congress Catalog Card Number: 94-76464

23456789-B-98 97 96 95

Credits

"Hair" by Marcia Aldrich. First published in *Northwest Review*. Copyright © 1992 by Marcia Aldrich. Reprinted by permission of the author.

Atwan, Robert, *The Best American Essays 1988.* Copyright © 1988 by Annie Dillard. Used with permission of Ticknor and Fields.

Atwan, Robert, *The Best American Essays 1993.* Copyright © 1993 by Joseph Epstein. Used with permission of Ticknor and Fields.

Atwan, Robert, *The Best American Essays 1986.* Copyright © 1986 by Elizabeth Hardwick. Used with permission of the author.

Atwan, Robert, *The Best American Essays 1990.* Copyright © 1990 by Justin Kaplan. Used with permission of Ticknor and Fields.

Atwan, Robert, *The Best American Essays 1991.* Copyright © 1991 by Joyce Carol Oates. Used with permission of Ticknor and Fields.

Atwan, Robert, *The Best American Essays 1992.* Copyright © 1992 by Susan Sontag. Used with permission of Ticknor and Fields.

Atwan, Robert, *The Best American Essays 1987.* Copyright © 1987 by Gay Talese. Used with permission of Ticknor and Fields.

troduction to *The Art of Mickey Mouse*, edited by Craig Yoe and Janet Morra-Yoe, published by Hyperion. Reprinted by permission of the author.

"How to Get Out of a Locked Trunk" by Philip Weiss. First published in *Harper's Magazine*. Copyright © 1992 by Philip Weiss. Reprinted by permission of the author.

"The Killing Game" by Joy Williams. First published in *Esquire*. Copyright © 1990 by Joy Williams. Reprinted by permission of the author.

In Memory of

Randy Shilts
(1951–1994)

Lewis Thomas
(1913–1993)

Contents

1. IDENTITY • 17

"In maturity, I'm incapable of assuming a coherent or consistent philosophy. I have wayward hair: it's always becoming something else."

"Black though I may be, it is impossible for me to sit in my single-family house with two cars in the driveway and a swing set in the back yard and *not* see the role class has played in my life."

"My fantasy, taken up in early adolescence and not quite dropped to this day, is that I can roam freely from social class to social class, comfortable everywhere and everywhere welcome."

"I tell him it's the rule, rather than the exception, that people from families like ours have very spooky sexual identity problems. He tells me that his sexuality is a birth defect."

"I was fifteen when I started my romance with Indians, and I only knew that I was in love with life outside the constricting white mainstream, and with all the energy that vibrates on the outer reaches of cultural stability."

2. HERITAGE • 83

"The men drank Palo Viejo rum, and some of the younger ones got weepy. The first time I saw a grown man cry was at a New Year's Eve party: he had been reminded of his mother by the smells in the kitchen."

"The tools in my workbench are a double inheritance, for each hammer and level and saw is wrapped in a cloud of knowing."

"He gave his testimony to me and I held it at first cautiously in my conscience like it was an heirloom too delicate to expose to strangers and anyone outside of the world Kubota made with his words."

"Somewhere close behind me the outline of Thoreau's small cabin plods along, a ghost set on haunting. It even has the same rueful eyes Henry David had in the portrait in his book. A wealthy woman with a floral breakfast nook once told me I would 'get over him' but I have not — documented here, I have not."

"Storytelling and make-believe, like war and agriculture, are among the arts of self-defense, and all of them are ways of enclosing otherness and claiming ownership."

"I had written a book to change the world, and here I was on talk shows throughout America, answering questions about mosquitoes and gay waiters."

"Dramatically perverse sexual signals are always powerful elements in the modern fashionable vocabulary; and the most sensational component among present trends is something referred to as androgyny."

"Justice Oliver Wendell Holmes's classic example of unprotected speech — falsely shouting 'Fire!' in a crowded theater — has been invoked so often, by so many people, in such diverse contexts, that it has become part of our national folk language."

5. SURVIVAL • 247

"People with sunny natures do seem to live longer than people who are nervous wrecks; yet mankind didn't evolve out of the animal kingdom by being unduly sunny-minded."

"For most of us, as people of crisis, it became clear that horror can last only a little while, and then it becomes commonplace."

"My legs were lifeless, useless, but their loss had created a dancing image in whose shadowy gyrations I recognized a strange but potentially interesting new self. I would survive."

"Last spring at this time I was coming out of a bout with pneumonia. I went to bed on January first and didn't get up until the end of February. Winter was a cocoon in which my gagging, basso cough shook the dark figures at the end of my bed."

"To kill is to put to death, extinguish, nullify, cancel, destroy. But from the hunter's point of view, it's just a tiny part of the experience."

6. JOURNEYS • 332

"When my teacher had pinned this map up on the blackboard, she said, 'This is England'—and she said it with authority, seriousness, and adoration, and we all sat up. It was as if she had said, "This is Jerusalem, the place you will go to when you die but only if you have been good.""

"I waited until I held his eye. I assured him I would not tell anyone else how to get there. He looked at me with stoical despair, like a man who had been robbed twice, whose belief in human beings was offered without conviction."

"Among sacred pilgrimage sites of the world—far-off snowy peaks on which gods are thought to dance, thronged temples by the Ganges, gold-domed cathedrals or humble country altars—the French shrine of Lourdes in its gloomy mountain setting may be one of the most instructive."

"Tourists are all children at history's knee, begging for some snatch of song or scrap of idea to play with. Though all the world's a stage, we prefer the sideshow."

"We also respect an authenticity of *place*. Genuine objects out of context and milieu may foster intrigue, but rarely inspiration. London Bridge dismantled and reassembled in America becomes a mere curiosity."

7. AMERICANA • 384

"Yet survival cannot be imposed through weight of publicity; Mickey's persistence springs from something unhyped, something timeless in the image that has allowed it to pass in status from a fad to an icon."

"Promotion was what made Elvis Presley. In 1977, the year of his death, his likeness was more widely reproduced than any other save that of Mickey Mouse, and it has been reported that the news of his demise was greeted by one cynic with the words "Good career move!""

"The Miss America pageant is the worst sort of 'Americanism,' the soft smile of sex and the hard sell of toothpaste and hair dye ads wrapped in the dreamy ideological gauze of 'making it through one's own effort.' "

"For nearly thirty years, platoons of conspiricists have concertedly scavenged the record, floating their appalling and thrilling might-have-beens, unfazed by the contradictions and absurdities in their own wantonly selective accounts, often consciously, cunningly deceitful."

"Animal-rights publications are illustrated largely with photographs of two kinds of animals —"Helpless Fluff" and "Agonized Fluff," the two conditions in which some people seem to prefer their animals, because any other version of an animal is too complicated for propaganda."

ALTERNATIVE ARRANGEMENTS • 463

Preface

Back in the 1970s Edward Hoagland wondered why no one compiled an annual collection of the year's best essays, especially since comparable short story volumes had been around for decades. I agreed with Hoagland, and after a few false starts (I thought at first of calling the series "The E. B. White Awards" and later "The Emerson Awards"), I founded *The Best American Essays* as a companion volume to Houghton Mifflin's *The Best American Short Stories.* The first volume was published in 1986. Since then, the series has grown in popularity; each year more and more readers seem drawn to the vitality and versatility of the contemporary American essay.

For readers unfamiliar with the series, a brief introduction may be useful. As the series editor, I screen hundreds of essays from an enormous variety of general, specialized, and literary magazines: I then turn over a large number of candidates to a guest editor, a prominent American writer, who makes the final selection of approximately twenty essays. To qualify for selection, the essays must be works of high literary quality intended as fully developed, independent essays on subjects of general interest, originally written in English for first appearance in an American periodical during a calendar year. In general, selections for the book are included on the basis of literary achievement: they must be admirably written and demonstrate an awareness of craft as well as a forcefulness of thought. Since each guest editor, of course, possesses a different idea about what comprises a fine essay, each book also represents a unique literary sensibility. This variety of literary taste and opinion (which can be sampled in the prologue, "On the Essay") keeps the series healthy and diverse.

This edition of *The Best American Essays* is designed for college students and classroom use. Essays have long been a staple of writing courses, so why not a collection of "the best" contemporary essays for today's students? I believe that many writing instructors wish to expose their students to high-quality, relevant, and intellectually challenging prose. With this end in mind, I selected thirty-five essays from the first eight volumes in the series — 1986–1993. From the pool of one hundred and sixty-two essays published during that period, I chose those essays that, for a variety of reasons (length, topicality, rhetorical and thematic diversity, etc.), would work best for writing instructors and their classes. Still, *The Best American Essays, College Edition* represents work from each of the annual volumes and contains many essays that have — if repeated publication is any indication — been among the most popular of the series.

To make this edition more suitable to writing courses, I arranged the essays within seven thematic chapters. The themes were not arbitrarily imposed on the essays; as I went through the eight volumes, I noticed a number of recurring themes which I used to organize this edition. The themes, I believe, not only reveal some of the contemporary essay's major preoccupations (such as identity conflicts, cultural heritages, and self-recovery), but they also introduce readers to the dominant types of essay published in our time (personal, expository, and argumentative).

For instructors who prefer to teach essays along different lines, I've included three alternative arrangements: (a) a rhetorical table of contents that rearranges the essays into ten traditional modes or patterns; (b) a table of contents that focuses on salient literary and journalistic features; and (c) a topical organization that places the essays in a context of current issues. I've also drawn from the various "Forewords" I contribute to the annual volumes to develop an introduction to the literary and compositional features of the contemporary American essay. And, though space would not permit the inclusion of the eight guest-editor introductions, I orchestrated twenty incisive excerpts into a prologue that should stimulate critical discussion of the genre and lead to writing assignments.

In addition, to help orient student readers, the volume contains an informative "lead-in" to each essay and a brief biographical note. "Reflections and Responses," a set of questions designed to assist class discussion or to instigate ideas for papers follows each selection. The questions range from a consideration of compositional details to broader reflections on theme and issue. Instructors who wish to delve deeper into the literary and rhetorical features of the essays will appreciate the thorough and perceptive instructor's manual prepared by Elizabeth Huyck (Princton University).

Although anthologies such as this one may appear simple to construct, they actually involve the professional efforts of many people. I wish to extend my thanks, first of all, to the distinguished guest editors I've worked with and whose presence is felt throughout this edition: Elizabeth Hardwick, Gay Talese, Annie Dillard, Geoffrey Wolff, Justin Kaplan, Joyce Carol Oates, Susan Sontag, and Joseph Epstein. Without them there would be no series. I appreciate the enthusiasm for the project and the help I've received from the Houghton Mifflin college staff: from my editors Kristin Watts Peri and Nandana Sen, and from Stefanie Jacobs, who saw the book through production, and Jeff Smith, who copyedited the manuscript and provided many helpful details. George Kane also offered many helpful suggestions. I'm especially grateful to Elizabeth Huyck for producing a superb instructor's manual. I'm much obliged to my assistant, Peter Krass, who managed to keep a thousand moving parts efficiently in place. I appreciate the suggestions of four good friends, Donald McQuade (University of California, Berkeley), Charles O'Neill and Jack Roberts (both of St. Thomas Aquinas College), and William Vesterman (Rutgers University). As always, I'm indebted to my wife, Hélène, for her indispensable support and advice.

—R.A.

The Best AMERICAN ESSAYS College Edition

Encountering the Essay

What Are Essays?

Like poems, plays, and short stories, essays resist simple definition or classification. There are so many types of essays that any attempt to come up with a single, authoritative description of *the* essay is likely to be overly general or critically useless. A well-known handbook to literary terms, for example, doesn't even attempt to define the form: "A moderately brief prose discussion of a restricted topic,'' the entry begins. But it then goes on to say: "Because of the wide application of the term, no satisfactory definition can be arrived at; nor can a wholly acceptable 'classification' of essay types be made." So much writing today goes under the name of essay — celebrity profiles, interviews, political commentary, reviews, reportage, scientific papers, scholarly articles, snippets of humor, and newspaper columns — that it's virtually impossible for readers to obtain any clear and consistent impression of the form.

Though many illustrious examples of "brief prose discussion" can be found in classical Greek and Latin literature, the modern essay had its origins in the European Renaissance. At a time when writers and artists throughout Europe were exploring ways to express their personalities more freely in painting and literature, a French magistrate, Michel de Montaigne, retired to his Bordeaux estate in 1570 and began experimenting with a new kind of prose. Impatient with formal philosophy and academic disquisition, he soon found a way to create a more flexible and personal discourse. Realizing that his efforts fit no conventional category — they could not be termed letters, or memoirs, or treatises — he simply referred to them by the French word *essais,* meaning *attempts, trials,* or *experiments.* By adopting a casual, everyday word to describe his endeavors, Montaigne called attention to the informal character of this new literary genre. His essays were personal, tentative, highly digressive, and wholly unsystematic in their approach to a topic.

Montaigne's brand of essay became for many later writers *the* genuine essay. For William Hazlitt, Virginia Woolf, and E. B. White, this was the only type of essay that could be considered a literary form. It went under different names; sometimes it was called the periodical, informal, or familiar essay. This was to differentiate it from types of prose discourse composed in a more systematic and formal fashion, writing that conformed to objective rather than subjective standards. Some examples of the formal essay are philosophical and ethical arguments, historical and scientific papers, dissertations and critical articles. Today the informal essay is best represented by the personal essay, whereas the most popular type of formal essay is the magazine article. Although writers and editors may use the terms interchangeably, many periodicals routinely distinguish between essay and article in their tables of contents, a distinction that usually boils down to personal memoir or reflection as opposed to reportage or feature stories.

Essays and Articles

If it's impossible to produce an airtight definition of an essay, it's equally impossible to define an article. Like "essay," this all-purpose literary label has a long, complex history. The word goes back to the Latin term for a joint *(artus)* connecting two parts of a body, and its literal use was eventually extended to include the components of writing and discourse. By the eighteenth century, "article" was used regularly for literary compositions that treated a specific topic. The first to use the term in its modern journalistic sense was one of English literature's foremost essayists, Joseph Addison.

Articles require not just a topic, but a timely topic. Unlike essays, articles are usually (a) about something specific and (b) about something of *current* interest. Essays, on the other hand, can take large liberties with subject, theme, organization, and point of view. Essayists tend to be personal, reflective, leisurely; article writers (they used to be called "articlers") usually stay close to the facts, rarely stray from "the point," and seldom interrupt the flow of information with personal opinion or reflection. The essayist will feel comfortable writing about various general topics — friendship, envy, manners, nature. The article writer is often looking for an angle, or "hook," that will directly relate the article to some current event or fashionable trend.

For example: assign the topic of "revenge" to two authors — one who prefers to write personal or familiar essays and one who specializes in journalistic articles or feature stories. Chances are the essayist will take a first-person, reflective look at the nature of revenge, blending together personal experience and literary references. The journalist will most likely conduct several interviews with psychologists and then skillfully choreograph these into an informative piece on how to deal constructively with vengeful emotions. These are, of course, extremes, but they suggest the divergent routes of the essay and article in today's literature. In general, the personal, reflective essay is often found in the literary quarterlies and periodicals; articles, like the example above, are the mainstay of popular magazines.

With a few exceptions, our major magazines print relatively few personal essays. Editors believe that their readers want news and information, not personal reminiscence or leisurely reflection. As a result, the weekly and monthly magazines depend on hard news stories, interviews, profiles, and "service articles" that offer readers practical advice on everything from child rearing to the latest diet. Few of these pieces could be called "literary"; most of them fall rapidly out of date and are not likely to be read even a few months after their appearance. If the personal essayist faces the challenge of making his or her experiences and reflections interesting and relevant, the article writer faces a different challenge: how to handle current issues and topics in such a way that people will still read the work with pleasure long after those issues and topics have vanished from public discussion.

Yet, as the selections in this volume show, most good prose is not easy to pigeonhole. At either end of the spectrum, it's fairly easy to distinguish a literary essay from a journalistic article. But as we move toward the center of the spectrum, the distinctions become less clear. We begin to find a compositional mix: personal essays that depend on research and reporting, topical articles that feature a personal voice and individual viewpoint. Such literary mixtures have become increasingly prevalent in today's magazines and literary periodicals. Note, for example, the selection by the late Randy Shilts, "Talking AIDS to Death." In this superb account of his encounters with the media, Shilts moves deftly between the personal essay and the journalistic article as he shifts from an account of his private experiences with a dying friend to his public confrontations with talk-show personalities and lecture audiences. In a number of the essays collected here, the writers move between the topical requirements of an article and the literary demands of an essay, adroitly balancing fact and observation with the nuances of voice and style, irony and wit.

Personal Essays and Stories

What ultimately makes a piece of prose an essay is usually found in the personal quality of its writing. Many of the essays in this book are not only written in the first-person singular but they are also *about* the first-person singular. As Montaigne proved long ago, the essay is the perfect literary vehicle for both self-disclosure and self-discovery: "The wisdom of my lesson," he wrote, "is wholly in truth, in freedom, in reality." Writers today use the essay to explore their personal relationships, their individual identities, and their ethnic or racial heritages. Personal essays like Judith Ortiz Cofer's "Silent Dancing" and Scott Sanders's "The Inheritance of Tools" are intimate, candid, revealing, close to the pulse of everyday human experience.

Yet "personal" can be a tricky term. Its roots reach back to the Latin *"persona,"* the literal term for "mask." The word was traditionally used for a theatrical character, a *dramatis persona*. Thus, oddly enough, the word we use to convey intimacy and sincerity — we often approvingly speak of someone's *personal* touch — has hidden overtones of disguise and performance. Readers may overlook this double sense of the term, but personal essayists rarely do. They know that the first-person singular is not a simple equivalent of the self, a mere matter of slapping down the word "I" in front of every sentence. They know that the single letter "I" is one of the English language's most complex words.

Who is the "I" of the essay — a real person or a *dramatis persona?* Did Scott Sanders really bang his thumb with a hammer just before learning of his father's death? Did Ann Hodgman actually sample Gaines-burgers to see if they tasted like human food? Does Gerald Early truly enjoy watching Miss America pageants with his wife and children? Or have these essayists contrived incidents and fabricated moods in the interests of creating a story or endorsing a position? Unless we personally know the writers, how can we verify their accounts?

When the essay is philosophical or argumentative, we can decide whether we accept an essayist's opinions or not on the basis of logic, evidence, proof, or internal consistency. For example, we would base our agreement or disagreement with Jacob Cohen's "Yes, Oswald Alone Killed Kennedy" entirely on information that has nothing to do with the author's personal life. But once essayists begin to tell stories — about sampling dog food or playing with their children — they move dangerously close to fiction, especially when they add characters, dialogue, episodes, and climaxes. When constructing personal narratives, the essayist confronts the toughest challenge of the craft: telling stories that are at once artful, true, and *believable*. One of the essayist's most frustrating moments is when he or she relates a true story with the utmost candor and discovers that nobody believes it.

The personal essayist, then, must balance craft and credibility, aesthetics and accuracy. The first-person singular is both person and *persona*, a real person and a literary construct. The "I" is both reporting a story and simultaneously *shaping* one. If essayists hope to be wholly believable, however, they need to worry about too much shaping. A true story doesn't usually come prepackaged in a compellingly dramatic shape — many elements just don't fit in. To be believable, the essayist may narrate a story that doesn't — like much of life itself — possess a satisfying narrative closure. Sometimes what one expects to happen doesn't happen. "The writer in me," writes Frank Conroy in "Think About It," "is tempted to create a scene here — to invent one for dramatic purposes — but of course I can't do that." His literary impulse as a novelist is to create a scene; his honesty as an essayist won't let him. An essay like "Think About It" places the reader directly inside the conflict between essay and story. In fact, the tension between personal essays and stories recurs throughout this collection and is especially apparent in such selections as Garrett Hongo's "Kubota" and William Kittredge's "Home."

The Contemporary American Essay

The personal essay has long existed in a literary twilight zone. Because it presumes to tell a true story yet often employs fictional techniques, it stands awkwardly with one foot in and one foot out of "imaginative" literature. It was partially for this reason that one of America's foremost essayists, E. B. White, complained in 1977 that the essayist "unlike the novelist, the poet, and the playwright, must be content in his self-imposed role of second-class citizen." Writers who have their eyes on a Nobel Prize or "other earthly triumphs," White continued, "had best write a novel, a poem, or a play." White was responding not only to the critical reception of his own work but to a general decline in the literary quality of the American essay. Essays struck a lot of readers as "old-fashioned." When readers thought of essays, they thought of writing that was stiff, stuffy, textbookish — things teachers forced them to read and write in school.

One reason that essays seemed old-fashioned to the American reader was that they were slow in coming to terms with the twentieth century. While William Faulkner, T. S. Eliot, and Eugene O'Neill were radically transforming fiction, poetry, and drama, the essay retained much of its relaxed, genteel, Victorian manner. The essay — with few exceptions — broke no new ground, violated no literary conventions. Instead of trying to become modern works of literature in themselves, essays seemed content with simply trying to explain those works. For the academic community as well as for many general readers, the essay gradually became synonymous with literary criticism. Essays were written *about* literature; they weren't written *as* literature.

Since E. B. White issued his complaint, however, the literary status of the essay has dramatically improved. As Annie Dillard says, the essay "has joined the modern world." Essays are now being written in the same imaginative spirit as fiction and poetry. The contemporary essay can rival the best fiction and poetry in artistic accomplishment. Far from being hesitant about literary aims and methods, today's essayists delight in the use of imagery, symbol, and metaphor, often interweaving them into such complex mosaic patterns as those we find in Judy Ruiz's "Oranges and Sweet Sister Boy" or Gretel Ehrlich's "Spring."

This volume collects and celebrates the contemporary American essay. Never before — except perhaps in the days of Ralph Waldo Emerson and Henry David Thoreau — have so many fine young American writers begun to explore the essay's literary possibilities. They come to the form with a renewed enthusiasm for its astonishing flexibility and versatility — the essay can incorporate an enormously wide range of subjects and styles. The personal essay has grown increasingly candid, more intimate, less polite. Essayists seem willing to take greater emotional risks. Essayists today seem less relaxed and more eager to confront urgent social questions. Journalism has contributed to this sense of risk and urgency, encouraging essayists to fuse within a single style both personal experience and public issues, dual themes that Barry Lopez brilliantly combines in "The Stone Horse."

A Diversity of Voices

We "relish diversity," writes Stephen Jay Gould, speaking as an evolutionary biologist in "Counters and Cable Cars," a selection that in many ways captures the spirit of the contemporary essay. Gould here is writing not about his usual scientific subjects — paleontology and natural history — but about the special joys of a busy San Francisco breakfast counter and an early-morning cable-car ride. For Gould, as for many contemporary essayists, regional and cultural diversity satisfies a fundamental human need — the need for authenticity.

The essays collected in this book represent what Joyce Carol Oates in a perceptive account of today's essay called "the diversity of voices that now constitute the American literary community." Though surprisingly diverse, these essays are nevertheless united in their quest for authenticity, their demand for genuine emotions and experiences, and their sense of urgency. The essay is alive and well in large part because writers like the ones collected here have dared to resist the encroachments of artificiality and standardization, whether it be social, cultural, or academic. "Don't spread it around," Joseph Epstein wrote a few years ago, "but it's a sweet time to be an essayist." This unique and diverse collection goes a long way in proving him right.

On the Essay

Each edition of The Best American Essays *features a guest editor who makes the final selections and writes an introduction to the volume. The guest editors themselves are distinguished American writers, many of whom have excelled in a variety of literary forms. In their introductions, they almost always address the question of the essay: its history, definition, style, audience, composition. Their essays on the essay would in themselves make an interesting collection. What follows are some of their most incisive remarks.*

What Is an Essay?

What *is* an essay, and what, if anything, is it about? "Formal" and "informal," "personal," "familiar," "review-essay," "article-essay," "critical essay," essays literary, biographical, polemic, and historical — the standard lit-crit lexicon and similar attempts at genre definition and subclassification in the end simply tell you how like an eel this essay creature is. It wriggles between narcissism and detachment, opinion and fact, the private party and the public meeting, omphalos and brain, analysis and polemics, confession and reportage, persuasion and provocation. All you can safely say is that it's not poetry and it's not fiction.

—Justin Kaplan

Essays and the Real World

The essay can do everything a poem can do, and everything a short story can do — everything but fake it. The elements in any nonfiction should be true not only artistically — the connections must hold at base and must be veracious, for that is the convention and the covenant between the nonfiction writer and his reader. Veracity isn't much of a drawback to the writer; there's a lot of truth out there to work with. And veracity isn't much of a drawback to the reader. The real world arguably exerts a greater fascination on people than any fictional one; many people, at least, spend their whole lives there, apparently by choice. The essayist does what we do with our lives; the essayist thinks about actual things. He can make sense of them analytically or artistically. In either case he renders the real world coherent and meaningful, even if only bits of it, and even if that coherence and meaning reside only inside small texts.

— Annie Dillard

No Standard Essay

As there is no standard human type who writes essays, so is there no standard essay: no set style, length, or subject. But what does unite almost all successful essays, no matter how divergent the subject, is that a strong personal presence is felt behind them. This is so even if the essayist never comes out to tell you his view of the matter being discussed, never attempts directly to assert his personality, never even slips into the first-person singular. Without that strong personal presence, the essay doesn't quite exist; it becomes an article, a piece, or some other indefinable verbal construction. Even when the subject seems a distant and impersonal one, the self of the writer is in good part what the essay is about.

— Joseph Epstein

The Essay's Diversity

It is not only that the essay *could* be about anything. It usually was. The good health of essay writing depends on writers continuing to address eccentric subjects. In contrast to poetry and fiction, the nature of the essay is diversity — diversity of level, subject, tone, diction. Essays on being old and falling in love and the nature of poetry are still being written. And there are also essays on Rita Hayworth's zipper and Mickey Mouse's ears.

— Susan Sontag

The Memorable Essay

I am predisposed to the essay with knowledge to impart — but, unlike journalism, which exists primarily to present facts, the essays transcend their data, or transmute it into personal meaning. The memorable essay, unlike the article, is not place- or time-bound; it survives the occasion of its original composition. Indeed, in the most brilliant essays, language is not merely the medium of communication, it *is* communication.

— Joyce Carol Oates

What Distinguishes Essays from Articles

Given the confusion of genre minglings and overlaps, what finally distinguishes an essay from an article may just be the author's gumption, the extent to which personal voice, vision, and style are the prime movers and shapers, even though the authorial "I" may be only a remote energy, nowhere visible but everywhere present. ("We commonly do not remember," Thoreau wrote in the opening paragraphs of *Walden,* "that it is, after all, always the first person that is speaking.")

— Justin Kaplan

Essays versus Stories

In some ways the essay can deal in both events and ideas better than the short story can, because the essayist — unlike the poet — may introduce the plain, unadorned thought without the contrived entrances of long-winded characters who mouth discourses.

This sort of awful device killed "the novel of idea." (But eschewing it served to limit fiction's materials a little further, and likely contributed to our being left with the short story of scant idea.) The essayist may reason; he may treat of historical, cultural, or natural events, as well as personal events, for their interest and meaning alone, without resort to fabricated dramatic occasions. So the essay's materials are larger than the story's.

—Annie Dillard

Essays versus Poems

The essay may deal in metaphor better than the poem can, in some ways, because prose may expand what the lyric poem must compress. Instead of confining a metaphor to half a line, the essayist can devote to it a narrative, descriptive, or reflective couple of pages, and bring forth vividly its meanings. Prose welcomes all sorts of figurative language, of course, as well as alliteration, and even rhyme. The range of rhythms in prose is larger and grander than that of poetry. And it can handle discursive idea, and plain fact, as well as character and story.

—Annie Dillard

The Essayist's Defensiveness

No poet has a problem saying, I am a poet. No fiction writer hesitates to say, I am writing a story. "Poem" and "story" are still relatively stable, easily identified literary forms or genres. The essay is not, in that sense, a genre. Rather, "essay" is just one name, the most sonorous name, bestowed on a wide range of writings. Writers and editors usually call them "pieces." This is not just modesty or American casualness. A certain defensiveness now surrounds the notion of the essay. And many of the best essayists today are quick to declare that their best work lies elsewhere: in writing that is more "creative" (fiction, poetry) or more exacting (scholarship, theory, philosophy).

—Susan Sontag

On Being an Essayist

As someone who takes some pride in being known as "Joseph Epstein, an essayist" — or, even better, "the essayist Joseph Epstein" — who takes the term "essayist" as an honorific, I have both an interest and a stake in the form. I hate to see it put down, defamed, spat upon, even mildly slighted. The best luck that any writer can have is to find his or her form, and I feel fortunate in having found mine some twenty years ago in the familiar essay. It happened quite by luck: I was not then a frequent reader of Montaigne and Hazlitt; in those days I was even put off by Charles Lamb, who sometimes seemed to me a bit precious. For me the novel was the form or forms, and easily the one I most admired and should most have liked to master. Although I have published a dozen or so short stories, I have not yet written a novel — nor have I one in mind to write — and so I have to conclude that despite my enormous regard for that form, it just isn't mine. Perhaps it is quite useless for a writer to search for his perfect form; that form, it may well be, has to find him.

—Joseph Epstein

Essayists Must Tell the Truth

I work by Hemingway's precept that a writer's root charge is to distinguish what you really felt in the moment from the false sentiment of what you now believe you should have felt. The personal essay, autobiography, has been a red flag to professional classifiers and epistemologists; a critical industry has flourished for the refinement of generic protocols (many in French, with as much fine print as an installment purchase agreement), subcontracted principally to skeptics. In the judgment of Northrop Frye, for instance, a piece of work is shelved with autobiography or with fiction according to whether the librarian chooses to believe it.

Well. I've written one, and I've written the other, and I'm here to testify that the issue is at once weightier and simpler: a personal essayist means to tell the truth. The contract between a personal essayist and a reader is absolute, an agreement about intention. Because memory is fallible, and point of view by its nature biased, the personal essayist will tell a slant tale, willy-nilly. But not by design.

— Geoffrey Wolff

The Essayist's Voice

The influential essayist is someone with an acute sense of what has not been (properly) talked about, what should be talked about (but differently). But what makes essays last is less their argument than the display of a complex mind and a distinctive prose voice.

— Susan Sontag

The "Who Cares?" Factor

Not every voice a great soliloquy makes, a truth at odds with the education of many an American writer, with the education of *this* American writer. I remember (see how difficult, even now, to break the habit of that pronoun, that solipsistic verb), at boarding school in England, writing about Cordelia in the moment when she recognizes how mistaken is her father's measurement of affection. I spent the greater part of my allotted space telling about a tangled misunderstanding between my dad and myself: "So I understand just how Cordelia felt." Of course my teacher wrote "who cares?" Of course he was right to write that: to filter all data through the mesh of personal relevance is the voice's tyrannical sway over listener and speaker alike. Sometimes it should be okay to take facts in, quietly manipulate them behind an opaque scrim, and display them as though the arranger never arranged. It should be all right to mediate, let another voice speak through your spirit medium, pretend as a writer not to be front and center on stage.

— Geoffrey Wolff

The Conversational Style

While there is no firmly set, single style for the essayist, styles varying with each particular essayist, the best general description of essayistic style was written in 1827 by William Hazlitt in his essay "Familiar Style." "To write a genuine familiar or truly English style," Hazlitt wrote, "is to write as any one would speak in common conversation who had a thorough command and choice of words, who could discourse with ease, force, and perspicuity, setting aside all pedantic and oratorical flourishes." The style of the essayist is that of an extremely intelligent, highly commonsensical person talking, without stammer and with impressive coherence, to him- or herself and to anyone else who cares to eavesdrop. This self-reflexivity, this notion of talking to oneself, has always seemed to me to mark the essay off from the lecture. The lecturer is always teaching; so, too, frequently is the critic. If the essayist does so, it is usually only indirectly.

—Joseph Epstein

The Essayist's Audience

Essays are addressed to a public in which some degree or equity exists between the writer and the reader. Shared knowledge is a necessity, although the information need not be concrete. Perhaps it is more to be thought of as a sharing of the experience of reading certain kinds of texts, texts with omissions and elisions, leaps. The essayist does not stop to identify the common ground; he will not write, "Picasso, the great Spanish painter who lived long in France." On the other hand, essays are about something, something we may not have had reason to study and master, often matters about which we are quite ignorant. Elegance of presentation, reflection made interesting and significant, easily lead us to engage our reading minds with Zulus, herbaceous borders in the English garden, marriage records in eighteenth-century France, Japanese scrolls.

—Elizabeth Hardwick

Essays Start Out in Magazines

Essays end up in books, but they start their lives in magazines. (It's hard to imagine a book of recent but previously unpublished essays.) The perennial comes now mainly in the guise of the topi-

cal and, in the short run, no literary form has as great and immediate an impact on contemporary readers. Many essays are discussed, debated, reacted to in a way that poets and writers of
fiction can only envy.

—Susan Sontag

On Certain Magazine Interviews

I myself have been interviewed by writers carrying recorders,
and as I sit answering their questions, I see them half-listening,
nodding pleasantly, and relaxing in the knowledge that the little
wheels are rolling. But what they are getting from me (and I assume from other people they talk to) is not the insight that comes
from deep probing and perceptive analysis and old-fashioned
legwork; it is rather the first-draft drift of my mind, a once-over-
lightly dialogue that — while perhaps symptomatic of a society permeated by fast-food computerized bottom-line impersonalized
workmanship — too frequently reduces the once-artful craft of
magazine writing to the level of talk radio on paper.

—Gay Talese

Listening to People Think

Quoting people verbatim, to be sure, has rarely blended well
with my narrative style of writing or with my wish to observe and
describe people actively engaged in ordinary but revealing situations rather than to confine them to a room and present them in
the passive posture of a monologist. Since my earliest days in journalism, I was far less interested in the exact words that came out of
people's mouths than in the essence of their meaning. More important than what people say is what they think, even though the
latter may initially be difficult for them to articulate and may require much pondering and reworking within the interviewee's
mind — which is what I gently try to prod and stimulate as I query,
interrelate, and identify with my subjects as I personally accompany them whenever possible, be it on their errands, their
appointments, their aimless peregrinations before dinner or after
work. Wherever it is, I try physically to be there in my role as a

curious confidant, a trustworthy fellow traveler searching into their interior, seeking to discover, clarify, and finally to describe in words (my words) what they personify and how they think.

—Gay Talese

On the Subjects of Essays

Those with the least gift are most anxious to receive a commission. It seems to them that there lies waiting a topic, a new book, a performance, and that this is known as material. The true prose writer knows there is nothing given, no idea, no text or play seen last evening until an assault has taken place, the forced domination that we call "putting it in your own words." Talking about, thinking about a project bears little relation to the composition; enthusiasm boils down with distressing speed to a paragraph, often one of mischievous banality. To proceed from musing to writing is to feel a robbery has taken place. And certainly there has been a loss; the loss of the smiles and ramblings and discussions so much friendlier to ambition than the cold hardship of writing.

—Elizabeth Hardwick

The Essay's Unlimited Possibilities

The essay is, and has been, all over the map. There's nothing you cannot do with it; no subject matter is forbidden, no structure is proscribed. You get to make up your own structure every time, a structure that arises from the materials and best contains them. The material is the world itself, which, so far, keeps on keeping on. The thinking mind will analyze, and the creative imagination will link instances, and time itself will churn out scenes — scenes unnoticed and lost, or scenes remembered, written, and saved.

In his essay "Home," William Kittredge remembers Jack Ray, his boyhood hero, whom he later hired as a hand on his Oregon ranch. After a bout in jail, Jack Ray would show up in the bunkhouse grinning. "Well, hell, Jack," Kittredge would say. "It's a new day."

"Kid," he would say, "she's a new world every morning."

—Annie Dillard

1

Identity

MARCIA ALDRICH

Hair

Montaigne, the first essayist, would have enjoyed Marcia Aldrich's wonder-ful meditation on hairstyles and the way they reflect our personal identity. When Montaigne began writing personal essays in the 1570s, he initiated a new style of self-portrayal. He brought his whole body into his writing, inviting his readers to see his essays not simply as thoughts on a page but as an extension of his physical being. Not having (as he put it) an "imposing presence" in actual life, he tried to create one in and through his remark-able essays. A very "physical" writer, he would discuss his looks, height, voice, and complexion, the way he walked and his habit of scratching the inside of his ears. A persistent self-reviser, Montaigne would also appreciate Aldrich's resistance to a settled style ("a new hair style," she says, "will write over the last") and to a coherent philosophy.

Marcia Aldrich is an assistant professor of English who specializes in twentieth-century poetry at Michigan State University. "Hair" will form part of The X Woman, *a longer work of prose pieces inspired by letters of the alphabet. She is also working on a study of the poet Louise Bogan. "Hair" originally appeared in* The Northwest Review *(1992) and was selected by Joseph Epstein for* The Best American Essays 1993.

I've been around and seen the Taj Mahal and the Grand Canyon and Marilyn Monroe's footprints outside Grauman's Chinese The-ater, but I've never seen my mother wash her own hair. After my mother married, she never washed her own hair again. As a girl and an unmarried woman — yes — but, in my lifetime, she never washed her hair with her own two hands. Upon matrimony, she began weekly treks to the beauty salon where Julie washed and styled her hair. Her appointment on Fridays at two o'clock was never cancelled or rescheduled; it was the bedrock of her week, around which she pivoted and planned. These two hours were indispensable to my mother's routine, to her sense of herself and what, as a woman, she should concern herself with — not to mention their being her primary source of information about all sorts of things she wouldn't otherwise come to know. With Julie my mother discussed momentous decisions concerning hair color and the advancement of age and what could be done about it, hair length and its effect upon maturity, when to perm and when not to perm, the need to proceed with caution when a woman desperately wanted a major change in her life like dumping her husband or sending back her newborn baby and the only change she could effect was a change in her hair. That was what Julie called a "dangerous time" in a woman's life. When my mother spoke to Julie, she spoke in conspiratorial, almost confessional, tones I had never heard before. Her voice was usually tense, on guard, the laughter forced, but with Julie it dropped much lower, the timbre darker than the upper-register shrills sounded at home. And most remarkably, she listened to everything Julie said.

As a child I was puzzled by the way my mother's sense of self-worth and mood seemed dependent upon how she thought her hair looked, how the search for the perfect hairstyle never ended. Just as Mother seemed to like her latest color and cut, she began to agitate for a new look. The cut seemed to have become a melancholy testimony, in my mother's eyes, to time's inexorable passage. Her hair never stood in and of itself; it was always moored to a complex set of needs and desires her hair couldn't in itself satisfy. She wanted her hair to illuminate the relationship between herself and the idea of motion while appearing still, for example. My mother wanted her hair to be fashioned into an event with a complicated narrative past. However, the more my mother attempted to impose a hairstyle pulled from an idealized image of herself, the more the hairstyle seemed to be at odds with my mother. The more the hairstyle became substantial, the more the woman underneath was obscured. She'd riffle through women's magazines and stare for long dreamy hours at a particular woman's coiffure. Then she'd ask my father in an artificially casual voice: "How do you think I'd look with really short hair?" or "Would blonde become me?" My father never committed himself to an opinion. He had learned from long experience that no response he made could turn out well; anything he said would be used against him, if not in the immediate circumstances, down the line, for my mother never forgot anything anyone ever said about her hair. My father's refusal to engage the "hair question" irritated her.

So too, I was puzzled to see that unmarried women washed their own hair, and married women, in my mother's circle at least, by some unwritten dictum never touched their own hair. I began studying before and after photographs of my mother's friends. These photographs were all the same. In the pre-married mode, their hair was soft and unformed. After the wedding, the women's hairstyles bore the stamp of property, looked constructed from grooming talents not their own, hairstyles I'd call produced, requiring constant upkeep and technique to sustain the considerable loft and rigidity — in short, the antithesis of anything I might naively call natural. This was hair no one touched, crushed, or ran fingers through. One poked and prodded various hair masses back into formation. This hair presented obstacles to embrace, the scent of the hair spray alone warded off man, child, and pests. I never saw my father stroke my mother's head. Children whimpered when my mother came home fresh from the salon with a potent do. Just when a woman's life was supposed to be opening out into daily affection, *the* sanctioned affection of husband and children, the women of my mother's circle encased themselves in a helmet of hair not unlike Medusa's.

In so called middle age, my mother's hair never moved, never blew, never fell in her face: her hair became a museum piece. When she went to bed, she wore a blue net, and when she took short showers, short because, after all, she wasn't washing her hair and she was seldom dirty, she wore a blue plastic cap for the sake of preservation. From one appointment to the next, the only change her hair could be said to undergo was to become crestfallen. Taking extended vacations presented problems sufficiently troublesome to rule out countries where she feared no beauty parlors existed. In the beginning, my parents took overnighters, then week jaunts, and thereby avoided the whole hair dilemma. Extending their vacations to two weeks was eventually managed by my mother applying more hair spray and sleeping sitting up. But after the two week mark had been reached, she was forced to either re-

turn home or venture into an unfamiliar salon and subject herself
to scrutiny, the kind of scrutiny that leaves no woman unscathed.
Then she faced Julie's disapproval, for no matter how expensive
and expert the salon, my mother's hair was to be lamented. Speaking just for myself, I had difficulty distinguishing Julie's cunning
from the stranger's. In these years my mother's hair looked curled,
teased, and sprayed into a waved tossed monument with holes
poked through for glasses. She believed the damage done to her
hair was tangible proof she had been somewhere, like stickers on
her suitcases.

My older sisters have worked out their hair positions differently.
My oldest sister's solution has been to fix upon one hairstyle and
never change it. She wants to be thought of in a singular fashion.
She may vary the length from long to longer, but that is the extent
of her alteration. Once, after having her first baby, the "dangerous
time" for women, she recklessly cut her hair to just below the ear.
She immediately regretted the decision and began growing it back
as she walked home from the salon, vowing not to repeat the mistake. Her signature is dark, straight hair pulled heavily off her face
in a large silver clip, found at any Woolworth's. When one clip
breaks, she buys another just like it. My mother hates the timeless-
ness of my sister's hair. She equates it with a refusal to face growing
old. My mother says, "It's immature to wear your hair the same way
all your life." My sister replies,

"It's immature to never stop thinking about your hair. If this
hairstyle was good enough when I was twenty, it's good enough
when I'm forty, if not better."

"But what about change?" my mother asks.

"Change is overrated," my sister says flipping her long hair over
her shoulder definitively. "I feel my hair."

My other sister was born with thin, lifeless, nondescript hair: a
cross she has had to bear. Even in the baby pictures, the limp
strands plastered on her forehead in question marks wear her
down. Shame and self-effacement are especially plain in the pictures where she posed with our eldest sister, whose dark hair dom-
inates the frame. She's spent her life attempting to disguise the
real state of her hair. Some years she'd focus on style, pulling it
back in ponytails so that from the front no one could see there
wasn't much hair in the back. She tried artless, even messy styles —

as if she had just tied it up any old way before taking a bath or bunched it to look deliberately snarled. There were the weird years punctuated by styles that looked as if she had taken sugar water and lemon juice and squeezed them onto her wet hair and then let them crystallize. The worst style was when she took her hair and piled it on the top of her head in a cone shape and then crimped the ponytail into a zigzag. Personally, I thought she had gone too far. No single approach solved the hair problem, and so now, in maturity, she combines the various phases of attack in hope something will work. She frosts both the grey strands and the pale brown, and then perms for added body and thickness. She's forced to keep her hair short because chemicals do tend to destroy. My mother admires my sister's determination to transform herself, and never more than in my sister's latest assault upon middle age. No one has known for many years nor does anyone remember what the untreated color or texture of either my mother's or my sister's hair might be.

As the youngest by twelve years, there was little to distract Mother's considerable attention from the problem of my hair. I had cowlicks, a remarkable number of them, which like little arrows shot across my scalp. They refused to be trained, to lie down quietly in the same direction as the rest of my hair. One at the front insisted on sticking straight up while two on either side of my ears jutted out seeking sun. The lack of uniformity, the fact that my hair had a mind of its own, infuriated my mother and she saw to it that Julie cut my hair as short as possible in order to curtail its wanton expression. Sitting in the swivel chair before the mirror while Julie snipped, I felt invisible, as if I was unattached to my hair.

Just when I started to menstruate, my mother decided the battle plan needed a change, and presto, the page boy replaced the pixie. Having not outgrown the thicket of cowlicks, Mother bought a spectrum of brightly colored stretch bands to hold my hair back off my face. Then she attached thin pink plastic curlers with snap on lids to the ends of my hair to make them flip up or under, depending on her mood. The stretch bands pressed my hair flat until the very bottom, at which point the ends formed a tunnel with ridges from the roller caps — a point of emphasis, she called it. Coupled with the aquamarine eyeglasses, newly acquired, I looked like an overgrown insect that had none of its kind to bond with.

However, I was not alone. Unless you were the last in a long line of sisters, chances were good that your hair would not go unnoticed by your mother. Each of my best friends was subjected to her mother's hair dictatorship, although with entirely different results. Perry Jensen's mother insisted that all five of her daughters peroxide their hair blonde and pull it back into high ponytails. All the girls' hair turned green in the summer from chlorine. Melissa Matson underwent a look-alike "home perm" with her mother, an experience she never did recover from. She developed a phobic reaction to anything synthetic, which made life very expensive. Not only did mother and daughter have identical tight curls and wear mother-daughter outfits, later they had look-alike nose jobs.

In my generation, many women who survived hair bondage to their mothers now experiment with hairstyles as one would test a new design: to see how it works, what it will withstand, and how it can be improved. Testing requires boldness, for often the style fails dramatically, as when I had my hair cut about a half inch long at the top, and it stood straight up like a tacky shag carpet. I had to live with the results, bear daily witness to the kinks in its design for nine months until strategies of damage control could be deployed. But sometimes women I know create a look that startles in its originality and suggests a future not yet realized.

The women in my family divide into two general groups: those who fasten upon one style, become identified with a look, and are impervious to change, weathering the years steadfastly, and those who, for a variety of reasons, are in the business of transforming themselves. In my sister's case, the quest for perfect hair originates in a need to mask her own appearance; in my mother's case, she wants to achieve a beauty of person unavailable in her own life story. Some women seek transformation, not out of dissatisfaction with themselves, but because hair change is a means of moving along in their lives. These women create portraits of themselves that won't last forever, a new hairstyle will write over the last.

Since my mother dictated my hair, I never took a stand on the hair issue. In maturity, I'm incapable of assuming a coherent or consistent philosophy. I have wayward hair: it's always becoming something else. The moment it arrives at a recognizable style, it begins to undo itself, it grows, the sun colors it, it waves. When one hair pin goes in, another seems to come out. Sometimes I think I should follow my oldest sister — she claims to never give more than a passing thought to her hair and can't see what all the angst is about. She asks, "Don't women have better things to think about than their hair?"

I bite back: "But don't you think hair should reflect who you are?"

"To be honest, I've never thought about it. I don't think so. Cut your hair the same way, and lose your self in something else. You're distracted from the real action."

I want to do what my sister says, but when I walk out into shop-lined streets, I automatically study women's hair and always with the same question: How did they arrive at their hair? Lately, I've been feeling more and more like my mother. I hadn't known how to resolve the dilemma until I found Rhonda. I don't know if I found Rhonda or made her up. She is not a normally trained hair-dresser: she has a different set of eyes, unaffected. One day while out driving around to no place in particular, at the bottom of a hill, I found: "Rhonda's Hair Salon — Don't Look Back" written on a life-size cardboard image of Rhonda. Her shop was on the top of this steep orchard planted hill, on a plateau with a great view that opened out and went on forever. I parked my car at the bottom and walked up. Zigzagging all the way up the hill, leaning against or sticking out from behind the apple trees were more life-sized cardboard likenesses of Rhonda. Except for the explosive sun-bursts in her hair, no two signs were the same. At the bottom, she wore long red hair falling below her knees and covering her entire body like a shawl. As I climbed the hill, Rhonda's hair gradually be-came shorter and shorter, and each length was cut differently, until when I reached the top, her head was shaved and glistening in the sun. I found Rhonda herself out under one of the apple trees wearing running shoes. Her hair was long and red and looked as if it had never been cut. She told me she had no aspira-tions to be a hairdresser, "she just fell into it." "I see hair," she con-tinued, "as an extension of the head and therefore I try to do hair with a lot of thought." Inside there were no mirrors, no swivel chairs, no machines of torture with their accompanying stink. She said, "Nothing is permanent, nothing is forever. Don't feel ham-pered or hemmed in by the shape of your face or the shape of your past. Hair is vital, sustains mistakes, can be born again. You don't have to marry it. Now tip back and put your head into my hands."

Reflections and Responses

1. Consider how Aldrich invites you to see hairstyles in terms of personal identity. Compare the different female members of her family. How does each reflect a different philosophical attitude through her hairstyle? What are they? Why do you think Aldrich left her father out of these reflections?

2. How does Aldrich establish a relationship between hairstyle and writing style? For Aldrich, what do the two have in common? In going through her essay, identify some features of her writing style that also reflect her attitude toward her hair.

3. Reread Aldrich's final paragraph carefully. It's tricky. What do you think is happening? Is "Rhonda" real or fictitious? What makes you think she is real? Alternatively, what makes you think Aldrich made her up? Why do you think Aldrich concluded her essay with this visit to Rhonda's Hair Salon?

SHELBY STEELE

On Being Black and Middle Class

One of the most controversial selections to have appeared in The Best American Essay *series, Shelby Steele's 1988 essay disturbed readers who saw it not as a black writer's candid account of his divided identity but rather as an assimilationist endorsement of white America. In refusing to define himself solely along racial lines, Steele appeared to be turning his back on his own people. His essay, however, calls into question this very dilemma: Steele wonders why black middle-class Americans are somehow expected to celebrate the black underclass as the "purest" representation of African American identity. While maintaining that he has more in common with middle-class Americans than with underclass blacks, Steele confesses that he often finds himself contriving to be black, aligning himself with a "victim-focused black identity." He concludes his essay with a distinction he believes African Americans must make if they are to enjoy the opportunities open to them: they must learn, he says, to distinguish between "actual victimization" and "identification with the victim's status." In his resistance to that kind of "identification," Steele establishes his own "identity" as a writer and individual.*

Shelby Steele is a professor of English at San Jose State University. His collection of essays, The Content of Our Character, *won the National Book Critics Circle Award for general nonfiction in 1991. His essays have appeared in a wide variety of periodicals, including* Harper's, The American Scholar, Commentary, The New Republic, Confrontation, Black World, *and* The New York Times Magazine. *"On Being Black and Middle Class" originally appeared in* Commentary *(1988) and was selected by Geoffrey Wolff for* The Best American Essays 1989.

Not long ago, a friend of mine, black like myself, said to me that the term "black middle class" was actually a contradiction in terms. Race, he insisted, blurred class distinctions among blacks. If you were black, you were just black and that was that. When I argued, he let his eyes roll at my naiveté. Then he went on. For us, as black professionals, it was an exercise in self-flattery, a pathetic pretension, to give meaning to such a distinction. Worse, the very idea of class threatened the unity that was vital to the black community as a whole. After all, since when had white America taken note of anything but color when it came to blacks? He then reminded me of an old Malcolm X line that had been popular in the sixties. Question: What is a black man with a Ph.D.? Answer: A nigger.

For many years I had been on my friend's side of this argument. Much of my conscious thinking on the old conundrum of race and class was shaped during my high school and college years in the race-charged sixties, when the fact of my race took on an almost religious significance. Progressively, from the mid-sixties on, more and more aspects of my life found their explanation, their justification, and their motivation in race. My youthful concerns about career, romance, money, values, and even styles of dress became a subject to consultation with various oracular sources of racial wisdom. And these ranged from a figure as ennobling as Martin Luther King, Jr., to the underworld elegance of dress I found in jazz clubs on the South Side of Chicago. Everywhere there were signals, and in those days I considered myself so blessed with clarity and direction that I pitied my white classmates who found more embarrassment than guidance in the fact of *their* race. In 1968, inflated by my new power, I took a mischievous delight in calling them culturally disadvantaged.

But now, hearing my friend's comment was like hearing a priest from a church I'd grown disenchanted with. I understood him, but my faith was weak. What had sustained me in the sixties sounded monotonous and off the mark in the eighties. For me, race had lost much of its juju, its singular capacity to conjure meaning. And today, when I honestly look at my life and the lives of many other middle-class blacks I know, I can see that race never fully explained our situation in American society. Black though I may be, it is impossible for me to sit in my single-family house with two cars in the driveway and a swing set in the back yard and *not* see the role class has played in my life. And how can my friend, similarly raised and similarly situated, not see it?

Yet despite my certainty I felt a sharp tug of guilt as I tried to explain myself over my friend's skepticism. He is a man of many comedic facial expressions and, as I spoke, his brow lifted in extreme moral alarm as if I were uttering the unspeakable. His clear implication was that I was being elitist and possibly (dare he suggest?) anti-black — crimes for which there might well be no redemption. He pretended to fear for me. I chuckled along with him, but inwardly I did wonder at myself. Though I never doubted the validity of what I was saying, I felt guilty saying it. Why?

After he left (to retrieve his daughter from a dance lesson) I realized that the trap I felt myself in had a tiresome familiarity and, in a sort of slow-motion epiphany, I began to see its outline. It was like the suddenly sharp vision one has at the end of a burdensome marriage when all the long-repressed incompatibilities come undeniably to light.

What became clear to me is that people like myself, my friend, and middle-class blacks generally are caught in a very specific double bind that keeps two equally powerful elements of our identity at odds with each other. The middle-class values by which we were raised — the work ethic, the importance of education, the value of property ownership, of respectability, of "getting ahead," of stable family life, of initiative, of self-reliance, etc. — are, in themselves, raceless and even assimilationist. They urge us toward participation in the American mainstream, toward integration, toward a strong identification with the society — and toward the entire constellation of qualities that are implied in the word "individualism." These values are almost rules for how to prosper in a democratic, free-enterprise society that admires and rewards individual effort. They tell us to work hard for ourselves and our families and to seek our opportunities whenever they appear, inside or outside the confines of whatever ethnic group we may belong to.

But the particular pattern of racial identification that emerged in the sixties and that still prevails today urges middle-class blacks (and all blacks) in the opposite direction. This pattern asks us to see ourselves as an embattled minority, and it urges an adversarial stance toward the mainstream, an emphasis on ethnic consciousness over individualism. It is organized around an implied separatism.

The opposing thrust of these two parts of our identity results in the double bind of middle-class blacks. There is no forward movement on either plane that does not constitute backward movement on the other. This was the familiar trap I felt myself in while talking with my friend. As I spoke about class, his eyes reminded me that I was betraying race. Clearly, the two indispensable parts of my identity were a threat to each other.

Of course when you think about it, class and race are both similar in some ways and also naturally opposed. They are two forms of collective identity with boundaries that intersect. But whether they clash or peacefully coexist has much to do with how they are defined. Being both black and middle class becomes a double bind when class and race are defined in sharply antagonistic terms, so that one must be repressed to appease the other.

But what is the "substance" of these two identities, and how does each establish itself in an individual's overall identity? It seems to me that when we identify with any collective we are basically identifying with images that tell us what it means to be a member of that collective. Identity is not the same thing as the fact of membership in a collective; it is, rather, a form of self-definition, facilitated by images of what we wish our membership in the collective to mean. In this sense, the images we identify with may reflect the aspirations of the collective more than they reflect reality, and their content can vary with shifts in those aspirations.

But the process of identification is usually dialectical. It is just as necessary to say what we are *not* as it is to say what we are — so that finally identification comes about by embracing a polarity of positive and negative images. To identify as middle class, for example, I must have both positive and negative images of what being middle class entails; then I will know what I should and should not be doing in order to be middle class. The same goes for racial identity.

In the racially turbulent sixties the polarity of images that came to define racial identification was very antagonistic to the polarity that defined middle-class identification. One might say that the positive images of one lined up with the negative images of the other, so that to identify with both required either a contortionist's flexibility or a dangerous splitting of the self. The double bind of the black middle class was in place. . . .

The black middle class has always defined its class identity by means of positive images gleaned from middle- and upper-class white society, and by means of negative images of lower-class blacks. This habit goes back to the institution of slavery itself, when "house" slaves both mimicked the whites they served and held themselves above the "field" slaves. But in the sixties the old bourgeois impulse to dissociate from the lower classes (the "we-they" distinction) backfired when racial identity suddenly called for the celebration of this same black lower class. One of the qualities of a double bind is that one feels it more than sees it, and I distinctly remember the tension and strange sense of dishonesty I felt in those days as I moved back and forth like a bigamist between the demands of class and race.

Though my father was born poor, he achieved middle-class standing through much hard work and sacrifice (one of his favorite words) and by identifying fully with solid middle-class values — mainly hard work, family life, property ownership, and education for his children (all four of whom have advanced degrees). In his mind these were not so much values as laws of nature. People who embodied them made up the positive images in his class polarity. The negative images came largely from the blacks he had left behind because they were "going nowhere."

No one in my family remembers how it happened, but as time went on, the negative images congealed into an imaginary character named Sam, who, from the extensive service we put him to, quickly grew to mythic proportions. In our family lore he was sometimes a trickster, sometimes a boob, but always possessed of a catalogue of sly faults that gave up graphic images of everything we should not be. On sacrifice: "Sam never thinks about tomorrow. He wants it now or he doesn't care about it." On work: "Sam doesn't favor it too much." On children: "Sam likes to have them but not to raise them." On money: "Sam drinks it up and pisses it out." On fidelity: "Sam has to have two or three women." On clothes: "Sam features loud clothes. He likes to see and be seen." And so on. Sam's persona amounted to a negative instruction manual in class identity.

I don't think that any of us believed Sam's faults were accurate representations of lower-class black life. He was an instrument of self-definition, not of sociological accuracy. It never occurred to us that he looked very much like the white racist stereotype of blacks, or that he might have been a manifestation of our own racial self-hatred. He simply gave us a counterpoint against which to express our aspirations. If self-hatred was a factor, it was not, for us, a matter of hating lower-class blacks but of hating what we did not want to be.

Still, hate or love aside, it is fundamentally true that my middle-class identity involved a dissociation from images of lower-class black life and a corresponding identification with values and patterns of responsibility that are common to the middle class everywhere. These values sent me a clear message: be both an individual and a responsible citizen; understand that the quality of your life will approximately reflect the quality of effort you put into it; know that individual responsibility is the basis of freedom and that the limitations imposed by fate (whether fair or unfair) are no excuse for passivity.

Whether I live up to these values or not, I know that my acceptance of them is the result of lifelong conditioning. I know also that I share this conditioning with middle-class people of all races and that I can no more easily be free of it than I can be free of my race. Whether all this got started because the black middle class modeled itself on the white middle class is no longer relevant. For the middle-class black, conditioned by these values from birth, the sense of meaning they provide is as immutable as the color of his skin.

I started the sixties in high school feeling that my class-conditioning was the surest way to overcome racial barriers. My racial identity was pretty much taken for granted. After all, it was obvious to the world that I was black. Yet I ended the sixties in graduate school a little embarrassed by my class background and with an almost desperate need to be "black." The tables had turned. I knew very clearly (though I struggled to repress it) that my aspirations and my sense of how to operate in the world came from my class background, yet "being black" required certain attitudes and stances that made me feel secretly a little duplicitous. The inner compatibility of class and race I had known in 1960 was gone.

For blacks, the decade between 1960 and 1969 saw racial identification undergo the same sort of transformation that national identity undergoes in times of war. It became more self-conscious, more narrowly focused, more prescribed, less tolerant of opposition. It spawned an implicit party line, which tended to disallow competing forms of identity. Race-as-identity was lifted from the relative slumber it knew in the fifties and pressed into service in a social and political war against oppression. It was redefined along sharp adversarial lines and directed toward the goal of mobilizing the great mass of black Americans in this warlike effort. It was imbued with a strong moral authority, useful for denouncing those who opposed it and for celebrating those who honored it as a positive achievement rather than as a mere birthright.

The form of racial identification that quickly evolved to meet this challenge presented blacks as a racial monolith, a singular people with a common experience of oppression. Differences within the race, no matter how ineradicable, had to be minimized. Class distinctions were one of the first such differences to be sacrificed, since they not only threatened racial unity but also seemed to stand in contradiction to the principle of equality which was the announced goal of the movement for racial progress. The discomfort I felt in 1969, the vague but relentless sense of duplicity, was the result of a historical necessity that put my race and class at odds, that was asking me to cast aside the distinction of my class and identify with a monolithic view of my race.

If the form of this racial identity was the monolith, its substance was victimization. The civil rights movement and the more radical splinter groups of the late sixties were all dedicated to ending racial victimization, and the form of black identity that emerged to facilitate this goal made blackness and victimization virtually synonymous. Since it was our victimization more than any other variable that identified and unified us, moreover, it followed logically that the purest black was the poor black. It was images of him that clustered around the positive pole of the race polarity; all other blacks were, in effect, required to identify with him in order to confirm their own blackness.

Certainly there were more dimensions to the black experience than victimization, but no other had the same capacity to fire the indignation needed for war. So, again out of historical necessity, victimization became the overriding focus of racial identity. But this only deepened the double bind for middle-class blacks like me. When it came to class we were accustomed to defining ourselves against lower-class blacks and identifying with at least the values of middle-class whites; when it came to race we were now being asked to identify with images of lower-class blacks and to see whites, middle class or otherwise, as victimizers. Negative lining up with positive, we were called upon to reject what we had previously embraced and to embrace what we had previously rejected. To put it still more personally, the Sam figure I had been raised to define myself against had now become the "real" black I was expected to identify with.

The fact that the poor black's new status was only passively earned by the condition of his victimization, not by assertive, positive action, made little difference. Status was status apart from the means by which it was achieved, and along with it came a certain power — the power to define the terms of access to that status, to say who was black and who was not. If a lower-class black said you were not really "black" — a sellout, an Uncle Tom — the judgment was all the more devastating because it carried the authority of his status. And this judgment soon enough came to be accepted by many whites as well.

In graduate school I was once told by a white professor, "Well, but . . . you're not really black. I mean, you're not disadvantaged." In his mind my lack of victim status disqualified me from the race itself. More recently I was complimented by a black student for speaking reasonably correct English, "proper" English as he put it. "But I don't know if I really want to talk like that," he went on. "Why not?" I asked. "Because then I wouldn't be black no more," he replied without a pause.

To overcome his marginal status, the middle-class black had to identify with a degree of victimization that was beyond his actual experience. In college (and well beyond) we used to play a game called "nap matching." It was a game of one-upmanship, in which we sat around outdoing each other with stories of racial victimization, symbolically measured by the naps of our hair. Most of us were middle class and so had few personal stories to relate, but if we could not match naps with our own biographies, we would move on to those legendary tales of victimization that came to us from the public domain.

The single story that sat atop the pinnacle of racial victimization for us was that of Emmett Till, the Northern black teenager who, on a visit to the South in 1955, was killed and grotesquely mutilated for supposedly looking at or whistling at (we were never sure which, though we argued the point endlessly) a white woman. Oh, how we probed his story, finding in his youth and Northern up-bringing the quintessential embodiment of black innocence, brought down by a white evil so portentous and apocalyptic, so gnarled and hideous, that it left us with a feeling not far from awe. By telling his story and others like it, we came to *feel* the immutability of our victimization, its utter indigenousness, as a thing on this earth like dirt or sand or water.

Of course, these sessions were a ritual of group identification, a means by which we, as middle-class blacks, could be at one with our race. But why were we, who had only a moderate experience of victimization (and that offset by opportunities our parents never had), so intent on assimilating or appropriating an identity that in so many ways contradicted our own? Because, I think, the sense of innocence that is always entailed in feeling victimized filled us with a corresponding feeling of entitlement, or even license, that helped us endure our vulnerability on a largely white college campus.

In my junior year in college I rode to a debate tournament with three white students and our faculty coach, an elderly English professor. The experience of being the lone black in a group of whites was so familiar to me that I thought nothing of it as our trip began. But then halfway through the trip the professor casually turned to me and, in an isn't-the-world-funny sort of tone, said that he had just refused to rent an apartment in a house he owned to a "very nice" black couple because their color would "offend" the white couple who lived downstairs. His eyebrows lifted helplessly over his hawkish nose, suggesting that he too, like me, was a victim of America's racial farce. His look assumed a kind of comradeship: he and I were above this grimy business of race, though for expediency we had occasionally to concede the world its madness.

My vulnerability in this situation came not so much from the professor's blindness to his own racism as from his assumption that I would participate in it, that I would conspire with him against my own race so that he might remain comfortably blind. Why did he think I would be amenable to this? I can only guess that he assumed my middle-class identity was so complete and all-encompassing that I would see his action as nothing more than a trifling concession to the folkways of our land, that I would in fact applaud his decision not to disturb propriety. Blind to both his own racism and to me — one blindness serving the other — he could not recognize that he was asking me to betray my race in the name of my class.

His blindness made me feel vulnerable because it threatened to expose my own repressed ambivalence. His comment pressured me to choose between my class identification, which had contributed to my being a college student and a member of the debating team, and my desperate desire to be "black." I could have one but not both; I was double-bound.

Because double binds are repressed there is always an element of terror in them: the terror of bringing to the conscious mind the buried duplicity, self-deception, and pretense involved in serving two masters. This terror is the stuff of vulnerability, and since vulnerability is one of the least tolerable of all human feelings, we usually transform it into an emotion that seems to restore the control of which it has robbed us; most often, that emotion is anger. And so, before the professor had even finished his little story, I had become a furnace of rage. The year was 1967, and I had been primed by endless hours of nap-matching to feel, at least consciously, completely at one with the victim-focused black identity. This identity gave me the license, and the impunity, to unleash upon this professor one of those volcanic eruptions of racial indignation familiar to us from the novels of Richard Wright. Like Cross Damon in *Outsider,* who kills in perfectly righteous anger, I tried to annihilate the man. I punished him not according to the measure of his crime but according to the measure of my vulnerability, a measure set by the cumulative tension of years of repressed terror. Soon I saw that terror in *his* face, as he stared hollow-eyed at the road ahead. My white friends in the back seat, knowing no conflict between their own class and race, were astonished that someone they had taken to be so much like themselves could harbor a rage that for all the world looked murderous.

Though my rage was triggered by the professor's comment, it was deepened and sustained by a complex of need, conflict, and repression in myself of which I had been wholly unaware. Out of my racial vulnerability I had developed the strong need of an identity with which to defend myself. The only such identity available was that of me as victim, him as victimizer. Once in the grip of this paradigm, I began to do far more damage to myself than he had done.

Seeing myself as a victim meant that I clung all the harder to my racial identity, which, in turn, meant that I suppressed my class identity. This cut me off from all the resources my class values might have offered me. In those values, for instance, I might have found the means to a more dispassionate response, the response less of a victim attacked by a victimizer than of an individual offended by a foolish old man. As an individual I might have reported this professor to the college dean. Or I might have calmly tried to reveal his blindness to him, and possibly won a convert. (The flagrancy of his remark suggested a hidden guilt and even self-recognition on which I might have capitalized. Doesn't confession usually signal a willingness to face oneself?) Or I might have simply chuckled and then let my silence serve as an answer to his provocation. Would not my composure, in any form it might take, deflect into his own heart the arrow he'd shot at me?

Instead, my anger, itself the hair-trigger expression of a long-repressed double bind, not only cut me off from the best of my own resources, it also distorted the nature of my true racial problem. The righteousness of this anger and the easy catharsis it brought buoyed the delusion of my victimization and left me as blind as the professor himself.

As a middle-class black I have often felt myself *contriving* to be "black." And I have noticed this same contrivance in others — a certain stretching away from the natural flow of one's life to align oneself with a victim-focused black identity. Our particular needs are out of sync with the form of identity available to meet those needs. Middle-class blacks need to identify racially; it is better to think of ourselves as black and victimized than not black at all; so we contrive (more unconsciously than consciously) to fit ourselves into an identity that denies our class and fails to address the true source of our vulnerability.

For me this once meant spending inordinate amounts of time at black faculty meetings, though these meetings had little to do with my real racial anxieties or my professional life. I was new to the university, one of two blacks in an English department of over seventy, and I felt a little isolated and vulnerable, though I did not admit it to myself. But at these meetings we discussed the problems of black faculty and students within a framework of victimization. The real vulnerability we felt was covered over by all the adversarial drama the victim/victimized polarity inspired, and hence went unseen and unassuaged. And this, I think, explains our rather chronic ineffectiveness as a group. Since victimization was not our primary problem — the university had long ago opened its doors to us — we had to contrive to make it so, and there is not much energy in contrivance. What I got at these meetings was ultimately an object lesson in how fruitless struggle can be when it is not grounded in actual need.

At our black faculty meetings, the old equation of blackness with victimization was ever present — to be black was to be a victim; therefore, not to be a victim was not to be black. As we contrived to meet the terms of this formula there was an inevitable distortion of both ourselves and the larger university. Through the prism of victimization the university seemed more impenetrable than it actually was, and we more limited in our powers. We fell prey to the victim's myopia, making the university an institution from which we could seek redress but which we could never fully join. And this mind-set often led us to look more for compensations for our supposed victimization than for opportunities we could pursue as individuals.

The discomfort and vulnerability felt by middle-class blacks in the sixties, it could be argued, was a worthwhile price to pay considering the progress achieved during that time of racial confrontation. But what may have been tolerable then is intolerable now. Though changes in American society have made it an anachronism, the monolithic form of racial identification that came out of the sixties is still very much with us. It may be more loosely held, and its power to punish heretics has probably diminished, but it continues to catch middle-class blacks in a double bind, thus impeding not only their own advancement but even, I would contend, that of blacks as a group.

The victim-focused black identity encourages the individual to feel that his advancement depends almost entirely on that of the group. Thus he loses sight not only of his own possibilities but of the inextricable connection between individual effort and individual advancement. This is a profound encumbrance today, when there is more opportunity for blacks than ever before, for it reimposes limitations that can have the same oppressive effect as those the society has only recently begun to remove.

It was the emphasis on mass action in the sixties that made the victim-focused black identity a necessity. But in the eighties and beyond, when racial advancement will come only through a multitude of individual advancements, this form of identity inadvertently adds itself to the forces that hold us back. Hard work, education, individual initiative, stable family life, property ownership — these have always been the means by which ethnic groups have moved ahead in America. Regardless of past or present victimization, these "laws" of advancement apply absolutely to black Americans also. There is no getting around this. What we need is a form of racial identity that energizes the individual by putting him in touch with both his possibilities and his responsibilities.

It has always annoyed me to hear from the mouths of certain arbiters of blackness that middle-class blacks should "reach back" and pull up those blacks less fortunate than they — as though middle-class status were an unearned and essentially passive condition in which one needed a large measure of noblesse oblige to occupy one's time. My own image is of reaching back from a moving train to lift on board those who have no tickets. A noble enough sentiment — but might it not be wiser to show them the entire structure of principles, efforts, and sacrifice that puts one in a position to buy a ticket any time one likes? This, I think, is something members of the black middle class can realistically offer to other blacks. Their example is not only a testament to possibility but also a lesson in method. But they cannot lead by example until they are released from a black identity that regards that example as suspect, that sees them as "marginally" black, indeed that holds *them* back by catching them in a double bind.

To move beyond the victim-focused black identity we must learn to make a difficult but crucial distinction: between actual victimization, which we must resist with every resource, and identification with the victim's status. Until we do this we will continue to wrestle more with ourselves than with the new opportunities which so many paid so dearly to win.

Reflections and Responses

---

1. Consider the two people Steele introduces us to in his essay — a black friend (pages 27–28) and a white college professor (pages 34–36). What does each person represent? Of what importance are they to Steele's own self-identity? How does he establish his differences toward each one? Why are these differences important to Steele's own identity?

2. What do you think of Steele's contention that poorer and less-educated African Americans are generally considered more "black" than those from the middle class? What evidence does Steele offer to support this idea? On what grounds is black "authenticity" or "purity" based? Do you think the media — especially film, music, and television — reinforce certain images of "blackness"?

3. Note that toward the conclusion of his essay Steele uses the word "we." What is the significance of this shift? What identification is he establishing and with whom?

JOSEPH EPSTEIN

They Said You Was High Class

For many personal essayists, authorial identity leads to a literary predicament. On the one hand, the writer hopes — through candor, voice, and style — to establish a vigorous personal identity. On the other hand, the essayist's resistance to simple labels can lead to the mistrust of a settled identity. Watch how Joseph Epstein slips in and out of whatever category he momentarily chooses for himself. As Epstein would have it, an essayist should "dislike being labeled too easily, being understood too quickly." For Epstein, the essayist's mind should be a "great wanderer," moving robustly among all sorts of ideas and opinions without intellectual rigidity or emotional fixations. Such essays, however, though free-ranging, are not undemanding; they require that their readers, too, be willing to entertain divergent opinions and be patient with numerous and often unfamiliar literary references. Essayists like Epstein are often voluminous readers and enjoy interlacing their prose with appealing quotations.

Joseph Epstein's essays have so far been selected three times for The Best American Essays, *and in 1993 he served as the annual's guest editor. One of the best-known American essayists, Epstein's work has appeared in* The New Yorker, Commentary, Harper's, The New York Times Magazine, The New Republic, *and many other leading magazines. The author of nine volumes of fiction and nonfiction, Epstein has taught at Northwestern University since 1974 and has been the editor of* The American Scholar *since 1975. "They Said You Was High Class" originally appeared in* The American Scholar *(1986) and was selected by Gay Talese for* The Best American Essays 1987.

"Look, I know it's a dodgy topic, but you are lower class, aren't you, darling? Just between ourselves, naturally."

"I was before I came up in the world, true, but lower-middle class, not working class. Very important distinction. My old dad got really wild if you said he was working class. Worse than calling him a Jew."

—Kingsley Amis, *Stanley and the Women*

Karl, Friedrich, forgive me, fellas, for never having taken much interest in your class struggle, but the truth is that for the better part of my life I have been a bit unclear about what class I myself belong to. If the phrase didn't imply that I was of a higher social class than I am — and make me sound like an Englishman into the bargain — I should call the whole thing a frightful muddle. More than a mite confusing it is, though. How nice to be able to say with confidence, as George Orwell once did, that one is "lower-upper-middle class." Yet, unless I am quite wrong, such terms have now lost much of their descriptive power. The social pace has quickened; nowadays people move in and out of social classes with greater rapidity than ever before. Sometimes I wonder if today social class, at least as we used to think of it in this country, has about as much relevance as an electric salad fork and as bright a future as a cha-cha instructor in Montana.

Social mobility — the jumping or, more commonly, sliding from one class to another — is scarcely a new phenomenon. Chekhov, to cite an interesting instance, had a grandfather who bought himself out of serfdom and a nephew who became a Hollywood producer. I myself have a cousin, ten years older than I, named Moe and a niece, thirty years younger than I, named Nicole; and to go from Moe to Nicole in only forty years is in some respects to travel farther than the Chekhovs did from Voronezh Province to Beverly Hills. Other evidence of our whirring social flux can readily be adduced. The janitor of the apartment building I live in has published a book; it is not, granted, a slender little volume on the poetry of the Comte Robert de Montesquiou but instead a book about the martial arts; yet the same man is a janitor and a published author. The other day, in Manhattan, I had the bite put on me by a panhandler wearing a rumpled but still a real Ralph Lauren shirt; and it occurred to me shortly afterward that, should I ever hit the skids, I may not have the wardrobe to go on the bum.

Just when you begin to think you understand a thing or two about the drama of life, they change the scenery and send in a whole new cast of characters.

Cracks, major fault lines, in the class system, may be a worldwide phenomenon. Peregrine Worsthorne, the British political writer, recently noted in *The Spectator* that "the class system has changed out of all recognition in my lifetime." Certainly, social distinctions in America have become vastly less clear in my own. When does a child first notice such distinctions? My own first realization that the world was a place filled with social differences might have been the gross recognition that some people lived rather better than we and others rather worse. It might have been the woman, whose name was Emma, who came in to clean for us on Tuesdays, for I seem to recall thinking it peculiar that someone would clean a place not her own. It might have had to do with automobiles, for we lived on a street that was a thoroughfare, and the first organized knowledge I acquired as a child had to do with telling the difference between cars; and it could not have been long before I also learned that some cars (Cadillacs, Packards, Lincolns) were held in higher regard than others (Fords, Studebakers, Plymouths). These were the years of World War II, during which my father drove a green 1942 Dodge sedan.

If our family had a crest, that green 1942 Dodge sedan ought to be at its center. That car placed us — socially, financially, and stylistically — and where it placed us was slam-bang in the middle. Our family was not so much socially uninteresting as socially uninterested. If life is in some sense a status race, my parents never noticed the flag drop. While we owned possessions roughly comparable to those owned by our neighbors, we showed no passion for the subtleties of social life. Even when the money was there to do so, it would never have occurred to my parents to join a city club or country club or to move to a fashionable address — a residence with social resonance. Their notion of the good life was to live comfortably, always well within their means, and insofar as possible never to pay for pretension. Then as now that seems to me quite sensible — though I must add, I myself have not had the character to live up to it.

I have omitted a social fact of no small significance and even greater complication. The fact is that I am Jewish. I was born thus, and thus I shall remain; and it is exceedingly difficult to be Jewish and not have a somewhat heightened sense of social and class distinctions. Not for nothing was the keenest modern observer of such distinctions, Marcel Proust, half Jewish and fully homosexual; after all, a man who is in danger of being despised from two difference directions learns to devise sensitive antennae. Another sharp observer of social gradations, Anton Chekhov, was neither Jewish nor homosexual; but he was low born, the son of a bankrupt grocer, the grandson of a serf, and that put the antennae permanently on his roof. In a famous letter to his friend and publisher, Alexey Suvorin, Chekhov explained his own social unease when he wrote that "what aristocratic writers take from nature gratis, the less privileged must pay for with their youth," adding that he had had to squeeze "the slave out of himself drop by drop" before he "finds that the blood coursing through his veins is no longer the blood of a slave, but that of a real human being."

Let me hasten to insert that I never for a moment felt the least like a slave. Doubtless this was in large part owing to having a father who was successful yet in no way tyrannical or crushing, on the model, say, of Papa Kafka. My father, along with giving me the reassuring sense that I was working with a net under me, encouraged me to believe that I came of a family capable of serious achievement. But my father also alerted me early to the alarming fact that people might detest me for reasons having nothing to do with my character or conduct and everything to do with my religion. I must have been four or five years old when the potential social consequences of being Jewish were thus impinged upon me. In the 1940s and early 1950s the word — the euphemism, really — for de facto anti-Semitic arrangements was "restricted"; and in those years many neighborhoods and suburbs, clubs and resorts, fraternities and sororities were restricted.

I would be a liar if I said that knowledge of such things didn't bother me. But I would be an even greater liar if I said that it bothered me very much. When I was growing up, we lived in neighborhoods that tended to be at least 50 percent Jewish, and the same was true of the public schools I attended. If anything, this encouraged me in the belief that Jews were rather superior — a belief based, unknowingly, on social class. What I didn't know was that the non-Jews who remained in the neighborhoods we lived in were mainly people who for one reason or another were probably unable to depart them. In other words, most of the non-Jews I went to grade school and high school with were the sons and daughters of the working class or the lower white-collar classes, while the Jews tended to be among the newly surging middle classes, still very much on the make.

Although so far as I know I have never been the victim of any serious anti-Semitic acts, the first time I recall feeling rather out of the social mainstream because I was Jewish was during a year I spent as a freshman student at the University of Illinois in the middle *1950*s. Illinois was very much a school of fraternities and sororities — a "Greek campus," as it was called — and I, who had not yet developed socially to the point of knowing there was something in the world called nonconformity, accepted an invitation to join what was thought to be the best of the Jewish fraternities. (All non-Jewish fraternities and sororities at Illinois were then "restricted.") The reigning spirit at the university in those days, far from being the Jewish and metropolitan one I was used to, was Protestant and small town — a midwestern, somewhat more yokelish version of the muscular Christianity* that George Santayana found several decades earlier prevailing at Yale. The student who seemed to me best to represent this spirit was a young man from Peoria named Hiles Stout. Stout was a Sigma Chi and played three major sports for the university and resembled e. e. cummings's conscientious objector Olaf only in being "more brave than me:more blond than you"— though perhaps it would be more accurate to say that he was "more Hiles than me:more Stout than you."

I did not so much feel outclassed or declassed at the University of Illinois as I felt myself on the outside of a house I had no particular desire to enter. For while attending the University of Illinois, I had informally enrolled at good old Mencken-Lewis-Dreiser University,† where I learned a haughty if not especially original dis-

---

*muscular Christianity: A mildly satirical name given to an informal Christian revivalist movement, concentrated around schools and college campuses in Britain and the United States in the first half of this century, which encouraged an "active," outdoorsy, sports-oriented faith with an eye to bringing more young people to the church.

†Mencken-Lewis-Dreiser University: A joke. Referring to three twentieth-century American writers and activists: Louis Mencken (1880–1956), Sinclair Lewis (1885–1951), and Theodore Dreiser (1871–1945).

dain for the middle class, that inartistic and uninspired group also
known as the booboisie — that is to say, a disdain for the social
class and culture from which, apart from being Jewish, I myself
had derived. From MLDU, beloved alma mater, I learned not to
join the class struggle but instead to disassociate myself, insofar as
possible, from my own class.

As a step in that direction, I transferred to the University of
Chicago, which was perhaps as close as I have ever come to living
in a classless society — I refer to the student segment of university
society — and rather closer than I ever again care to come. A few
fraternities remained at the University of Chicago at that time, but
far from being thought in any way admirable, the chief attitude toward them was a mixture of mild contempt and apathy. Wealth
and genteel birth counted for naught at the University of Chicago;
apart from books and classical records, material possessions were
thought the sign of a cramped spirit. Physical beauty and social
graces were held to be beside the point, and the standard joke of
the day had it that a panty raid on one of the women's dormitories
netted a fatigue jacket and a single combat boot. A passionate bo-
hemianism was what the University of Chicago student body as-
pired to; a grim scruffiness was what it often achieved.

Intellectually, the University of Chicago strove much higher,
holding four tasks in life to be worthwhile: to be an artist, to be a
scientist, to be a statesman, or to be a teacher of artists, scientists,
or statesmen. In this regard the University of Chicago was not anti-
middle class in the abrasive manner of Sinclair Lewis and H. L.
Mencken; it was para-middle class by its tacit implication that
there were higher things in life than getting a good job, earning a
living, raising a family, and getting on. Chamfort once said that society was divided between those who had more dinners than appetite and those who had more appetite than dinners, but at the
University of Chicago the division was between those who loved
art and learning and those who did not, and those who loved it
were thought better.

If the University of Chicago was relatively free of conventional
social-class considerations, the United States Army, the institution
in which I was to spend the next two years of my life, was, at least
formally, as class-bound as any society I have ever lived in. The
first — and chief — class distinction was the patent one between

officers and enlisted men. Officers ate, slept, dressed, and were paid better. Obeisance needed to be paid them in the form of salutes and in addressing them as "sir." Theirs was a strikingly better deal; one didn't have to be Alexis de Tocqueville* to notice that. As an enlisted man who as a boy was never required to learn the habits of obeisance, I could not help marveling at the vast social discrepancies between officers and enlisted men. I did not so much resent them as wonder how career noncommissioned officers managed to tolerate them, especially in a peacetime army, when an officer's responsibilities were less and the call on his bravery nonexistent. Confronted for the first time with a codified class system, I found myself more of a democrat than I had imagined.

At the same time that the U.S. Army was rigidly hierarchical and held together by the idea of rank, no American institution was, at its core, more democratic. Well in advance of the larger society of which it was a part, the U.S. Army had integrated its facilities and was color-blind in its promotions and other procedures. As an enlisted man, one was really thrown into the stew of American life. In my own basic-training platoon I lived with Missouri farmers, Appalachian miners, an American Indian auto mechanic, a black car salesman from Detroit, a Jewish lawyer from Chicago, a fundamentalist high school teacher from Kansas, and others no less varied but now lost to memory. It felt, at moments, like living in a badly directed screen version of *Leaves of Grass.* Although I groaned and cursed, questioning the heavens for putting me through the torture in tedium that I then took my time in the Army to be, I have since come to view that time as one of the most interesting interludes in my life — among other reasons because it jerked me free, if only for a few years, from the social classes in which I have otherwise spent nearly all my days. It jerked everyone free from his social class, however high or low that class may have been, and yet somehow, despite the jolt, it seemed to work.

Or at least it seemed to work most of the time. A case where it didn't was that of Samuel Schuyler III, whom I worked with as a fellow enlisted man in the Public Information Office at Fort Hood, Texas. The Third, as I always thought of him, had gone to the

---

*Alexis de Tocqueville:** (1805–1859) French statesman and author, who published a popular account of the "character" of the new American nation.

Wharton School of Business, hungered for the country-club ease he was missing while in the Army, and drove a black Cadillac convertible, the current year's model. Despite the numeral affixed to his name, the Third was without social pretensions; he was a simple hedonist and a straight money man. How he had come to own that Cadillac convertible at the age of twenty-three I never discovered — my own social-class manners, I now suppose, prevented me from asking — but he played the stock market fairly often, calling his broker in Pittsburgh to place his orders.

What was not difficult to discover was the Third's contempt for everyone around him, officers and enlisted men both. (Only a few acquaintances, of whom for some reason I was one, were spared.) Forms through which to express this contempt were not wanting to him. The Third had developed a salute that, while formally correct, made every officer to whom he tendered it think at least twice about it; there was about this salute the faint yet almost unmistakable suggestion that its recipient go forth to exercise an anatomical impossibility upon himself. Driving on the post in his black Cadillac, the Third was everywhere taken for the post commander — who himself drove a more modest car, a Buick — and everyone, even up to the rank of bird colonel, dropped everything to salute him, only to receive in turn the Third's own extraordinary salute. The Third even dressed with contempt. If there is a word that is the antonym of "panache," I should avail myself of it to describe the deliberately slovenly way that he wore his uniform. In mufti, meanwhile, no muted Ivy League dresser, the Third preferred draped trousers, alligator shoes, and in shirts showed an unfortunate penchant for the color known as dubonnet. Toward the close of his enlistment, the Third was promoted from Pfc. to Sp4c. but refused the promotion on the grounds that the additional money wasn't worth the trouble of sewing new patches on his uniforms. No gesture better summed up his refusal to partake of military class arrangements; he scoffed at them every chance he got, making clear that, short of doing anything that could land him in the stockade, he chose not to play the game. His lofty contempt earned him a great deal of not-so-lofty-hatred. The Third knew he was hated and felt about this much as he did about his promotion — he could not, that is, have cared less.

I cared rather more, in the Army and elsewhere, because social class has always seemed to me intrinsically fascinating. I have inevitably been interested in attempting to take the measure of any class system in which I found myself, though when young I must often have been, as Henry James might have put it, destitute of the materials requisite for measurement. A fantasy about social class said to be common among children, especially children fed ample rations of fairy tales, is that one's parents are not one's real parents but instead that one is much higher born — and is probably, as will surely one day be revealed, a prince or princess. My fantasy, taken up in early adolescence and not quite dropped to this day, is that I can roam freely from social class to social class, comfortable everywhere and everywhere welcome. Sometimes I think it would be more realistic to believe that one is the last of the Romanovs.*

Not that I am a proletarian fancier, the American equivalent of a Narodnik or a Slavophile. There is something inherently condescending in assigning special qualities to the lower class. Dorothy Parker, after being told that Clare Boothe Luce was always kind to her inferiors, is supposed to have asked, "And where does she find them?" But I like to view myself as being able to slip from class to class because I detest the notion of one's destiny being absolutely determined by birth and social upbringing; I readily grant the importance of both but not their decisiveness. I myself dislike being labeled too easily, being understood too quickly. Neither a strict Marxist nor a straight Freudian be — such is the advice of this old Polonius.† Accept the possibility of all influences; reject the fiats of all absolute determinants.

The old, received wisdom about social class is that one is supposed to dislike the class just below one's own and gaze yearningly upon those above one's own. But I find that the only class whose members can sometimes get me worked up are the upper classes, or what is left of them after taxes and the Zeitgeist have done their work. A plummy upper-class English accent with nothing behind it but enormous self-satisfaction can, in the proper mood, still bring out the residual Red in me. My Anglo-philia, which may have had behind it a certain social-class longing, seems to have slipped

---

***Romanovs:** The royal family of Russia, deposed during the 1917 Soviet revolution. After the revolution, the czar and his entire family were imprisoned and later shot.

†**Polonius:** Character in *Hamlet;* a comically self-important old man who spouts clichéd advice.

badly in recent years; today, apart from being somewhat regretful about not having gone to an Oxbridge college when a boy, I have only one regret about not being English, which is that, because I am not, I cannot be permitted to use the word "whilst" without seeming affected. The upper class of my own country now seems to me, when it is not sad, mostly comic. The traditional WASP-ocracy seems to have left the field without firing a shot; they resemble nothing so much as white Russians,* with the serious proviso that they appear to have been forced into exile without actually leaving their own country. One reads about them nowadays at play in Newport or in Charleston, or in repose at the Somerset Club in Boston, or sees them decked out for a photographer from *Town & Country*, but they seem rather desiccated and plain tuckered out.

It is a bit difficult to have a serious class system when, as in this country at present, you don't have a convincing upper class. So long as there is a convincing upper class, other classes in the society at least know what to imitate, however absurd the imitation. I can attest to this when I recall that, in 1950, as a boy of thirteen growing up in a middle-class, mostly Jewish neighborhood, I and several of my pals attended a class in ballrooom dancing called Fortnightly. It was held at the field house of a public park, was taught by a couple of very correct posture and general deportment whom I now think would be best described as "shabby genteel," and, despite the name Fortnightly, met every Saturday afternoon. What we did in this class was, in effect, prepare for a cotillion none of us would ever attend. Young ladies sat on one side of the room, young gentlemen on the other; young gentlemen crossed the room to ask young ladies to dance, and to dance waltzes, fox trots, and other, rather intricate dances and steps that this young gentleman, aging fast, has still never had to press into service.

The decisive movement in the defeat of upper-class, capital-*S* Society may have come when, in newspapers all over the nation, what used to be called the Society page was replaced by the Style section. The old Society page, with its accounts of engagements and weddings, charity balls and coming-out parties, tended to be boring and silly; while the new Style section, with its accounts of designer

---

*white Russians: Russian Monarchists; mostly wealthy aristocrats, many went into fashionable exile after the communist revolution, where they thought of many but acted on few half-baked plots to restore the czar.

clothing, gourmandizing, and the trend of the moment, tends to be lively and silly. The Society page, like Society itself, began to go under sometime in the middle 1960s, which was not exactly a felicitous time for establishments of many kinds. Not that the sixties did away with class consciousness; it attempted instead to reorient such consciousness in favor of other classes. The animus of the sixties generation, expressed in its popular culture, was against both upper- and middle-class life. In their place it wished to substitute ethnic pride and, as expressed by such groups as the Beatles and the Rolling Stones, something of a working-class ethos, with sexual freedom and drug use added. Even in England, that most traditional of class-bound countries, according to the English journalist Jilly Cooper, "working-class became beautiful and everyone from Princess Anne downwards spat the plums out of their mouths, embraced the flat 'a' and talked with a working-class accent."

Not many people outside of it are likely to have been sorry to see the old upper class in this country pushed rudely to the sidelines. The upper class had a lot to apologize for, and in many ways it is still apologizing. In wealthy Fairfield County, Connecticut, in the town of Darien (the setting for Laura Hobson's novel about genteel anti-Semitism, *Gentleman's Agreement*), a local newspaper, according to the *New York Times*, ran an article by a high school girl attacking the town for its lack of social diversity. "I am," this girl wrote, "a white Protestant living in a basically white Protestant community. I lack the richness and cultural background gained from a diversified environment. What are you, the townspeople, going to do about it?" Few things so lower the morale, and raise the gorge, as being lectured to by one's own children. One of these things may be being lectured to on the same grounds by the clergymen of one's church, and no church in America has gone at this task more relentlessly than the Episcopalian church, once *the* church of the old upper classes if there is truth in the one-sentence sociology of religion that holds: A Methodist is a Baptist with shoes, a Presbyterian is a Methodist who has gone to college, and an Episcopalian is a Prebyterian living off his investments.

Although much that was once thought to represent upper-class life appears to have been routed, much more lives on, often in attenuated and snobbish form. Contemned the old upper class may be, yet the line of people hopefully awaiting their children's enrollment in such formerly exclusively upper-class prep schools as Choate, Groton, Exeter, and Saint Paul's has not, my guess is, in any serious way diminished. Most middle-class students who have a wide choice will tend to choose universities favored by the old upper classes; and most university professors, given a similiar choice in institutions, will do the same — a tenured professor who has left Princeton for Purdue, or Harvard for Hofstra, or Yale for Ypsilanti Community College is a fit candidate for the television show called "That's Incredible."

Freud said that it was better to be an ancestor, which he turns out to have been, than to have ancestors, which he lacked. But surely better still is both to be an ancestor and to have ancestors. In literary life I can think of at least three living writers whose careers owe more than a little to upper-class cachet: Gore Vidal, who at every opportunity brings his family connections into his writing; William F. Buckley, who attempts to live like an aristocrat, though without much in the way of aristocratic leisure; and George Plimpton, whose many autobiographical books on the subject of sports have about them something of the aura of slumming. (I do not count Louis Auchincloss, a novelist whose subject is often the eclipse of the upper class in which he grew up.) All three men are, in accent, neither chummy nor unplummy.

If he were still alive, I should most certainly count in Robert Lowell, whose ancestors were reputed to speak only to God and who, before his death, was generally conceded to be this country's first poet. Without for a moment claiming that Lowell set out to exploit his upper-class genealogy, neither can one for another moment disclaim the importance of that genealogy to Lowell's poetry. Elizabeth Bishop once told Lowell: "All you have to do is put down the names! And the fact that it seems significant, illustrative, American, etc., gives you, I think, the confidence you display about tackling any idea or theme, *seriously*, in both writing and conversation. In some ways you are the luckiest poet I know." Was Elizabeth Bishop correct? Let us change some of those names she claimed Lowell had only to mention. What if Lowell's poem "My Last Afternoon with Uncle Devereux Winslow" were instead entitled "My Last Afternoon with Uncle Morris Shapiro," or his "Terminal Days at Beverly Farms" were instead entitled "Terminal Days at Grossinger's"? (Actually, given that resort's famously rich pro-

vender, any day at Grossinger's could be terminal.) Not quite the
same, perhaps you will agree.

But then neither is anti-Semitism in the United States quite the
same as it once was, or else I could not make the kind of easy joke
that I just did about the titles of Robert Lowell's poems, at least not
in print. Whether anti-Semitism is today less, whether racism has
greatly diminished, cannot be known with certainty; my sense is
that they both are much reduced. But what can be known is that
neither is any longer officially recognized in restricted or segre-
gated arrangements, and this, along with marking impressive
progress, has made for significant changes in the American class
system. Whereas the retreat of the older upper class has blown the
roof off the system, the demise of official and quasi-official discrimination has uprooted the basement. The metaphor I seem to
be building toward here is a class system that resembles an open-
air ranch house. Strange edifice, this, but then socially many
strange things appear to have taken place in recent years. In many
industries union wages have placed many union workers, financially at least, into the upper reaches of the middle class, while
attending college, once the ultimate rite of passage into solid middle-class respectability, no longer inevitably accomplishes this
task — owing doubtless to the spread and watering down of higher
education. There is a great deal of senseless and haphazard luxury
in the land. Athletes and rock stars, many of them made million-
aires before they are thirty, are removed from the financial wars
for all their days. Meanwhile a servant class has all but disappeared. A daughter from the working class uses part of her wages
from working at the supermarket to buy designer jeans, while a
son of Scarsdale comes into Manhattan to acquire his duds at a
Salvation Army thrift shop. The other day, in a parking lot near
where I live, I noted a rather dingy Saab automobile, with an antenna for a telephone on its roof, an Oberlin College decal on its
back window, and bumper stickers reading "National Computer
Camp" and "I Support Greenpeace." Now there is a vehicle with a
lot of class — and, symbolic of our time, a lot of class confusions.

If that car isn't owned by someone from what today passes for
the upper-middle class, I'll buy you a salmon mousse and a manual
on how your children can raise their SAT scores fully thirty points.
"The upper-middle classes," writes Jilly Cooper, "are the most in-

telligent and highly educated of all the classes, and therefore the silliest and most sensitive to every new trend: radical chic, health food, ethnic clothes, bra-lessness, gifted children, French cooking." The members of the upper-middle class that Miss Cooper has in mind are mostly newly risen and, not always sure where they are, insecure about where they are headed. This upper-middle class is not to be confused with the noveau riche. The former tends to be rather better educated, immensely concerned with what it understands to be good taste, and serious if also a little worried about culture — very little that one could think of, in fact, would be more wounding to members of this upper-middle class than to be taken for nouveau riche. I think I know what I am talking about here; this upper-middle class is my milieu — or, as the writer Josephine Herbst used to call it, my "maloo."

When I say that the upper-middle class is my maloo, I do not mean that I am quite of that class. Strictly speaking, I am fairly sure that I do not qualify financially. I do not drive a BMW, a Mercedes, or a Jaguar; I do not dream of driving such cars, and if I leave the earth without owning one or the other of them, I shall not, for that reason, die with a frown on my face (I cannot otherwise promise to depart smiling). I own no works of art, nor do I aspire to own anything above the level of an unnumbered print. No espresso machine sits on the counter of my kitchen, no mousse molds sit upon the shelves of my cabinets. From the tax standpoint, I do not earn enough money now, nor do I soon expect to earn enough, to cry out, in the words of the rock 'n' roll song, "Gimme shelter." Do not get me wrong. I should not in the least mind driving off in a Mercedes 380 SL, a Turner watercolor locked in its trunk, on my way to have a cappuccino with my tax lawyer. But my mind, the great wanderer, does not linger long on such things. Expensive good taste, that sine qua non* of the new upper-middle class, is not my sine qua non. I do not despise it; I am not in the least uncomfortable around it; but I do not live for it.

What, then, do I live for? Apart from love for my family and friends, I live for words. I live for the delights of talking and reading and writing. I am content when talking with people I adore or

---

*__sine qua non:__ Literally, "without which there is nothing"; something of fundamental importance.

admire or at least feel I can learn a little something from; I am happy when I am reading something fine or subtle or powerful; and I am delirious when I am writing something of which I am not altogether ashamed. If one's social class is defined, at least in part, by one's wishes, then I ought perhaps to be defined as a member of what I think of as the verbal class — someone, that is, who both earns his livelihood and derives his greatest pleasure from words. Membership in the verbal class has its advantages and its disadvantages: the hours are a bit crazy, but, like the village idiot posted at the town gates to await the arrival of the messiah, at least you are never out of work.

The term "verbal class" is meant to be almost purely descriptive; nothing, certainly, honorific is intended by it. Orwell, who did not use the term "verbal class," did once refer to "the new aristocracy" of professors, publicists, and journalists who in large part comprise the verbal class; he did so in the portion of *1984* that purports to be from Emmanuel Goldstein's manuscript, where this new aristocracy is described as "less tempted by luxury, hungrier for pure power" than their opposite numbers in past ages. In Chekhov's time the verbal class of our day and the new aristocracy of *1984* would have been described as the intelligentsia. This is the same intelligentsia of whom Chekhov, in a letter to a friend, writes: "I have no faith in our intelligentsia; it is hypocritical, dishonest, hysterical, ill-bred, and lazy." Which made them, in Chekhov's view, quite as wretched as any other social class, though perhaps a bit worse because the pretensions of the intelligentsia were more extravagant and its complaints better formulated and more insistently expressed. Read Chekhov and, in questions of social class, one soon becomes a Chekhovian. "I have faith in individuals," he wrote. "I see salvation in individuals scattered here and there . . . be they intellectuals or peasants, for they're the ones who really matter, though they are few."

Yet my sense is that the verbal class has risen slightly in recent years. It has not done so, near as I can make out, because of any improvement in its members' general mental acuity or civic valor. The verbal class appears instead to be rising by default. Members of the verbal class, odd fish that they are, seem able to swim easily through a fluid social scene — and the American social scene at present seems extremely fluid. John Adams spoke of his studying

"politics and war that my sons may have the liberty to study mathematics and philosophy," but what would he have thought of men
who studied real estate and the stock market that their daughters
may have the liberty to study Marxist historiography and their sons
become, through downward mobility, carpenters in Vancouver?
He would probably think his wife, Abigail, very clever for describing the American people as "the mobility."

"Classless Soviet Is Far Off, Siberian Scholar Says." So read a recent headline in the *New York Times*. It is difficult to doubt such authority, for surely one of the quickest ways of telling that a classless
society is far off is merely to live in Siberia. My guess is that a classless society is roughly as near completion in the Soviet Union as it
is in the United States — which isn't very near at all. Not that this
even remotely suggests the need for intensifying the class struggle.
Take it from a member of the verbal class: in a real class struggle
one is lucky to end up with a draw, except that it inevitably turns
out to have been a very bloody draw.

I see the serious class struggle as that of men and women singly
fighting off being entirely shaped by the social class into which
they were born. Insularity, unimaginativeness, self-satisfaction —
each social class has its own special drawbacks, blindnesses, vices.
"Vices" reminds me of a story a friend of mine, a man born into
the English working class, used to tell about a shop class he was required to take at a grammar school in London. It was taught by a
flinty little Scotsman who, when he wanted the class's attention in
order to make an announcement, used to cry out, "Stand by your
vices, boys!" When we think too exclusively as members of our social class, we all, essentially, stand by our vices. I should have
thought the trick of becoming a human being is to stand away
from them.

Reflections and Responses

1. Consider Epstein's opening paragraph. How does he establish a
humorous attitude toward his topic? How is that attitude reflected
in his title? What elements of mimicry can you detect in the first
paragraph? What is the purpose of Epstein's mimicry?

2. What do you think Epstein means by the "verbal class"? How does it compare with other, more traditional, types of social class? Do you think this category liberates Epstein from the restrictions of more conventional class categories?

3. At one point, Epstein says that he has "omitted a social fact of no small significance and even greater complication." This fact is that he is Jewish. In what ways does this fact complicate his situation? Does he find a conflict between class and ethnic identity? Explain.

JUDY RUIZ

Oranges and Sweet Sister Boy

The investigation of sexual identity has been a favorite theme among contemporary essayists. One of the most adventurous explorations along these lines in recent years is Judy Ruiz's "Oranges and Sweet Sister Boy." Contemporary not only in its theme but in its literary technique, Ruiz's remarkable essay weaves together autobiographical narrative and fragments of imagery into a moving personal memoir of a brother and sister's "spooky sexual identity problems." Like many of America's new essays, this one dramatizes not so much a quest for a settled identity but a struggle against one. An unusual essay of self-transformation, it stands as one of the most penetrating and memorable identity essays of our time.

A widely published poet, Judy Ruiz earned an M.F.A. in Poetry from the University of Arkansas in 1988 and teaches creative writing at Southwest Missouri State University. She is the author of a book of poetry, Talking Razzmatazz *(1991). "Oranges and Sweet Sister Boy" originally appeared in* Iowa Woman *(1988) and was selected by Geoffrey Wolff for* The Best American Essays 1989.

I am sleeping, hard, when the telephone rings. It's my brother, and he's calling to say he is now my sister. I feel something fry a little, deep behind my eyes. Knowing how sometimes dreams get mixed up with not-dreams, I decide to do a reality test at once. "Let me get a cigarette," I say, knowing that if I reach for a Marlboro and it turns into a trombone or a snake or anything else on the way to my lips that I'm still out in the large world of dreams.

The cigarette stays a cigarette. I light it. I ask my brother to run that stuff by me again.

It is the Texas Zephyr at midnight — the woman in a white suit, the man in a blue uniform; she carries flowers — I know they are flowers. The petals spill and spill into the aisle, and a child goes past this couple who have just come from their own wedding — goes past them and past them, going always to the toilet but really just going past them; and the child could be a horse or she could be the police and they'd not notice her any more than they do, which is not at all — the man's hands high up on the woman's legs, her skirt up, her stockings and garters, the petals and finally all the flowers spilling out into the aisle and his mouth open on her. My mother. My father. I am conceived near Dallas in the dark while a child passes, a young girl who knows and doesn't know, who witnesses, in glimpses, the creation of the universe, who feels an odd hurt as her own mother, fat and empty, snores with her mouth open, her false teeth slipping down, snores and snores just two seats behind the Creators.

News can make a person stupid. It can make you think you can do something. So I ask The Blade question, thinking that if he hasn't had the operation yet that I can fly to him, rent a cabin out on Puget Sound. That we can talk. That I can get him to touch base with reality.

"Begin with an orange," I would tell him. "Because oranges are mildly intrusive by nature, put the orange somewhere so that it will not bother you — in the cupboard, in a drawer, even a pocket or a handbag will do. The orange, being a patient fruit, will wait for you much longer than say a banana or a peach."

I would hold an orange out to him. I would say, "This is the one that will save your life." And I would tell him about the woman I saw in a bus station who bit right into her orange like it was an apple. She was wild looking, as if she'd been outside for too long in a wind that blew the same way all the time. One of the dregs of humanity, our mother would have called her, the same mother who never brought fruit into the house except in cans. My children used to ask me to "start" their oranges for them. That meant to make a hole in the orange so they could peel the rind away, and their small hands weren't equipped with fingernails that were long enough or strong enough to do the job. Sometimes they would suck the juice out of the hole my thumbnail had made, leaving the orange flat and sad.

The earrings are as big as dessert plates, filigree gold-plated with thin dangles hanging down that touch her bare shoulders. She stands in front of the Alamo while a bald man takes her picture. The sun is absorbed by the earrings so quickly that by the time she feels the heat, it is too late. The hanging dangles make small blisters on her shoulders, as if a centipede had traveled there. She takes the famous river walk in spiked heels, rides in a boat, eats some Italian noodles, returns to the motel room, soaks her feet, and applies small band-aids to her toes. She is briefly concerned about the gun on the nightstand. The toilet flushes. She pretends to be sleeping. The gun is just large and heavy. A .45? A .357 magnum? She's never been good with names. She hopes he doesn't try to. Or that if he does, that it's not loaded. But he'll say it's loaded just for fun. Or he'll pull the trigger and the bullet will lodge in her medulla oblongata, ripping through her womb first, taking everything else vital on the way.

In the magazine articles, you don't see this: "Well, yes. The testicles have to come out. And yes. The penis is cut off." What you get is tonsils. So-and-so has had a "sex change" operation. A sex change operation. How precious. How benign. Doctor, just what do you people do with those penises?

News can make a person a little crazy also. News like, "We regret to inform you that you have failed your sanity hearing."

The bracelet on my wrist bears the necessary information about me, but there is one small error. The receptionist typing the information asked me my religious preference. I said, "None." She typed, "Neon."

Pearl doesn't have any teeth and her tongue looks weird. She says, "Pumpkin pie." That's all she says. Sometimes she runs her hands over my bed sheets and says pumpkin pie. Sometimes I am under the sheets. Marsha got stabbed in the chest, but she tells everyone she fell on a knife. Elizabeth — she's the one who thinks her shoe is a baby — hit me in the back with a tray right after one of the cooks gave me extra toast. There's a note on the bulletin board about a class for the nurses: "How Putting A Towel On Sometime's Face Makes Them Stop Banging Their Spoon/OR Reduction of Disruptive Mealtime Behavior By Facial Screening — 7 P.M. — Conference Room." Another note announces the topic for remotivation class: "COWS." All the paranoid schizophrenics will be there.

Here, in the place for the permanently bewildered, I fit right in. Not because I stood at the window that first night and listened to the trains. Not because I imagined those trains were bracelets, the jewelry of earth. Not even because I imagined that one of those bracelets was on my own arm and was the Texas Zephyr where a young couple made love and conceived me. I am eighteen and beautiful and committed to the state hospital by a district court judge for a period of one day to life. Because I am a paranoid schizophrenic.

I will learn about cows.

So I'm being very quiet in the back of the classroom, and I'm peeling an orange. It's the smell that makes the others begin to turn around, that mildly intrusive nature. The course is called "Women and Modern Literature," and the diaries of Virginia Woolf are up for discussion except nobody has anything to say. I, of course, am making a mess with the orange; and I'm wanting to say that my brother is now my sister.

Later, with my hands still orangey, I wander in to leave something on a desk in a professor's office, and he's reading so I'm being very quiet, and then he says, sort of out of nowhere, "Emily Dickinson up there in her room making poems while her brother was making love to her best friend right downstairs on the dining room table. A regular thing. Think of it. And Walt Whitman out sniffing around the boys. Our two great American poets." And I want to grab this professor's arm and say, "Listen. My brother called me and now he's my sister, and I'm having trouble making sense out of my life right now, so would you mind not telling me any more stuff about sex." And I want my knuckles to turn white while the pressure of my fingers leaves imprints right through his jacket, little indentations he can interpret as urgent. But I don't say anything. And I don't grab his arm. I go read a magazine. I find this:

"I've never found an explanation for why the human race has so many languages. When the brain became a language brain, it obviously needed to develop an intense degree of plasticity. Such plasticity allows languages to be logical, coherent systems and yet be extremely variable. The same brain that thinks in words and symbols is also a brain that has to be freed up with regard to sexual turn-on and partnering. God knows why sex attitudes have been subject to the corresponding degrees of modification and variety as language. I suspect there's a close parallel between the two. The brain doesn't seem incredibly efficient with regard to sex."

John Money said that. The same John Money who, with surgeon Howard W. Jones, performed the first sex change operation in the United States in 1965 at Johns Hopkins University and Hospital in Baltimore.

Money also tells us about the *hijra* of India who disgrace their families because they are too effeminate: "The ultimate stage of the *hijra* is to get up the courage to go through the amputation of penis and testicles. They had no anesthetic." Money also answers anyone who might think that "heartless members of the medical profession are forcing these poor darlings to go and get themselves cut up and mutilated," or who think the medical profession should leave them alone. "You'd have lots of patients willing to get a gun and blow off their own genitals if you don't do it. I've had several who got knives and cut themselves trying to get rid of their sex organs. That's their obsession!"

Perhaps better than all else, I understand obsession. It is of the mind. And it is language-bound. Sex is of the body. It has no words. I am stunned to learn that someone with an obsession of the mind can have parts of the body surgically removed. This is my brother I speak of. This is not some lunatic named Carl who becomes Carlene. This is my brother.

So while we're out in that cabin on Puget Sound, I'll tell him about LuAnn. She is the sort of woman who orders the inseason fruit and a little cottage cheese. I am the sort of woman who orders a double cheeseburger and fries. LuAnn and I are sitting in her car. She has a huge orange, and she peels it so the peel falls off in one neat strip. I have a sack of oranges, the small ones. The peel of my orange comes off in hunks about the size of a baby's nail. "Oh, you bought the *juice* oranges," LuAnn says to me. Her emphasis on the word "juice" makes me want to die or something. I lack the courage to admit my ignorance, so I smile and breathe "yes," as if I know some secret, when I'm wanting to scream at her about how my mother didn't teach me about fruit and my own blood pounds in my head wanting out, out.

There is a pattern to this thought as there is a pattern for a jumpsuit. Sew the sleeve to the leg, sew the leg to the collar. Put the garment on. Sew the mouth shut. This is how I tell about being quiet because I am bad, and because I cannot stand it when he beats me or my brother.

"The first time I got caught in your clothes was when I was four years old and you were over at Sarah what's-her-name's babysitting. Dad beat me so hard I thought I was going to die. I really thought I was going to die. That was the day I made up my mind I would *never* get caught again. And I never got caught again." My brother goes on to say he continued to go through my things until I was hospitalized. A mystery is solved.

He wore my clothes. He played in my makeup. I kept saying, back then, that someone was going through my stuff. I kept saying it and saying it. I told the counselor at school. "Someone goes in my room when I'm not there, and I *know* it — goes in there and wears my clothes and goes through my stuff." I was assured by the counselor that this was not so. I was assured by my mother that this was not so. I thought my mother was doing it, snooping around for clues like mothers do. It made me a little crazy, so I started deliberately leaving things in a certain order so that I would be able to prove to myself that someone, indeed, was going through my belongings. No one, not one person, ever believed that my room was being ransacked; I was accused of just making it up. A paranoid fixation.

And all the time it was old Goldilocks.

So I tell my brother to promise me he'll see someone who counsels adult children from dysfunctional families. I tell him he needs to deal with the fact that he was physically abused on a daily basis. He tells me he doesn't remember being beaten except on three occasions. He wants me to get into a support group for families of people who are having a sex change. Support groups are people who are in the same boat. Except no one has any oars in the water.

I tell him I know how it feels to think you are in the wrong body. I tell him how I wanted my boyfriend to put a gun up inside me and blow the woman out, how I thought wearing spiked heels and low-cut dresses would somehow help my crisis, that putting on an ultrafeminine outside would mask the maleness I felt needed hiding. I tell him it's the rule, rather than the exception, that people from families like ours have very spooky sexual identity problems. He tells me that his sexuality is a birth defect. I recognize the lingo. It's support-group-for-transsexuals lingo. He tells me he sits down to pee. He told his therapist that he used to wet all over the floor. His therapist said, "You can't aim the bullets if you don't touch the gun." Lingo. My brother is hell-bent for castration, the castration that started before he had language: the castration of abuse. He will simply finish what was set in motion long ago.

I will tell my brother about the time I took ten sacks of oranges into a school so that I could teach metaphor. The school was for special students — those who were socially or intellectually impaired. I had planned to have them peel the oranges as I spoke about how much the world is like the orange. I handed out the oranges. The students refused to peel them, not because they wanted to make life difficult for me — they were enchanted with the gift. One child asked if he could have an orange to take home to his little brother. Another said he would bring me ten dollars the next day if I would give him a sack of oranges. And I knew I was at home, that these children and I shared something that *makes* the leap of mind the metaphor attempts. And something in me healed.

A neighbor of mine takes pantyhose and cuts them up and sews them up after stuffing them. Then she puts these things into Mason jars and sells them, you know, to put out on the mantel for conversation. They are little penises and little scrotums, complete with hair. She calls them "Pickled Peters."

A friend of mine had a sister who had a sex change operation. This young woman had her breasts removed and ran around the house with no shirt on before the stitches were taken out. She answered the door one evening. A young man had come to call on my friend. The sex-changed sister invited him in and offered him some black bean soup as if she were perfectly normal with her red surgical wounds and her black stitches. The young man left and never went back. A couple years later, my friend's sister/brother died when s/he ran a car into a concrete bridge railing. I hope for a happier ending. For my brother, for myself, for all of us.

My brother calls. He's done his toenails: Shimmering Cinnamon. And he's left his wife and children and purchased some nightgowns at a yard sale. His hair is getting longer. He wears a special bra. Most of the people he works with know about the changes in his life. His voice is not the same voice I've heard for years; he sounds happy.

My brother calls. He's always envied me, my woman's body. The same body I live in and have cursed for its softness. He asks me how I feel about myself. He says, "You know, you are really our father's first-born son." He tells me he used to want to be me because I was the only person our father almost loved.

The drama of life. After I saw that woman in the bus station eat an orange as if it were an apple, I went out into the street and smoked a joint with some guy I'd met on the bus. Then I hailed a cab and went to a tattoo parlor. The tattoo artist tried to talk me into getting a nice bird or butterfly design; I had chosen a design on his wall that appealed to me — a symbol I didn't know the meaning of. It is the Yin-Yang, and it's tattooed above my right ankle bone. I suppose my drugged, crazed consciousness knew more than I knew: that yin combines with yang to produce all that comes to be. I am drawn to androgyny.

Of course there is the nagging possibility that my brother's dilemma is genetic. Our father used to dress in drag on Halloween, and he made a beautiful woman. One year, the year my mother cut my brother's blond curls off, my father taped those curls to his own head and tied a silk scarf over the tape. Even his close friends didn't know it was him. And my youngest daughter was a body builder for a while, her lean body as muscular as a man's. And my sons are beautiful, not handsome: they look androgynous.

Then there's my grandson. I saw him when he was less than an hour old. He was naked and had hiccups. I watched as he had his first bath, and I heard him cry. He had not been named yet, but his little crib had a blue card affixed to it with tape. And on the card were the words "Baby Boy." There was no doubt in me that the words were true.

When my brother was born, my father was off flying jets in Korea. I went to the hospital with my grandfather to get my mother and this new brother. I remember how I wanted a sister, and I remember looking at him as my mother held him in the front seat of the car. I was certain he was a sister, certain that my mother was joking. She removed his diaper to show me that he was a boy. I still didn't believe her. Considering what has happened lately, I wonder if my child-skewed consciousness knew more than the anatomical proof suggested.

I try to make peace with myself. I try to understand his decision to alter himself. I try to think of him as her. I write his woman name, and I feel like I'm betraying myself. I try to be open-minded, but something in me shuts down. I think we humans are in big trouble, that many of us don't really have a clue as to what acceptable human behavior is. Something in me says no to all this, that this surgery business is the ultimate betrayal of the self. And yet, I want my brother to be happy.

It was in the city of San Antonio that my father had his surgery. I rode the bus from Kansas to Texas, and arrived at the hospital two days after the operation to find my father sitting in the solarium playing solitaire. He had a type of cancer that particularly thrived on testosterone. And so he was castrated in order to ease his pain and to stop the growth of tumors. He died six months later.

Back in the sleep of the large world of dreams, I have done surgeries under water in which I float my father's testicles back into him, and he — the brutal man he was — emerges from the pool a tan and smiling man, parting the surface of the water with his perfect head. He loves all the grief away.

I will tell my brother all I know of oranges, that if you squeeze the orange peel into a flame, small fires happen because of the volatile oil in the peel. Also, if you squeeze the peel and it gets into your cat's eyes, the cat will blink and blink. I will tell him there is no perfect rhyme for the word "orange," and that if we can just make up a good word we can be immortal. We will become obsessed with finding the right word, and I will be joyous at our legitimate pursuit.

I have purchased a black camisole with lace to send to my new sister. And a card. On the outside of the card there's a drawing of a woman sitting by a pond and a zebra is off to the left. Inside are these words; "The past is ended. Be happy." And I have asked my companions to hold me and I have cried. My self is wet and small. But it is not dark. Sometimes, if no one touches me, I will die.

Sister, you are the best craziness of the family. Brother, love what you love.

Reflections and Responses

1. Ruiz opens her essay with references to sleep and dreams. How do these states appear and reappear throughout the essay? What effect do they have on your reading of the essay?

2. Consider the different kinds of errors and mistakes that Ruiz refers to throughout the essay. Identify a few of these. How do they reinforce her theme? Observe, too, the references to names, labels, and writing. How are these related to the theme of the essay?

3. At the center of this essay is the writer's brother. Why, then, does Ruiz introduce oranges? Identify their many occurrences. What do they have to do with her subject?

DIANA HUME GEORGE

Wounded Chevy at
Wounded Knee

*This is not so much an essay of mixed identity as of mixed identification.
As a white teenager, Diana Hume George hung out with Senecan Indians
on a reservation in western New York State. She married a young Senecan
carnival worker and lived deep inside Native American culture for five
years. Her "romance with Indians" left her with a very unromantic view of
Native American life today and a "contempt for the white liberal intellectual's romance with all things Indian." In this tough-minded essay, she
writes of how years later she finally came to terms with "confusion, rejection, and ambivalence" as a result of a chance encounter one day at
Wounded Knee in South Dakota, the historical site of the 1890 U.S. Cavalry massacre of the Lakota.*

*Diana Hume George is a professor of English and Women's Studies at
Pennsylvania State University, Erie Behrend College. She is the author of
several books of literary criticism, including* Blake and Freud *(1980)
and* Oedipus Anne: The Poetry of Anne Sexton *(1987), as well as
several volumes of poetry, including* The Resurrection of the Body
*(1989). Her critical essays on poetry and psychoanalytic feminism have
been published in a variety of literary periodicals. Her latest collection of essays is* The Lonely Other: A Woman Watching America *(1994).
"Wounded Chevy at Wounded Knee" originally appeared in* The Missouri Review *(1990) and was selected by Joyce Carol Oates for* The Best
American Essays 1991.

Pine Ridge Sioux Reservation, July 1989
"If you break down on that reservation, your car belongs to the
Indians. They don't like white people out there." This was our ami-
able motel proprietor in Custer, South Dakota, who asked where

we were headed and then propped a conspiratorial white elbow on the counter and said we'd better make sure our vehicle was in good shape. To get to Wounded Knee, site of the last cavalry massacre of the Lakota in 1890 and of more recent confrontations between the FBI and the American Indian Movement, you take a road out of Pine Ridge on the Lakota reservation and go about eight miles. If you weren't watching for it you could miss it, because nothing is there but a hill, a painted board explaining what happened, a tiny church, and a cemetery.

The motel man told us stories about his trucking times, when by day his gas stops were friendly, but by night groups of Indian men who'd been drinking used to circle his truck looking for something to steal — or so he assumed. He began carrying a .357 Magnum with him "just in case." Once he took his wife out to Pine Ridge. "She broke out in hives before we even got there." And when they were stopped on the roadside and a reservation policeman asked if they needed help, she was sure he was going to order her out of the car, steal it, and, I suppose, rape and scalp her while he was at it. As the motel man told us these contradictory stories, he seemed to be unaware of the irony of warning us that the Indians would steal our car if they got a chance and following with a story about an Indian who tried to help them just in case they might be having trouble.

He did make a distinction between the reservation toughs and the police. He wasn't a racist creep, but rather a basically decent fellow whose view of the world was narrowly white. I briefly entertained the notion of staying awhile, pouring another cup of coffee, and asking him a few questions that would make him address the assumptions behind his little sermon, but I really wanted to get on my way, and I knew he wasn't going to change his mind about Indians here in the middle of his life in the middle of the Black Hills.

Mac and I exchanged a few rueful remarks about it while we drove. But we both knew that the real resistance to dealing with Indian culture on these trips that have taken us through both Pueblo and Plains Indian territories hasn't come from outside of our car or our minds, but rather from within them. More specifically, from within me. For years Mac has read about the Plains Indians with real attentiveness and with an openness to learning what he can about the indigenous peoples of North America. He reads histo-

ries, biographies, novels, and essays, thinks carefully about the issues involved, remembers what he has read, informs himself with
curiosity and respect about tribes that have occupied the areas we
visit. For a couple of years he urged me toward these materials,
many of which have been visible around our home for years: *Black
Elk Speaks, In a Sacred Manner We Live, Bury My Heart at Wounded
Knee,* studies of Indian spiritual and cultural life. While we were in
Lakota country this time, he was reading Mari Sandoz's biography
of Crazy Horse. But he has long since given up on getting me to
pay sustained attention to these rich materials, because my resistance has been firm and long-standing. I am probably better informed about Indian life than most Americans ever thought of
being, but not informed enough for a thoughtful reader and writer.
My resistance has taken the form of a mixture of pride and contempt: pride that I already know more than these books can tell
me, and contempt for the white liberal intellectual's romance with
all things Indian. But my position has been very strange perhaps,
given that I was married to an American Indian for five years, lived
on a reservation, and am the mother of a half-Indian son.

I've been mostly wrong in my attitudes, but it's taken me years to
understand that. Wounded Knee is where I came to terms with my
confusion, rejection, and ambivalence, and it happened in a direct
confrontation with past events that are now twenty years old. My
resistance broke down because of an encounter with a young
Lakota named Mark, who is just about my own son's age.

I grew up in the 1950s and 1960s in a small white community
on the edge of the Cattaraugus Seneca Indian Reservation in western New York State. Relations between Indians and whites in my
world were bitter, and in many respects replicated the dynamics
between whites and blacks in the South, with many exceptions due
to the very different functions and circumstances of these two
groups of people of color in white America. The school system had
recently been integrated after the closing of the Thomas Indian
School on the reservation. The middle-class whites wanted nothing to do with the Indians, whom they saw as drunkards and de-
generates, in many cases subhuman. When I rebelled against the
restraints of my white upbringing, the medium for asserting myself against my parents and my world was ready-made, and I
grabbed it.

I began hanging out on the reserve with young Indians and shifted my social and sexual arena entirely to the Indian world. I fell in love with an idea of noble darkness in the form of an Indian carnival worker, got pregnant by him, married him, left the white world completely, and moved into his. Despite the fact that this was the sixties, my actions weren't politically motivated; or, rather, my politics were entirely personal at that point. While my more aware counterparts might have done some of the same things as conscious political and spiritual statements, I was fifteen when I started my romance with Indians, and I only knew that I was in love with life outside the constricting white mainstream, and with all the energy that vibrates on the outer reaches of cultural stability. My heart and what would later become my politics were definitely in the right place, and I have never regretted where I went or what I came to know. But for twenty years that knowledge spoiled me for another kind of knowing.

Whatever my romantic notions were about the ideal forms of American Indian wisdom — closeness to the land, respect for other living creatures, a sense of harmony with natural cycles, a way of walking lightly in the world, a manner of living that could make the ordinary and profane into the sacred — I learned that on the reservation I was inhabiting a world that was contrary to all these values. American Indian culture at the end of the road has virtually none of these qualities. White America has destroyed them. Any culture in its death throes is a grim spectacle, and there can be no grimmer reality than that endured by people on their way to annihilation.

I did not live among the scattered wise people or political activists of the Seneca Nation. I did not marry a nominal American Indian from a middle-class family. I married an illiterate man who dropped out of school in the seventh grade and was in school only intermittently before that. He traveled around the East with carnivals, running a Ferris wheel during the summer months, and logged wood on the reservation during the winter — when he could get work. Home base was an old trailer without plumbing in the woods, where his mother lived. He drank sporadically but heavily, and his weekends, often his weekdays, were full of pool tables, bar brawls, the endlessness of hanging out with little to do. He didn't talk much. How I built this dismal life into a romanti-

cized myth about still waters running deep gives me an enduring respect for the mythopoeic, self-deluding power of desire, wish,
will.

When I was married to him my world was a blur of old cars
driven by drunk men in the middle of the night, of honky-tonk
bars, country music, late night fights with furniture flying, food
stamps and welfare lines, stories of injury and death. The smell of
beer still sickens me slightly. I was sober as a saint through all of
this, so I didn't have the insulation of liquor, only of love. I lived
the contrary of every white myth about Indian life, both the myths
of the small-town white racists and those of the smitten hippies.
When I finally left that life behind, extricating myself and my child
in the certain knowledge that to stay would mean something very
like death for both of us, I removed myself in every respect. I knew
how stupid white prejudice was, understood the real story about
why Indians drank and wasted their lives, felt the complexities so
keenly that I couldn't even try to explain them to anyone white.
But similarly, I knew how birdbrained the lovechild generation's
romance with Indian culture was.

My husband went on to a career of raping white women that had
begun during — or maybe before — our marriage. When he was
finally caught, convicted, and sent to Attica, I was long since done
with that part of my life. My son pulled me back toward it with his
own love for his father, and I still keep in touch with my husband's
mother on the reservation, sometimes helping her to handle white
bureaucracy, but that's all. I heard at a remove of miles, of eons, it
seemed, about the early deaths of young men I'd known well —
deaths due to diabetes, to lost limbs, or to car wrecks at high
speed — and I felt something, but I didn't have to deal with it.
When I tried to think about that past life in order to put it into
some kind of perspective, no whole picture emerged. When I tried
to write about it, no words would come. And when I tried to be
open to learning something new about Indians in America on my
trips, my heart closed up tight, and with it my mind. When I went
to Wounded Knee, the wounds of these other Indians half a continent and half a lifetime away were a part of the landscape.

We pull off to the side of the road to read the billboard that tells
what happened here. "Massacre of Wounded Knee" is the header,

but upon close inspection you see that "Massacre" is a new addition, painted over something else. "Battle," perhaps? What did it used to say, I wonder, and hope I'll run into a local who can tell me. While I'm puzzling over this, an old Chevy sputters into the pull-off and shakes to a stop. It's loaded with dark faces, a young man and an older woman with many small children. The man gets out and walks slowly to the front of the car, rolling up his T-shirt over his stomach to get air on his skin. As he raises the hood, a Comanche truck pulls in beside him with one woman inside. It's very hot, and I weave a little in the glare of sun. Suddenly I see the past, superimposed on this hot moment. I've seen it before, again and again, cars full of little Indian kids in the heat of summer on the sides of roads. I glance again, see the woman in the front seat, know that she's their mother or their aunt. She looks weary and resigned, not really sad. She expects this.

And then in another blink it's not only that I have seen this woman; I have *been* this woman, my old car or someone else's packed with little kids who are almost preternaturally quiet, wide-eyed and dark-skinned and already knowing that this is a big part of what life is about, sitting in boiling back seats, their arms jammed against the arms of their brother, their sister, their cousin. There is no use asking when they'll get there, wherever "there" is. It will happen when it happens, when the adults as helpless as they are, figure out what to do. In the meantime they sweat and stare. But I am not this woman anymore, not responsible for these children, some of whose intelligent faces will blank into a permanent sheen of resignation before they're five. I am a tourist in a new Plymouth Voyager, my luggage rack packed with fine camping equipment, my Minolta in my hand to snap pictures of the places I can afford to go.

When Mac suggests that we offer to help them, I am not surprised at my flat negative feeling. He doesn't know what that means, I surmise, and I don't have any way to tell him. Help them? Do you want to get anywhere today, do you have the whole afternoon? The young man's shoulders bend over the motor. He is fit and beautiful, his good torso moves knowingly but powerlessly over the heat rising from beneath the hood. I recognize him, as well as the woman. He has no job. He talks about getting off the reservation, finding work, living the dreams he still has. He'll talk this way for a few more years, then give up entirely. He drinks too much. He has nothing to do. Drinking is the only thing that makes him really laugh, and his only way to release rage. I also know that whatever else is wrong with it the car is out of gas, and that these people have no money. Okay, sure, I say to Mac, standing to one side while he asks how we can help. Close to the car now, I see that the woman is the young man's mother. These kids are his brothers and sisters.

The car is out of gas and it needs a jump. The battery is bad. The woman in the other car is the young man's aunt, who can give him a jump but has no money to give him for gas — or so she says. I know her, too. She is more prosperous than her relatives, and has learned the hard way never to give them any money because she needs it herself, and if she gives it to them she'll never see it again. She made her policy years ago, and makes it stick no matter what. She has to.

Well, then, we'll take them to the nearest gas station. Do they have a gas can? No, just a plastic washer-fluid jug with no top. Okay, that will have to do. How far is the nearest gas? Just up the road a couple of miles. But they don't have any money because they were on their way to cash his mother's unemployment check when they ran out of gas, and the town where they can do that is many miles away. So can we loan them some money for gas? We can. He gets in the front seat. I get in the back, and as we pull away from the windy parking area, I look at the woman and the kids who will be sitting in the car waiting until we return. She knows she can't figure out how soon that will be. She stares straight ahead. I don't want to catch her eye, nor will she catch mine.

Right here up this road. Mark is in his early twenties. Mac asks him questions. He is careful and restrained in his answers at first, then begins to open up. No there's no work around here. Sometimes he does a little horse breaking or fence mending for the ranchers. All the ranches here are run by whites who had the money to make the grim land yield a living. They lease it from the Lakota. Mark went away to a Job Corps camp last year, but he had to come back because his twenty-one-year-old brother died last winter, leaving his mother alone with the little ones. He froze to death. He was drinking at a party and went outside to take a leak. Mark said they figured he must have just stopped for a minute to rest, and then he fell asleep. They found him frozen in the morning. Mark had to come back home to bury his brother and help his mother with the kids.

As we bounce over the dirt road, I stare at the back of Mark's head and at his good Indian profile when he turns toward Mac to speak. He is so familiar to me that I could almost reach out to touch his black straight hair, his brown shoulder. He is my husband, he is my son. I want to give him hope. He speaks about getting out of here, going to "Rapid" — Lakota shorthand for Rapid City — and making a life. He is sick of having nothing to do, he wants work, wants an apartment. But he can't leave yet; he has to stay to help his mother. But things are going to be okay, because he has just won a hundred thousand dollars and is waiting for them to send the check.

What?

"You know the Baja Sweepstakes?" He pronounces it "Bay-jah." "Well, I won it, I think I won it, I got a letter. My little brother sent in the entry form we got with my CD club and he put my name on it, and it came back saying that I'm one of a select few chosen people who've won a hundred thousand dollars. That's what it said, it said that, and I had to scratch out the letters and if three of them matched it means I win, and they matched, and so I sent it back in and now I'm just waiting for my money. It should come pretty soon and then everything will be okay." He repeats it over and over again in the next few minutes: he's one of a select few chosen people.

As he speaks of this, his flat voice becomes animated. Slowly I begin to believe that he believes this. Whatever part of him knows better is firmly shelved for now. This hope, this belief that hundreds of thousands of dollars are on the way, is what keeps him going, what keeps him from walking out into the sky — or to the outhouse in the winter to take a leak and a nap in the snow. What will you do with the money, I ask. Well, first he is going to buy his mother and the kids a house.

The first gas stop is a little shack that's closed when we finally get there. Sandy wind and no sign of life. Miles on down the road is a small Lakota grocery store with only a few items on the shelves and a sign that reads "Stealing is not the Lakota way." Mac hands Mark a five dollar bill. You can kiss that five bucks goodbye, I say to Mac. I know, he nods. When Mark comes back out he has the gas, and

also a big cup of 7-Up and a bag of nachos. You want some, he asks
me? He hands Mac a buck fifty in change. On the way back I hold
the gas can in the back seat, placing my hand over the opening.
Despite the open windows, the van fills with fumes. My head begins to ache. I am riding in a dream of flatness, ranch fences,
Mark's dark head in front of me wishing away his life, waiting for
the break that takes him to Rapid. Later I learn that we are in Man-
derson, and this is the road where Black Elk lived.

Mark is talking about white people now. Yes, they get along okay.
For "yes" he has an expression of affirmation that sounds sort of
like "huh." Mari Sandoz spells it "hou" in her books on the Lakota.
The Lakota are infiltrated in every way by whites, according to
Mark. Lots of people in charge are white, the ranchers are white.
And there's a place in Rapid called Lakota Hills, fancy houses
meant for Lakotas, but whites live in them. Later it occurs to us
that this is probably a development named Lakota Hills that has
nothing at all to do with the Indians, but it has their name and so
Mark thinks it belongs to them. I am angry for him that we borrow
their name this way and paste it on our air-conditioned prosperity.
I don't have anything to say to him. I lean back and close my eyes.
It would be easy to be one of them again. I remember now how it's
done. You just let everything flatten inside.

And when we return to Wounded Knee, the pull-off is empty.
Mother, children, car, aunt, all are gone. There's nothing but wind
and dust. This doesn't surprise me. Mark's mother knows better
than to wait for her son's return if other help comes along. Mark
means well, but maybe she has learned that sometimes it's hours
before he gets back with gas — hours and a couple of six-packs if
he has the chance. Now we face the prospect of driving Mark
around the reservation until we can find them. I have just resigned
myself to this when his aunt pulls back in and says they're broken
down again a couple of miles up. We can leave now. Mark thanks
us, smiles, and shyly allows us the liberty of having his aunt take a
picture of all three of us. I am feeling a strange kind of shame, as
though I had seen him naked, because he told us his secret and I
knew it was a lie.

Unemployment, high rates of suicide and infant mortality, fetal
alcohol syndrome, death by accident, and drinking-related dis-

eases such as diabetes: these are now the ways that American Indians are approaching their collective demise. Over a century ago, American whites began this destruction by displacing and killing the *pte*, the Indian name for the buffalo the Plains Indians depended upon. We herded them together in far crueler ways than they had herded the bison, whose sacredness the Indians respected even as they killed them for food and shelter. The history of our genocide is available in many historical and imaginative sources. What is still elusive, still amazingly misunderstood, is how and why the Indians seem to have participated in their own destruction by their failure to adapt to changed circumstances.

Whites can point to the phenomenal adjustments of other non-Caucasian groups in America, most recently the Asians, who were badly mistreated and who have nevertheless not only adapted but excelled. Indians even come off badly in comparison to the group in some respects most parallel to them, American blacks, whose slowness in adapting seems at first glance to have more justification. Blacks were, after all, our slaves, brought here against their will, without close cultural ties to keep them bound together in a tradition of strength; and on the whole blacks are doing better than Indians. However slowly, a black middle class is emerging in America. What's the matter with Indians? Why haven't they adjusted better as a group?

The American Indian Movement is of course strong in some areas, and Indians have articulate, tough leaders and savvy representatives of their cause who are fighting hard against the tide of despair gripping the heart of their race. But they're still losing, and they know it. Estimates of unemployment on the Pine Ridge and Rosebud reservations run as high as 85 percent. Health officials at Pine Ridge estimate that as many as 25 percent of babies born on the reservation now have fetal alcohol syndrome. This culturally lethal condition cannot be overemphasized, since it means that the next generation of Lakota are genetically as well as socioeconomically crippled; one of the consequences of fetal alcohol syndrome is not only physical disability but mental retardation. The prospects are extremely depressing for Lakota leaders whose traditional values are associated with mental acuity and imaginative wisdom. Mark is vastly ignorant and gullible, but he is intelligent enough. Many of his younger brothers and sisters are not only underprivileged and without educational advantages, but also — let the word be spoken — stupid. When the light of inquiry, curiosity, mental energy, dies out in the eyes of young Indians early in their stunted lives because they have nowhere to go and nothing to do, it is one kind of tragedy. When it is never present to die out in the first place, the magnitude of the waste and devastation is exponentially increased. Indian leaders who are now concentrating on anti-alcohol campaigns among their people are doing so for good reasons.

Indian leaders disagree about culpability at this point. Essentially the arguments become theories of genocide or suicide. On one end of the spectrum of blame is the theory that it is all the fault of white America. The evidence that can be marshaled for this point of view is massive: broken treaties, complete destruction of the Indian ways of life, welfare dependency established as the cheapest and easiest form of guilt payment, continued undermining of Indian autonomy and rights. The problem with this perspective, say others, is that it perpetuates Indian desperation and permits the easy way out — spend your life complaining that white America put you here, and drink yourself into the oblivion of martyrdom instead of taking responsibility for your own life. Some Indians say they've heard enough about white America's culpability, and prefer to transfer responsibility — not blame, but responsibility — to the shoulders of their own people. "White people aren't doing this to us — we're doing it to ourselves," said one Pine Ridge health official on National Public Radio's *Morning Edition* recently. She sees the victim stance as the lethal enemy now.

The situation is as nearly hopeless as it is possible to be. Assimilation failed the first time and would fail if tried concertedly again, because Indian culture is rural and tribal and tied to open land, not urban airlessness. The Indian model is the encampment or village — the latter more recently and under duress — and not the city. Even the more stationary pueblo model is by definition not urban. The only real hope for Indian prosperity would be connected to vast tracts of land — not wasteland, but rich land. Nor are most Indians farmers in the sense that white America defines the farm. Though they might be, and have been, successful farmers under pressure, this is not their traditional milieu. Supposing that many tribes could adapt to the farming model over hunting and gathering, they would need large tracts of fine land to farm, and there are none left to grant them.

When the American government gave the Lakota 160 acres apiece and said "Farm this," they misunderstood the Indians completely; and even if Indians had been able to adapt readily — a change approximately as difficult as asking a yuppie to become a nomad moving from encampment to encampment — the land they were given was inadequate to the purpose. Grubbing a living out of the land we have given them, in what John Wesley Powell called "the arid region" west of the one hundredth meridian — takes a kind of know-how developed and perfected by white Americans, and it also takes capital. It is no coincidence that the large ranches on Pine Ridge are almost entirely leased by whites who had the initial wherewithal to make the land yield.

The Sioux were a people whose lives were shaped by a sense of seeking and vision that white America could barely understand even if we were to try, and we do not try. The life of a Sioux of a century and a half ago was framed by the Vision Quest, a search for goals, identity, purpose. One primary means of fulfillment was self-sacrifice. Now, as Royal Hassrick has written, "No longer is there anything which they can deny themselves, and so they have sacrificed themselves in pity." Whereas they were once people whose idea of being human was bound to creative self-expression, their faces now reflect what Hassrick calls "apathy and psychic emaciation." Collectively and individually they have become a people without a vision.

Why do they drink themselves into obliteration and erasure? Why not? When white America approaches the problem from within our own ethnocentric biases, we can't see why people would allow themselves to be wasted in this way, why they would not take the initiative to better themselves, to save themselves through the capitalist individuality that says, "*I* will make it out of this." But in fact part of their problem is that they have tried to do this, as have most Indian peoples. They've bought the American dream in part, and become greedy for money and material goods. Life on an Indian reservation — almost any reservation — is a despairing imitation of white middle-class values. In this respect Indians are like all other minority groups in ghettos in America, and this explains why Mark has a CD player instead of the more modest possessions we would not have begrudged him. If he is anything like the Indians I lived with, he also has a color TV, though he may well live in a shack or trailer without plumbing and without siding.

Their own dreams have evaded them, and so have ours. Mark and his brothers and sisters have been nourished on memories of a culture that vanished long before they were born and on the promises of a different one, from whose advantages they are forever excluded. Does Mark really believe he has won the sweepstakes? What he got was obviously one of those computer letters that invite the recipient to believe he has won something. Without the education that could teach him to read its language critically, or to read it adequately at all, he has been deceived into believing that a *deus ex machina* in the form of the Baja Sweepstakes will take him out of his despair.

In 1890, the year of the final defeat of the Sioux at Wounded Knee, the Ghost Dance was sweeping the plains. Begun by a few leaders, especially the Paiute seer Wovoka, the Ghost Dance promised its practitioners among the warriors that the buffalo would return and the white man would be defeated. Ghost Dancers believed that their ceremonial dancing and the shirts they wore would make them proof against the white man's bullets. Among the Sioux warriors at Wounded Knee, the willing suspension of disbelief was complete. It made the warriors reckless and abandoned, throwing normal caution and survival strategy to the wind.

A tragically inverted form of the self-delusion embodied in the Ghost Dance is practiced today on the Pine Ridge and other Sioux reservations. The original Ghost Dance has beauty and vitality, as well as desperation, as its sources. Now many Sioux men who would have been warriors in another time behave as though liquor and passivity will not kill them. Mark chooses to suspend his disbelief in white promises and to wait for a hundred thousand dollars to arrive in the mail.

Hank Doctor was my husband's best friend on the Seneca reservation. He was raunchy, hard drinking, outrageous in behavior and looks. His hair was long and scraggly, his nearly black eyes were genuinely wild, and his blue jeans were always caked with dust and falling down his hips. His wit was wicked, his laugh raucous, dangerous, infectious. Hank was merciless toward me, always making white-girl jokes, telling me maybe I better go home to my mama, where I'd be safe from all these dark men. He wanted me to feel a little afraid in his world, told me horrible stories about ghost-dogs that would get me on the reservation if I ventured out at night — and then he'd laugh in a way that said hey, white girl, just joking, but not entirely. He alternated his affection toward me with edgy threats, made fun of the too-white way I talked or walked, took every opportunity to make me feel foolish and out of place. He was suspicious that I was just slumming it as a temporary rebellion — maybe taking notes in my head — and that I'd probably run for home when the going got too tough. Of course he was right, even though I didn't know it at the time. I liked him a lot.

A few years ago, my son Bernie went through a period when he chose to remove himself from my world and go live in his father's, from which I'd taken him when he was three. I didn't try to stop him, even though I knew he was hanging out with people who lived dangerously. I used to lie in bed unable to go to sleep because I was wondering what tree he'd end up wrapped around with his dad. He was a minor, but I was essentially helpless to prevent this. If I'd forced the issue, it would only have made his desire to know a forbidden world more intense. He lived there for months, and I slowly learned to get to sleep at night. Mothers can't save their children. And he had a right.

The day I knew he'd ultimately be okay was when he came home and told me about Hank. He wondered if I'd known Hank. He'd never met him before because Hank had been out west for years. Now he was back home, living in a shack way out in the country, terribly crippled with diabetes and other ailments from drinking, barely able to walk. Hank would have been in his mid-forties at this time. Bernie and his dad took rabbits to Hank when they went hunting so that Hank would have something to eat. During these visits, Hank talked nonstop about the old days, reminding big Bernard of all their bar brawls, crowing to young Bernie that the two of them could beat anyone when they fought as a team, recounting the times they'd dismantled the insides of buildings at four in the morning. He told his stories in vivid, loving detail. His gift for metaphor was precise and fine, his memory perfect even if hyperbolic. He recalled the conversations leading up to fights, the way a person had leaned over the bar, and who had said what to whom just before the furniture flew.

Bernie was impressed with him, but mostly he thought it was pathetic, this not-yet-old man who looked like he was in his seventies, with nothing to remember but brawls. I told Bernie to value Hank for the way he remembered, the way he could make a night from twenty years ago intensely present again, his gift for swagger and characterization, his poetry, his laughter. In another time Hank would have been a tribal narrator, a story catcher with better exploits to recount. He would have occupied a special place in Seneca life because of his gifts.

My son left the reservation valuing and understanding important things about his father's world, but not interested in living in its grip. He lives in Florida where he's a chef in a resort, and he's going to college. A month ago his daughter, my granddaughter, was born. She is named Sequoia, after the Cherokee chief who gave his people an alphabet and a written language. Bernie took her to the reservation on his recent visit north and introduced the infant Sequoia to her great-grandmother. My husband's mother says that big Bernard is drinking again, using up her money, and she doesn't know how much more she can take. I know she'll take as much as she has to. I hope I'll see Bernard someday soon to say hello, and maybe we can bend together over our granddaughter, for whom I know we both have many hopes.

Just before we leave Wounded Knee, I walk over to Aunt Lena's Comanche and point to the tribal sign that tells the story. "It says 'Massacre' there, but it used to say something else." I ask her if she knows what it said before. She looks over my shoulder and laughs. "That's funny," she says, "I've lived here all my life, but you know, I never did read that sign." We're miles down the road before I realize that I never finished reading it myself.

Reflections and Responses

1. What do you think Diana Hume George means by the "white liberal intellectual's romance with all things Indian"? What are some examples of this romance in our culture? Can you find any examples of it in her essay? In what ways does she herself try to resist this romance? How well do you think she succeeds?

2. Do you think the author is being unfair or harsh to Native American males? How would you summarize her attitude toward them? Does her attitude seem to be based solely on her personal experience? Explain your answer. What evidence from the essay would you introduce to counter the charge that she is treating Native American men unjustly?

3. Consider the essay's final paragraph. How does it comment on the opening paragraph? Of what significance is it that Aunt Lena admits that she's never read the sign? How is that detail — and the author's final sentence — relevant to the essay as a whole?

2

Heritage

JUDITH ORTIZ COFER

Silent Dancing

Nothing rekindles childhood memories better than old photographs or home movies. In this vivid essay, a grainy and poorly focused five-minute home movie of a New Year's Eve party helps a writer capture the spirit of a Puerto Rican community in Paterson, New Jersey. That the movie is fragmented and silent adds to its documentary value and, for a lyrical essayist, it evokes much more than it can possibly reveal. "Even the home movie," Cofer writes, "cannot fill in the sensory details such a gathering left imprinted in a child's brain." Those sensory details — "the flavor of Puerto Rico" — must be supplied through the art of writing.

An assistant professor of English and creative writing at the University of Georgia, Judith Ortiz Cofer has published prize-winning books in a number of genres: a novel, The Line of the Sun *(1989); two poetry collections,* Terms of Survival *(1987) and* Reaching for the Mainland *(1986); and two autobiographical books combining prose and poetry,* Silent Dancing *(1990) and* The Latin Deli *(1993). Cofer has received many prestigious awards, including fellowships from the National Endowment for the Arts, the Witter Bynner Foundation for Poetry, and the Bread Loaf Writers' Conference. "Silent Dancing" originally appeared in* The Georgia Review *(1990) and was selected by Joyce Carol Oates for* The Best American Essays *1991. Ms. Cofer courteously supplied the notes to this selection.*

We have a home movie of this party. Several times my mother and I have watched it together, and I have asked questions about the silent revelers coming in and out of focus. It is grainy and of short duration, but it's a great visual aid to my memory of life at that time. And it is in color — the only complete scene in color I can recall from those years.

We lived in Puerto Rico until my brother was born in 1954. Soon after, because of economic pressures on our growing family, my father joined the United States Navy. He was assigned to duty on a ship in Brooklyn Yard — a place of cement and steel that was to be his home base in the States until his retirement more than twenty years later. He left the Island first, alone, going to New York City and tracking down his uncle who lived with his family across the Hudson River in Paterson, New Jersey. There my father found a tiny apartment in a huge tenement that had once housed Jewish families but was just being taken over and transformed by Puerto Ricans, overflowing from New York City. In 1955 he sent for us. My mother was only twenty years old, I was not quite three, and my brother was a toddler when we arrived at *El Building*, as the place had been christened by its newest residents.

My memories of life in Paterson during those first few years are all in shades of gray. Maybe I was too young to absorb vivid colors and details, or to discriminate between the slate blue of the winter sky and the darker hues of the snow-bearing clouds, but that single color washes over the whole period. The building we lived in was gray, as were the streets, filled with slush the first few months of my life there. The coat my father had bought for me was similar in color and too big; it sat heavily on my thin frame.

I do remember the way the heater pipes banged and rattled, startling all of us out of sleep until we got so used to the sound that we automatically shut it out or raised our voices above the racket. The hiss from the valve punctuated my sleep (which has always been fitful) like a nonhuman presence in the room — a dragon sleeping at the entrance of my childhood. But the pipes were also a connection to all the other lives being lived around us. Having come from a house designed for a single family back in Puerto Rico — my mother's extended-family home — it was curious to know that strangers lived under our floor and above our heads, and that the heater pipe went through everyone's apartments. (My first spanking in Paterson came as a result of playing tunes on the pipes in my room to see if there would be an answer.) My mother was as new to this concept of beehive life as I was, but she had been given strict orders by my father to keep the doors locked, the noise down, ourselves to ourselves.

It seems that Father had learned some painful lessons about prejudice while searching for an apartment in Paterson. Not until years later did I hear how much resistance he had encountered with landlords who were panicking at the influx of Latinos into a neighborhood that had been Jewish for a couple of generations. It made no difference that it was the American phenomenon of ethnic turnover which was changing the urban core of Paterson, and that the human flood could not be held back with an accusing finger.

"You Cuban?" one man had asked my father, pointing at his name tag on the Navy uniform — even though my father had the fair skin and light-brown hair of his northern Spanish background, and the name Ortiz is as common in Puerto Rico as Johnson is in the U.S.

"No," my father had answered, looking past the finger into his adversary's angry eyes. "I'm Puerto Rican."

"Same shit." And the door closed.

My father could have passed as European, but we couldn't. My brother and I both have our mother's black hair and olive skin, and so we lived in El Building and visited our great-uncle and his fair children on the next block. It was their private joke that they were the German branch of the family. Not many years later that area too would be mainly Puerto Rican. It was as if the heart of the city map were being gradually colored brown — *café con leche* brown. Our color.

The movie opens with a sweep of the living room. It is "typical" immigrant Puerto Rican decor for the time: the sofa and chairs are square and hard-looking, upholstered in bright colors (blue and yellow in this instance), and covered with the transparent plastic that furniture salesmen then were so adept at convincing women to buy. The linoleum on the floor is light blue; if it had been subjected to spike heels (as it was in most places), there were dime-sized indentations all over it that cannot be seen in this movie. The room is full of people dressed up: dark suits for the men, red dresses for the women. When I have asked my mother why most of the women are in red that night, she has shrugged, "I don't remember. Just a coincidence." She doesn't have my obsession for assigning symbolism to everything.

The three women in red sitting on the couch are my mother, my eighteen-year-old cousin, and her brother's girlfriend. The novia *is just up from the Island, which is apparent in her body language. She sits up formally, her dress pulled over her knees. She is a pretty girl, but her posture makes her look insecure, lost in her full-skirted dress, which she has carefully tucked around her to make room for my gorgeous cousin, her future sister-in-law. My cousin has grown up in Paterson and is in her last year of high school. She doesn't have a trace of what Puerto Ricans call* la mancha *(literally, the stain: the mark of the new immigrant — something about the posture, the voice, or the humble demeanor that makes it obvious to everyone the person has just arrived on the mainland). My cousin is wearing a tight, sequined, cocktail dress. Her brown hair has been lightened with peroxide around the bangs, and she is holding a cigarette expertly between her fingers, bringing it up to her mouth in a sensuous arc of her arm as she talks animatedly. My mother, who has come up to sit between the two women, both only a few years younger than herself, is somewhere between the poles they represent in our culture.*

It became my father's obsession to get out of the barrio, and thus we were never permitted to form bonds with the place or with the people who lived there. Yet El Building was a comfort to my mother, who never got over yearning for *la isla.* She felt surrounded by her language: the walls were thin, and voices speaking and arguing in Spanish could be heard all day. *Salsas* blasted out of radios, turned on early in the morning and left on for company. Women seemed to cook rice and beans perpetually — the strong aroma of boiling red kidney beans permeated the hallways.

Though Father preferred that we do our grocery shopping at the supermarket when he came home on weekend leaves, my mother insisted that she could cook only with products whose labels she could read. Consequently, during the week I accompanied her and my little brother to *La Bodega* — a hole-in-the-wall grocery store across the street from El Building. There we squeezed down three narrow aisles jammed with various products. Goya's and Libby's — those were the trademarks that were trusted by *her mamá,* so my mother bought many cans of Goya beans, soups, and condiments, as well as little cans of Libby's fruit juices for us. And she also bought Colgate toothpaste and Palmolive soap. (The final *e* is pronounced in both these products in Spanish, so for many years I believed that they were manufactured on the Island. I remember my surprise at first hearing a commercial on television in which Colgate rhymed with "ate.") We always lingered at La Bodega, for it was there that Mother breathed best, taking in the familiar aromas of the foods she knew from Mamá's kitchen. It was also there that she got to speak to the other women of El Building without violating outright Father's dictates against fraternizing with our neighbors.

Yet Father did his best to make our "assimilation" painless. I can still see him carrying a real Christmas tree up several flights of stairs to our apartment, leaving a trail of aromatic pine. He carried it formally, as if it were a flag in a parade. We were the only ones in El Building that I knew of who got presents on both Christmas day AND *día de Reyes,* the day when the Three Kings brought gifts to Christ and to Hispanic children.

Our supreme luxury in El Building was having our own television set. It must have been a result of Father's guilt feelings over the isolation he had imposed on us, but we were among the first in the barrio to have one. My brother quickly became an avid watcher of Captain Kangaroo and Jungle Jim, while I loved all the series showing families. By the time I started first grade, I could have drawn a map of Middle America as exemplified by the lives of characters in *Father Knows Best, The Donna Reed Show, Leave It to Beaver, My Three Sons,* and (my favorite) *Bachelor Father,* where John Forsythe treated his adopted teenage daughter like a princess because he was rich and had a Chinese houseboy to do everything for him. In truth, compared to our neighbors in El Building, *we* were rich. My father's Navy check provided us with financial security and a standard of life that the factory workers envied. The only thing his money could not buy us was a place to live away from the barrio — his greatest wish, Mother's greatest fear.

In the home movie the men are shown next, sitting around a card table set up in one corner of the living room, playing dominoes. The clack of the ivory pieces was a familiar sound. I heard it in many houses on the Island and in many apartments in Paterson. In Leave It to Beaver, *the Cleavers*

played bridge in every other episode; in my childhood, the men started every
social occasion with a hotly debated round of dominoes. The women would
sit around and watch, but they never participated in the games.

Here and there you can see a small child. Children were always brought
to parties and, whenever they got sleepy, were put to bed in the host's bed-
room. Babysitting was a concept unrecognized by the Puerto Rican women I
knew: a responsible mother did not leave her children with any stranger.
And in a culture where children are not considered intrusive, there was no
need to leave the children at home. We went where our mother went.

Of my preschool years I have only impressions: the sharp bite of
the wind in December as we walked with our parents towards the
brightly lit stores downtown; how I felt like a stuffed doll in my
heavy coat, boots, and mittens; how good it was to walk into the
five-and-dime and sit at the counter drinking hot chocolate. On
Saturdays our whole family would walk downtown to shop at the
big department stores on Broadway. Mother bought all our clothes
at Penney's and Sears, and she liked to buy her dresses at the wom-
en's specialty shops like Lerner's and Diana's. At some point we'd
go into Woolworth's and sit at the soda fountain to eat.

We never ran into other Latinos at these stores or when eating
out, and it became clear to me only years later that the women
from El Building shopped mainly in other places — stores owned
by other Puerto Ricans or by Jewish merchants who had philo-
sophically accepted our presence in the city and decided to make
us their good customers, if not real neighbors and friends. These
establishments were located not downtown but in the blocks
around our street, and they were referred to generically as *La
Tienda, El Bazar, La Bodega, La Botánica.* Everyone knew what was
meant. These were the stores where your face did not turn a clerk
to stone, where your money was as green as anyone else's.

One New Year's Eve we were dressed up like child models in the
Sears catalogue: my brother in a miniature man's suit and bow tie,
and I in black patent-leather shoes and a frilly dress with several
layers of crinoline underneath. My mother wore a bright-red dress
that night, I remember, and spike heels; her long black hair hung
to her waist. Father, who usually wore his Navy uniform during his
short visits home, had put on a dark civilian suit for the occasion:

we had been invited to his uncle's house for a big celebration. Everyone was excited because my mother's brother Hernan — a bachelor who could indulge himself with luxuries — had bought a home movie camera, which he would be trying out that night.

Even the home movie cannot fill in the sensory details such a gathering left imprinted in a child's brain. The thick sweetness of women's perfumes mixing with the ever-present smells of food cooking in the kitchen: meat and plantain *pasteles,* as well as the ubiquitous rice dish made special with pigeon peas — *gandules* — and seasoned with precious *sofrito** sent up from the Island by somebody's mother or smuggled in by a recent traveler. *Sofrito* was one of the items that women hoarded, since it was hardly ever in stock at La Bodega. It was the flavor of Puerto Rico.

The men drank Palo Viejo rum, and some of the younger ones got weepy. The first time I saw a grown man cry was at a New Year's Eve party: he had been reminded of his mother by the smells in the kitchen. But what I remember most were the boiled *pasteles* — plantain or yucca rectangles stuffed with corned beef or other meats, olives, and many other savory ingredients, all wrapped in banana leaves. Everybody had to fish one out with a fork. There was always a "trick" pastel — one without stuffing — and whoever got that one was the "New Year's Fool."

There was also the music. Long-playing albums were treated like precious china in these homes. Mexican recordings were popular, but the songs that brought tears to my mother's eyes were sung by the melancholy Daniel Santos, whose life as a drug addict was the stuff of legend. Felipe Rodríguez was a particular favorite of couples, since he sang about faithless women and brokenhearted men. There is a snatch of one lyric that has stuck in my mind like a needle on a worn groove: *De piedra ha de ser mi cama, de piedra la cabezera . . . la mujer que a mi me quiera . . . ha de quererme de veras. Ay, Ay, Ay, corazón, porque no amas*†. . . . I must

---

***sofrito:** A cooked condiment. A sauce composed of a mixture of fatback, ham, tomatoes, and many island spices and herbs. It is added to many typical Puerto Rican dishes for a distinctive flavor.

†**De piedra ha de ser . . .** Lyrics from a popular romantic ballad (called a *bolero* in Puerto Rico). Freely translated: "My bed will be made of stone, of stone also my headrest (or pillow), the woman who (dares to) loves me, will have to love me for real. Ay, Ay, Ay, my heart, why can't you (let me) love. . . ."

have heard it a thousand times since the idea of a bed made of stone, and its connection to love, first troubled me with its disturbing images.

The five-minute home movie ends with people dancing in a circle — the creative filmmaker must have set it up, so that all of them could file past him. It is both comical and sad to watch silent dancing. Since there is no justification for the absurd movements that music provides for some of us, people appear frantic, their faces embarrassingly intense. It's as if you were watching sex. Yet for years, I've had dreams in the form of this home movie. In a recurring scene, familiar faces push themselves forward into my mind's eye, plastering their features into distorted close-ups. And I'm asking them: "Who is she? Who is the old woman I don't recognize? Is she an aunt? Somebody's wife? Tell me who she is."

"See the beauty mark on her cheek as big as a hill on the lunar landscape of her face — well, that runs in the family. The women on your father's side of the family wrinkle early; it's the price they pay for that fair skin. The young girl with the green stain on her wedding dress is *La Novia* — just up from the Island. See, she lowers her eyes when she approaches the camera, as she's supposed to. Decent girls never look at you directly in the face. *Humilde,* humble, a girl should express humility in all her actions. She will make a good wife for your cousin. He should consider himself lucky to have met her only weeks after she arrived here. If he marries her quickly, she will make him a good Puerto Rican-style wife; but if he waits too long, she will be corrupted by the city — just like your cousin there."

"She means me. I do what I want. This is not some primitive island I live on. Do they expect me to wear a black mantilla on my head and go to mass every day? Not me. I'm an American woman, and I will do as I please. I can type faster than anyone in my senior class at Central High, and I'm going to be a secretary to a lawyer when I graduate. I can pass for an American girl anywhere — I've tried it. At least for Italian, anyway — I never speak Spanish in public. I hate these parties, but I wanted the dress. I look better than any of these *humildes* here. *My* life is going to be different. I have an American boyfriend. He is older and has a car. My parents don't know it, but I sneak out of the house late at night sometimes to be with him. If I marry him, even my name will be American. I hate rice and beans — that's what makes these women fat."

"Your *prima** is pregnant by that man she's been sneaking around with. Would I lie to you? I'm your *Tiá Política,*† your great-uncle's common-law wife — the one he abandoned on the Island to go marry your cousin's mother. *I* was not invited to this party, of course, but I came anyway. I came to tell you that story about your cousin that you've always wanted to hear. Do you remember the comment your mother made to a neighbor that has always haunted you? The only thing you heard was your cousin's name, and then you saw your mother pick up your doll from the couch and say: 'It was as big as this doll when they flushed it down the toilet.' This image has bothered you for years, hasn't it? You had nightmares about babies being flushed down the toilet, and you wondered why anyone would do such a horrible thing. You didn't dare ask your mother about it. She would only tell you that you had not heard her right, and yell at you for listening to adult conversations. But later, when you were old enough to know about abortions, you suspected.

I am here to tell you that you were right. Your cousin was growing an *Americanito* in her belly when this movie was made. Soon after she put something long and pointy into her pretty self, thinking maybe she could get rid of the problem before breakfast and still make it to her first class at the high school. Well, *Niña,*‡ her screams could be heard downtown. Your aunt, her mamá, who had been a midwife on the Island, managed to pull the little thing out. Yes, they probably flushed it down the toilet. What else could they do with it — give it a Christian burial in a little white casket with blue bows and ribbons? Nobody wanted that baby — least of all the father, a teacher at her school with a house in West Paterson that he was filling with real children, and a wife who was a natural blond.

Girl, the scandal sent your uncle back to the bottle. And guess where your cousin ended up? Irony of ironies. She was sent to a village in Puerto Rico to live with a relative on her mother's side: a place so far away from civilization that you have to ride a mule to reach it. A real change in scenery. She found a man there — women like that cannot live without male company — but believe me, the men in Puerto Rico know how to put a saddle on a woman like her. *La Gringa,*§ they call her. Ha, ha, ha. *La Gringa* is what she always wanted to be. . . ."

---

*prima: Female cousin.
†tía política: Aunt by marriage.
‡niña: Girl.
§La gringa: Derogatory epithet used here to ridicule a Puerto Rican girl who wants to look like a blonde North American.

The old woman's mouth becomes a cavernous black hole I fall into. And as I fall, I can feel the reverberations of her laughter. I hear the echoes of her last mocking words: *La Gringa, La Gringa!* And the conga line keeps moving silently past me. There is no music in my dream for the dancers.

When Odysseus visits Hades to see the spirit of his mother, he makes an offering of sacrificial blood, but since all the souls crave an audience with the living, he has to listen to many of them before he can ask questions. I, too, have to hear the dead and the forgotten speak in my dream. Those who are still part of my life remain silent, going around and around in their dance. The others keep pressing their faces forward to say things about the past.

My father's uncle is last in line. He is dying of alcoholism, shrunken and shriveled like a monkey, his face a mass of wrinkles and broken arteries. As he comes closer I realize that in his features I can see my whole family. If you were to stretch that rubbery flesh, you could find my father's face, and deep within *that* face — my own. I don't want to look into those eyes ringed in purple. In a few years he will retreat into silence, and take a long, long time to die. *Move back, Tío,* I tell him. *I don't want to hear what you have to say. Give the dancers room to move. Soon it will be midnight. Who is the New Year's Fool this time?*

Reflections and Responses

1. Consider the idea of "silence" in the essay. Why is it significant that the home movie has no soundtrack? What does Cofer do with that missing element? How does silence contribute to the theme of the essay?

2. What connections does Cofer make between the home movie and her dreams? In what ways is the movie dreamlike? In what ways does the essay become more nightmarish as it proceeds?

3. Consider Cofer's final paragraph. How does it pull together the various strands of the essay?

SCOTT RUSSELL SANDERS

The Inheritance of Tools

A heritage is not only ethnic or cultural; it can also be a code of behavior, a system of manners, or even the practical skills that grandparents and parents often pass along to their children. In this widely reprinted personal essay, a writer, upon hearing of his father's sudden death, is reminded of the tools and techniques he inherited from his grandfather and father, which he in turn is now passing along to his own children. Though these tools and techniques have literally to do with carpentry, they take on extra duty in this finely crafted essay in which the hand tools themselves become equivalent to works of art: "I look at my claw hammer, the distillation of a hundred generations of carpenters, and consider that it holds up well beside those other classics — Greek vases, Gregorian chants, Don Quixote, *barbed fish hooks, candles, spoons."*

Scott Russell Sanders is the author of more than a dozen books of fiction, science fiction, essays, and nonfiction; these include Stone Country *(1985),* The Paradise of Bombs *(1987),* Secrets of the Universe *(1991), and* Staying Put *(1993). His latest book,* Writing from the Center *(1994), is a volume of essays about living and working in the Midwest. The recipient of many prestigious writing awards and fellowships, Sanders is a professor of English at Indiana University. "The Inheritance of Tools" originally appeared in* The North American Review *(1986) and was selected by Gay Talese for* The Best American Essays 1987.

At just about the hour when my father died, soon after dawn one February morning when ice coated the windows like cataracts, I banged my thumb with a hammer. Naturally I swore at the hammer, the reckless thing, and in the moment of swearing I thought of what my father would say: "If you'd try hitting the nail it would go in a whole lot faster. Don't you know your thumb's not as hard as that hammer?" We both were doing carpentry that day, but far apart. He was building cupboards at my brother's place in Oklahoma; I was at home in Indiana, putting up a wall in the basement to make a bedroom for my daughter. By the time my mother called with news of his death — the long distance wires whittling her voice until it seemed too thin to bear the weight of what she had to say — my thumb was swollen. A week or so later a white scar in the shape of a crescent moon began to show above the cuticle, and month by month it rose across the pink sky of my thumbnail. It took the better part of a year for the scar to disappear, and every time I noticed it I thought of my father.

The hammer had belonged to him, and to his father before him. The three of us have used it to build houses and barns and chicken coops, to upholster chairs and crack walnuts, to make doll furniture and bookshelves and jewelry boxes. The head is scratched and pockmarked, like an old plowshare that has been working rocky fields, and it gives off the sort of dull sheen you see on fast creek water in the shade. It is a finishing hammer, about the weight of a bread loaf, too light, really, for framing walls, too heavy for cabinet work, with a curved claw for pulling nails, a rounded head for pounding, a fluted neck for looks, and a hickory handle for strength.

The present handle is my third one, bought from a lumberyard in Tennessee, down the road from where my brother and I were helping my father build his retirement house. I broke the previous one by trying to pull sixteen-penny nails out of floor joists — a foolish thing to do with a finishing hammer, as my father pointed out. "You ever hear of a crowbar?" he said. No telling how many handles he and my grandfather had gone through before me. My grandfather used to cut down hickory trees on his farm, saw them into slabs, cure the planks in his hayloft, and carve handles with a drawknife. The grain in hickory is crooked and knotty, and therefore tough, hard to split, like the grain in the two men who owned this hammer before me.

After proposing marriage to a neighbor girl, my grandfather used this hammer to build a house for his bride on a stretch of river bottom in northern Mississippi. The lumber for the place, like the hickory for the handle, was cut on his own land. By the day of the wedding he had not quite finished the house, and so right after the ceremony he took his wife home and put her to work. My grandmother had worn her Sunday dress for the wedding, with a fringe of lace tacked on around the hem in honor of the occasion. She removed this lace and folded it away before going out to help my grandfather nail siding on the house. "There she was in her good dress," he told me some fifty-odd years after that wedding day, "holding up them long pieces of clapboard while I hammered, and together we got the place covered up before dark." As the family grew to four, six, eight, and eventually thirteen, my grandfather used this hammer to enlarge his house room by room, like a chambered nautilus expanding its shell.

By and by the hammer was passed along to my father. One day he was up on the roof of our pony barn nailing shingles with it, when I stepped out the kitchen door to call him for supper. Before I could yell, something about the sight of him straddling the spine of that roof and swinging the hammer caught my eye and made me hold my tongue. I was five or six years old, and the world's commonplaces were still news to me. He would pull a nail from the pouch at his waist, bring the hammer down, and a moment later the *thunk* of the blow would reach my ears. And that is what had stopped me in my tracks and stilled my tongue, that momentary gap between seeing and hearing the blow. Instead of yelling from the kitchen door, I ran to the barn and climbed two rungs up the ladder — as far as I was allowed to go — and spoke quietly to my father. On our walk to the house he explained that sound takes time to make its way through air. Suddenly the world seemed larger, the air more dense, if sound could be held back like any ordinary traveler.

By the time I started using this hammer, at about the age when I discovered the speed of sound, it already contained houses and mysteries for me. The smooth handle was one my grandfather had made. In those days I needed both hands to swing it. My father would start a nail in a scrap of wood, and I would pound away until I bent it over.

"Looks like you got ahold of some of those rubber nails," he would tell me. "Here, let me see if I can find you some stiff ones." And he would rummage in a drawer until he came up with a fistful of more cooperative nails. "Look at the head," he would tell me. "Don't look at your hands, don't look at the hammer. Just look at the head of that nail and pretty soon you'll learn to hit it square."

Pretty soon I did learn. While he worked in the garage cutting dovetail joints for a drawer or skinning a deer or tuning an engine, I would hammer nails. I made innocent blocks of wood look like porcupines. He did not talk much in the midst of his tools, but he kept up a nearly ceaseless humming, slipping in and out of a dozen tunes in an afternoon, often running back over the same stretch of melody again and again, as if searching for a way out. When the humming did cease, I knew he was faced with a task requiring great delicacy or concentration, and I took care not to distract him.

He kept scraps of wood in a cardboard box — the ends of two-by-fours, slabs of shelving and plywood, odd pieces of molding — and everything in it was fair game. I nailed scraps together to fashion what I called boats or houses, but the results usually bore only faint resemblance to the visions I carried in my head. I would hold up these constructions to show my father, and he would turn them over in his hands admiringly, speculating about what they might be. My cobbled-together guitars might have been alien spaceships, my barns might have been models of Aztec temples, each wooden contraption might have been anything but what I had set out to make.

Now and again I would feel the need to have a chunk of wood shaped or shortened before I riddled it with nails, and I would clamp it in a vise and scrape at it with a handsaw. My father would let me lacerate the board until my arm gave out, and then he would wrap his hand around mine and help me finish the cut, showing me how to use my thumb to guide the blade, how to pull back on the saw to keep it from binding, how to let my shoulder do the work.

"Don't force it," he would say, "just drag it easy and give the teeth a chance to bite."

As the saw teeth bit down, the wood released its smell, each kind with its own fragrance, oak or walnut or cherry or pine — usually pine because it was the softest, easiest for a child to work. No matter how weathered or gray the board, no matter how warped and cracked, inside there was this smell waiting, as of something freshly baked. I gathered every smidgen of sawdust and stored it

away in coffee cans, which I kept in a drawer of the workbench.
When I did not feel like hammering nails, I would dump my sawdust on the concrete floor of the garage and landscape it into
highways and farms and towns, running miniature cars and trucks
along miniature roads. Looming as huge as a colossus, my father
worked over and around me, now and again bending down to inspect my work, careful not to trample my creations. It was a landscape that smelled dizzyingly of wood. Even after a bath my skin
would carry the smell, and so would my father's hair, when he
lifted me for a bedtime hug.

I tell these things not only from memory but also from recent observation, because my own son now turns blocks of wood into
nailed porcupines, dumps cans full of sawdust at my feet and
sculpts highways on the floor. He learns how to swing a hammer
from the elbow instead of the wrist, how to lay his thumb beside
the blade to guide a saw, how to tap a chisel with a wooden mallet,
how to mark a hole with an awl before starting a drill bit. My
daughter did the same before him, and even now, on the brink of
teenage aloofness, she will occasionally drag out my box of wood
scraps and carpenter something. So I have seen my apprenticeship
to wood and tools re-enacted in each of my children, as my father
saw his own apprenticeship renewed in me.

The saw I use belonged to him, as did my level and both of my
squares, and all four tools had belonged to his father. The blade of
the saw is the bluish color of gun barrels, and the maple handle,
dark from the sweat of hands, is inscribed with curving leaf designs. The level is a shaft of walnut two feet long, edged with brass
and pierced by three round windows in which air bubbles float in
oil-filled tubes of glass. The middle window serves for testing if a
surface is horizontal, the others for testing if a surface is plumb or
vertical. My grandfather used to carry this level on the gun rack
behind the seat in his pickup, and when I rode with him I would
turn around to watch the bubbles dance. The larger of the two
squares is called a framing square, a flat steel elbow, so beat up
and tarnished you can barely make out the rows of numbers that
show how to figure the cuts on rafters. The smaller one is called a
try square, for marking right angles, with a blued steel blade for
the shank and a brass-faced block of cherry for the head.

I was taught early on that a saw is not to be used apart from a square: "If you're going to cut a piece of wood," my father insisted, "you owe it to the tree to cut it straight."

Long before studying geometry, I learned there is a mystical virtue in right angles. There is an unspoken morality in seeking the level and the plumb. A house will stand, a table will bear weight, the sides of a box will hold together, only if the joints are square and the members upright. When the bubble is lined up between two marks etched in the glass tube of a level, you have aligned yourself with the forces that hold the universe together. When you miter the corners of a picture frame, each angle must be exactly forty-five degrees, as they are in the perfect triangles of Pythagoras, not a degree more or less. Otherwise the frame will hang crookedly, as if ashamed of itself and of its maker. No matter if the joints you are cutting do not show. Even if you are butting two pieces of wood together inside a cabinet, where no one except a wrecking crew will ever see them, you must take pains to ensure that the ends are square and the studs are plumb.

I took pains over the wall I was building on the day my father died. Not long after that wall was finished — paneled with tongue-and-groove boards of yellow pine, the nail holes filled with putty and the wood all stained and sealed — I came close to wrecking it one afternoon when my daughter ran howling up the stairs to announce that her gerbils had escaped from their cage and were hiding in my brand new wall. She could hear them scratching and squeaking behind her bed. Impossible! I said. How on earth could they get inside my drum-tight wall? Through the heating vent, she answered. I went downstairs, pressed my ear to the honey-colored wood, and heard the *scritch scritch* of tiny feet.

"What can we do?" my daughter wailed. "They'll starve to death, they'll die of thirst, they'll suffocate."

"Hold on," I soothed. "I'll think of something."

While I thought and she fretted, the radio on her bedside table delivered us the headlines: Several thousand people had died in a city in India from a poisonous cloud that had leaked overnight from a chemical plant. A nuclear-powered submarine had been launched. Rioting continued in South Africa. An airplane had been hijacked in the Mediterranean. Authorities calculated that several thousand homeless people slept on the streets within sight of the Washington Monument. I felt my usual helplessness in the face of all these calamities. But here was my daughter, weeping because her gerbils were holed up in a wall. This calamity I could handle.

"Don't worry," I told her. "We'll set food and water by the heating vent and lure them out. And if that doesn't do the trick, I'll tear the wall apart until we find them."

She stopped crying and gazed at me. "You'd really tear it apart? Just for my gerbils? The wall?" Astonishment slowed her down only for a second, however, before she ran to the workbench and began tugging at drawers, saying, "Let's see, what'll we need? Crowbar. Hammer. Chisels. I hope we don't have to use them — but just in case."

We didn't need the wrecking tools. I never had to assault my handsome wall, because the gerbils eventually came out to nibble at a dish of popcorn. But for several hours I studied the tongue-and-groove skin I had nailed up on the day of my father's death, considering where to begin prying. There were no gaps in that wall, no crooked joints.

I had botched a great many pieces of wood before I mastered the right angle with a saw, botched even more before I learned to miter a joint. The knowledge of these things resides in my hands and eyes and the webwork of muscles, not in the tools. There are machines for sale — powered miter boxes and radial arm saws, for instance — that will enable any casual soul to cut proper angles in boards. The skill is invested in the gadget instead of the person who uses it, and this is what distinguishes a machine from a tool. If I had to earn my keep by making furniture or building houses, I suppose I would buy powered saws and pneumatic nailers; the need for speed would drive me to it. But since I carpenter only for my own pleasure or to help neighbors or to remake the house around the ears of my family, I stick with hand tools. Most of the ones I own were given to me by my father, who also taught me how to wield them. The tools in my workbench are a double inheritance, for each hammer and level and saw is wrapped in a cloud of knowing.

All of these tools are a pleasure to look at and to hold. Merchants would never paste NEW NEW NEW! signs of them in stores. Their designs are old because they work, because they serve their purpose well. Like folk songs and aphorisms and the grainy bits of language, these tools have been pared down to essentials. I look at my claw hammer, the distillation of a hundred generations of carpenters, and consider that it holds up well beside those other classics — Greek vases, Gregorian chants, *Don Quixote,* barbed fish hooks, candles, spoons. Knowledge of hammering stretches back to the earliest humans who squatted beside fires, chipping flints. Anthropologists have a lovely name for those unworked rocks that served as the earliest hammers. "Dawn stones," they are called. Their only qualification for the work, aside from hardness, is that they fit the hand. Our ancestors used them for grinding corn, tapping awls, smashing bones. From dawn stones to this claw hammer is a great leap in time, but no great distance in design or imagination.

On that iced-over February morning when I smashed my thumb with the hammer, I was down in the basement framing the wall that my daughter's gerbils would later hide in. I was thinking of my father, as I always did whenever I built anything, thinking how he would have gone about the work, hearing in memory what he would have said about the wisdom of hitting the nail instead of my thumb. I had the studs and plates nailed together all square and trim, and was lifting the wall into place when the phone rang upstairs. My wife answered, and in a moment she came to the basement door and called down softly to me. The stillness in her voice made me drop the framed wall and hurry upstairs. She told me my father was dead. Then I heard the details over the phone from my mother. Building a set of cupboards for my brother in Oklahoma, he had knocked off work early the previous afternoon because of cramps in his stomach. Early this morning, on his way into the kitchen of my brother's trailer, maybe going for a glass of water, so early that no one else was awake, he slumped down on the linoleum and his heart quit.

For several hours I paced around inside my house, upstairs and down, in and out of every room, looking for the right door to open and knowing there was no such door. My wife and children followed me and wrapped me in arms and backed away again, circling and staring as if I were on fire. Where was the door, the door, the door? I kept wondering. My smashed thumb turned purple and throbbed, making me furious. I wanted to cut it off and rush outside and scrape away the snow and hack a hole in the frozen earth and bury the shameful thing.

I went down into the basement, opened a drawer in my workbench, and stared at the ranks of chisels and knives. Oiled and sharp, as my father would have kept them, they gleamed at me like teeth. I took up a clasp knife, pried out the longest blade, and tested the edge on the hair of my forearm. A tuft came away cleanly, and I saw my father testing the sharpness of tools on his own skin, the blades of axes and knives and gouges and hoes, saw the red hair shaved off in patches from his arms and the backs of his hands. "That will cut bear," he would say. He never cut a bear with his blades, now my blades, but he cut deer, dirt, wood. I closed the knife and put it away. Then I took up the hammer and went back to work on my daughter's wall, snugging the bottom plate against a chalk line on the floor, shimming the top plate against the joists overhead, plumbing the studs with my level, making sure before I drove the first nail that every line was square and true.

Reflections and Responses

1. Consider the way Sanders opens the essay. Given the significance of his father's death, why does he mention his injured thumb in the same sentence? Why is this a relevant detail? How does it figure later in the essay?

2. Note the many concrete references to carpentry in the essay. In what ways is the language of tools and carpentry related to other aspects of life? Why is there "a mystical virtue in right angles"?

3. In rereading the essay, try to reconstruct the chronology of the February day that Sanders's father died. First, consider how Sanders constructs his narrative. Why does he deviate from a straightforward, hour-by-hour account? Why, for example, does he introduce the story about his daughter's gerbils? In what ways does that anecdote deepen the essay's theme?

GARRETT HONGO

Kubota

"I was not made yet, and he was determined that his stories be part of my making," Garrett Hongo says of his Hawaiian-born Japanese grandfather, Kubota, whose nightly "talk story" bore testimony to the trials endured by Japanese Americans soon after the attack on Pearl Harbor. Hongo's essay is more than a personal recollection; it is a fulfillment of his grandfather's injunction to retain these stories as part of his heritage. Having encouraged Hongo to "learn speak dah good Ing-rish," Kubota then leaves him with the command: "You tell story." Such injunctions, Hongo reminds us, are the inspiration behind many enduring works of literature — a character frequently encountered in the classics is the "witness who gives personal testimony about an event the rest of his community cannot even imagine."

Garrett Hongo is a poet born in Volcano, Hawaii, where he has been at work on a memoir entitled Volcano Journal. *He was educated at Pomona College, the University of Michigan, and the University of California, Irvine, where he received an M.F.A. in English. The author of two highly praised volumes of poetry,* Yellow Light *(1982) and* The River of Heaven *(1988), and the editor of* The Open Boat: Poems from Asian America *(1993), Hongo is Professor of Creative Writing at the University of Oregon. He has received many literary awards, including fellowships from the National Endowment for the Arts and the John Simon Guggenheim Foundation. "Kubota" originally appeared in* Ploughshares *(1990) and was selected by Joyce Carol Oates for* The Best American Essays *1991.*

On December 8, 1941, the day after the Japanese attack on Pearl Harbor in Hawaii, my grandfather barricaded himself with his family — my grandmother, my teenage mother, her two sisters and two brothers — inside of his home in La'ie, a sugar plantation village on Oahu's North Shore. This was my maternal grandfather, a man most villagers called by his last name, Kubota. It could mean either "Wayside Field" or else "Broken Dreams," depending on which ideograms he used. Kubota ran La'ie's general store, and the previous night, after a long day of bad news on the radio, some locals had come by, pounded on the front door, and made threats. One was said to have brandished a machete. They were angry and shocked, as the whole nation was in the aftermath of the surprise attack. Kubota was one of the few Japanese Americans in the village and president of the local Japanese language school. He had become a target for their rage and suspicion. A wise man, he locked all his doors and windows and did not open his store the next day, but stayed closed and waited for news from some official.

He was a *kibei*, a Japanese American born in Hawaii (a U.S. territory then, so he was thus a citizen) but who was subsequently sent back by his father for formal education in Hiroshima, Japan, their home province. *Kibei* is written with two ideograms in Japanese: one is the word for "return" and the other is the word for "rice." Poetically, it means one who returns from America, known as the Land of Rice in Japanese (by contrast, Chinese immigrants called their new home Mountain of Gold).

Kubota was graduated from a Japanese high school and then came back to Hawaii as a teenager. He spoke English — and a Hawaiian creole version of it at that — with a Japanese accent. But he was well liked and good at numbers, scrupulous and hard working like so many immigrants and children of immigrants. Castle & Cook, a grower's company that ran the sugarcane business along the North Shore, hired him on first as a stock boy and then appointed him to run one of its company stores. He did well, had the trust of management and labor — not an easy accomplishment in any day — married, had children, and had begun to exert himself in community affairs and excel in his own recreations. He put together a Japanese community organization that backed a Japanese language school for children and sponsored teachers from Japan. Kubota boarded many of them, in succession, in his own home. This made dinners a silent affair for his talkative, Hawaiian-bred children, as their stern *sensei*, or teacher, was nearly always at the table and their own abilities in the Japanese language were as delinquent as their attendance. While Kubota and the *sensei* rattled on about things Japanese, speaking Japanese, his children hurried through their suppers and tried to run off early to listen to the radio shows.

After dinner, while the *sensei* graded exams seated in a wicker chair in the spare room and his wife and children gathered around the radio in the front parlor, Kubota sat on the screened porch outside, reading the local Japanese newspapers. He finished reading about the same time as he finished the tea he drank for his digestion — a habit he'd learned in Japan — and then he'd get out his fishing gear and spread it out on the plank floors. The wraps on his rods needed to be redone, gears in his reels needed oil, and, once through with those tasks, he'd painstakingly wind on hundreds of yards of new line. Fishing was his hobby and his passion. He spent weekends camping along the North Shore beaches with his children, setting up umbrella tents, packing a rice pot and hibachi along for meals. And he caught fish. *Ulu'a* mostly, the huge surf-feeding fish known on the mainland as the jack crevalle, but he'd go after almost anything in its season. In Kawela, a plantation-owned bay nearby, he fished for mullet Hawaiian-style with a throw net, stalking the bottom-hugging, gray-backed schools as they gathered at the stream mouths and in the freshwater springs. In an outrigger out beyond the reef, he'd try for *aku* — the skipjack tuna prized for steaks and, sliced raw and mixed with fresh seaweed and cut onions, for *sashimi* salad. In Kahaluu and Ka'awa and on an offshore rock locals called Goat Island, he loved to go torching, stringing lanterns on bamboo poles stuck in the sand to attract *kumu'u,* the red goatfish, as they schooled at night just inside the reef. But in Lai'e on Laniloa Point near Kahuku, the northernmost tip of Oahu, he cast twelve- and fourteen-foot surf rods for the huge, varicolored, and fast-running *ulu'a* as they ran for schools of squid and baitfish just beyond the biggest breakers and past the low sand flats wadable from the shore to nearly a half mile out. At sunset, against the western light, he looked as if he walked on water as he came back, fish and rods slung over his shoulders, stepping along the rock and coral path just inches under the surface of a running tide.

When it was torching season, in December or January, he'd drive out the afternoon before and stay with old friends, the

Tanakas or Yoshikawas, shopkeepers like him who ran stores near the fishing grounds. They'd have been preparing for weeks, selecting and cutting their bamboo poles, cleaning the hurricane lanterns, tearing up burlap sacks for the cloths they'd soak with kerosene and tie onto sticks they'd poke into the soft sand of the shallows. Once lit, touched off with a Zippo lighter, these would be the torches they'd use as beacons to attract the schooling fish. In another time, they might have made up a dozen paper lanterns of the kind mostly used for decorating the summer folk dances outdoors on the grounds of the Buddhist church during O-Bon, the Festival for the Dead. But now, wealthy and modern and efficient killers of fish, Tanaka and Kubota used rag torches and Colemans and cast rods with tips made of Tonkin bamboo and butts of American-spun fiberglass. After just one good night, they might bring back a prize bounty of a dozen burlap bags filled with scores of bloody, rigid fish delicious to eat and even better to give away as gifts to friends, family, and special customers.

It was a Monday night, the day after Pearl Harbor, and there was a rattling knock at the front door. Two FBI agents presented themselves, showed identification, and took my grandfather in for questioning in Honolulu. He didn't return home for days. No one knew what had happened or what was wrong. But there was a roundup going on of all those in the Japanese-American community suspected of sympathizing with the enemy and worse. My grandfather was suspected of espionage, of communicating with offshore Japanese submarines launched from the attack fleet days before war began. Torpedo planes and escort fighters, decorated with the insignia of the Rising Sun, had taken an approach route from northwest of Oahu directly across Kahuku Point and on toward Pearl. They had strafed an auxiliary air station near the fishing grounds my grandfather loved and destroyed a small gun battery there, killing three men. Kubota was known to have sponsored and harbored Japanese nationals in his own home. He had a radio. He had wholesale access to firearms. Circumstances and an undertone of racial resentment had combined with wartime hysteria in the aftermath of the tragic naval battle to cast suspicion on the loyalties of my grandfather and all other Japanese Americans. The FBI reached out and pulled hundreds of them in for questioning in dragnets cast throughout the West Coast and Hawaii.

My grandfather was lucky; he'd somehow been let go after only a few days. Others were not as fortunate. Hundreds, from small communities in Washington, California, Oregon, and Hawaii, were rounded up and, after what appeared to be routine questioning, shipped off under Justice Department orders to holding centers in Leuppe on the Navaho reservation in Arizona, in Fort Missoula in Montana, and on Sand Island in Honolulu Harbor. There were other special camps on Maui in Ha'iku and on Hawaii — the Big Island — in my own home village of Volcano.

Many of these men — it was exclusively the Japanese-American men suspected of ties to Japan who were initially rounded up — did not see their families again for more than four years. Under a suspension of due process that was only after the fact ruled as warranted by military necessity, they were, if only temporarily, "disappeared" in Justice Department prison camps scattered in particularly desolate areas of the United States designated as militarily "safe." These were grim forerunners of the assembly centers and concentration camps for the 120,000 Japanese-American evacuees that were to come later.

I am Kubota's eldest grandchild, and I remember him as a lonely, habitually silent old man who lived with us in our home near Los Angeles for most of my childhood and adolescence. It was the fifties, and my parents had emigrated from Hawaii to the mainland in the hope of a better life away from the old sugar plantation. After some success, they had sent back for my grandparents and taken them in. And it was my grandparents who did the work of the household while my mother and father worked their salaried city jobs. My grandmother cooked and sewed, washed our clothes, and knitted in the front room under the light of a huge lamp with a bright three-way bulb. Kubota raised a flower garden, read up on soils and grasses in gardening books, and planted a zoysia lawn in front and a dichondra one in back. He planted a small patch near the rear block wall with green onions, eggplant, white Japanese radishes, and cucumber. While he hoed and spaded the loamless, clayey earth of Los Angeles, he sang particularly plangent songs in Japanese about plum blossoms and bamboo groves.

Once, in the mid-sixties, after a dinner during which, as always, he had been silent while he worked away at a meal of fish and rice spiced with dabs of Chinese mustard and catsup thinned with soy sauce, Kubota took his own dishes to the kitchen sink and washed them up. He took a clean jelly jar out of the cupboard — the glass was thick and its shape squatty like an old-fashioned. He reached around to the hutch below where he kept his bourbon. He made himself a drink and retired to the living room where I was expected to join him for "talk story," the Hawaiian idiom for chewing the fat.

I was a teenager and, though I was bored listening to stories I'd heard often enough before at holiday dinners, I was dutiful. I took my spot on the couch next to Kubota and heard him out. Usually, he'd tell me about his schooling in Japan where he learned judo along with mathematics and literature. He'd learned the *soroban* there — the abacus, which was the original pocket calculator of the Far East — and that, along with his strong, judo-trained back, got him his first job in Hawaii. This was the moral. "Study *ha-ahd*," he'd say with pidgin emphasis. "Learn read good. Learn speak da kine *good* English." The message is the familiar one taught to any children of immigrants: succeed through education. And imitation. But this time, Kubota reached down into his past and told me a different story. I was thirteen by then, and I suppose he thought me ready for it. He told me about Pearl Harbor, how the planes flew in wing after wing of formations over his old house in La'ie in Hawaii, and how, the next day, after Roosevelt had made his famous "Day of Infamy" speech about the treachery of the Japanese, the FBI agents had come to his door and taken him in, hauled him off to Honolulu for questioning, and held him without charge for several days. I thought he was lying. I thought he was making up a kind of horror story to shock me and give his moral that much more starch. But it was true. I asked around. I brought it up during history class in junior high school, and my teacher, after silencing me and stepping me off to the back of the room, told me that it was indeed so. I asked my mother and she said it was true. I asked my schoolmates, who laughed and ridiculed me for being so ignorant. We lived in a Japanese-American community, and the parents of most of my classmates were the *nisei* who had been interned as teenagers all through the war. But there was a strange silence around all of this. There was a hush, as if one were invoking the ill powers of the dead when one brought it up. No one cared to speak about the evacuation and relocation for very long. It wasn't in our history books, though we were studying World War II at the time. It wasn't in the family albums of the people I knew and whom I'd visit staying over weekends with friends. And it wasn't anything that the family talked about or allowed me to keep bringing up either. I was given the facts, told sternly and pointedly that "it was war" and that "nothing could be done." *"Shikatta ga nai"* is the phrase in Japanese, a kind of resolute and determinist pronouncement on how to deal with inexplicable tragedy. I was to know it but not to dwell on it. Japanese Americans were busy trying to forget it ever happened and were having a hard enough time building their new lives after "camp." It was as if we had no history for four years and the relocation was something unspeakable.

But Kubota would not let it go. In session after session, for months it seemed, he pounded away at his story. He wanted to tell me the names of the FBI agents. He went over their questions and his responses again and again. He'd tell me how one would try to act friendly toward him, offering him cigarettes while the other, who hounded him with accusations and threats, left the interrogation room. Good cop, bad cop, I thought to myself, already superficially streetwise from stories black classmates told of the Watts riots and from my having watched too many episodes of *Dragnet* and *The Mod Squad*. But Kubota was not interested in my experiences. I was not made yet, and he was determined that his stories be part of my making. He spoke quietly at first, mildly, but once into his narrative and after his drink was down, his voice would rise and quaver with resentment and he'd make his accusations. He gave his testimony to me and I held it at first cautiously in my conscience like it was an heirloom too delicate to expose to strangers and anyone outside of the world Kubota made with his words. "I give you story now," he once said, "and you learn speak good, eh?" It was my job, as the disciple of his preaching I had then become, Ananda to his Buddha, to reassure him with a promise. "You learn speak good like the Dillingham," he'd say another time, referring to the wealthy scion of the grower family who had once run, unsuccessfully, for one of Hawaii's first senatorial seats. Or he'd then invoke a magical name, the name of one of his heroes, a man he thought particularly exemplary and righteous. "Learn speak dah good Ing-rish like *Mistah Inouye*," Kubota shouted. "He *lick* dah Dillingham even in debate. I saw on *terre-bision* myself." He was remembering the debates before the first senatorial election just before Hawaii was admitted to the Union as its fiftieth state. "You *tell* story," Kubota would end. And I had my injunction.

The town we settled in after the move from Hawaii is called Gardena, the independently incorporated city south of Los Angeles and north of San Pedro harbor. At its northern limit, it borders on Watts and Compton, black towns. To the southwest are Torrance and Redondo Beach, white towns. To the rest of L.A., Gardena is primarily famous for having legalized five-card draw poker after the war. On Vermont Boulevard, its eastern border, there is a dingy little Vegas-like strip of card clubs with huge parking lots and flickering neon signs that spell out "The Rainbow" and "The Horseshoe" in timed sequences of varicolored lights. The town is only secondarily famous as the largest community of Japanese Americans in the United States outside of Honolulu, Hawaii. When I was in high school there, it seemed to me that every *sansei* kid I knew wanted to be a doctor, an engineer, or a pharmacist. Our fathers were gardeners or electricians or nurserymen or ran small businesses catering to other Japanese Americans. Our mothers worked in civil service for the city or as cashiers for Thrifty Drug. What the kids wanted was a good job, good pay, a fine home, and no troubles. No one wanted to mess with the law — from either side — and no one wanted to mess with language or art. They all talked about getting into the right clubs so that they could go to the right schools. There was a certain kind of sameness, an intensely enforced system of conformity. Style was all. Boys wore moccasin-sewn shoes from Flagg Brothers, black A-1 slacks, and Kensington shirts with high collars. Girls wore their hair up in stiff bouffants solidified in hairspray and knew all the latest dances from the slauson to the funky chicken. We did well in chemistry and in math, no one who was Japanese but me spoke in English class or in history unless called upon, and no one talked about World War II. The day after Robert Kennedy was assassinated, after winning the California Democratic primary, we worked on calculus and elected class coordinators for the prom, featuring the 5th Dimension. We avoided grief. We avoided government. We avoided strong feelings and dangers of any kind. Once punished, we tried to maintain a concerted emotional and social discipline and would not willingly seek to fall out of the narrow margin of protective favor again.

But when I was thirteen, in junior high, I'd not understood why it was so difficult for my classmates, those who were themselves Japanese American, to talk about the relocation. They had cringed, too, when I tried to bring it up during our discussions of World War II. I was Hawaiian-born. They were mainland-born. Their parents had been in camp, had been the ones to suffer the complicated experience of having to distance themselves from their own history and all things Japanese in order to make their way back and into the American social and economic mainstream. It was out of this sense of shame and a fear of stigma I was only beginning to understand that the *nisei* had silenced themselves. And, for their children, among whom I grew up, they wanted no heritage, no culture, no contact with a defiled history. I recall the silence very well. The Japanese-American children around me were burdened in a way I was not. Their injunction was silence. Mine was to speak.

Away at college, in another protected world in its own way as magical to me as the Hawaii of my childhood, I dreamed about my grandfather. Tired from studying languages, practicing German conjugations or scripting an army's worth of Chinese ideograms on a single sheet of paper, Kubota would come to me as I drifted off into sleep. Or I would walk across the newly mown ball field in back of my dormitory, cutting through a street-side phalanx of ancient eucalyptus trees on my way to visit friends off campus, and I would think of him, his anger, and his sadness.

I don't know myself what makes someone feel that kind of need to have a story they've lived through be deposited somewhere, but I can guess. I think about *The Iliad, The Odyssey, The Peloponnesian Wars* of Thucydides, and a myriad of the works of literature I've studied. A character, almost a *topoi* he occurs so often, is frequently the witness who gives personal testimony about an event the rest of his community cannot even imagine. The sibyl is such a character. And Procne, the maid whose tongue is cut out so that she will not tell that she has been raped by her own brother-in-law, the king of Thebes. There are the dime novels, the epic blockbusters Hollywood makes into miniseries, and then there are the plain, relentless stories of witnesses who have suffered through horrors major and minor that have marked and changed their lives. I myself haven't talked to Holocaust victims. But I've read their survival stories and their stories of witness and been revolted and moved by them. My father-in-law, Al Thiessen, tells me his war stories again and again and I listen. A Mennonite who set aside the strictures of his own church in order to serve, he was a Marine codeman in the Pacific during World War II, in the Signal Corps on Guadalcanal, Morotai, and Bougainville. He was part of the island-hopping maneuver MacArthur had devised to win the war in the Pacific. He saw friends die from bombs which exploded not ten yards away. When he was with the 298th Signal Corps attached to the Thirteenth Air Force, he saw plane after plane come in and crash, just short of the runway, killing their crews, setting the jungle ablaze with oil and gas fires. Emergency wagons would scramble, bouncing over newly bulldozed land men used just the afternoon before for a football game. Every time we go fishing together, whether it's in a McKenzie boat drifting for salmon in Tillamook Bay or taking a lunch break from wading the riffles of a stream in the Cascades, he tells me about what happened to him and the young men in his unit. One was a Jewish boy from Brooklyn. One was a foul-mouthed kid from Kansas. They died. And he *has* to tell me. And I *have* to listen. It's a ritual payment the young owe their elders who have survived. The evacuation and relocation is something like that.

Kubota, my grandfather, had been ill with Alzheimer's disease for some time before he died. At the house he'd built on Kamehameha Highway in Hau'ula, a seacoast village just down the road from La'ie where he had his store, he'd wander out from the garage or greenhouse where he'd set up a workbench, and trudge down to the beach or up toward the line of pines he'd planted while employed by the Work Projects Administration during the thirties. Kubota thought he was going fishing. Or he thought he was back at work for Roosevelt, planting pines as a windbreak or soilbreak on the windward flank of the Ko'olau Mountains, emerald monoliths rising out of sea and cane fields from Waialua to Kaneohe. When I visited, my grandmother would send me down to the beach to fetch him. Or I'd run down Kam Highway a quarter mile or so and find him hiding in the cane field by the roadside, counting stalks, measuring circumferences in the claw of his thumb and forefinger. The look on his face was confused or concentrated, I didn't know which. But I guessed he was going fishing again. I'd grab him and walk him back to his house on the highway. My grandmother would shut him in a room.

Within a few years, Kubota had a stroke and survived it, then he had another one and was completely debilitated. The family decided to put him in a nursing home in Kahuku, just set back from the highway, within a mile or so of Kahuku Point and the Tanaka Store where he had his first job as a stock boy. He lived there three years, and I visited him once with my aunt. He was like a potato that had been worn down by cooking. Everything on him — his eyes, his teeth, his legs and torso — seemed like it had been sloughed away. What he had been was mostly gone now and I was looking at the nub of a man. In a wheelchair, he grasped my hands and tugged on them — violently. His hands were still thick and, I believed, strong enough to lift me out of my own seat into his lap. He murmured something in Japanese — he'd long ago ceased to speak any English. My aunt and I cried a little, and we left him.

I remember walking out on the black asphalt of the parking lot of the nursing home. It was heat-cracked and eroded already, and grass had veined itself into the interstices. There were coconut trees around, a cane field I could see across the street, and the ocean I knew was pitching a surf just beyond it. The green Ko'olaus came up behind us. Somewhere nearby, alongside the beach, there was an abandoned airfield in the middle of the canes. As a child, I'd come upon it playing one day, and my friends and I kept returning to it, day after day, playing war or sprinting games or coming to fly kites. I recognize it even now when I see it on TV — it's used as a site for action scenes in the detective shows Hollywood always sets in the islands: a helicopter chasing the hero racing away in a Ferrari, or gun dealers making a clandestine rendezvous on the abandoned runway. It was the old airfield strafed by Japanese planes the day the major flight attacked Pearl Harbor. It was the airfield the FBI thought my grandfather had targeted in his night fishing and signaling with the long surf poles he'd stuck in the sandy bays near Kahuku Point.

Kubota died a short while after I visited him, but not, I thought, without giving me a final message. I was on the mainland, in

California studying for Ph.D. exams, when my grandmother called me with the news. It was a relief. He'd suffered from his debilitation a long time and I was grateful he'd gone. I went home for the funeral and gave the eulogy. My grandmother and I took his ashes home in a small, heavy metal box wrapped in a black *furoshiki*, a large silk scarf. She showed me the name the priest had given to him on his death, scripted with a calligraphy brush on a long, narrow talent of plain wood. Buddhist commoners, at death, are given priestly names, received symbolically into the clergy. The idea is that, in their next life, one of scholarship and leisure, they might meditate and attain the enlightenment the religion is aimed at. "*Shaku Shūchi,*" the ideograms read. It was Kubota's Buddhist name, incorporating characters from his family and given names. It meant "Shining Wisdom of the Law." He died on Pearl Harbor Day, December 7, 1983.

After years, after I'd finally come back to live in Hawaii again, only once did I dream of Kubota, my grandfather. It was the same night I'd heard HR 442, the redress bill for Japanese Americans, had been signed into law. In my dream that night Kubota was "torching," and he sang a Japanese song, a querulous and wavery folk ballad, as he hung paper lanterns on bamboo poles stuck into the sand in the shallow water of the lagoon behind the reef near Kahuku Point. Then he was at a work table, smoking a hand-rolled cigarette, letting it dangle from his lips Bogart-style as he drew, daintily and skillfully, with a narrow trim brush, ideogram after ideogram on a score of paper lanterns he had hung in a dark shed to dry. He had painted a talismanic mantra onto each lantern, the ideogram for the word "red" in Japanese, a bit of art blended with some superstition, a piece of sympathetic magic appealing to the magenta coloring on the rough skins of the schooling, night-feeding fish he wanted to attract to his baited hooks. He strung them from pole to pole in the dream then, hiking up his khaki worker's pants so his white ankles showed and wading through the shimmering black waters of the sand flats and then the reef. "The moon is leaving, leaving," he sang in Japanese. "Take me deeper in the savage sea." He turned and crouched like an ice racer then, leaning forward so that his unshaven face almost touched the light film of water. I could see the light stubble of beard like a fine, gray ash covering the lower half of his face. I could see his gold-rimmed spectacles. He held a small wooden boat in his cupped hands and placed it lightly on the sea and pushed it away. One of his lanterns was on it and, written in small neat rows like a sutra scroll, it had been decorated with the silvery names of all our dead.

Reflections and Responses

1. What do you think Hongo means when he states that his grandfather "was determined that his stories be part of my making"? What is being "made" and how do family stories contribute?

2. Why do you think Hongo places his grandfather's stories in the context of "a myriad of the works of literature" he studied? What effect does this have on the way we consider both the stories and works of literature?

3. Why do you think Hongo decided to conclude his essay with a dream? What does the imagery suggest? How does it refer to other images in the essay?

NAOMI SHIHAB NYE

Maintenance

*Though Naomi Shihab Nye frequently writes from a Palestinian American
perspective, that heritage appears to form only a peripheral part of this meditative essay on the small tasks of daily household life, which in its mosaic
pattern and enigmatic connections resembles a modern prose poem. Nye
never directly states the way her childhood background has helped shape her
experiences and predispositions, but rather invites the reader to find the
shaping principle in the juxtaposition of anecdotes and encounters (often
humorous) that form the essay. Growing up with parents who often entertained strange dinner guests, Nye writes that she "hungrily savored the
tales told by the guests, the wild immigrant fables and metaphysical links."
Fables and their metaphysical links are at the core of "Maintenance."*

Naomi Shihab Nye is the author of three collections of poems, Different
Ways to Pray *(1980),* Hugging the Jukebox *(1982), and* Yellow
Glove *(1986). She edited a collection of poems from around the world,*
This Same Sky *(1993), which was selected as a Notable Book by the
American Library Association. The recipient of the I. B. Lavan Award for
Younger Poets from the Academy of American Poets and the Charity Ran-
dall Citation for Spoken Poetry from the International Poetry Forum, she is
the author of four forthcoming children's books and the editor of an anthol-
ogy of poems and stories from Mexico. "Maintenance" originally appeared
in* The Georgia Review *(1990) and was selected by Joyce Carol Oates for*
The Best American Essays 1991.

The only maid I ever had left messages throughout our house:
*Lady as I was cleaning your room I heard a mouse and all the clothes in
your closet fell down to the floor there is too many dresses in there take a few
off. Your friend Marta Alejandro.* Sometimes I'd find notes stuck into

the couch with straight pins. *I cannot do this room today bec. St. Jude came to me in a dream and say it is not safe.* Our darkroom was never safe because the devil liked dark places and also the enlarger had an eye that picked up light and threw it on Marta. She got sick and had to go to a doctor who gave her green medicine that tasted like leaves.

Sometimes I'd come home to find her lounging in the bamboo chair on the back porch, eating melon, or lying on the couch with a bowl of half-melted ice cream balanced on her chest. She seemed depressed by my house. She didn't like the noise the vacuum made. Once she waxed the bathtub with floor wax. I think she was experimenting.

Each Wednesday I paid Marta ten dollars — that's what she asked for. When I raised it to eleven, then thirteen, she held the single dollars away from the ten as if they might contaminate it. She did not seem happy to get raises, and my friends (who paid her ten dollars each for the other days of the week) were clearly unhappy to hear about it. After a while I had less work of my own and less need for help, so I found her a position with two gay men who lived in the neighborhood. She called once to say she liked them very much because mostly what they wanted her to do was shine. Shine?

"You know, silver. They have a lot of bowls. They have real beautiful spoons not like your spoons. They have a big circle tray that shines like the moon."

My friend Kathy had no maid and wanted none. She ran ten miles a day and lived an organized life. Once I brought her a gift — a blue weaving from Guatemala, diagonal patterns of thread on sticks — and she looked at it dubiously. "Give it to someone else," she said. "I really appreciate your thinking of me, but I try not to keep things around here." Then I realized how bare her mantel was. Who among us would fail to place *something* on a mantel? A few shelves in her kitchen also stood empty, and not the highest ones either.

Kathy had very definite methods of housekeeping. When we'd eat dinner with her she'd rise quickly, before dessert, to scrape each plate and place it in one side of her sink to soak. She had Tupperware containers already lined up for leftovers and a soup pan with suds ready for the silverware. If I tried to help she'd slap at my hand. "Take care of your own kitchen," she'd say, not at all harshly. After dessert she'd fold up the card table we'd just eaten on and place it against the wall. Dining rooms needed to be swept after meals, and a stationary table just made sweeping more difficult.

Kathy could listen to any conversation and ask meaningful questions. She always seemed to remember what anybody said — maybe because she'd left space for it. One day she described having grown up in west Texas in a house of twelve children, the air jammed with voices, crosscurrents, the floors piled with grocery bags, mountains of tossed-off clothes, toys, blankets, the clutter of her sisters' shoes. That's when she decided to have only one pair of shoes at any time, running shoes, though she later revised this to include a pair of sandals.

Somehow I understood her better then, her tank tops and wiry arms . . . She ran to shake off dust. She ran to leave it all behind.

Another friend, Barbara, lived in an apartment but wanted to live in a house. Secretly I loved her spacious domain, perched high above the city with a wide sweep of view, but I could understand the wish to plant one's feet more firmly on the ground. Barbara has the best taste of any person I've ever known — the best khaki-colored linen clothing, the best books, the name of the best masseuse. When I'm with her I feel uplifted, excited by life; there's so much to know about that I haven't heard of yet, and Barbara probably has. So I agreed to help her look.

We saw one house where walls and windows had been sheathed in various patterns of gloomy brocade. We visited another where the kitchen had been removed because the owners only ate in restaurants. They had a tiny office refrigerator next to their bed which I peeked into after they'd left the room: orange juice in a carton, coffee beans. A Krups coffee maker on the sink in their bathroom. They seemed unashamed, shrugging, "You could put a new kitchen wherever you like."

Then we entered a house that felt unusually vivid, airy, and hard-to-define until the realtor mentioned, "Have you noticed there's not a stick of wood anywhere in this place? No wood furniture, not even a wooden salad bowl, I'd bet. These people, very hip, you'd like them, want wood to stay in forests. The man says wood makes him feel heavy."

Barbara and her husband bought that house — complete with pear-shaped swimming pool, terraces of pansies, plum trees, white limestone rock gardens lush with succulents — but they brought wood into it. Never before had I been so conscious of things like wooden cutting boards. I helped them unpack and stroked the sanded ebony backs of African animals.

Then, after about a year and a half, Barbara called to tell me they were selling the house. "You won't believe this," she said, "but we've decided. It's the maintenance — the yardmen, little things always breaking — I'm so busy assigning chores I hardly have time for my own work anymore. A house really seems ridiculous to me now. If I want earth I can go walk in a park."

I had a new baby at the time and everything surprised me. My mouth dropped open, oh yes. I was living between a mound of fresh cloth diapers and a bucket of soiled ones, but I agreed to participate in the huge garage sale Barbara was having.

"That day," Barbara said later, "humanity sank to a new lowest level." We had made signs declaring the sale would start at 9 A.M., but by 8, middle-aged women and men were already ripping our boxes open, lunging into the back of my loaded pickup truck to see what I had. Two women argued in front of me over my stained dish drainer. I sold a kerosene heater which we'd never lit and a stack of my great-uncle's rumpled tablecloths, so large they completely engulfed an ironing board. One woman flashed a charm with my initial on it under my nose, saying, "I'd think twice about selling this, sweetheart — don't you realize it's ten carat?"

Afterwards we counted our wads of small bills and felt drained, diluted. We had spent the whole day bartering in a driveway, releasing ourselves from the burden of things we did not need. We even felt disgusted by the thought of eating — yet another means of accumulation — and would derive no pleasure from shopping, or catalogues, for at least a month.

While their new apartment was being refurbished, Barbara and her husband lived in a grand hotel downtown. She said it felt marvelous to use all the towels and have fresh ones appear on the racks within hours. Life seemed to regain its old recklessness. Soon they moved back to the same windswept apartment building they'd left, but to a higher floor. Sometimes I stood in their living room staring out at the horizon, which always seemed flawlessly clean.

My mother liked to sing along to records while she did house-work — Mahalia Jackson, the Hallelujah Chorus. Sometimes we would sing duets, "Tell Me Why" and "Nobody Knows the Trouble I've Seen." I felt lucky my mother was such a clear soprano. We also sang while preparing for the big dinners my parents often gave, while folding the napkins or decorating little plates of hummus with olives and radishes.

I hungrily savored the tales told by the guests, the wild immigrant fables and metaphysical links. My mother's favorite friend, a rail-thin vegetarian who had once been secretary to Aldous Huxley, conversed passionately with a Syrian who was translating the Bible from Aramaic, then scolded me for leaving a mound of carrots on my plate.

"I'm not going to waste them!" I said. "I always save carrots for last because I love them best."

I thought this would please her, but she frowned. "Never save what you love, dear. You know what might happen? You may lose it while you are waiting."

It was difficult to imagine losing the carrots — what were they going to do, leap off my plate? — but she continued.

"Long ago I loved a man very much. He had gone on a far journey — our relationship had been delicate — and I waited anxiously for word from him. Finally a letter arrived and I stuffed it into my bag, trembling, thinking I would read it later on the train. Would rejoice in every word, was what I thought, but you know what happened? My purse was snatched away from me — stolen! — before I boarded the train. Things like that didn't even happen much in those days. I never saw the letter again — and I never saw my friend again either."

A pause swallowed the room. My mother rose to clear the dishes. Meaningful glances passed. I knew this woman had never married. When I asked why she hadn't written him to say she lost the letter, she said, "Don't you see, I also lost the only address I had for him."

I thought about this for days. Couldn't she have tracked him down? Didn't she know anyone else who might have known him and forwarded a message? I asked my mother, who replied that love was not easy.

Later my mother told me about a man who had carried a brief-case of important papers on a hike because he was afraid they might get stolen from the car. The trail wove high up the side of a mountain, between stands of majestic piñon. As he leaned over a rocky gorge to breathe the fragrant air, his fingers slipped and the briefcase dropped down into a narrow crevasse. They heard it far below, clunking into a deep underground pool. My mother said the man fell to the ground and sobbed.

The forest ranger whistled when they brought him up to the spot. "Hell of an aim!" He said there were some lost things you just had to say goodbye to, "like a wedding ring down a commode." My parents took the man to Western Union so he could telegraph about the lost papers, and the clerk said, "Don't feel bad, every woman drops an earring down a drain once in her life." The man glared. "This was not an earring — *I am not a woman!*"

I thought of the carrots, and the letter, when I heard his story. And of my American grandmother's vintage furniture, sold to in-different buyers when I was still a child, too young even to think of antique wardrobes or bed frames. And I also thought of an-other friend of my parents, Peace Pilgrim, who walked across America for years, lecturing about inner peace and world peace. A single, broad pocket in her tunic contained all her worldly pos-sessions: a toothbrush, a few postage stamps, a ballpoint pen. She had no bank account behind her and nothing in storage. Her motto was, "I walk till given shelter, I fast till given food." My fa-ther used to call her a freeloader behind her back, but my mother recognized a prophet when she saw one. I grappled with the de-tails. How would it help humanity if I slept in a cardboard box under a bridge?

Peace Pilgrim told a story about a woman who worked hard so she could afford a certain style of furniture — French provincial, I think. She struggled to pay for insurance to protect it and rooms large enough to house it. She worked so much she hardly ever got to sit on it. "Then her life was over. And what kind of a life was that?"

Peace Pilgrim lived so deliberately she didn't even have colds. Shortly before her death in a car accident — for years she hadn't even ridden in cars — she sat on the fold-out bed in our living

room, hugging her knees. I was grown by then, but all our furniture was still from thrift stores. She invited me to play the piano
and sing for her, which I did, as she stared calmly around the
room. "I loved to sing as a child," she said. "It is nice to have a
piano."

In my grandmother's Palestinian village, the family has accumu-
lated vast mounds and heaps of woolly comforters, stacking them
in great wooden cupboards along the walls. The blankets smell
pleasantly like sheep and wear coverings of cheerful gingham, but
no family — not even our huge one on the coldest night — could
possibly use that many blankets. My grandmother smiled when I
asked her about them. She said people should have many blankets
and head scarves to feel secure.

I took a photograph of her modern refrigerator, bought by one
of the emigrant sons on a visit home from America, unplugged in a
corner and stuffed with extra yardages of cloth and old magazines.
I felt like one of those governmental watchdogs who asks how do
you feel knowing your money is being used this way? My grandmother seemed nervous whenever we sat near the refrigerator, as if
a stranger who refused to say his name had entered the room.

I never felt women were more doomed to housework than men;
I thought women were lucky. Men had to maintain questionably
pleasurable associations with less tangible elements — mortgage
payments, fan belts and alternators, the IRS. I preferred sinks, and
the way people who washed dishes immediately became exempt
from after-dinner conversation. I loved to plunge my hands into
tubs of scalding bubbles. Once my father reached in to retrieve
something and reeled back, yelling, "Do you always make it this
hot?" My parents got a dishwasher as soon as they could, but luck-
ily I was out of college by then and never had to touch it. To me it
only seemed to extend the task. You rinse, you bend and arrange,
you measure soap — and it hasn't even started yet. How many
other gratifications were as instant as the old method of washing
dishes?

But it's hard to determine how much pleasure someone else gets
from an addiction to a task. The neighbor woman who spends
hours pinching off dead roses and browned lilies, wearing her

housecoat and dragging a hose, may be as close as she comes to bliss, or she may be feeling utterly miserable. I weigh her sighs, her monosyllables about weather. Endlessly I compliment her yard. She shakes her head — "It's a lot of work." For more than a year she tries to get her husband to dig out an old stump at one corner but finally gives up and plants bougainvillea in it. The vibrant splash of pink seems to make her happier than anything else has in a long time.

Certain bylaws: If you have it, you will have to clean it. Nothing stays clean long. No one else notices your messy house as much as you do; they don't know where things are supposed to go anyway. It takes much longer to clean a house than to mess it up. Be suspicious of any cleaning agent (often designated with a single alphabetical letter, like *C* or *M*) that claims to clean everything from floors to dogs. Never install white floor tiles in the bathroom if your family members have brown hair. Cloth diapers eventually make the best rags — another reason beyond ecology. Other people's homes have charisma, charm, because you don't have to know them inside out. If you want high ceilings you may have to give up closets. (Still, as a neighbor once insisted to me, "high ceilings make you a better person.") Be wary of vacuums with headlights; they burn out in a month. A broom, as one of my starry-eyed newlywed sisters-in-law once said, *does a lot*. So does a dustpan. Whatever you haven't touched, worn, or eaten off of in a year should be passed on; something will pop up immediately to take its place.

I can't help thinking about these things — I live in the same town where Heloise lives. And down the street, in a shed behind his house, a man produces orange-scented wood moisturizer containing beeswax. You rub it on three times, let it sit, then buff it off. Your house smells like a hive in an orchard for twenty-four hours.

I'd like to say a word, just a short one, for the background hum of lesser, unexpected maintenances that can devour a day or days — or a life, if one is not careful. The scrubbing of the little ledge above the doorway belongs in this category, along with the thin lines of dust that quietly gather on bookshelves in front of the books. It took me an hour working with a bent wire to unplug the bird feeder, which had become clogged with fuzzy damp seed —

no dove could get a beak in. And who would ever notice? The doves would notice. I am reminded of Buddhism whenever I undertake one of these invisible tasks: one acts, without any thought of reward or foolish notion of glory.

Perhaps all cleaning products should be labeled with additional warnings, as some natural-soap companies have taken to philosophizing right above the price tag. Bottles of guitar polish might read: "If you polish your guitar, it will not play any better. People who close their eyes to listen to your song will not see the gleaming wood. But you may feel more intimate with the instrument you are holding."

Sometimes I like the preparation for maintenance, the motions of preface, better than the developed story. I like to move all the chairs off the back porch many hours before I sweep it. I drag the mop and bucket into the house in the morning even if I don't intend to mop until dusk. This is related to addressing envelopes months before I write the letters to go inside.

Such extended prefacing drives my husband wild. He comes home and can read the house like a mystery story — small half-baked clues in every room. I get out the bowl for the birthday cake two days early. I like the sense of house as still life, on the road to becoming. Why rush to finish? You will only have to do it over again, sooner. I keep a proverb from Thailand above my towel rack: "Life is so short / we must move very slowly." I believe what it says.

My Palestinian father was furious with me when, as a teenager, I impulsively answered a newspaper ad and took a job as a maid. A woman, bedfast with a difficult pregnancy, ordered me to scrub, rearrange, and cook — for a dollar an hour. She sat propped on pillows, clicking her remote control, glaring suspiciously whenever I passed her doorway. She said her husband liked green Jell-O with fresh fruit. I was slicing peaches when the oven next to me exploded, filling the house with heavy black smoke. My meat loaf was only half baked. She shrieked and cried, blaming it on me, but how was I responsible for her oven?

It took me a long time to get over my negative feelings about pregnant women. I found a job scooping ice cream and had to wrap my swollen wrists in heavy elastic bands because they hurt so much. I had never considered what ice cream servers went through.

These days I wake up with good intentions. I pretend to be my own maid. I know the secret of travelers: each time you leave your home with a few suitcases, books, and note pads, your maintenance shrinks to a lovely tiny size. All you need to take care of is your own body and a few changes of clothes. Now and then, if you're driving, you brush the pistachio shells off the seat. I love ice chests and miniature bottles of shampoo. Note the expansive breath veteran travelers take when they feel the road spinning open beneath them again.

Somewhere close behind me the outline of Thoreau's small cabin plods along, a ghost set on haunting. It even has the same rueful eyes Henry David had in the portrait in his book. A wealthy woman with a floral breakfast nook once told me I would "get over him" but I have not — documented here, I have not.

Marta Alejandro, my former maid, now lives in a green outbuilding at the corner of Beauregard and Madison. I saw her recently, walking a skinny wisp of a dog and wearing a bandanna twisted and tied around her waist. I called to her from my car. Maybe I only imagined she approached me reluctantly. Maybe she couldn't see who I was.

But then she started talking as if we had paused only a second ago. "Oh hi I was very sick were you? The doctor said it has to come to everybody. Don't think you can escape! Is your house still as big as it used to be?"

Reflections and Responses

1. How does the essay's title relate to the essay itself? In what way does the idea of "maintenance" hold together the various episodes Nye relates? What are the various meanings in which Nye uses the term?

2. Why does Nye introduce at the beginning of the essay several friends and their attitudes toward possessions and living

accommodations? What relationship do these anecdotes bear to the essay as a whole? How do they help us understand Nye's own attitudes?

3. Consider the story Nye tells about the woman who scolded her for not eating her carrots. In what way does it sound like a fable? What links can you establish between the woman's story and other parts of Nye's essay? Can you detect any connection between the story and the mother's story about the man who lost his briefcase? Can you find any connections between these two stories and the overall theme of "maintenance"?

WILLIAM KITTREDGE

Home

Above all, a heritage is an intricate web of stories, some factual, others leg-endary, yet often without clear and distinct boundaries between the two. In this essay, a Montana writer digs deep into his childhood memories and finds an abundance of stories that help him invent a coherency to enclose the stupendous and bewildering otherness we face every day. "It is a skill," Kittredge writes, "we learn early, the art of inventing stories to explain away the fearful sacred strangeness of the world." Like Robert Frost, who claimed that poetry is "a momentary stay against confusion," Kittredge finds in the anecdotes that shape his personal essays an artistically longed for coherency. But there's a literary price an essayist must pay: "This keeps becoming fiction," Kittredge says of his writing. Must we then think he's made everything up, that his memoirs are sheer fabrications? To confront this question is to confront one of the perennial problems of the narrative essay.

William Kittredge grew up on a ranch in southeastern Oregon, stayed home with the farming until he was thirty-five, studied at the Iowa Writers' Workshop, and is a professor of English at the University of Montana. Among his many literary awards are a Stegner Fellowship at Stanford Uni-versity and two Creative Writing Fellowships from the National Endow-ment for the Arts. He is the author of a collection of stories, We Are Not in This Together *(1984), collection of essays,* Owning It All *(1987) and a memoir,* Hole in the Sky *(1992). "Home" originally appeared in* Owning It All *(1987) and was selected by Annie Dillard for* The Best American Essays 1988.

In the long-ago land of my childhood we clearly understood the high desert country of southeastern Oregon as the actual world. The rest of creation was distant as news on the radio.

In 1945, the summer I turned thirteen, my grandfather sentenced his chuckwagon cow outfit to a month of haying on the IXL, a little ranch he had leased from the Sheldon Antelope Refuge in Nevada. Along in August we came in to lunch one noontime, and found the cook, a woman named Hannah, flabbergasted by news that some bomb had just blown up a whole city in Japan. Everybody figured she had been into the vanilla extract, a frailty of cooks in those days. As we know, it was no joke. Nagasaki and then V-J Day. We all listened to that radio. Great changes and possibilities floated and cut in the air. But such far-off strange events remained the concern of people who lived in cities. We might get drunk and celebrate, but we knew such news really had nothing to do with us. Not in the far outback of southeastern Oregon.

When I came home from the Air Force in 1958, I found our backland country rich with television from the Great World. But that old attitude from my childhood, the notion that my people live in a separate kingdom where they own it all, secure from the world, is still powerful and troublesome. When people ask where I'm from I still say southeastern Oregon, expecting them to understand my obvious pride.

Jack Ray was one of the heroes of my boyhood. A slope-shouldered balding little man, Jack dominated the late roughhouse craziness at our mid-July country dances. The Harvest Moon Ball.

"He can hit like a mule kicking," my father used to say after those dances, winking at us kids and grinning at my mother's back while she served up a very late Sunday breakfast of steak and fried mush and biscuits and thick sausage gravy.

At that time I was maybe five or six years old, and I would have been asleep in the back seat of our car for a couple of hours when the shouting and fighting started around midnight. So I recall those scenes with a newly awakened child's kind of strobe-light clarity, a flash here and there, all illuminated in the headlights of 1930s automobiles. The ranch women would be crowded outside on the porch where they could see, some wife weeping, the men out closer to the battle in the parking lot, passing bottles.

But what I see mainly is Jack Ray getting up off the ground, wiping a little trickle of blood from the corner of his mouth, glancing down at the smear on his hand, his eyes gone hard while some

sweating farm boy moved at him again; and torn shirts, the little
puffs of dust their feet kicked there in the headlights. At that point
my memory goes fragile. There is some quick slippery violence,
and the farm boy is on his knees. Jack Ray is standing above him,
waiting, wheezing as he breathes.

It's over, everybody knows, and soon it is. Two more grunting
punches, and the farm boy is down again, and Jack Ray steps back,
his eyes gone soft and almost bewildered in the light as a little
shudder moves through the crowd, and someone shouts, and the
bottles pass again. I see Jack Ray, there in those headlights, smiling
like a child now that it's finished, the farm boy up on his knees,
shaking his head.

No harm done, the air clear. I see it over and over, summer
dance after summer dance. I see the kind of heroism my boyhood
educated me to understand and respect.

And I hate the part that comes next. I grew up and ran the haying and combine crews on our ranch, and there eventually came a
time when I hired Jack Ray to work for me. He had worked a lot of
seasons for my father, and such men always had a job with us. Jack
was maybe fifty by that time, and crippled by his life, the magic
gone, a peaceable man who seemed to have turned a little simple.
He did what he could, chores around the cook house, and once in
a while he drank. After a bout in town which earned him some
time in the county jail, he would show up grinning in the bunk
house. "Well, hell, Jack," I would say, "it's a new day."

"Kid," he would say, "she's a new world every morning."

Looking backward is one of our main hobbies here in the American West, as we age. And we are aging, which could mean we are
growing up. Or not. It's a difficult process for a culture which has
always been so insistently boyish. Jack Ray has been dead a long
time now. As my father said, he drank his liver right into the
ground. "But, by God," my father said, "he was something once."

Possibility is the oldest American story. Head west for freedom
and the chance of inventing a spanking new life for yourself. Our
citizens are always leaping the traces when their territory gets too
small and cramped.

Back in the late fifties, living with my wife and our small children in our little cattle-ranch house, when things would get too

tight on a rainy Sunday afternoon in November I always had the excuse of work. "I got to go out," I would say, and I would duck away to the peacefulness of driving the muddy fields and levee banks in my old Ford pickup. Or, if the roads were too bad, I would go down to the blacksmith shop and bang on some damned thing.

Whenever I find myself growing grim about the mouth; whenever it is damp, drizzly November in my soul; whenever I find myself involuntarily pausing before coffin warehouses, and bringing up the rear of every funeral I meet . . . Then he runs away to sea. *Ishmael.*

". . . lighting out for territory," says Huckleberry Finn, with his broken-hearted optimism, right at the end of his getaway down the Mississippi.

And it wasn't just the runaway boys in books. John Colter left Ohio at the age of thirty, to head up the Missouri with Lewis and Clark in 1804. He stayed west another five years, earning his keep as a fur trapper in pursuit of the beaver. One fearsome Montana winter he took a legendary walk from Fort Lisa on the Yellowstone, traveling through what is Yellowstone Park to circumnavigate the Tetons — about a thousand miles on snowshoes through country where no white man had ever been before. A thing both wondrous and powerful drove him. Maybe it was a need so simple as being out, away.

Imagine those shining snowy mountains burning against the sheltering endless bowl of clean sky, and Colter alone there in Jackson Hole. We will not see such things again, not any of us, ever. It's gone. We know it is. Only one man ever got to be Colter. Not even Bridger or Joe Meek or Jedediah Smith had a world so absolutely to themselves. Except for some natives, who maybe never thought they were alone.

In 1836 Narcissa and Marcus Whitman came west with Eliza and Henry Spalding. The first white women had crossed the Rockies. Along the way they witnessed one of the last fur-trapper rendezvous, on the Green River in Wyoming. Think of those Presbyterian women among the inhabitants of wilderness. Less than ten years later Marcus Whitman was leading one of the first wagon trains west from St. Louis to the Oregon country.

The New York newspaper editor Horace Greeley worried about the exodus, wondering what those families could be seeking, leaving behind the best of climates and agricultural lands, schools and churches and markets: "For what, then, do they brave the desert, the wilderness, the savage, the snowy precipices of the Rocky Mountains, the early summer march, the storm-drenched bivouac, and the gnawings of famine? Only to fulfill their destiny! There is probably not one among them whose outward circumstances will be improved by this perilous pilgrimage."

Anybody sensible, Greeley suggested, would stop "this side of the jumping-off place." The only practice stupider than such migration, he said, was suicide.

It's easy to understand his puzzlement. The wagon trains were predominantly middle-class ventures. Poor folks couldn't afford a wagon, much less provisions. The basic outfitting cost up toward a thousand dollars. And in those long-gone days that was some real money. But seemingly sensible people persisted in selling their good farms and heading west.

Imagine half the population of Ohio picking up sticks, selling out, and heading for one of our latter-day mythological frontiers, Alaska or Australia. Greeley was right, it was crazy, it was a mania.

What was pushing them? Lots of things. Among them a quite legitimate fear of mortal corruption and death. Cholera. By the spring of 1849 an epidemic had reached St. Louis. Ten percent of the population died of the disease. The road west from Independence was likened to traveling through a graveyard.

But mostly, we have to believe, they were lured west by promises. Promises of paradise for the taking. Free land, crystalline water, great herds of game roaming the natural meadowlands, good fishing, gold, all in unfettered abundance, a new world every morning.

What compelled men to believe promises of paradise on earth with such simpleminded devotion? Well, for openers, a gut yearning for the chance of becoming someone else, and freedom from the terrible weight of responsibilities, freedom too often equaling free, without cost.

My own great-grandfather on my father's side left Michigan in 1849 to travel down the Mississippi and across to Panama, where he hiked west through the jungles on the route Balboa had blazed, and caught a ship north to California and the gold camps. After a long and bootless career of chasing mineral trace in the mountain streams, first in the central Sierra and then up around the foothills of Mount Shasta, he gave it up and turned to ranching and school teaching in one place after another around the Northwest, until in 1897 he died white-trash poor in the sagebrush backlands near Silver Lake, Oregon, leaving a family determined to shake his suicidal despair.

It wasn't just the gold that he never found — such instant boomer riches were to have been only the beginning. The green and easy dreamland fields of some home place were to have been the ultimate reward for his searching, the grape arbor beside the white house he would own outright, where he could rest out some last serene years while the hordes of grandchildren played down across the lawns by the sod-banked pond where the tame ducks swam and fed and squawked in their happy, idiot way. The pastoral heaven on this earth — some particular secret and h eart's-desire version of it — has time and again proved to be the absolute heart in American dreams. All this we promise you.

II

Childhood, it has been said, is always partly a lie of poetry. When I was maybe eight years old, in the fall of the year, I would have to go out in the garden after school with damp burlap sacks and cover the long rows of cucumber and tomato plants, so they wouldn't freeze.

It was a hated, cold-handed job which had to be done every evening. I daydreamed along in a halfhearted, distracted way, flopping the sacks onto the plants, sorry for myself and angry because I was alone at my boring work. No doubt my younger brother and sister were in the house and warm. Eating cookies.

But then a great strutting bird appeared out from the dry remnants of our corn, black tail feathers flaring and a monstrous yellow-orange air sac pulsating from its white breast, its throat croaking with popping sounds like rust in a joint.

The bird looked to be stalking me with grave slow intensity, coming after me from a place I could not understand as real, and yet quite recognizable, the sort of terrifying creature which would sometimes spawn in the incoherent world of my night dreams. In my story, now, I say it looked like death, come to say hello. Then, it was simply an apparition.

The moment demanded all my boyish courage, but I stood my ground, holding one of those wet sacks out before me like a shield, stepping slowly backwards, listening as the terrible creature croaked, its bright preposterous throat pulsating — and then the great bird flapped its wings in an angry way, raising a little commonplace dust.

It was the dust, I think, that did it, convincing me that this could not be a dream. My fear collapsed, and I felt foolish as I understood this was a creature I had heard my father talk about, a courting sage grouse, we called them prairie chickens. This was only a bird, and not much interested in me at all. But for an instant it had been both phantom and real, the thing I deserved, come to punish me for my anger.

For that childhood moment I believed the world to be absolutely inhabited by an otherness which was utterly demonic and natural, not of my own making. But soon as that bird was enclosed in a story which defined it as a commonplace prairie chicken, I was no longer frightened. It is a skill we learn early, the art of inventing stories to explain away the fearful sacred strangeness of the world. Storytelling and make-believe, like war and agriculture, are among the arts of self-defense, and all of them are ways of enclosing otherness and claiming ownership.

Such emblematic memories continue to surface, as I grow older and find ways to accept them into the fiction of myself. One of the earliest, from a time before I ever went to school, is of studying the worn oiled softwood flooring in the Warner Valley store where my mother took me when she picked up the mail three times a week. I have no idea how many years that floor had been tromped and dirtied and swept, but by the time I recall it was worn into a topography of swales and buttes, traffic patterns and hard knots, much like the land, if you will, under the wear of a glacier. For a child, as his mother gossiped with the postmistress, it was a place, high ground and valleys, prospects and sanctuaries, and I in my boredom could invent stories about it — finding a coherency I loved, a place which was mine. They tore up that floor somewhere around the time I started school, and I had the sense to grieve.

The coherency I found worn into those floorboards was mirrored a few years later, just before the war began, when I was seven or eight, in the summertime play of my brother and sister and cousins and myself, as we laid out roads to drive and rectangular fields to work with our toy trucks in the dirt under the huge old box elder which also functioned as a swing tree near the kitchen door to our house. It was a little play world we made for ourselves, and it was, we believed, just like the vast world beyond. In it we imitated the kind of ordering we watched each spring while our father laid out the garden with such measured precision, and the kind of planning we could not help but sense while riding with him along the levee banks in his dusty Chevrolet pickup truck. All the world we knew was visible from the front porch of our house, inside the valley, and all the work he did was directed toward making it orderly, functional, and productive — and of course that work seemed sacred.

Our play ended when a small rattlesnake showed up in our midst, undulating in sweeping little curving lines across our dusty make-believe fields. A young woman who cooked for my mother killed the snake in a matter-of-fact way with a shovel. But the next spring my mother insisted, and my father hauled in topsoil and planted the packed dirt, where we had played at our toylike world of fields, into a lawn where rattlesnakes would never come. We hated him for it.

These stories suggest reasons why, during childhood winters through the Second World War, such an important segment of my imagination lived amid maps of Europe and the Pacific. Maps delineated the dimensions of that dream which was the war for me, maps and traced drawings of aircraft camouflaged for combat. I collected them like peacetime city boys collect baseball cards, and I colored them in with crayons, my far South Pacific and Europe invaded and shaped by dreams and invisible forces I could not hope to make sense of in any other way.

In the spring of 1942, just before I turned ten years old, we opened every first-period class in our one-room Warner Valley schoolhouse singing "Praise the Lord and Pass the Ammunition." We embraced the war. We heard it every morning on the Zenith Trans-Oceanic radio while we got ready for school, and during recess we ran endless games of gunfighter pursuit and justifiably merciless death in the playgrounds. Mostly we killed Hitler and Mister Tojo.

Fall down, you're dead.

When it came your turn to play Nazi, you were honor bound eventually to fall killed through the long adult agony, twisting and staggering to heedless collapse in the dirt. Out in our landlocked, end-of-the-road, rancher valley, the air was bright and clean with purpose.

Always, at least in memory, those running battles involve my cousins and my younger brother and my even younger sister, and a black-and-white dog named Victory. Out back of the house in the summer of 1942 we circled and shot our ways through groves of wild plum in heavy fruit, and we swung to ambush from gnarled limbs in the apple orchard where the blue flies and the yellowjack-ets were mostly interested in having their way with the rotting fallen fruit: yellowjackets flitting to a hive in the hollow trunk of a Lombardy poplar along the irrigation ditch, burning the air with their going, and near to the secret, stinging, irreligious heart of *my* paradise.

In late September our dog named Victory was crushed under the rear duals of a semi truck flatbed hauling one-hundred-pound burlap sacks of my father's newly combined oats across forty twist-ing miles of gravel road over the Warner Mountains to town and the railroad. My sister ran shrieking to the kitchen door, and my mother came to the roadside in her apron, and I was stoic and tough-minded as that poor animal panted and died. *Beyond the crys-tal sea, undreamed shores, precious angels.*

This was a time when our national life was gone to war against U-boats and Bataan and the death march, betrayal reeking every-where. The death of that dog with cockleburrs matted into his coat must have shimmered with significance past heartbreak. We were American and proud, and we were steeled to deal with these mat-ters.

So we unearthed a shallow grave in the good loam soil at the upper end of the huge rancher garden my father laid out each spring in those days, before it became cheaper to feed our crews from truckloads of canned goods bought wholesale in the cities. We gathered late-blooming flowers from the border beneath my mother's bedroom window, we loaded the stiffening carcass of that dead dog on a red wagon, and we staged a funeral with full sym-bolic honors.

My older cousin blew taps through his fist, my brother hid his face, and my six-year-old sister wept openly, which was all right since she was a little child. I waved a leafy bough of willow over the slope-sided grave while my other cousins shoveled the loose dry soil down on the corpse.

It is impossible to know what the child who was myself felt, gazing east across the valley which I can still envision so clearly — the ordered garden and the sage-covered slope running down to the slough-cut meadows of the Thompson Field, willows there concealing secret hideaway places where I would burrow away from the world for hours, imagining I was some animal, hidden and watching the stock cows graze the open islands of meadow grass.

On the far side of the valley lay the great level distances of the plow-ground fields which had so recently been tule swamps, reaching to the rise of barren eastern ridges. That enclosed valley is the home I imagine walking when someday I fall into the dream which is my death. My real, particular, vivid and populated solace for that irrevocable moment of utter loss when the mind stops forever. The chill of that remembered September evening feels right as I imagine that heartbreakingly distant boy.

It's hard for me to know where I got the notion of waving that willow branch over our burial of that poor dog unless I find it in this other memory, from about the same time. A Paiute girl of roughly my own age died of measles in the ramshackle encampment her people maintained alongside the irrigation ditch which eventually led to our vast garden. A dozen or so people lived there, and true or not, I keep thinking of them as in touch with some remnant memories of hunting and gathering forebears who summered so many generations in the valley we had so recently come to own.

In the fall of 1890 a man named James Mooney went west under the auspices of the Bureau of Ethnology to investigate the rise of Native American religious fervor which culminated in the massacre at Wounded Knee on December 29. In Mooney's report, *The Ghost Dance Religion and the Sioux Outbreak of 1890,* there is a statement delivered by a Paiute man named Captain Dick at Fort Bidwell in Surprise Valley — right in the home territory I am talking about, at the junction on maps where California and Nevada come together at the Oregon border.

All Indians must dance, everywhere, keep on dancing. Pretty soon in the next spring Big Man come. He bring back game of every kind. The game be thick everywhere. All dead Indians come back and live again. They all be strong just like young men, be young again. Old blind Indians see again and get young and have fine time. When the Old Man comes this way, then all the Indians go to the mountains, high up away from the whites. Whites can't hurt the Indians then. Then while Indians way up high, big flood comes like water and all white people die, get drowned. After that water go away and then nobody but Indians everywhere game all kinds thick. Then medicine-man tell Indians to send word to all Indians to keep up dancing and the good time will come. Indians who don't dance, who don't believe in this word, will grow little, just about a foot high, and stay that way. Some of them will turn into wood and will be burned in the fire.

In the 1950s and '60s a Paiute named Conlan Dick lived in a cabin on our ranch in Warner Valley, and helped to look after the irrigation and fences. Conlan was reputed to be a kind of medicine man in our local mythology, related to the man who delivered that statement. His wife, whose name I cannot recall, did ironing for women in the valley. And there was a son, a young man named Virgil Dick, who sometimes came to Warner for a few weeks and helped his father with the field work.

In the early 1960s my cousin, the one who blew taps through his fist in 1942, was riding horseback across the swampy spring meadows alongside Conlan. He asked if Virgil was Conlan's only child.

Conlan grinned. "Naw," he said. "But you know, those kids, they play outside, and they get sick and they die."

Story after story. Is it possible to claim that proceeding through some incidents in this free-associative manner is in fact a technique, a way of discovery? Probably. One of our model narrators these days is the patient spinning and respinning the past and trying to resolve it into a story that makes sense.

". . . they get sick and they die." Once I had the romance in me to think that this was the mature comment of a man who had grown up healed into wholeness and connection with the ways of nature to a degree I would never understand. Now I think it was more likely the statement of a man trying to forget his wounds — so many of which were inflicted by schoolyard warriors like us. A healthy culture could never have taught him to forgo sorrow.

In any event, Captain Dick's magic was dead.

All these stories are part of my own story about a place called Home, and a time in which I imagined we owned it all. The girl who died was named Pearl. I recall her name with that particular exactness which occasionally hovers in memories. She was of enormous interest to us because she so obviously disdained our foolish play with make-believe weapons and miniature trucks. Or so it seemed. Maybe she was only shy, or had been warned away from us. But to our minds she lived with adults and shared in the realities of adult lives in ways we did not, and now she was being paid the attention of burial.

Try to imagine their singing that spring morning. I cannot. I like to think our running brigade of warrior children might have been touched by dim sorrow-filled wailing in the crystalline brightness of her morning, but the memory is silent.

Maybe it's enough to recall the sight of people she loved, carrying her elaborately clothed body in an open home-built casket. Not that we saw it up close, or that we ever really saw a body, clothed or unclothed.

They were making their slow parade up a sandy path through the sagebrush to her burial in the brushy plot, loosely fenced with barbed wire, which we knew as the "Indian Graveyard." I see them high on the banking sand-hill behind our house, and beyond them the abrupt two-thousand-foot lift of rimrock which forms the great western lip of our Warner Valley. That rim is always there, the table of lava flow at the top breaking so abruptly, dropping through long scree slopes clustered with juniper. As I grow older it is always at my back. The sun sets there, summer and winter. I can turn and squint my eyes, and see it.

From the flowering trees in the homesteader's orchard behind our house we watched that astonishing processional through my father's binoculars, and then we ran out through the brush beyond the garden, tasting the perfect spring morning and leaping along the small animal trails, filled with thrilling purpose, and silent and urgent. We had to be closer.

The procession was just above us on the sandy trail when we halted, those people paying us no mind but frightening us anyway, mourning men and women in their dark castaway clothing and bright blankets and strange robes made of animal skins, clutching at spring blossoms and sweeping at the air with thick sheaves of willow in new leaf. It is now that I would like to hear the faint singsong of their chanting. I would like to think we studied them through the dancing waves of oncoming heat, and found in them the only models we had ever had for such primal ceremonies.

But this keeps becoming fiction. Ours was a rising class of agricultural people, new to that part of the world, too preoccupied with an endless ambition toward perfection in their work to care at all for any tradition of religion. No one in our immediate families had ever died, and no one ever would so far as we knew. None of us, in those days, had any interest in religion or ritual.

So I have this story of those shrouded people proceeding through my imagination. I feel them celebrating as that young girl entered into the ripe fruit of another paradise, lamenting the dole-food exigencies of their own lives, some of them likely thinking she was lucky to have escaped.

But I don't really have much idea what was going on behind the story I've made of that morning. It was as if those people were trailing along that sandy path toward tomorrow-morrow land themselves. Some of them, somewhere, are likely still alive.

In a book called *Shoshone,* the poet Ed Dorn tells of interviewing an ancient man and woman in a trailer house on the Duck Valley Reservation, a couple of hundred miles east of us but still deep in the high basin and range desert, along the border between Idaho and Nevada. They were both more than one hundred years old, and told Dorn they had never heard of white men until past the age of thirty. Which is possible.

It's easy to imagine those ancient people grinning in what looks to be a toothless old way in their aluminum-sided trailer house, with screens on the windows, on the Duck Valley Reservation. They must have understood the value of stories. Dorn says they demanded cartons of cigarettes before they allowed themselves to be photographed. The point is, they were willing to be part of any make-believe anybody could invent for them, willing to tell their stories and let us make of them what we could. But not for nothing. Stories are valuable precisely to the degree that they are for the moment useful in our ongoing task of finding coherency in the world, and those old people must have known that whatever story Dorn was imagining was worth at least the price of some smokes.

My father's catskinners bulldozed the shacktown Indian camp with its willow-roofed ramada into a pile of old posts and lumber, and burned it, after the last of those people had gone to wherever they went. Our children? In the fall of 1942, the same year that girl named Pearl was buried, they learned something about the emotional thrust of a warrior code as the news from the Zenith Trans-Oceanic radio was translated into singing in first-period music class, and they loaded that dead dog named Victory in a red wagon, and trailed him toward burial at the upper end of the garden. And I waved sweeps of willow over the ceremony while my cousin blew taps through his fist.

Reflections and Responses

1. "Childhood, it has been said, is always partly a lie of poetry." Why does Kittredge cite this adage? What do you think it means? What episode does the quotation introduce? In what other ways does the concept of lying enter the essay?

2. Consider how literature or literary attitudes find their way into Kittredge's recollection of his childhood. To what extent does Kittredge welcome or challenge these attitudes? What does the story of the Paiute girl who died have to do with literature? What prompts Kittredge to include that story?

3. Look carefully at the conclusion of the essay. What details and strands of imagery that have appeared earlier in the essay are interwoven here? Of what importance to Kittredge's theme is this interweaving?

3

Insight

FRANK CONROY

Think About It

Though educators don't like to think so, education is very often a mysterious process. How we come to understand something—both in and out of school — can be far less direct and systematic than methodically minded teachers might acknowledge. Illumination sometimes takes time: "The light bulb may appear over your head," Frank Conroy writes, "but it may be a while before it actually goes on." In this brief but deeply intriguing essay, Conroy explores several episodes from his younger years and shows how some puzzling things he couldn't quite understand at first finally revealed their meaning to him long afterward. But not every such illumination came with "a resolving kind of click." Conroy also recalls a series of enigmatic meetings with two of America's most famous legal minds and how they led to the strange satisfaction of an unresolved problem.

Conroy, director of the prestigious Iowa Writers' Workshop, is the author of Stop-Time *(1967) and* Midair *(1985). His stories and essays have appeared in* The New Yorker, Esquire, Harper's Magazine, GQ, *and many other publications. He has worked as a jazz pianist and has often written about American music. Music is the theme of his latest novel,* Body & Soul *(1993). "Think About It" originally appeared in* Harper's Magazine *(1988) and was selected by Geoffrey Wolff for* The Best American Essays 1989.

When I was sixteen I worked selling hot dogs at a stand in the Fourteenth Street subway station in New York City, one level above the trains and one below the street, where the crowds continually flowed back and forth. I worked with three Puerto Rican men who could not speak English. I had no Spanish, and although we understood each other well with regard to the tasks at hand, sensing and adjusting to each other's body movements in the extremely confined space in which we operated, I felt isolated with no one to talk to. On my break I came out from behind the counter and passed the time with two old black men who ran a shoeshine stand in a dark corner of the corridor. It was a poor location, half hidden by columns, and they didn't have much business. I would sit with my back against the wall while they stood or moved around their ancient elevated stand, talking to each other or to me, but always staring into the distance as they did so.

As the weeks went by I realized that they never looked at anything in their immediate vicinity — not at me or their stand or anybody who might come within ten or fifteen feet. They did not look at approaching customers once they were inside the perimeter. Save for the instant it took to discern the color of the shoes, they did not even look at what they were doing while they worked, but rubbed in polish, brushed, and buffed by feel while looking over their shoulders, into the distance, as if awaiting the arrival of an important person. Of course there wasn't all that much distance in the underground station, but their behavior was so focused and consistent they seemed somehow to transcend the physical. A powerful mood was created, and I came almost to believe that these men could see through walls, through girders, and around corners to whatever hyperspace it was where whoever it was they were waiting and watching for would finally emerge. Their scattered talk was hip, elliptical, and hinted at mysteries beyond my white boy's ken, but it was the staring off, the long, steady staring off, that had me hypnotized. I left for a better job, with handshakes from both of them, without understanding what I had seen.

Perhaps ten years later, after playing jazz with black musicians in various Harlem clubs, hanging out uptown with a few young artists and intellectuals, I began to learn from them something of the extraordinarily varied and complex riffs and rituals embraced by different people to help themselves get through life in the ghetto. Fantasy of all kinds — from playful to dangerous — was in the very air of Harlem. It was the spice of uptown life.

Only then did I understand the two shoeshine men. They were trapped in a demeaning situation in a dark corner in an underground corridor in a filthy subway system. Their continuous staring off was a kind of statement, a kind of dance. Our bodies are here, went the statement, but our souls are receiving nourishment from distant sources only we can see. They were powerful magic dancers, sorcerers almost, and thirty-five years later I can still feel the pressure of their spell.

The light bulb may appear over your head, is what I'm saying, but it may be a while before it actually goes on. Early in my attempts to learn jazz piano, I used to listen to recordings of a fine player named Red Garland, whose music I admired. I couldn't quite figure out what he was doing with his left hand, however; the chords eluded me. I went uptown to an obscure club where he was playing with his trio, caught him on his break, and simply asked him. "Sixths," he said cheerfully. And then he went away.

I didn't know what to make of it. The basic jazz chord is the seventh, which comes in various configurations, but it is what it is. I was a self-taught pianist, pretty shaky on theory and harmony, and when he said sixths I kept trying to fit the information into what I already knew, and it didn't fit. But it stuck in my mind — a tantalizing mystery.

A couple of years later, when I began playing with a bass player, I discovered more or less by accident that if the bass played the root and I played a sixth based on the fifth note of the scale, a very interesting chord involving both instruments emerged. Ordinarily, I suppose I would have skipped over the matter and not paid much attention, but I remembered Garland's remark and so I stopped and spent a week or two working out the voicings, and greatly strengthened my foundations as a player. I had remembered what I hadn't understood, you might say, until my life caught up with the information and the light bulb went on.

I remember another, more complicated example from my sophomore year at the small liberal-arts college outside Philadelphia. I seemed never to be able to get up in time for breakfast in the dining hall. I would get coffee and a doughnut in the Coop instead — a basement area with about a dozen small tables where students could get something to eat at odd hours. Several mornings in a row I noticed a strange man sitting by himself with a cup of coffee. He was in his sixties, perhaps, and sat straight in his chair with very little extraneous movement. I guessed he was some sort of distinguished visitor to the college who had decided to put in some time at a student hangout. But no one ever sat with him. One morning I approached his table and asked if I could join him.

"Certainly," he said. "Please do." He had perhaps the clearest eyes I had ever seen, like blue ice, and to be held in their steady gaze was not, at first, an entirely comfortable experience. His eyes gave nothing away about himself while at the same time creating in me the eerie impression that he was looking directly into my soul. He asked a few quick questions, as if to put me at my ease, and we fell into conversation. He was William O. Douglas from the Supreme Court, and when he saw how startled I was he said, "Call me Bill. Now tell me what you're studying and why you get up so late in the morning." Thus began a series of talks that stretched over many weeks. The fact that I was an ignorant sophomore with literary pretensions who knew nothing about the law didn't seem to bother him. We talked about everything from Shakespeare to the possibility of life on other planets. One day I mentioned that I was going to have dinner with Judge Learned Hand. I explained that Hand was my girlfriend's grandfather. Douglas nodded, but I could tell he was surprised at the coincidence of my knowing the chief judge of the most important court in the country save the Supreme Court itself. After fifty years on the bench Judge Hand had become a famous man, both in and out of legal circles — a living legend, to his own dismay. "Tell him hello and give him my best regards," Douglas said.

Learned Hand, in his eighties, was a short, barrel-chested man with a large, square head, huge, thick, bristling eyebrows, and soft brown eyes. He radiated energy and would sometimes bark out remarks or questions in the living room as if he were in court. His humor was sharp, but often leavened with a touch of self-mockery. When something caught his funny bone he would burst out with explosive laughter — the laughter of a man who enjoyed laughing. He had a large repertoire of dramatic expressions involving the use of his eyebrows — very useful, he told me conspiratorially, when looking down on things from behind the bench. (The court stenographer could not record the movement of his eyebrows.) When I told him I'd been talking to William O. Douglas, they first shot up in exaggerated surprise, and then lowered and moved forward in a glower.

"*Justice* William O. Douglas, young man," he admonished.

"Justice Douglas, if you please." About the Supreme Court in general, Hand insisted on a tone of profound respect. Little did I know that in private correspondence he had referred to the Court as "The Blessed Saints, Cherubim and Seraphim," "The Jolly Boys," "The Nine Tin Jesuses," "The Nine Blameless Ethiopians," and my particular favorite, "The Nine Blessed Chalices of the Sacred Effluvium."

Hand was badly stooped and had a lot of pain in his lower back. Martinis helped, but his strict Yankee wife approved of only one before dinner. It was my job to make the second and somehow slip it to him. If the pain was particularly acute he would get out of his chair and lie flat on the rug, still talking, and finish his point without missing a beat. He flattered me by asking for my impression of Justice Douglas, instructed me to convey his warmest regards, and then began talking about the Dennis case, which he described as a particularly tricky and difficult case involving the prosecution of eleven leaders of the Communist party. He had just started in on the First Amendment and free speech when we were called in to dinner.

William O. Douglas loved the outdoors with a passion, and we fell into the habit of having coffee in the Coop and then strolling under the trees down toward the duck pond. About the Dennis case, he said something to this effect: "Eleven Communists arrested by the government. Up to no good, said the government; dangerous people, violent overthrow, etc. First Amendment, said the defense, freedom of speech, etc." Douglas stopped walking. "Clear and present danger."

"What?" I asked. He often talked in a telegraphic manner, and one was expected to keep up with him. It was sometimes like listening to a man thinking out loud.

"Clear and present danger," he said. "That was the issue. Did they constitute a clear and present danger? I don't think so. I think everybody took the language pretty far in Dennis." He began walking, striding along quickly. Again, one was expected to keep up with him. "The FBI was all over them. Phones tapped, constant surveillance. How could it be clear and present danger with the FBI watching every move they made? That's a ginkgo," he said suddenly, pointing at a tree. "A beauty. You don't see those every day. Ask Hand about clear and present danger."

I was in fact reluctant to do so. Douglas's argument seemed to me to be crushing — the last word, really — and I didn't want to embarrass Judge Hand. But back in the living room, on the second martini, the old man asked about Douglas. I sort of scratched my nose and recapitulated the conversation by the ginkgo tree.

"What?" Hand shouted. "Speak up, sir, for heaven's sake."

"He said the FBI was watching them all the time so there couldn't be a clear and present danger," I blurted out, blushing as I said it.

A terrible silence filled the room. Hand's eyebrows writhed on his face like two huge caterpillars. He leaned forward in the wing chair, his face settling, finally, into a grim expression. "I am astonished," he said softly, his eyes holding mine, "at Justice Douglas's newfound faith in the Federal Bureau of Investigation." His big, granite head moved even closer to mine, until I could smell the martini. "I had understood him to consider it a politically corrupt, incompetent organization, directed by a power-crazed lunatic." I realized I had been holding my breath throughout all of this, and as I relaxed, I saw the faintest trace of a smile cross Hand's face. Things are sometimes more complicated than they first appear, his smile seemed to say. The old man leaned back. "The proximity of the danger is something to think about. Ask him about that. See what he says."

I chewed the matter over as I returned to campus. Hand had pointed out some of Douglas's language about the FBI from other sources that seemed to bear out his point. I thought about the words "clear and present danger," and the fact that if you looked at them closely they might not be as simple as they had first appeared. What degree of danger? Did the word "present" allude to the proximity of the danger, or just the fact that the danger was there at all — that it wasn't an anticipated danger? Were there other hidden factors these great men were weighing of which I was unaware?

But Douglas was gone, back to Washington. (The writer in me is tempted to create a scene here — to invent one for dramatic purposes — but of course I can't do that.) My brief time as a messenger boy was over, and I felt a certain frustration, as if, with a few more exchanges, the matter of *Dennis* v. *United States* might have been resolved to my satisfaction. They'd left me high and dry. But, of course, it is precisely because the matter did not resolve that has caused me to think about it, off and on, all these years. "The Constitution," Hand used to say to me flatly, "is a piece of paper. The Bill of Rights is a piece of paper." It was many years before I understood what he meant. Documents alone do not keep democracy alive, nor maintain the state of law. There is no particular safety in them. Living men and women, generation after generation, must continually remake democracy and the law, and that involves an ongoing state of tension between the past and the present which will never completely resolve.

Education doesn't end until life ends, because you never know when you're going to understand something you hadn't understood before. For me, the magic dance of the shoeshine men was the kind of experience in which understanding came with a kind of click, a resolving kind of click. The same with the experience at the piano. What happened with Justice Douglas and Judge Hand was different, and makes the point that understanding does not always mean resolution. Indeed, in our intellectual lives, our creative lives, it is perhaps those problems that will never resolve that rightly claim the lion's share of our energies. The physical body exists in a constant state of tension as it maintains homeostasis, and so too does the active mind embrace the tension of never being certain, never being absolutely sure, never being done, as it engages the world. That is our special fate, our inexpressibly valuable condition.

Reflections and Responses

1. How does Conroy finally come to understand the reason the two shoeshine men always seemed to be looking into the distance? What has Conroy learned that illuminates their behavior? Can you think of other explanations?

2. What connections can you see between Conroy's insight into the behavior of the shoeshine men and his later understanding of

the elusive jazz chords? In what ways does the insight go beyond
music?

3. Consider the conclusion of the episode involving William O.
Douglas and Learned Hand. How does it end? Conroy says: "The
writer in me is tempted to create a scene here — to invent one for
dramatic purposes — but of course I can't do that." What do you
think he means by the "writer in me"? Why is the refusal to "create
a scene" significant to both Conroy's theme and his technique?

PHILIP WEISS

How to Get Out
of a Locked Trunk

"There [are] some things you could only learn by doing," Philip Weiss discovers in this brief essay that entertainingly parodies the "how-to" genre. But there's more at stake here than finding out what to do if you happen to get locked inside the trunk of your car. The deeper issue is: Why does Weiss become obsessed with locked trunks? The theme of escape informs the selection, taking us far past the typical "how-to" article and into the world of the imaginative essay.

Weiss, whose essays have appeared in a wide variety of national publications, is a contributing editor at Harper's Magazine *and* Esquire. *Weiss, who was born and raised in Baltimore, supported himself for ten years as a magazine journalist. He is working on a novel,* The Thinking Parts. *"How to Get Out of a Locked Trunk" originally appeared in* Harper's Magazine *(1992) and was selected by Joseph Epstein for* The Best American Essays *1993.*

On a hot Sunday last summer my friend Tony and I drove my rental car, a '91 Buick, from St. Paul to the small town of Waconia, Minnesota, forty miles southwest. We each had a project. Waconia is Tony's boyhood home, and his sister had recently given him a panoramic postcard of Lake Waconia as seen from a high point in the town early in the century. He wanted to duplicate the photograph's vantage point, then hang the two pictures together in his house in Frogtown. I was hoping to see Tony's father, Emmett, a retired mechanic, in order to settle a question that had been nagging me: Is it possible to get out of a locked car trunk?

We tried to call ahead to Emmett twice, but he wasn't home.

Tony thought he was probably golfing but that there was a good chance he'd be back by the time we got there. So we set out.

I parked the Buick, which was a silver sedan with a red interior, by the graveyard near where Tony thought the picture had been taken. He took his picture and I wandered among the headstones, reading the epitaphs. One of them was chillingly anti-individualist. It said, "Not to do my will, but thine."

Trunk lockings had been on my mind for a few weeks. It seemed to me that the fear of being locked in a car trunk had a particular hold on the American imagination. Trunk lockings occur in many movies and books — from *Goodfellas* to *Thelma and Louise* to *Humboldt's Gift*. And while the highbrow national newspapers generally shy away from trunk lockings, the attention they receive in local papers suggests a widespread anxiety surrounding the subject. In an afternoon at the New York Public Library I found numerous stories about trunk lockings. A Los Angeles man is discovered, bloodshot, banging the trunk of his white Eldorado following a night and a day trapped inside; he says his captors went on joyrides and picked up women. A forty-eight-year-old Houston doctor is forced into her trunk at a bank ATM and then the car is abandoned, parked near the Astrodome. A New Orleans woman tells police she gave birth in a trunk while being abducted to Texas. Tests undermine her story, the police drop the investigation. But so what if it's a fantasy? That only shows the idea's hold on us.

Every culture comes up with tests of a person's ability to get out of a sticky situation. The English plant mazes. Tropical resorts market those straw finger-grabbers that tighten their grip the harder you pull on them, and Viennese intellectuals gave us the concept of childhood sexuality — figure it out, or remain neurotic for life.

At least you could puzzle your way out of those predicaments. When they slam the trunk, though, you're helpless unless someone finds you. You would think that such a common worry should have a ready fix, and that the secret of getting out of a locked trunk is something we should all know about.

I phoned experts but they were very discouraging.

"You cannot get out. If you got a pair of pliers and bat's eyes, yes. But you have to have a lot of knowledge of the lock," said James Foote at Automotive Locksmiths in New York City.

Jim Frens, whom I reached at the technical section of *Car and Driver* in Detroit, told me the magazine had not dealt with this question. But he echoed the opinion of experts elsewhere when he said that the best hope for escape would be to try and kick out the panel between the trunk and the backseat. That angle didn't seem worth pursuing. What if your enemies were in the car, crumpling beer cans and laughing at your fate? It didn't make sense to join them.

The people who deal with rules on auto design were uncomfortable with my scenarios. Debra Barclay of the Center for Auto Safety, an organization founded by Ralph Nader, had certainly heard of cases, but she was not aware of any regulations on the matter. "Now, if there was a defect involved —" she said, her voice trailing off, implying that trunk locking was all phobia. This must be one of the few issues on which she and the auto industry agree. Ann Carlson of the Motor Vehicle Manufacturing Association became alarmed at the thought that I was going to play up a non-problem: "In reality this very rarely happens. As you say, in the movies it's a wonderful plot device," she said. "But in reality apparently this is not that frequent an occurrence. So they have not designed that feature into vehicles in a specific way."

When we got to Emmett's one-story house it was full of people. Tony's sister, Carol, was on the floor with her two small children. Her husband, Charlie, had one eye on the golf tournament on TV, and Emmett was at the kitchen counter, trimming fat from meat for lunch. I have known Emmett for fifteen years. He looked better than ever. In his retirement he had sharply changed his diet and lost a lot of weight. He had on shorts. His legs were tanned and muscular. As always, his manner was humorous, if opaque.

Tony told his family my news: I was getting married in three weeks. Charlie wanted to know where my fiancée was. Back East, getting everything ready. A big-time hatter was fitting her for a new hat.

Emmett sat on the couch, watching me. "Do you want my advice?"

"Sure."

He just grinned. A gold tooth glinted. Carol and Charlie pressed him to yield his wisdom.

Finally he said, "Once you get to be thirty, you make your own mistakes."

He got out several cans of beer, and then I brought up what was on my mind.

Emmett nodded and took off his glasses, then cleaned them and put them back on.

We went out to his car, a Mercury Grand Marquis, and Emmett opened the trunk. His golf clubs were sitting on top of the spare tire in a green golf bag. Next to them was a toolbox and what he called his "burglar tools," a set of elbowed rods with red plastic handles he used to open door locks when people locked their keys inside.

Tony and Charlie stood watching. Charlie is a banker in Minneapolis. He enjoys gizmos and is extremely practical. I would describe him as unflappable. That's a word I always wanted to apply to myself, but my fiancée had recently informed me that I am high-strung. Though that surprised me, I didn't quarrel with her.

For a while we studied the latch assembly. The lock closed in much the same way that a lobster might clamp on to a pencil. The claw portion, the jaws of the lock, was mounted inside the trunk lid. When you shut the lid, the jaws locked on to the bend of a U-shaped piece of metal mounted on the body of the car. Emmett said my best bet would be to unscrew the bolts. That way the U-shaped piece would come loose and the lock's jaws would swing up with it still in their grasp.

"But you'd need a wrench," he said.

It was already getting too technical. Emmett had an air of endless patience, but I felt defeated. I could only imagine bloodied fingers, cracked teeth. I had hoped for a simple trick.

Charlie stepped forward. He reached out and squeezed the lock's jaws. They clicked shut in the air, bound together by heavy springs. Charlie now prodded the upper part of the left-hand jaw, the thicker part. With a rough flick of his thumb, he was able to force the jaws to snap open. Great.

Unfortunately, the jaws were mounted behind a steel plate the size of your palm in such a way that while they were accessible to us, standing outside the car, had we been inside the trunk the plate would be in our way, blocking the jaws.

This time Emmett saw the way out. He fingered a hole in the

plate. It was no bigger than the tip of your little finger. But the hole was close enough to the latch itself that it might be possible to angle something through the hole from inside the trunk and nudge the jaws apart. We tried with one of my keys. The lock jumped open.

It was time for a full-dress test. Emmett swung the clubs out of the trunk, and I set my can of Schmidt's on the rear bumper and climbed in. Everyone gathered around, and Emmett lowered the trunk on me, then pressed it shut with his meaty hands. Total darkness. I couldn't hear the people outside. I thought I was going to panic. But the big trunk felt comfortable. I was pressed against a sort of black carpet that softened the angles against my back.

I could almost stretch out in the trunk, and it seemed to me I could make them sweat if I took my time. Even Emmett, that sphinx, would give way to curiosity. Once I was out he'd ask how it had been and I'd just grin. There were some things you could only learn by doing.

It took a while to find the hole. I slipped the key in and angled it to one side. The trunk gasped open.

Emmett motioned the others away, then levered me out with his big right forearm. Though I'd only been inside for a minute, I was disoriented — as much as anything because someone had moved my beer while I was gone, setting it down on the cement floor of the garage. It was just a little thing, but I could not be entirely sure I had gotten my own beer back.

Charlie was now raring to try other cars. We examined the latch on his Toyota, which was entirely shielded to the trunk occupant (i.e., no hole in the plate), and on the neighbor's Honda (ditto). But a 1991 Dodge Dynasty was doable. The trunk was tight, but its lock had a feature one of the mechanics I'd phoned described as a "tailpiece": a finger-like extension of the lock mechanism itself that stuck out a half inch into the trunk cavity: simply by twisting the tailpiece I could free the lock. I was even faster on a 1984 Subaru that had a little lever device on the latch.

We went out to my rental on Oak Street. The Skylark was in direct sun and the trunk was hot to the touch, but when we got it open we could see that its latch plate had a perfect hole, a square in which the edge of the lock's jaw appeared like a face in a window.

The trunk was shallow and hot. Emmett had to push my knees down before he could close the lid. This one was a little suffocating. I imagined being trapped for hours, and even before he had got it closed I regretted the decision with a slightly nauseous feeling. I thought of Edgar Allan Poe's live burials, and then about something my fiancée had said more than a year and a half before. I had been on her case to get married. She was divorced, and at every opportunity I would reissue my proposal — even during a commercial. She'd interrupted one of these chirps to tell me, in a cold, throaty voice, that she had no intention of ever going through another divorce: "This time, it's death out." I'd carried those words around like a lump of wet clay.

As it happened, the Skylark trunk was the easiest of all. The hole was right where it was supposed to be. The trunk popped open, and I felt great satisfaction that we'd been able to figure out a rule that seemed to apply about 60 percent of the time. If we publicized our success, it might get the attention it deserved. All trunks would be fitted with such a hole. Kids would learn about it in school. The grip of the fear would relax. Before long a successful trunk-locking scene would date a movie like a fedora dates one today.

When I got back East I was caught up in wedding preparations. I live in New York, and the wedding was to take place in Philadelphia. We set up camp there with five days to go. A friend had lent my fiancée her BMW, and we drove it south with all our things. I unloaded the car in my parents' driveway. The last thing I pulled out of the trunk was my fiancée's hat in its heavy cardboard shipping box. She'd warned me I was not allowed to look. The lid was free but I didn't open it. I was willing to be surprised.

When the trunk was empty it occurred to me I might hop in and give it a try. First I looked over the mechanism. The jaws of the BMW's lock were shielded, but there seemed to be some kind of cable coming off it that you might be able to manipulate so as to cause the lock to open. The same cable that allowed the driver to open the trunk remotely . . .

I fingered it for a moment or two but decided I didn't need to test out the theory.

Reflections and Responses

1. Do you think that Weiss's title wholly describes the purpose of his essay? Does the title fit into a genre? If so, what is it? Is this genre appropriate to the essay? Would this essay have appeared in a popular automotive magazine? What elements of Weiss's essay do not conform to the typical "how-to" or "service" article?

2. How does Weiss's impending marriage figure in the essay? Of what significance is it to his theme?

3. Consider the way Weiss ends his essay. Why does he decide not "to test out the theory"?

ANN HODGMAN

No Wonder They Call Me a Bitch

Whether gently funny or savagely comic, the humorous essay has one of the longest traditions in the history of the essay genre. Decades ago, in the days of James Thurber, E. B. White, Robert Benchley, Dorothy Parker, and S. J. Perelman, the American essay thrived on an urbane wit and humor. For whatever reasons (political correctness? sensitivity? entrenched academic seriousness?), our era seems less accommodating to funny essays. There are far fewer humor magazines now, and the periodicals that ordinarily feature humor include less of it than they once did. Today's best-known humor writers usually work within the restrictions of 750-word newspaper columns and seldom expand the literary possibilities of humor as did S. J. Perelman, who died in 1979. Still, every now and then a humorous essay — like Ann Hodgman's deliciously comic tidbit—finds its way into The Best American Essays. *Reminiscent of Perelman's zany investigations, Hodgman's courageous essay pushes self-education past the point most of us would go.*

A former contributing editor to the now defunct Spy *magazine, Ann Hodgman is the author of* Beat This! *(1993), a cookbook, several humor books, including* True Tiny Tales of Terror *(1982), and more than forty children's books, including a six-book series for middle schoolers called* My Babysitter Is a Vampire *(1991). She is currently at work on a cookbook sequel and a gothic series for high schoolers. "No Wonder They Call Me a Bitch" originally appeared in* Spy *(1989) and was selected by Justin Kaplan for* The Best American Essays *1990.*

I've always wondered about dog food. Is a Gaines-burger really like a hamburger? Can you fry it? Does dog food "cheese" taste like real cheese? Does Gravy Train actually make gravy in the dog's bowl, or is that brown liquid just dissolved crumbs? And exactly what *are* by-products?

Having spent the better part of a week eating dog food, I'm sorry to say that I now know the answers to these questions. While my dachshund, Shortie, watched in agonies of yearning, I gagged my way through can after can of stinky, white-flecked mush and bag after bag of stinky, fat-drenched nuggets. And now I understand exactly why Shortie's breath is so bad.

Of course, Gaines-burgers are neither mush nor nuggets. They are, rather, a miracle of beauty and packaging — or at least that's what I thought when I was little. I used to beg my mother to get them for our dogs, but she always said they were too expensive. When I finally bought a box of cheese-flavored Gaines-burgers — after 20 years of longing — I felt deliciously wicked.

"Dogs love real beef," the back of the box proclaimed proudly. "That's why Gaines-burgers is the only beef burger for dogs with real beef and no meat by-products!" The copy was accurate: meat by-products did not appear in the list of ingredients. Poultry by-products did, though — right there next to preserved animal fat.

One Purina spokesman told me that poultry by-products consist of necks, intestines, undeveloped eggs and other "carcass remnants," but not feathers, heads or feet. When I told him I'd been eating dog food, he said, "Oh, you're kidding! Oh no!" (I came to share his alarm when, weeks later, a second Purina spokesman said that Gaines-burgers *do* contain poultry heads and feet — but *not* undeveloped eggs.)

Up close my Gaines-burger didn't much resemble chopped beef. Rather, it looked — and felt — like a single long, extruded piece of redness that had been chopped into segments and formed into a patty. You could make one at home if you had a Play-Doh Fun Factory.

I turned on the skillet. While I waited for it to heat up I pulled out a shred of cheese-colored material and palpated it. Again, like Play-Doh, it was quite malleable. I made a little cheese bird out of it; then I counted to three and ate the bird.

There was a horrifying rush of cheddar taste, followed immediately by the dull tang of soybean flour — the main ingredient in Gaines-burgers. Next I tried a piece of red extrusion. The main difference between the meat-flavored and cheese-flavored extrusions is one of texture. The "cheese" chews like fresh Play-Doh, whereas the "meat" chews like Play-Doh that's been sitting out on a rug for a couple of hours.

Frying only turned the Gaines-burger black. There was no melting, no sizzling, no warm meat smells. A cherished childhood illusion was gone. I flipped the patty into the sink, where it immediately began leaking rivulets of red dye.

As alarming as the Gaines-burgers were, their soy meal began to seem like an old friend when the time came to try some *canned* dog foods. I decided to try the Cycle foods first. When I opened them, I thought about how rarely I use can openers these days, and I was suddenly visited by a long-forgotten sensation of can-opener distaste. *This* is the kind of unsavory place can openers spend their time when you're not watching! Every time you open a can of, say, Italian plum tomatoes, you infect them with invisible particles of by-product.

I had been expecting to see the usual homogeneous scrapple inside, but each can of Cycle was packed with smooth, round, oily nuggets. As if someone at Gaines had been tipped off that a human would be tasting the stuff, the four Cycles really were different from one another. Cycle-1, for puppies, is wet and soyish. Cycle-2, for adults, glistens nastily with fat, but it's passably edible — a lot like some canned Swedish meatballs I once got in a care package at college. Cycle-3, the "lite" one, for fatties, had no specific flavor; it just tasted like dog food. But at least it didn't make me fat.

Cycle-4, for senior dogs, had the smallest nuggets. Maybe old dogs can't open their mouths as wide. This kind was far sweeter than the other three Cycles — almost like baked beans. It was also the only one to contain "dried beef digest," a mysterious substance that the Purina spokesman defined as "enzymes" and my dictionary defined as "the products of digestion."

Next on the menu was a can of Kal-Kan Pedigree with Chunky Chicken. Chunky chicken? There were chunks in the can, certainly — big, purplish-brown chunks. I forked one chunk out (by now I was becoming more callous) and found that while it had no discernible chicken flavor, it wasn't bad except for its texture — like meat loaf with ground-up chicken bones.

In the world of canned dog food, a smooth consistency is a sign of low quality — lots of cereal. A lumpy, frightening, bloody, stringy horror is a sign of high quality — lots of meat. Nowhere in the world of wet dog foods was this demonstrated better than in the fanciest I tried —Kal Kan's Pedigree Select Dinners. These came not in a can but in a tiny foil packet with a picture of an imperious Yorkie. When I pulled open the container, juice spurted all over my hand, and the first chunk I speared was trailing a long gray vein. I shrieked and went instead for a plain chunk, which I was able to swallow only after taking a break to read some suddenly fascinating office equipment catalogs. Once again, though, it tasted no more alarming than, say, canned hash.

Still, how pleasant it was to turn to *dry* dog food! Gravy Train was the first I tried, and I'm happy to report that it really does make a "thick, rich, real beef gravy" when you mix it with water. Thick and rich, anyway. Except for a lingering rancid-fat flavor, the gravy wasn't beefy, but since it tasted primarily like tap water, it wasn't nauseating either.

My poor dachshund just gets plain old Purina Dog Chow, but Purina also makes a dry food called Butcher's Blend that comes in Beef, Bacon & Chicken flavor. Here we see dog food's arcane semiotics at its best: a red triangle with a *T* stamped into it is supposed to suggest beef; a tan curl, chicken; and a brown *S*, a piece of bacon. Only dogs understand these messages. But Butcher's Blend does have an endearing slogan: "Great Meaty Tastes — without bothering the Butcher!" *You know, I wanted to buy some meat, but I just couldn't bring myself to bother the butcher. . . .*

Purina O.N.E. ("Optimum Nutritional Effectiveness") is targeted at people who are unlikely ever to worry about bothering a tradesperson. "We chose chicken as a primary ingredient in Purina O.N.E. for several reasonings," the long, long essay on the back of the bag announces. Chief among these reasonings, I'd guess, is the fact that chicken appeals to people who are — you know —*like us.* Although our dogs do nothing but spend 18-hour days alone in the apartment, we still want them to be *premium* dogs. We want them to cut down on red meat, too. We also want dog food that comes in a bag with an attractive design, a subtle typeface and no kitschy pictures of slobbering golden retrievers.

Besides that, we want a list of the Nutritional Benefits of our dog food — and we get it on O.N.E. One thing I especially like about this list is its constant references to a dog's "hair coat," as in "Beef tallow is good for the dog's skin and hair coat." (On the other hand, beef tallow merely provides palatability, while the dried beef digest in Cycle provides palatability *enhancement.*)

I hate to say it, but O.N.E. was pretty palatable. Maybe that's because it has about 100 percent more fat than, say, Butcher's Blend. Or maybe I'd been duped by the packaging; that's been known to happen before.

As with people food, dog snacks taste much better than dog meals. They're better-looking too. Take Milk-Bone Flavor Snacks. The loving-hands-at-home prose describing each flavor is colorful; the writers practically choke on their own exuberance. Of bacon they say, "It's so good, your dog will think it's hot off the frying pan." Of liver: "The only taste your dog wants more than liver — is even more liver!" Of poultry: "All those farm fresh flavors deliciously mixed in one biscuit. Your dog will bark with delight!" And of vegetable: "Gardens of taste! Specially blended to give your dog that vegetable flavor he wants — but can rarely get!"

Well, I may be a sucker, but advertising *this* emphatic just doesn't convince me. I lined up all seven flavors of Milk-Bone Flavor Snacks on the floor. Unless my dog's palate is a lot more sensitive than mine — and considering that she steals dirty diapers out of the trash and eats them, I'm loath to think it is — she doesn't detect any more difference in the seven flavors than I did when I tried them.

I much preferred Bonz, the hard-baked, bone-shaped snack stuffed with simulated marrow. I liked the bone part, that is; it tasted almost exactly like the cornmeal it was made of. The mock-marrow inside was a bit more problematic: in addition to looking like the sludge that collects in the treads of my running shoes, it was bursting with tiny hairs.

I'm sure you have a few dog food questions of your own. To save us time, I've answered them in advance.

Q. Are those little cans of Mighty Dog actually branded with the sizzling word BEEF, *the way they show in the commercials?*

A. You should know by now that that kind of thing never happens.

Q. Does chicken-flavored dog food taste like chicken-flavored cat food?

A. To my surprise, chicken cat food was actually a little better —
more chickeny. It tasted like inferior canned pâté.

Q. Was there any dog food that you just couldn't bring yourself to try?

A. Alas, it was a can of Mighty Dog called Prime Entree with
Bone Marrow. The meat was dark, dark brown, and it was surrounded by gelatin that was almost black. I knew I would die if I
tasted it, so I put it outside for the raccoons.

Reflections and Responses

1. What is Ann Hodgman making fun of? Is the essay a satire on
dog food products alone or does she have other targets?

2. Of what importance is the "packaging" of dog food? How does
Hodgman use the language of the packaging for comic effect?

3. Consider the advertising language that Hodgman cites. According to the ads, what similarities exist between the eating habits of
dogs and people? What has Hodgman learned from her experiment?

KENNETH A. McCLANE

Walls

At its best, education is a reciprocal process: Good teachers often learn surprising things from their students. And if the students are prisoners, the surprises can be especially enlightening, as Kenneth McClane discovered when he visited an "Inmate Higher Education Program" at New York's Auburn Correctional Facility. In an essay reminiscent of James Baldwin, McClane sees how fragile the idea of humanity can be and how some prisoners — as much as society would like to dehumanize them — must struggle for a human presence.

Kenneth McClane is the W. E. B. Du Bois Professor of Literature at Cornell University. He is the author of seven books of poetry, including A Tree Beyond Telling *(1983) and* Take Five: Collected Poems, 1971–1986 *(1988).* Walls: Essays 1985–1990 *was published in 1991. "Walls" originally appeared in* Community Review *(1987) and was selected by Annie Dillard for* The Best American Essays 1988.

People are trapped in history and history is trapped in them.
— James Baldwin

PAUL

The willows are gold again
and now the season seems past thinking
seems past remembrance, seems past
the long lean taking of your breath:

I remember you Paul, always, how you strutted
among the city — Lord of the manor: how you
fought with the drivers, how you never
let one person call you *nigger*. I remember how

you struggled with Dad — loving him in the stridency
of your ill-covered conquest: you wanted to love him
and he you: Yours is the story too often repeated:
the city boy driven to alcohol, death:

But the willow once green is golden:
and I remember you part in desire, part in fact:
You would have hated the lie I make of you; you
would have hated the fact:

Still the willow turns green to golden and still
you visit me in mid-morning, telling me of this awful
place, of the omnipresent *them,* who would not let you live
and I listen:

You who were too proud to equivocate: you who loved as freely
and deeply, as messily, as the world could imagine:
Paul, I miss you. I miss your hear-bearing, stern confidence,
your anger which made ghettos of all of us:

No one struggled more; no one asked more; no one
took the risk of presence more sacredly: in your loss
I understood not only the shores of grief,
but how its walls seem forever rising.
— Kenneth A. McClane

At first glance, Auburn Correctional Facility calls to mind a feudal castle or a stone and brick edifice worthy of Humphrey Bogart or Edward G. Robinson. One readily envisions prisoners dragging their balls and chains, the late night prison break, or the lights slowly flickering, presaging the imminent electrocution. This is the stuff of movies, or prison lore. Yet for most of us, these images, dispatched out of Hollywood, are all we shall ever know about the real life in our nation's prisons. Most of us will certainly not be sentenced there; few of us will choose one as a place to visit.

Yet in every stereotype, there is also a residuum of truth: people employ generalizations to celebrate a certain verity about the world; and no myth would have any currency if it did not, to some unassailable extent, identify something in actual experience. Certainly these cinematic incarnations are not the prison's reality, but they contain a grain of truth, nonetheless. Undeniably, though we may not know what a prison is, our imaginings, however incompletely, convey that the prison is a *hellish* place. Indeed, nothing in our arsenal of national fictions suggests that the prison is other than horrific. In this case, it is not a matter of correctness but degree. The prisons — at least the prisons I have encountered — are infinitely more hellish than our Hollywood dream makers relate. Inmates in these places are not planning breakouts or prison riots; they are not planning anything. To dream of escape is to believe that one has something worthy of salvaging; to believe, that is, in the proposition of a self-orchestrated future. The prisons I have visited are spirit killers: the inmates — no matter how smart, capable, or engaging — have little sense of their own inextinguishable worth, their own human possibility. And this is not by accident.

Auburn Prison is certainly not the worst reformatory in this country, nor is it the best. Like most, it probably sits in the thick middle range: no inmate would ask to be sentenced there; certainly some might wish to be transferred out; a few of the hardnosed might even like it, its attraction resting in its utter banality. Neither good (that is, experimental) nor bad (and the word here has almost no meaning, since Auburn, at least to my eyes — and no doubt to those of its inmates — is bad enough), Auburn just is.

At bottom, to cast out is not to cast off, and the long trek to Auburn Prison — through the mill town and over the proverbial railroad tracks — is our reminder that the great prison is a great industry: people earn their livings there; whole towns, including Auburn, are built on the day-to-day catering to our national pariah. And like anything which both haunts and fascinates us, we come to the prison's gates armed with rocks and wonder.

Inescapably, and with great trepidation, we know that the inhabitants of our man-made Siberias are our brethren: indeed, it is this weighty realization, this sense that the murderer we so ruthlessly banish may not eternally quiet the potential murderer within, which so frightens us. For it takes but a few precious seconds for the mind's knife to become the hand's weapon. And all of us, at some terrible time, have walked that narrow footpath between the imagined and the horrific.

At Auburn, the first thing one confronts is its massive guard tower, with its rifle-shouldering, no-nonsense officer. By the time you have noticed him, he has noticed you. For a minute or so, he looks down at you, looks around you and, always unsmiling, moves back to his elevation and privacy. What is so astonishing is that *you* feel condemned. You sense in that coldly dismissive gaze, in the backdrop of the great prison, that Gandhi was right: *to think of evil is to act evilly.* And you feel — and this is essential to the prison's apparatus — that the common denominator of your humanity had been discovered: that you are a writer, or a college professor, or a dutiful husband is of little significance. Here, as the guard corroborates, there is no room for romanticism: he's seen your kind before.

One enters Auburn Prison through two gigantic brass doors, each heavily tooled with elaborate metalwork, at the center of which, like an uneasy coupling, sits the famous symbol of Justice, with its blindfolded woman supporting her two delicately balanced weights. The rest of the portraiture is oddly cherubic, even sexual, as it seems the neoclassical invariably is. It is a celebration of everything, or a reminder of how everything — be it lust or justice — fights in this great amphitheater of a world. I wonder how I might understand this, should I be a prisoner passing on my way to serve a life sentence. He, certainly, knows that life is a great chaos — though this, I hazard, was not the artist's intention. It is, however, a possible interpretation; and it certainly was mine.

The prison's receiving room is reminiscent of an airport security check area, with much the same ingenious technology. At Auburn, there are two guards who inspect both your clothing and carri-ables. Since I had come to read from my poetry, I had a canvas bag filled with books, and never have my works been so finely perused. Each page was rigorously examined; the bag was checked and rechecked.

After all of us had passed through the metal detector, the guard stamped our right hands with an invisible substance. Then we were counted. Indeed, at the next twelve checkpoints, we were counted and counted again. At each checkpoint there is a "lock in": a holding area where one must remain until a guard electroni-cally dislodges the massive gates. The twelve of us, eleven teachers from Elmira Community College's Inmate Higher Education Pro-gram and myself, journeyed from checkpoint to checkpoint like wary salmon. The group was a strange conglomeration. All, with the exception of myself, were white; two of the twelve were women. Six had taught at Auburn for the last two years, and four had worked at the prison for more than a decade. One of the teachers, who wore a jaunty red hat, was the frailest young man I had ever seen: I wondered how he had negotiated his twenty-five years, not to mention the prison's exactings. Yet no one was partic-ularly large or muscular. Sporting his Special Forces army jacket, one man nearly looked the part. But most were aging college and high school teachers, stomachs a notch wider, dreams a bit more remote, than all would like.

Finally we reached "the Yard," and began the long walk through the corridor by cell block D. I say long walk, but it was only a thou-sand yards. All of a sudden, as if a wall of sound, the prisoners began chanting "Baby, you're beautiful" to the two women with us. Loosened through the stone and Plexiglas, the sound recalled that haunting, terrifying Malabar Caves sojourn, in Forster's *A Passage to India,* where human inadequacy and racism are shown as help-meets. I kept thinking, *This is not sound; it is an indictment.* And then I realized, undeniably, shamefully, as if for the first time, what it must *cost* to be a woman: to have your body become, day in and day out, the receptable for so much need, so much ill-digested, in-choate, dangerously poised lust.

I watched as the two women bore it, the college-aged one as strong as a serf in a Breton painting. Quickly her thin face closed down; she walked with a studied, disciplined bearing. Then someone, everyone yelling: *I'll kill you white motherfuckers.* The sound booming and pounding, as if the prison were a giant tuning fork.

Auburn Prison, built in 1816, is one of the oldest maximum security institutions in the United States. A pioneer in penology, Auburn was constructed with individual cells for each inmate, although the original design for these cells, the so-called "Auburn System," was pernicious to say the least. During the early part of the nineteenth century, Auburn became the focus for a unique penal "experiment," in which the most incorrigible inmates were sentenced to absolute, uninterrupted solitary confinement. Permitted neither to leave their cells nor to read nor work, the one hundred "selected" inmates were forced to stand for eight hours a day in total silence. Moreover, in the disturbingly convoluted thinking of the time, this practice was considered "a humane gesture," since it was assumed that an eternity of forced motionlessness might lead to muscle atrophy. No one, of course, questioned whether solitary confinement was in itself inhumane. No, in the rigidly Calvinistic teaching of the day, a prisoner's lot was to be cruel. One burned in hell for one's sins; and prison, most certainly, was this earth's hell.

As might be surmised, in the first year of this heinous experiment, of the hundred prisoners involved, nearly a half went mad, while the others succumbed to tuberculosis and pneumonia. Yet, as is so often the case the prisons, the public was of two minds: on the one hand, it wanted its "custodial houses" to keep the dangerous miscreants away from the community and expected the prison to salve the commonwealth of a serious problem; on the other, it was only willing to permit the prison such "corrective leeway" as might preserve the community's conscience. Clearly, although the public had wanted these Auburn convicts to be severely punished, it did not wish to see them die in plaguelike numbers, at least not within *its* institution. And so, after its first barbarous year, the experiment was ended.

Yet ideas die slowly, and the Auburn penologists — zealots that they were — still believed that solitary confinement was the only way to discipline the abject criminal. Indeed, just two years after their first ill-fated attempt, they began a new, yet no less severe, improvisation on the same theme. Realizing that absolute, forced human isolation encouraged death and psychosis, the Auburn authorities proposed a modified system, where inmates would work in a closely monitored common area, while always returning to their individual cells to sleep. Although the prisoners might come in contact with one another at work and at meals, at no time would they be permitted to talk, exchange letters, or communicate. In 1822, this rigidly proscribed denial of human intercourse — which is still the rubric in many of the world's penal systems — found its most eloquent spokesperson in Auburn's Warden Gersham Powers:

> The demands of nature must indeed be complied with; their [the prisoners] bodies must be fed and clothed . . . but they ought to be deprived of every enjoyment arising from social or kindred feelings and affections; of all knowledge of each other, the world, and their connections with it. Force them to reflection, and let self-tormenting guilt harrow up the tortures of accusing conscience, keener than scorpion stings; until the intensity of their sufferings subdues their stubborn spirits, and humbles them to a realizing sense of the enormity of their crimes and their obligation to reform.

Thankfully, the Auburn Prison of 1822 is not the institution that one confronts today. In 1986, as a case in point, even the term "prison" is anachronistic: Auburn is a "correctional facility." Yet even though Warden Powers is long buried, his philosophy, I surmise, still informs these halls. For Auburn, like any architecturally planned, functional structure, was constructed to facilitate a certain notion of reality. When these long tiers of individual cells were created — small, dark, and cramped — certain expectations were being fulfilled; certain others, suggested. Hopefully, the prisoner in 1986 will not die from long hours of standing in his cell, as fifty of his brethren once did; but he still will find his room terribly constrictive; he still will notice how the walls of his cell jut out into the corridor, a further hindrance to "unwanted talk"; and he still will discover — and this he will relish, albeit silently — that this is *his* cell: however cramped, squalid, and dark.

This, of course, is no insignificant development. However small his quarters, the inmate possesses something which is *his:* he can hang something on the wall (provided he has something to hang) and can, as much as is humanly possible, leave his mark on his space. For a time, he does not have to worry about someone else's belongings, feelings, or privacy — at least while *they* are in *their* cells. And if you are a prisoner, this is essential and important rest. Certainly, one may murder oneself in one's own cell; but amongst the prison community, there are literally hundreds of people who might potentially murder you, and all for some supposed slight, and one not even necessarily directed at them, but at their friend, lover, or even, God knows, at someone who is just a resident of their cell block. In one's cell — for a few precious hours then — one can safely "watch one's back." Of course, there might be a fire and one might perish; but there might be a nuclear disaster in New York, and all New York might evaporate in the conflagration. A prisoner, like most New Yorkers, is willing to live with that possibility. But he does not relish placing his life in harm's way, amongst people who know all too much about harm. And thus his cell is, in this darkest of places, "heaven sent."

Yet none of this enlightened humanitarianism — that social architects might applaud and Anton Chekhov, weary of Sahalin, might, understandably, envy — has much effect on the visitor. He is far too much a victim of his own life, and the perilous nature of it. If he has not valued his freedom before coming to Auburn, if he has not thought about whom he is (and therefore what he must protect), he does so now. For whatever else a prison does, it demands that one confront it. If you are a prisoner, it might take you a dozen years to realize that the life you *hope* to create requires, above all else, that it be lived *within* these walls, for these *walls do not go away.* Here, of all the world's places, there is everything to accept.

For those of us who are *visiting* — and this, indeed, is the greatest privilege — our status is in our faces, our movements, our bowels. We know, and we cling to this as we might to our children, that *we shall walk out of here, tonight, at a certain hour.*

And it is just this privilege which both the prisoners and, to a lesser degree, the guards wish to cost us dear. When we walked through the corridors, the catcalls, the *Baby, you look beautiful,* and *I'll kill you white motherfuckers,* were an expression of lust, anger, and bitterness; but they were also an expression of our envious ability to put off that which the inmates could not elude. In our quick, stuttering movements, in our downturned faces, in our trying to

look courageous we possessed a vulnerability — and how powerfully, in a different way, we sensed it — that they could ill afford.
Indeed, it was this flabby indulgence, this possibility for openly
embracing fear (swimming in it, as one might a fur coat), for
which they despised us. Fear would set them to the barbells late at
night; fear would turn them taciturn; fear would cause them to
stuff the fork into another's ribs before he jabbed it into theirs;
fear was *not* that mad dash between buildings, that shrinking,
scared, trying-to-look-not-so movement which so claimed us.

I had been invited to Auburn Correctional Facility to read and
talk about my poetry for an incredible two-and-a-half-hour class. I
remember how my stomach tightened when I first learned that I
had to perform for that length of time. By nature I am a one-hour
person. Indeed, whenever I attend a lecture that swells on beyond
that point, I find myself imaginatively melding with the audience,
thinking how I must meet someone in three minutes, catch the
late bus, or do the laundry. But more accurately, I clung to the
question of time, because it was the easiest thing on which to
cling. Although it would be difficult to fill one hundred and fifty
minutes, my great confrontation was not with the clock, but with
those time would place before me.

The forty inmates who made up my class were participants in
Elmira Community College's Inmate Higher Education Program.
Most of the students were black and in their early twenties; one
man had gray hair. Conspicuously, the three white prisoners clustered together, in much the same way blacks often huddle together in the outer world. At Cornell, where I teach, this behavior
is often looked upon as unfriendly at best, and racist at worst. Few
whites would concede that blacks, like themselves, are merely de-
sirous of fraternizing with people with whom they share a common
interest and experience. Whites, because this is America, have
never had to justify their actions; they sit with and entertain
whomever they wish. Yet when blacks exercise the same human
prerogative, it is considered an act of dismissal, subterfuge, or war.

At Auburn I couldn't help but wonder what those white inmates
felt with the tables turned. Was their isolation that of the lonely island, or the citadel beyond assault? Clearly they were in the minority in the prison population, but they were also white; and I
sensed, even in this last outcrop of civilization, that their color still

had some sting. And even if it didn't call the heavens down, it did testify that they were, in prison parlance, some "bad muthafuckas." For the few whites who found themselves sent up to Auburn had been convicted of repeated, unusually brutal offenses. Indeed, the viciousness of whites' crimes seemed in inverse proportion to their numbers. As one of the black inmates described them, and not without a touch of envy, "If evil walked, them cats be Jesse Owens."

At Auburn one thing was immediately apparent: the inmates were delighted that I had come. In the first instance, I was someone they didn't know who took them away from the tedium of the ordinary; but, more importantly, I was the first black teacher they had encountered in twelve months. Once I read two poems, the questions began: Where had I been raised? What was my background? How had I managed to evade prison? I breathlessly explained that I had grown up in Harlem, amongst two good parents "who rode my ass"; but offered little else.

This, of course, was an oversimplification, if not a direct lie. I had been raised in Harlem, but in the most unusual of circumstances. My father was a physician, my mother was a brilliant artist and writer, and I had attended one of the finest — and personally, most ruinous — independent schools in the city. I lived in Harlem, which is to say that I saw much, but I certainly hadn't lived the lives these inmates had: indeed, I had spent my entire life keeping myself at a safe remove from anything which might bring me to Harlem's reality. Yes, I had done a little of this and a bit of that, but I was always at the sidelines. I knew where the deep water was — everyone knew that. But I remained a shore bird.

My brother, however, paid for my escape. A talented drummer who shared the same exact IQ as myself (something which my mother was always wont to remind me), he lived in those streets, and it, and the difficult contradictions he faced, broke him. My brother, Paul, would ultimately drink himself to death at twenty-nine. He was tough, independent, and full of bitterness. He was, as I read that evening, "hungry for the end of the world."

The inmates particularly liked my "brother" poems: they too had brothers they missed and loved, brothers whose ultimate lives might be even more menaced than their own. This I found oddly comforting: in our desire to transcend the horror of crime, we hasten to view the criminal as someone without any notion of family or community. Certainly, this is our clumsy way of insulating ourselves from *their* human truth: for it is far too frightening to imagine ourselves as potential criminals, and far more convenient, and comforting, to see the criminal as truly subhuman. Indeed, had they been born with twelve heads or twenty spikes, we might finally, irrevocably, divorce ourselves from them. But as they come with two arms, two legs, a pumping heart, and a wondrous mind, their profanation suggests our own ratty flesh; their banishment, our own ever possible exile.

In truth, the lies we fabricate to distance ourselves from others invariably rise to haunt us. We may lie *to* ourselves, but others are under no obligation to lie *for* us. Whatever these inmates were — and all of them were sentenced to Auburn for corporal crimes — they would not permit me to view them merely as maniacs, psychopaths, or what have you. They were people, cussed and joy-filled: people capable of tenderness and murder: people like me and yet unlike me, because I haven't yet, thank goodness, killed anyone.

I learned a great deal in those two hours and thirty minutes; much more, I trust, than those inmates learned from me. At one point, one of the students asked me to describe how it felt to enter the prison. I shall never forget how dangerous that question seemed to me, dangerous because it gave voice to all my inner disquiet. Quickly I found myself looking about the room, noticing that there were no guards within immediate reach. To this day I don't know what made me sense my immediate vulnerability: certainly it had to do with the poignancy of the question, for in some profound way, the inmate was asking me to unburden myself, to tell him how I had found a means to live with fear; yet just as centrally — and this was as palpable as air — he wanted to know if I thought he was a beast, if I had cast him beyond the shores of humanity (and if I had, he might make my suspicions *real*); but most fundamentally, most crucially, I realized that he, Lord knows how, had given language to my own questioning, my own inadequate "sew-work." I hadn't made peace with the prison, with him, or with myself. And he knew it.

After some time — it seemed like hours, it was merely seconds — I told him the truth. I stated that the prison was the most frightening, scary place I had ever seen. He was quiet for a

moment, and then he smiled. He agreed with me. *Agreed with me.*
Yes, this place was as hellish as he imagined. In my own terror, I
had thought that he had been holding me to my life; in truth, I
had been holding him to his. He, like all of us, needed to affirm
that his own powers of discrimination were accurate, that his experience might be mirrored by others. Although Auburn was brutal
and spirit-crushing, it had not yet destroyed his ability to perceive
and differentiate shades of horror; it had not yet destroyed him.
Of this, at least, I could bear witness.

There were two questions which were asked again and again of
me. Inmate after inmate wanted to know if I thought I would continue to write and to teach. At first, I was not at all surprised at this
question: it is a common one, asked eternally of writers. Yet on this
particular occasion, whenever I attempted to answer the question,
the audience would neither hear nor accept my response. Again
and again I would state that Yes, I thought I would continue to
teach, and again and again I would be presented with the same
question. It was maddening.

Finally I realized what was happening. To these inmates, my tacit
belief in the probability of an *assured* future, my notion that I
could reasonably expect to find myself in a *certain* circumstance, at
a *certain* time, was as mind-boggling as if I had just sprouted wings.
For them, there had never been *one* veritable day of certainty:
when they were in the streets, they had to live on mother wit; now,
in prison, every minute brought new perils. Indeed, if there was
one inexpugnable axiom for them, it was the present tense, the resounding I *am.* Of nothing else could they be certain.

Ultimately, their questions were, if you will, *pre-*questions: they
were the first, tentative vocalizations of wonder. The inmates
wanted me to repeat myself, because they could not understand
the specifics of my answer until they understood the astonishing
grammar from which it sprang. Miraculously, although we shared
the ability to make sounds, we had yet to forge a common language. And it was just this which made us tongue-tied at revelation:
having so much to say, and no means, no suitable lexicon for conveying it, we were exiles in a country more hideous, terrible, and
unreachable than any Kafka had ever imagined.

If Auburn cut the prisoner off from the world, it, more horribly, sealed them into their *futureless* self. Usually, thankfully,

human beings — because of imagination, spirit, and plain can-
tankerousness — evolve the means to transcend most anything,
even the grim ghetto of self. Yet at Auburn, and I trust at most
prisons, this could not be tolerated (*jails, we must remember, are to
keep people in*). As any jailer knows, the walls of the present are
always dismantled in the future; but there is *no* future, if there is
no ability to set aside and reconstitute, to interdict and reposi-
tion, then the present becomes the almighty, and the walls become unconquerable. Although I did not interview the jailors, I
did see the jailed. For most of them, the walls without had become
the walls within; and such walls never, no matter what Joshua
does, *come a-tumbling down.*

After I had finished reading, one student, who had heretofore
been silent, spoke up, reminding me that although "we prisoners
might seem like nice guys, we're here because we killed people,"
the last statement clearly intended to elicit a reaction from me, the
naïve college professor. Now, after two long hours, I found myself
getting angry: I wondered why he so wanted to frighten me, especially since it seemed that my easy fright was all he desired. But
then I realized that he might be attempting something far more
humanly essential and generous. As I had told him of my brother,
had offered that intimate bond of personal experience and blood,
so too would he share his only sacred gift — his experience — with
me. Difficult and tentative as his motions were (and confession, by
nature, is always stony), this man wanted to speak to me as man to
man, witness to witness.

What first I had taken as a vitriolic assault was merely this man's
life: he had offered it up, in the ready language at his disposal. I
might not like the life he had, or the brutal language by which he
expressed it, but I certainly should permit him his truth. It might
sting; I might refuse to listen; but this is the privilege of the listener. The teller, sadly, can only recount his tale: he can lie, but
that, in itself, is just another corner of revelation.

At bottom, this man was trying to claim his humanity as he
tested mine. If I had my naïveté to lose, he had something far
more essential to win, his personhood; and he would struggle for
that at all costs. Indeed, it was the lopsidedness of this battle, the
vast inequality of our two involvements, which so charged the moment. I, since I had not yet truly become pariah, had the privilege

of arguing over the nature of my privilege (or even tossing it away
if I so desired); while he, on the other hand, had no choice but to
plead for his essential humanity. He, certainly, would not choose
to walk into this prison — not with what he knew. Indeed, if there
was light at the end of the proverbial tunnel for him, he had not
only to create the light, but the instrument by which it might be
seen. And since our predicaments were far from being reciprocal,
the wolves loomed at every corner.

And yet remembering my childhood joy when I "acted the nigger" on the New York City bus, negotiating that delicious nether
world that only the marginalized are allowed, I understood what
that inmate felt. When those "high-class" whites saw me, the
chocolate-faced boy, they knew that I was the flesh and blood
repository of their assumptions — the authentic ghetto type; and
I, even though I attended the crème-de-la-crème private school in
the city, gave them a show worthy of their concern. Although I
didn't have any real power, I could certainly fool those people. I'd
talk jive, look evil, and "badmouth" the toughest looking white boy
I could find. And then, laughing all the way, I'd romp over to the
Collegiate School, the place where ninety percent of *their* children
failed to gain entrance.

Yet notwithstanding my minor triumph, I bitterly decried the
subterra in which it was purchased. Certainly one can, in extreme
cases, extricate some pleasure out of hell; but hell is nonetheless
hell; it is certainly never heaven. And thus the inmate, though he
needed me to facilitate his journey to self-announcement, could
excuse neither the brashness of my declaration — I was asking
him to justify himself — nor the insubstantiality of my presence.
Whatever else I was, to him and the rest of the prison population, my credentials were dubious at best. A Cornell professorship
might mean something in the outer world; but here, it was as valuable as an expired driver's license, or an old football ticket. Power,
we must remember, is negotiable only where it has validity: in the
prison, had I been physically strong or good at cards, I might expect a measure of admiration, respect, and fellowship; but *sans*
these talents, my degrees and professional standing, understandably, met with little interest. Indeed, the value system which had so
honored me had exiled them. For those who had been ritually cast
out, certainly, it would be an inhumanly bitter pill to swallow to be

expected to salute the son as they suffered under his father. Blake to the contrary, the cut worm does *not* forgive the plow.

Ultimately the human voice is a very wondrous thing: it can show, at rare moments, everything which propels it. That these men had once been murderers meant that they could also be something else; at least, that was what the new wavering in this young man's voice suggested. I watched him slowly negotiate the incline of possibility, his voice swelling into a trill of astonishment, at first slow, gravelly, and then steady. Certainly this wasn't a wave of spontaneous announcement: he had seen far too much for that. More, it was the hard, pruned, strained depth-taking of someone who sensed, albeit bitterly, that the world might return nothing. But still he, with no reason that I could fathom, kept speaking, his own narrative building, gathering. Suddenly, words suggested words, listening suggested listeners, confession suggested healing; and he said, both to himself and to me, "Man, you ain't bad." And that was enough.

At ten o'clock the bell rang, and the prisoners began to file back to their cells. Of the forty I spoke with, twenty or so came up to me, shook my hand, and asked if I might come back. None of these congratulations came from the three white prisoners, something which I can only presume to understand. My poems are not overly racial: I didn't read a large number of racial poems. Possibly I had neglected them; possibly they did not like my reading. I just do not know.

The journey out of the prison seemed more efficacious. When we entered the yard this time, it was filled with inmates pumping iron, smoking, and chatting. Again we were escorted by four guards. Now the towers, with their no-nonsense sentries, were well lighted, although the lights were not dancing over the grounds as in the movies. For the first time I looked at the one-hundred-year-old granite. These walls had been made to last; hell, as Gersham Powers had so wanted, would remain interminable.

Near the first checkpoint, I saw one of the inmates who had been at my seminar. He smiled — a long, good smile — a smile that seemed almost hungry, a smile much like my brother's. I wished him well.

Then we began the elaborate countings until we reached the last checkpoint, where they asked us to put our right hands under an

ultraviolet light. The light illuminated the invisible stamp that
had been placed on our wrists when we first entered the prison.
It seemed such a fitting way to leave this place: the once invisible stamp, now glowing luminously green, as yet again another
mystery.

Reflections and Responses

1. McClane precedes his essay with a poem about his brother
"Paul." In what way does the poem contribute to the theme and
spirit of the essay? What images from the poem are interwoven
into the essay?

2. Why do you think McClane interrupts his narrative with a historical account of Auburn prison? How does this information contribute to the essay's effect?

3. Upon entering the prison, McClane notes that at Auburn
"there is no room for romanticism." Explain what you think he
means by this. Do you think he means this positively or negatively?
Does "romanticism" play any part in the essay?

LEWIS THOMAS

Crickets, Bats, Cats, & Chaos

How do animals think*? Do they possess a consciousness like ours or is theirs entirely different? How can we enter into the mind of a cat or a cricket? In this insightful essay, a renowned medical researcher considers the mysterious world of animal awareness and discovers the important role that chaos and unpredictability play in the life and mind of nonhuman creatures. These biological considerations lead Dr. Lewis Thomas to a surprising idea about the human mind: If chaos is so important to a creature as lowly as the cricket, what might be its significance to more complex organisms? Chaos, he comes to believe, is not an occasional aspect of human thought but the norm: "Predictable, small-scale, orderly, cause-and-effect sequences are hard to come by and don't last long when they do turn up. Something else almost always turns up at the same time, and then another sequential thought intervenes alongside, and there come turbulence and chaos again." Out of this unpredictable jumble comes — when we are lucky — our insights and illuminations, our "good ideas."*

A celebrated physician, Lewis Thomas also wrote five outstanding collections of essays: The Lives of a Cell *(1974),* The Medusa and the Snail *(1979),* Late Night Thoughts on Listening to Mahler's Ninth Symphony *(1983),* Et Cetera, Et Cetera *(1990), and* The Fragile Species *(1992). Thomas's essays demonstrate an enormously wide range of interests as he roams expertly and entertainingly through biology, ecology, semantics, literature, and classical music. In addition to numerous scientific papers, he is also the author of a memoir,* The Youngest Science *(1983). Thomas died in 1993. "Crickets, Bats, Cats, & Chaos" originally appeared in* Audubon *(1992) and was selected by Joseph Epstein for* The Best American Essays *1993.*

I am not sure where to classify the mind of my cat Jeoffry. He is a small Abyssinian cat, a creature of elegance, grace, and poise, a piece of moving sculpture, and a total mystery. We named him Jeoffry after the eighteenth-century cat celebrated by the unpredictable poet Christopher Smart in a poem titled "Jubilate Agno," one section of which begins, "For I will consider my cat Jeoffry." The following lines are selected more or less at random:

> For he counteracts the powers of darkness by his electrical skin
>   and glaring eyes.
> For he counteracts the Devil, who is death, by brisking about
>   the life . . .
> For he is of the tribe of Tiger . . .
> For he purrs in thankfulness, when God tells him he's a good
>   Cat . . .
> For he is an instrument for the children to learn benevolence
>   upon . . .
> For he is a mixture of gravity and waggery . . .
> For there is nothing sweeter than his peace when at rest.
> For there is nothing brisker than his life when in motion.

I have not the slightest notion what goes on in the mind of my cat Jeoffry, beyond the conviction that it is a genuine mind, with genuine thoughts and a strong tendency to chaos, but in all other respects a mind totally unlike mine. I have a hunch, based on long moments of observing him stretched on the rug in sunlight, that his mind has more periods of geometric order, and a better facility for switching itself almost, but not quite, entirely off, and accordingly an easier access to pure pleasure. Just as he is able to hear sounds that I cannot hear, and smell important things of which I am unaware, and suddenly leap like a crazed gymnast from chair to chair, upstairs and downstairs through the house, flawless in every movement and searching for something he never finds, he has periods of meditation on matters I know nothing about.

While thinking about what nonhumans think is, in most biological quarters, an outlandish question, even an impermissible one, to which the quick and easy answer is nothing, or almost nothing, or certainly nothing like *thought* as we use the word, I still think about it. For while none of them may have real thoughts, foresee the future, regret the past, or be self-aware, most of us up here at the peak of evolution cannot manage the awareness of our own awareness, a state of mind only achieved when the mind succeeds in emptying itself of all other information and switches off all messages, interior and exterior. This is the state of mind for which the Chinese Taoists long ago used a term meaning, literally, no-knowledge. With no-knowledge, it is said, you get a different look at the world, an illumination.

Falling short of this, as I do, and dispossessed of anything I could call illumination, it has become my lesser satisfaction to learn secondhand whatever I can, and then to think, firsthand, about the behavior of other kinds of animals.

I think of crickets, for instance, and the thought of their unique, very small thoughts — principally about mating and bats — but also about the state of cricket society. The cricket seems to me an eminently suitable animal for sorting out some of the emotional issues bound to arise in any consideration of animal awareness. Nobody, so far as I know, not even an eighteenth-century minor poet, could imagine any connection between events in the mind of a cricket and those in the mind of a human. If there was ever a creature in nature meriting the dismissive description of a living machine, mindless and thoughtless, the cricket qualifies. So in talking about what crickets are up to when they communicate with each other, as they unmistakably do, by species-unique runs and rhythms of chirps and trills, there can be no question of *anthropomorphization,* that most awful of all terms for the deepest error a modern biologist can fall into.

If you reduce the temperature of a male cricket, the rate of his emission of chirping signals is correspondingly reduced. Indeed, some of the earlier naturalists used the technical term "thermometer crickets" because of the observation that you can make a close guess at the air temperature in a field by counting the rate of chirps of familiar crickets.

This is curious, but there is a much more curious thing going on when the weather changes. The female crickets in the same field, genetically coded to respond specifically to the chirp rhythm of their species, adjust their recognition mechanism to the same temperature change and the same new, slower rate of chirps. That is, as John Doherty and Ronald Hoy wrote on observing the phenomenon, "warm females responded best to the songs of warm males, and cold females responded best to the songs of cold males." The same phenomenon, known as temperature coupling, has been encountered in grasshoppers and tree frogs, and also in fireflies, with their flash communication system. The receiving mind of the female cricket, if you are willing to call it that, adjusts itself immediately to match the sending mind of the male. This has always struck me as one of the neatest examples of animals adjusting to a change in their environment.

But I started thinking about crickets with something quite different in mind, namely bats. It has long been known that bats feed voraciously on the nocturnal flights of crickets and moths, which they detect on the wing by their fantastically accurate ultrasound mechanism. What should have been guessed at, considering the ingenuity of nature, is that certain cricket species, green lacewings, and certain moths have ears that can detect the ultrasound emissions of a bat, and can analyze the distance and direction from which the ultrasound is coming. These insects can employ two separate and quite distinct defensive maneuvers for evading the bat's keen sonar.

The first is simply swerving away. This is useful behavior when the bat signal is coming from a safe distance, twenty to thirty meters away. At this range the insect can detect the bat, but the bat is too far off to receive the bounced ultrasound back to its own ears. So the cricket or moth needs to do nothing more, at least for the moment, than swing out of earshot.

But when the bat is nearby, three meters or less, the insect is in immediate and mortal danger, for now the bat's sonar provides an accurate localization. It is too late for swerving or veering; because of its superior speed the bat can easily track such simple evasions. What to do? The answer has been provided by Kenneth Roeder, who designed a marvelous laboratory model for field studies, including instruments to imitate the intensity and direction of bat signals.

The answer, for a cricket or moth or lacewing who hears a bat homing in close by, is *chaos*. Instead of swerving away, the insect launches into wild, totally erratic, random flight patterns, as unpredictable as possible. This kind of response tends to confuse the bat and results in escape for the insect frequently enough to have been selected by evolution as the final, stereotyped, "last-chance" response to the threat. It has the look of a very smart move, whether thought out or not.

So chaos is part of the useful, everyday mental equipment of a cricket or a moth, and that, I submit, is something new to think about. I don't wish to push the matter beyond its possible significance, but it seems to me to justify a modest nudge. The long debate over the problem of animal awareness is not touched by the observation, but it does bring up the opposite side of that argument, the opposite of anthropomorphization. It is this: Leaving aside the deep question as to whether the lower animals have anything going on in their mind that we might accept as conscious thought, are there important events occurring in our human minds that are matched by habits of the animal mind?

Surely chaos is a capacious area of common ground. I am convinced that my own mind spends much of its waking hours, not to mention its sleeping time, in a state of chaos directly analogous to that of the cricket hearing the sound of the nearby bat. But there is a big difference. My chaos is not induced by a bat; it is not suddenly switched on in order to facilitate escape; it is not an evasive tactic set off by any new danger. It is, I think, the normal state of affairs, and not just for my brain in particular but for human brains in general. The chaos that is my natural state of being is rather like the concept of chaos that has emerged in higher mathematical circles in recent years.

As I understand it, and I am quick to say that I understand it only quite superficially, chaos occurs when any complex, dynamic system is perturbed by a small uncertainty in one or another of its subunits. The inevitable result is an amplification of the disturbance and then the spread of unpredictable, random behavior throughout the whole system. It is the total unpredictability and randomness that makes the word "chaos" applicable as a technical term, but it is not true that the behavior of the system becomes disorderly. Indeed, as James P. Crutchfield and his associates have written, "There is order in chaos: underlying chaotic behavior there are elegant geometric forms that create randomness in the same way as a card dealer shuffles a deck of cards or a blender mixes cake batter." The random behavior of a turbulent stream of water, or of the weather, or of Brownian movement, or of the central nervous system of a cricket in flight from a bat, are all

determined by the same mathematical rules. Behavior of this sort
has been encountered in computer models of large cities: When a
small change was made in one small part of the city model, the amplification of the change resulted in enormous upheavals, none of
them predictable, in the municipal behavior at remote sites in the
models.

A moth or a cricket has a small enough nervous system to *seem*
predictable and orderly most of the time. There are not all that
many neurons, and the circuitry contains what seem to be mostly
simple reflex pathways. Laboratory experiments suggest that in a
normal day, one thing — the sound of a bat at a safe distance,
say — leads to another, predictable thing — a swerving off to one
side in flight. It is only when something immensely new and important happens — the bat sound at three meters away — that the
system is thrown into chaos.

I suggest that the difference with us is that chaos is the norm.
Predictable, small-scale, orderly, cause-and-effect sequences are
hard to come by and don't last long when they do turn up. Something else almost always turns up at the same time, and then another sequential thought intervenes alongside, and there come
turbulence and chaos again. When we are lucky, and the system
operates at its random best, something astonishing may suddenly
turn up, beyond predicting or imagining. Events like these we recognize as good ideas.

My cat Jeoffry's brain is vastly larger and more commodious
than that of a cricket, but I wonder if it is qualitatively all that different. The cricket lives with his two great ideas in mind, mating
and predators, and his world is a world of particular, specified
sounds. He is a tiny machine, I suppose, depending on what you
mean by "machine," but it is his occasional moments of randomness and unpredictability that entitle him to be called aware. In
order to achieve that feat of wild chaotic flight, and thus escape,
he has to make use, literally, of his brain. When Int 1, an auditory
interneuron, is activated by the sound of a bat closing in, the message is transmitted by an axon connected straight to the insect's
brain, and it is here, and only here, that the swerving is generated.
This I consider to be a thought, a very small thought, but still a
thought. Without knowing what to count as a thought, I figure that
Jeoffry, with his kind of brain, has a trillion thoughts of about the

same size in any waking moment. As for me, and my sort of brain, I can't think where to begin.

We like to think of our minds as containing trains of thought, or streams of consciousness, as though they were orderly arrangements of linear events, one notion leading in a cause-and-effect way to the next notion. Logic is the way to go; we set a high price on logic, unlike E. M. Forster's elderly lady in *Aspects of the Novel*, who, when accused of being illogical, replied, "Logic? Good gracious! What rubbish! How can I tell what I think till I see what I say?"

But with regard to our own awareness of nature, I believe we've lost sight of, lost track of, lost touch with, and to some measurable degree lost respect for, the chaotic and natural in recent years — and during the very period of history when we humans have been learning more about the detailed workings of nature than in all our previous millennia. The more we learn, the more we seem to distance ourselves from the rest of life, as though we were separate creatures, so different from other occupants of the biosphere as to have arrived from another galaxy. We seek too much to explain, we assert a duty to run the place, to dominate the planet, to govern its life, but at the same time we ourselves seem to be less a part of it than ever before.

We leave it whenever we can, we crowd ourselves from open green countrysides onto the concrete surfaces of massive cities, as far removed from the earth as we can get, staring at it from behind insulated glass, or by way of half-hour television clips.

At the same time, we talk a great game of concern. We shout at each other in high virtue, now more than ever before, about the befoulment of our nest and about whom to blame. We have mechanized our lives so extensively that most of us live with the illusion that our only connection with nature is the nagging fear that it may one day turn on us and do us in. Polluting our farmlands and streams, even the seas, worries us because of what it may be doing to the food and water supplies necessary for human beings. Raising the level of CO^2, methane, and hydrofluorocarbons in the atmosphere troubles us because of the projected effects of climate upheaval on human habitats. These anxieties do not extend, really, to nature at large. They are not the result of any new awareness.

Nature itself, that vast incomprehensible meditative being, has come to mean for most of us nothing much more than odd walks in the nearby woods, or flowers in the rooftop garden, or the soap opera stories of the last giant panda or whooping crane, or curiosities like the northward approach, from Florida, of the Asiatic flying cockroach.

I will begin to feel better about us, and about our future, when we finally start learning about some of the things that are still mystifications. Start with the events in the mind of a cricket, I'd say, and then go on from there. Comprehend my cat Jeoffry and we'll be on our way. Nowhere near home, but off and dancing, getting within a few millennia of understanding why the music of Bach is what it is, ready at last for open outer space. Give us time, I'd say, the kind of endless time we mean when we talk about the real world.

Reflections and Responses

1. Consider Thomas's use of *anthropomorphization*. What does the term mean? Why does Thomas refer to it as "that most awful of all terms for the deepest error a modern biologist can fall into"? What is that error? How serious an "error" does Thomas consider it?

2. If biologists don't normally approve of attempting to understand animal consciousness in human terms, then what might they make of viewing human consciousness in terms of animals? Would it be a scientific error either way? Explain what you think Thomas's position is in this matter.

3. Note that Thomas breaks his essay into three (unnumbered) parts. How would you summarize and characterize each part? In what way is the third part of the essay related to the first two?

4

Expression

AMY TAN

Mother Tongue

*For many American students, the language spoken at home is far different
from the one spoken in school. For that reason, many students learn to
switch back and forth between two languages, the one they use with their
family and the one required for their education. Such switching, however,
need not be confining or demoralizing. Rather, it can enhance one's sensitivity to language and can even be creatively enabling, as the Chinese
American novelist Amy Tan suggests in this charming personal essay.
"Language is the tool of my trade," Tan writes. "And I use them all — all
the Englishes I grew up with."*

*Born into a Chinese family that had recently arrived in California,
Amy Tan began writing as a child and after graduation from college
worked for several years as a freelance business writer. In the mid-eighties,
she began writing fiction, basing much of her work on family stories. She is
the author of two best-selling novels:* The Joy Luck Club *(1989), which
was a finalist for both the National Book Award and National Book Critics
Circle Award and was made into a motion picture directed by Wayne
Wang, and* The Kitchen God's Wife *(1991). In 1992 she published a
popular children's book,* The Moon Lady. *She lives in San Francisco,
where she is at work on a new novel. "Mother Tongue" originally appeared
in* The Threepenny Review *(1990) and was selected by Joyce Carol
Oates for* The Best American Essays 1991.

I am not a scholar of English or literature. I cannot give you much
more than personal opinions on the English language and its vari-
ations in this country or others.

I am a writer. And by that definition, I am someone who has always loved language. I am fascinated by language in daily life. I

spend a great deal of my time thinking about the power of language — the way it can evoke an emotion, a visual image, a complex idea, or a simple truth. Language is the tool of my trade. And I use them all — all the Englishes I grew up with.

Recently, I was made keenly aware of the different Englishes I do use. I was giving a talk to a large group of people, the same talk I had already given to half a dozen other groups. The nature of the talk was about my writing, my life, and my book, *The Joy Luck Club.* The talk was going along well enough, until I remembered one major difference that made the whole talk sound wrong. My mother was in the room. And it was perhaps the first time she had heard me give a lengthy speech, using the kind of English I have never used with her. I was saying things like, "The intersection of memory upon imagination" and "There is an aspect of my fiction that relates to thus-and-thus"— a speech filled with carefully wrought grammatical phrases, burdened, it suddenly seemed to me, with nominalized forms, past perfect tenses, conditional phrases, all the forms of standard English that I had learned in school and through books, the forms of English I did not use at home with my mother.

Just last week, I was walking down the street with my mother, and I again found myself conscious of the English I was using, the English I do use with her. We were talking about the price of new and used furniture and I heard myself saying this: "Not waste money that way." My husband was with us as well, and he didn't notice any switch in my English. And then I realized why. It's because over the twenty years we've been together I've often used that same kind of English with him, and sometimes he even uses it with me. It has become our language of intimacy, a different sort of English that relates to family talk, the language I grew up with.

So you'll have some idea of what this family talk I heard sounds like, I'll quote what my mother said during a recent conversation which I videotaped and then transcribed. During this conversation, my mother was talking about a political gangster in Shanghai who had the same last name as her family's, Du, and how the gangster in his early years wanted to be adopted by her family, which was rich by comparison. Later, the gangster became more powerful, far richer than my mother's family, and one day showed up at my mother's wedding to pay his respects. Here's what she said in part:

"Du Yusong having business like fruit stand. Like off the street kind. He is Du like Du Zong — but not Tsung-ming Island people. The local people call putong, the river east side, he belong to that side local people. That man want to ask Du Zong father take him in like become own family. Du Zong father wasn't look down on him, but didn't take seriously, until that man big like become a mafia. Now important person, very hard to inviting him. Chinese way, came only to show respect, don't stay for dinner. Respect for making big celebration, he shows up. Mean gives lots of respect. Chinese custom. Chinese social life that way. If too important won't have to stay too long. He come to my wedding. I didn't see, I heard it. I gone to boy's side, they have YMCA dinner. Chinese age I was nineteen."

You should know that my mother's expressive command of English belies how much she actually understands. She reads the *Forbes* report, listens to *Wall Street Week,* converses daily with her stockbroker, reads all of Shirley MacLaine's books with ease — all kinds of things I can't begin to understand. Yet some of my friends tell me they understand 50 percent of what my mother says. Some say they understand 80 to 90 percent. Some say they understand none of it, as if she were speaking pure Chinese. But to me, my mother's English is perfectly clear, perfectly natural. It's my mother tongue. Her language, as I hear it, is vivid, direct, full of observation and imagery. That was the language that helped shape the way I saw things, expressed things, made sense of the world.

Lately, I've been giving more thought to the kind of English my mother speaks. Like others, I have described it to people as "broken" or "fractured" English. But I wince when I say that. It has always bothered me that I can think of no way to describe it other than "broken," as if it were damaged and needed to be fixed, as if it lacked a certain wholeness and soundness. I've heard other terms used, "limited English," for example. But they seem just as bad, as if everything is limited, including people's perceptions of the limited English speaker.

I know this for a fact, because when I was growing up, my mother's "limited" English limited *my* perception of her. I was ashamed of her English. I believed that her English reflected the quality of what she had to say. That is, because she expressed them imperfectly her thoughts were imperfect. And I had plenty of empirical evidence to support me: the fact that people in department stores, at banks, and at restaurants did not take her seriously, did not give her good service, pretended not to understand her, or even acted as if they did not hear her.

My mother has long realized the limitations of her English as well. When I was fifteen, she used to have me call people on the phone to pretend I was she. In this guise, I was forced to ask for information or even to complain and yell at people who had been rude to her. One time it was a call to her stockbroker in New York. She had cashed out her small portfolio and it just so happened we were going to go to New York the next week, our very first trip outside California. I had to get on the phone and say in an adolescent voice that was not very convincing, "This is Mrs. Tan."

And my mother was standing in the back whispering loudly, "Why he don't send me check, already two weeks late. So mad he lie to me, losing me money."

And then I said in perfect English, "Yes, I'm getting rather concerned. You had agreed to send the check two weeks ago, but it hasn't arrived."

Then she began to talk more loudly. "What he want, I come to New York tell him front of his boss, you cheating me?" And I was trying to calm her down, make her be quiet, while telling the stockbroker, "I can't tolerate any more excuses. If I don't receive the check immediately, I am going to have to speak to your manager when I'm in New York next week." And sure enough, the following week there we were in front of this astonished stockbroker, and I was sitting there red-faced and quiet, and my mother, the real Mrs. Tan, was shouting at his boss in her impeccable broken English.

We used a similar routine just five days ago, for a situation that was far less humorous. My mother had gone to the hospital for an appointment, to find out about a benign brain tumor a CAT scan had revealed a month ago. She said she had spoken very good English, her best English, no mistakes. Still, she said, the hospital did not apologize when they said they had lost the CAT scan and she had come for nothing. She said they did not seem to have any sympathy when she told them she was anxious to know the exact diagnosis, since her husband and son had both died of brain tumors. She said they would not give her any more information until the next time and she would have to make another appointment for that. So she said she would not leave until the doctor called her daughter. She wouldn't budge. And when the doctor finally called her daughter, me, who spoke in perfect English — lo and behold — we had assurances the CAT scan would be found, promises that a conference call on Monday would be held, and apologies for any suffering my mother had gone through for a most regrettable mistake.

I think my mother's English almost had an effect on limiting my possibilities in life as well. Sociologists and linguists probably will tell you that a person's developing language skills are more influenced by peers. But I do think that the language spoken in the family, especially in immigrant families which are more insular, plays a large role in shaping the language of the child. And I believe that it affected my results on achievement tests, IQ tests, and the SAT. While my English skills were never judged as poor, compared to math, English could not be considered my strong suit. In grade school I did moderately well, getting perhaps B's, sometimes B-pluses, in English and scoring perhaps in the sixtieth or seventieth percentile on achievement tests. But those scores were not good enough to override the opinion that my true abilities lay in math and science, because in those areas I achieved A's and scored in the ninetieth percentile or higher.

This was understandable. Math is precise; there is only one correct answer. Whereas, for me at least, the answers on English tests were always a judgment call, a matter of opinion and personal experience. Those tests were constructed around items like fill-in-the-blank sentence completion, such as, "Even though Tom was ——, Mary thought he was ——." And the correct answer always seemed to be the most bland combinations of thoughts, for example, "Even though Tom was shy, Mary thought he was charming," with the grammatical structure "even though" limiting the correct answer to some sort of semantic opposites, so you wouldn't get answers like, "Even though Tom was foolish, Mary thought he was ridiculous." Well, according to my mother, there were very few limitations as to what Tom could have been and what Mary might have thought of him. So I never did well on tests like that.

The same was true with word analogies, pairs of words in which you were supposed to find some sort of logical, semantic relationship — for example, "*Sunset* is to *nightfall* as —— is to ——." And here you would be presented with a list of four possible pairs, one of which showed the same kind of relationship: *red* is to *stoplight, bus* is to *arrival, chills* is to *fever, yawn* is to *boring.* Well, I could never think that way. I knew what the tests were asking, but I could not block out of my mind the images already created by the first pair, "*sunset* is to *nightfall*"—and I would see a burst of colors against a darkening sky, the moon rising, the lowering of a curtain of stars. And all the other pairs of words — red, bus, stoplight, boring — just threw up a mass of confusing images, making it impossible for me to sort out something as logical as saying: "A sunset precedes nightfall" is the same as "a chill precedes a fever." The only way I would have gotten that answer right would have been to imagine an associative situation, for example, my being disobedient and staying out past sunset, catching a chill at night, which turns into feverish pneumonia as punishment, which indeed did happen to me.

I have been thinking about all this lately, about my mother's English, about achievement tests. Because lately I've been asked, as a writer, why there are not more Asian Americans represented in American literature. Why are there few Asian Americans enrolled in creative writing programs? Why do so many Chinese students go into engineering? Well, these are broad sociological questions I can't begin to answer. But I have noticed in surveys — in fact, just last week — that Asian students, as a whole, always do significantly better on math achievement tests than in English. And this makes me think that there are other Asian-American students whose English spoken in the home might also be described as "broken" or "lmited." And perhaps they also have teachers who are steering them away from writing and into math and science, which is what happened to me.

Fortunately, I happen to be rebellious in nature and enjoy the challenge of disproving assumptions made about me. I became an English major my first year in college, after being enrolled as pre-med. I started writing nonfiction as a freelancer the week after I was told by my former boss that writing was my worst skill and I should hone my talents toward account management.

But it wasn't until 1985 that I finally began to write fiction. And at first I wrote using what I thought to be wittily crafted sentences, sentences that would finally prove I had mastery over the English language. Here's an example from the first draft of a story that later made its way into *The Joy Luck Club,* but without this line: "That was my mental quandary in its nascent state." A terrible line, which I can barely pronounce.

Fortunately, for reasons I won't get into today, I later decided I should envision a reader for the stories I would write. And the reader I decided upon was my mother, because these were stories about mothers. So with this reader in mind — and in fact she did read my early drafts — I began to write stories using all the Englishes I grew up with: the English I spoke to my mother, which for lack of a better term might be described as "simple"; the English she used with me, which for lack of a better term might be described as "broken"; my translation of her Chinese, which could certainly be described as "watered down"; and what I imagined to be her translation of her Chinese if she could speak in perfect English, her internal language, and for that I sought to preserve the essence, but neither an English nor a Chinese structure. I wanted to capture what language ability tests can never reveal: her intent, her passion, her imagery, the rhythms of her speech and the nature of her thoughts.

Apart from what any critic had to say about my writing, I knew I had succeeded where it counted when my mother finished reading my book and gave me her verdict: "So easy to read."

Reflections and Responses

1. What are the "Englishes" that Amy Tan grew up with? Why does she feel uncomfortable with the term "broken" English? Why do you think she still uses that term toward the end of her essay?

2. What point is Tan making about language tests? Why did she not perform as well on them as she did on math and science? In her opinion, what aspects of language do the tests fail to take into account?

3. Tan cites a sentence —"That was my mental quandary in its nascent state"— that she deleted from *The Joy Luck Club*. What do you think she dislikes about that sentence? What kind of English does it represent? Does it or doesn't it demonstrate a "mastery" of the English language?

ANNIE DILLARD

The Stunt Pilot

Creative expression can take many forms; it need not refer only to literature, painting, or music. We can find creativity in craft and design, in the move-ments of dancers and athletes, and even — as the following essay reveals — in the aerobatics of a stunt pilot. Observing the breathtaking dives and spins, the "loops and arabesques" of a celebrated pilot, Annie Dillard is struck by their resemblance to artistic expression. She finds in the pilot's use of space a new kind of beauty, one that seems to encompass all the arts — poetry, painting, music, sculpture: "The black plane dropped spinning, and flattened out spinning the other way; it began to carve the air into forms that built wildly and musically on each other and never ended."

Annie Dillard is one of America's preeminent essayists, someone for whom, as she puts it, the essay is not an occasional piece but her "real work." The author of many award-winning books of essays and nonfiction, including Pilgrim at Tinker Creek, *which won the Pulitzer Prize for General Nonfiction in 1975,* Living by Fiction *(1982),* Teaching a Stone to Talk *(1982),* An American Childhood *(1987), and* The Writing Life *(1989), Dillard has taught creative writing at Wesleyan University in Middletown, Connecticut since 1979. In 1992, she pub-lished her first novel,* The Living. *"The Stunt Pilot" originally appeared in* Esquire *(1989) and was selected by Justin Kaplan for* The Best American Essays 1990.

Dave Rahm lived in Bellingham, Washington, north of Seattle. Bellingham, a harbor town, lies between the alpine North Cascade Mountains and the San Juan Islands in Haro Strait above Puget Sound. The latitude is that of Newfoundland. Dave Rahm was a stunt pilot, the air's own genius.

In 1975, with a newcomer's willingness to try anything once, I attended the Bellingham Air Show. The Bellingham airport was a wide clearing in a forest of tall Douglas firs; its runways suited small planes. It was June. People wearing blue or tan zipped jackets stood loosely on the concrete walkways and runways outside the coffee shop. At that latitude in June, you stayed outside because you could, even most of the night, if you could think up something to do. The sky did not darken until ten o'clock or so, and it never got very dark. Your life parted and opened in the sunlight. You tossed your dark winter routines, thought up mad projects, and improvised everything from hour to hour. Being a stunt pilot seemed the most reasonable thing in the world; you could wave your arms in the air all day and night, and sleep next winter.

I saw from the ground a dozen stunt pilots; the air show scheduled them one after the other, for an hour of aerobatics. Each pilot took up his or her plane and performed a batch of tricks. They were precise and impressive. They flew upside down, and straightened out; they did barrel rolls, and straightened out; they drilled through dives and spins, and landed gently on a far runway.

For the end of the day, separated from all other performances of every sort, the air show director had scheduled a program titled "Dave Rahm." The leaflet said that Rahm was a geologist who taught at Western Washington University. He had flown for King Hussein in Jordan. A tall man in the crowd told me Hussein had seen Rahm fly on a visit the king made to the United States; he had invited him to Jordan to perform at ceremonies. Hussein was a pilot, too. "Hussein thought he was the greatest thing in the world."

Idly, paying scant attention, I saw a medium-sized, rugged man dressed in brown leather, all begoggled, climb in a black biplane's open cockpit. The plane was a Bücker Jungman, built in the thirties. I saw a tall, dark-haired woman seize a propeller tip at the plane's nose and yank it down till the engine caught. He was off; he climbed high over the airport in his biplane, very high until he was barely visible as a mote, and then seemed to fall down the air, diving headlong, and streaming beauty in spirals behind him.

The black plane dropped spinning, and flattened out spinning the other way; it began to carve the air into forms that built wildly and musically on each other and never ended. Reluctantly, I started paying attention. Rahm drew high above the world an inexhaustibly glorious line; it piled over our heads in loops and arabesques. It was like a Saul Steinberg* fantasy; the plane was the pen. Like Steinberg's contracting and billowing pen line, the line Rahm spun moved to form new, punning shapes from the edges of the old. Like a Klee† line, it smattered the sky with landscapes and systems.

The air show announcer hushed. He had been squawking all day, and now he quit. The crowd stilled. Even the children watched dumbstruck as the slow, black biplane buzzed its way around the air. Rahm made beauty with his whole body; it was pure pattern, and you could watch it happen. The plane moved every way a line can move, and it controlled three dimensions, so the line carved massive and subtle slits in the air like sculptures. The plane looped the loop, seeming to arch its back like a gymnast; it stalled, dropped, and spun out of it climbing; it spiraled and knifed west on one side's wings and back east on another; it turned cartwheels, which must be physically impossible; it played with its own line like a cat with yarn. How did the pilot know where in the air he was? If he got lost, the ground would swat him.

Rahm did everything his plane could do: tailspins, four-point rolls, flat spins, figure eights, snap rolls, and hammerheads. He did pirouettes on the plane's tail. The other pilots could do these stunts too, skillfully, one at a time. But Rahm used the plane inexhaustibly, like a brush marking thin air.

His was pure energy and naked spirit. I have thought about it for years. Rahm's line unrolled in time. Like music, it split the bulging rim of the future along its seam. It pried out the present. We watchers waited for the split-second curve of beauty in the present to reveal itself. The human pilot, Dave Rahm, worked in the cockpit right at the plane's nose; his very body tore into the future for us and reeled it down upon us like a curling peel.

Like any fine artist, he controlled the tension of the audience's

---

*Saul Steinberg: Contemporary artist (b. 1914) who also created numerous covers for *The New Yorker* magazine.

†Klee: Paul Klee (1879–1940), a Swiss artist known for his highly distinctive abstract paintings.

longing. You desired, unwittingly, a certain kind of roll or climb, or a return to a certain portion of the air, and he fulfilled your hope slantingly, like a poet, or evaded it until you thought you would burst, and then fulfilled it surprisingly, so you gasped and cried out.

The oddest, most exhilarating and exhausting thing was this: he never quit. The music had no periods, no rests or endings; the poetry's beautiful sentence never ended; the line had no finish; the sculptured forms piled overhead, one into another without surcease. Who could breathe, in a world where rhythm itself had no periods?

It had taken me several minutes to understand what an extraordinary thing I was seeing. Rahm kept all that embellished space in mind at once. For another twenty minutes I watched the beauty unroll and grow more fantastic and unlikely before my eyes. Now Rahm brought the plane down slidingly, and just in time, for I thought I would snap from the effort to compass and remember the line's long intelligence; I could not add another curve. He brought the plane down on a far runway. After a pause, I saw him step out, an ordinary man, and make his way back to the terminal.

The show was over. It was late. Just as I turned from the runway, something caught my eye and made me laugh. It was a swallow, a blue-green swallow, having its own air show, apparently inspired by Rahm. The swallow climbed high over the runway, held its wings oddly, tipped them, and rolled down the air in loops. The inspired swallow. I always want to paint, too, after I see the Rembrandts. The blue-green swallow tumbled precisely, and caught itself and flew up again as if excited, and looped down again, the way swallows do, but tensely, holding its body carefully still. It was a stunt swallow.

I went home and thought about Rahm's performance that night, and the next day, and the next.

I had thought I knew my way around beauty a little bit. I knew I had devoted a good part of my life to it, memorizing poetry and focusing my attention on complexity of rhythm in particular, on force, movement, repetition, and surprise, in both poetry and prose. Now I had stood among dandelions between two asphalt runways in Bellingham, Washington, and begun learning about beauty. Even the Boston Museum of Fine Arts was never more in-spiriting than this small northwestern airport on this time-killing Sunday afternoon in June. Nothing on earth is more gladdening than knowing we must roll up our sleeves and move back the boundaries of the humanly possible once more.

Later I flew with Dave Rahm; he took me up. A generous geogra-pher, Dick Smith, at Western Washington University, arranged it, and came along. Rahm and Dick Smith were colleagues at the uni-versity. In geology, Rahm had published two books and many arti-cles. Rahm was handsome in a dull sort of way, blunt-featured, wide-jawed, wind-burned, keen-eyed, and taciturn. As anyone would expect. He was forty. He wanted to show me the Cascade Mountains; these enormous peaks, only fifty miles from the coast, rise over nine thousand feet; they are heavily glaciated. Whatcom County has more glaciers than the lower forty-eight states com-bined; the Cascades make the Rocky Mountains look like hills. Mount Baker is volcanic, like most Cascade peaks. That year, Mount Baker was acting up. Even from my house at the shore I could see, early in the morning on clear days, volcanic vapor rise near its peak. Often the vapor made a cloud that swelled all morn-ing and hid the snows. Every day the newspapers reported on Ba-ker's activity: Would it blow? (A few years later, Mount St. Helens did blow.)

Rahm was not flying his trick biplane that day, but a faster en-closed plane, a single-engine Cessna. We flew from a bumpy grass airstrip near my house, out over the coast and inland. There was coastal plain down there, but we could not see it for clouds. We were over the clouds at five hundred feet and inside them too, heading for an abrupt line of peaks we could not see. I gave up on everything, the way you do in airplanes; it was out of my hands. Every once in a while Rahm saw a peephole in the clouds and buzzed over for a look. "That's Larsen's pea farm," he said, or "That's Nooksack Road," and he changed our course with a heave.

When we got to the mountains, he slid us along Mount Baker's flanks sideways.

Our plane swiped at the mountain with a roar. I glimpsed a windshield view of dirty snow traveling fast. Our shaking, swoop-ing belly seemed to graze the snow. The wings shuddered; we peeled away and the mountain fell back and the engines whined.

We felt flung, because we were in fact flung; parts of our faces and internal organs trailed pressingly behind on the curves. We came back for another pass at the mountain, and another. We dove at the snow headlong like suicides; we jerked up, down, or away at the last second, so late we left our hearts, stomachs, and lungs behind. If I forced myself to hold my heavy head up against the G's,* and to raise my eyelids, heavy as barbells, and to notice what I saw, I could see the wrinkled green crevasses cracking the glaciers' snow.

Pitching snow filled all the windows, and shapes of dark rock. I had no notion which way was up. Everything was black or gray or white except the fatal crevasses; everything made noise and shook. I felt my face smashed sideways and saw rushing abstractions of snow in the windshield. Patches of cloud obscured the snow fleetingly. We straightened out, turned, and dashed at the mountainside for another pass, which we made, apparently, on our ear, an inch or two away from the slope. Icefalls and cornices jumbled and fell away. If a commercial plane's black box, such as the FAA painstakingly recovers from crash sites, could store videotapes as well as pilots' last words, some videotapes would look like this: a mountainside coming up at the windows from all directions, ice and snow and rock filling the screen up close and screaming by.

Rahm was just being polite. His geographer colleague wanted to see the fissure on Mount Baker from which steam escaped. Everybody in Bellingham wanted to see that sooty fissure, as did every geologist in the country; no one on earth could fly so close to it as Rahm. He knew the mountain by familiar love and feel, like a face; he knew what the plane could do and what he dared to do.

When Mount Baker inexplicably let us go, he jammed us into cloud again and soon tilted. "The Sisters!" someone shouted, and I saw the windshield fill with red rock. This mountain looked infernal, a drear and sheer plane of lifeless rock. It was red and sharp; its gritty blades cut through the clouds at random. The mountain was quiet. It was in shade. Careening, we made sideways passes at these brittle peaks too steep for snow. Their rock was full of iron, somebody shouted at me then or later; the iron had rusted, so they were red. Later, when I was back on the ground, I recalled that, from a distance, the two jagged peaks called the Twin Sisters

*G's: A measure of gravitational force.

looked translucent against the sky; they were sharp, tapered, and fragile as arrowheads.

I talked to Rahm. He was flying us out to the islands now. The islands were fifty or sixty miles away. Like many other people, I had picked Bellingham, Washington, by looking at an atlas. It was clear from the atlas that you could row in the salt water and see snow-covered mountains; you could scale a glaciated mountainside with an ice ax in August, skirting green crevasses two hundred feet deep, and look out on the islands in the sea. Now, in the air, the clouds had risen over us; dark forms lay on the glinting water. There was almost no color to the day, just blackened green and some yellow. I knew the islands were forested in dark Douglas firs the size of skyscrapers. Bald eagles scavenged on the beaches; robins the size of herring gulls sang in the clearings. We made our way out to the islands through the layer of air between the curving planet and its held, thick clouds.

"When I started trying to figure out what I was going to do with my life, I decided to become an expert on mountains. It wasn't much to be, it wasn't everything, but it was something. I was going to know everything about mountains from every point of view. So I started out in geography." Geography proved too pedestrian for Rahm, too concerned with "how many bushels of wheat an acre." So he ended up in geology. Smith had told me that geology departments throughout the country used Rahm's photographic slides — close-ups of geologic features from the air.

"I used to climb mountains. But you know, you can get a better feel for a mountain's power flying around it, flying all around it, then you can from climbing it tied to its side like a flea."

He talked about his flying performances. He thought of the air as a line, he said. "This end of the line, that end of the line — like a rope." He improvised. "I get a rhythm going and stick with it." While he was performing in a show, he paid attention, he said, to the lighting. He didn't play against the sun. That was all he said about what he did.

In aerobatic maneuvers, pilots pull about seven positive G's on some stunts and six negative G's on others. Some gyrations push; others pull. Pilots alternate the pressures carefully, so they do not gray out or black out.

Later I learned that some stunt pilots tune up by wearing gravity

boots. These are boots made to hook over a doorway; wearing
them, you hang in the doorway upside down. It must startle a pilot's children to run into their father or mother in the course of
their home wanderings — the parents hanging wide-eyed, upside
down in the doorway like a bat.

We were landing; here was the airstrip on Stuart Island — that
island to which Ferrar Burn was dragged by the tide. We put down,
climbed out of the plane, and walked. We wandered a dirt track
through fields to a lee shore where yellow sandstone ledges slid
into the sea. The salt chuck, people there called salt water. The
sun came out. I caught a snake in the salt chuck; the snake, eighteen inches long, was swimming in the green shallows.

I had a survivor's elation. Rahm had found Mount Baker in the
clouds before Mount Baker found the plane. He had wiped it with
the fast plane like a cloth and we had lived. When we took off from
Stuart Island and gained altitude, I asked if we could turn over —
could we do a barrel roll? The plane was making a lot of noise, and
Dick Smith did not hear any of this, I learned later. "Why not?"
Rahm said, and added surprisingly, "It won't hurt the plane." Without ado he leaned on the wheel and the wing went down and we
went somersaulting over it. We upended with a roar. We stuck to
the plane's sides like flung paint. All the blood in my body bulged
on my face; it piled between my skull and skin. Vaguely I could see
the chrome sea twirling over Rahm's head like a baton, and the
dark islands sliding down the skies like rain.

The G's slammed me into my seat like thugs and pinned me
while my heart pounded and the plane turned over slowly and
compacted each organ in turn. My eyeballs were newly spherical
and full of heartbeats. I seemed to hear a crescendo; the wing
rolled shuddering down the last 90 degrees and settled on the flat.
There were the islands, admirably below us, and the clouds, admirably above. When I could breathe, I asked if we could do it
again, and we did. He rolled the other way. The brilliant line of the
sea slid up the side window bearing its heavy islands. Through the
shriek of my blood and the plane's shakes I glimpsed the line of
the sea over the windshield, thin as a spear. How in performance
did Rahm keep track while his brain blurred and blood roared in
his ears without ceasing? Every performance was a tour de force

and a show of will, a *Machtspruch*.* I had seen the other stunt pilots straighten out after a trick or two; their blood could drop back and the planet simmer down. An Olympic gymnast, at peak form, strings out a line of spins ten stunts long across a mat, and is hard put to keep his footing at the end. Rahm endured much greater pressure on his faster spins using the plane's power, and he could spin in three dimensions and keep twirling till he ran out of sky room or luck.

When we straightened out, and had flown straightforwardly for ten minutes toward home, Dick Smith, clearing his throat, brought himself to speak. "What was that we did out there?"

"The barrel rolls?" Rahm said. "They were barrel rolls." He said nothing else. I looked at the back of his head; I could see the serious line of his cheek and jaw. He was in shirtsleeves, tanned, strong-wristed. I could not imagine loving him under any circumstance; he was alien to me, unfazed. He looked like GI Joe. He flew with that matter-of-fact, bored gesture pilots use. They click overhead switches and turn dials as if only their magnificent strength makes such dullness endurable. The half circle of wheel in their big hands looks like a toy they plan to crush in a minute; the wiggly stick the wheel mounts seems barely attached.

A crop-duster pilot in Wyoming told me the life expectancy of a crop-duster pilot is five years. They fly too low. They hit buildings and power lines. They have no space to fly out of trouble, and no space to recover from a stall. We were in Cody, Wyoming, out on the north fork of the Shoshone River. The crop duster had wakened me that morning flying over the ranch house and clearing my bedroom roof by half an inch. I saw the bolts on the wheel assembly a few feet from my face. He was spraying with pesticide the plain old grass. Over breakfast I asked him how long he had been dusting crops. "Four years," he said, and the figure stalled in the air between us for a moment. "You know you're going to die at it someday," he added. "We all know it. We accept that; it's part of it." I think now that, since the crop duster was in his twenties, he accepted only that he had to say such stuff; privately he counted on skewing the curve.

*Machtspruch: German, meaning "power speech."

I suppose Rahm knew the fact too. I do not know how he felt about it. "It's worth it," said the early French aviator Mermoz. He was Antoine de Saint-Exupéry's friend. "It's worth the final smashup."

Rahm smashed up in front of King Hussein, in Jordan, during a performance. The plane spun down and never came out of it; it nosedived into the ground and exploded. He bought the farm. I was living then with my husband out on that remote island in the San Juans, cut off from everything. Battery radios picked up the Canadian Broadcasting Company out of Toronto, half a continent away; island people would, in theory, learn if the United States blew up, but not much else. There were no newspapers. One friend got the Sunday *New York Times* by mail boat on the following Friday. He saved it until Sunday and had a party, every week; we all read the Sunday *Times* and no one mentioned that it was last week's.

One day, Paul Glenn's brother flew out from Bellingham to visit; he had a seaplane. He landed in the water in front of the cabin and tied up to our mooring. He came in for coffee, and he gave out news of this and that, and — Say, did we know that stunt pilot Dave Rahm had cracked up? In Jordan, during a performance: he never came out of a dive. He just dove right down into the ground, and his wife was there watching. "I saw it on CBS News last night." And then — with a sudden sharp look at my filling eyes — "What, did you know him?" But no, I did not know him. He took me up once. Several years ago. I admired his flying. I had thought that danger was the safest thing in the world, if you went about it right.

Later, I found a newspaper. Rahm was living in Jordan that year; King Hussein invited him to train the aerobatics team, the Royal Jordanian Falcons. He was also visiting professor of geology at the University of Jordan. In Amman that day he had been flying a Pitt Special, a plane he knew well. Katy Rahm, his wife of six months, was sitting beside Hussein in the viewing stands, with her daughter. Rahm died performing a Lomcevak combined with a tail slide and hammerhead. In a Lomcevak, the pilot brings the plane up on a slant and pirouettes. I had seen Rahm do this: the falling plane twirled slowly like a leaf. Like a ballerina, the plane seemed to hold its head back stiff in concentration at the music's slow, painful beauty. It was one of Rahm's favorite routines. Next the

pilot flies straight up, stalls the plane, and slides down the air on
his tail. He brings the nose down — the hammerhead — kicks the
engine, and finishes with a low loop.

It is a dangerous maneuver at any altitude, and Rahm was doing
it low. He hit the ground on the loop; the tail slide had left him no
height. When Rahm went down, King Hussein dashed to the burning plane to pull him out, but he was already dead.

A few months after the air show, and a month after I had flown
with Rahm, I was working at my desk near Bellingham, where I
lived, when I heard a sound so odd it finally penetrated my concentration. It was the buzz of an airplane, but it rose and fell musically, and it never quit; the plane never flew out of earshot. I
walked out on the porch and looked up: it was Rahm in the black
and gold biplane, looping all over the air. I had been wondering
about his performance flight: could it really have been so beautiful? It was, for here it was again. The little plane twisted all over the
air like a vine. It trailed a line like a very long mathematical proof
you could follow only so far, and then it lost you in its complexity. I
saw Rahm flying high over the Douglas firs, and out over the water,
and back over farms. The air was a fluid, and Rahm was an eel.

It was as if Mozart could move his body through his notes, and
you could walk out on the porch, look up, and see him in periwig
and breeches, flying around in the sky. You could hear the music
as he dove through it; it streamed after him like a contrail.

I lost myself; standing on the firm porch, I lost my direction and
reeled. My neck and spine rose and turned, so I followed the
plane's line kinesthetically. In his open-cockpit black plane, Rahm
demonstrated curved space. He slid down ramps of air, he vaulted
and wheeled. He piled loops in heaps and praised height. He unrolled the scroll of air, extended it, and bent it into Möbius strips;
he furled line in a thousand new ways, as if he were inventing a
script and writing it in one infinitely recurring utterance until I
thought the bounds of beauty must break.

From inside, the looping plane had sounded tinny, like a kazoo.
Outside, the buzz rose and fell to the Doppler effect as the plane
looped near or away. Rahm cleaved the sky like a prow and tossed
out time left and right in his wake. He performed for forty minutes; then he headed the plane, as small as a wasp, back to the airport inland. Later I learned Rahm often practiced acrobatic

flights over this shore. His idea was that if he lost control and was going to go down, he could ditch in the salt chuck, where no one else would get hurt.

If I had not turned two barrel rolls in an airplane, I might have fancied Rahm felt good up there, and playful. Maybe Jackson Pollock felt a sort of playfulness, in addition to the artist's usual deliberate and intelligent care. In my limited experience, painting, unlike writing, pleases the senses while you do it, and more while you do it than after it is done. Drawing lines with an airplane, unfortunately, tortures the senses. Jet bomber pilots black out. I knew Rahm felt as if his brain were bursting his eardrums, felt that if he let his jaws close as tight as centrifugal force pressed them, he would bite through his lungs.

"All virtue is a form of acting," Yeats said. Rahm deliberately turned himself into a figure. Sitting invisible at the controls of a distant airplane, he became the agent and the instrument of art and invention. He did not tell me how he felt when we spoke of his performance flying; he told me instead that he paid attention to how his plane and its line looked to the audience against the lighted sky. If he had noticed how he felt, he could not have done the work. Robed in his airplane, he was as featureless as a priest. He was lost in his figural aspect like an actor or a king. Of his flying, he had said only, "I get a rhythm and stick with it." In its reticence, this statement reminded me of Veronese's* "Given a large canvas, I enhanced it as I saw fit." But Veronese was ironic, and Rahm was not; he was as literal as an astronaut; the machine gave him tongue.

When Rahm flew, he sat down in the middle of art and strapped himself in. He spun it all around him. He could not see it himself. If he never saw it on film, he never saw it at all — as if Beethoven could not hear his final symphonies not because he was deaf but because he was inside the paper on which he wrote. Rahm must have felt it happen, that fusion of vision and metal, motion and idea. I think of this man as a figure, a college professor with a Ph.D. upside down in the loud band of beauty. What are we here for? *Propter chorum,* the monks say: for the sake of the choir.

---

*__Veronese:__ Paolo Veronese (1528–88), famous Venetian painter.

"Purity does not lie in separation from but in deeper penetration into the universe," Teilhard de Chardin* wrote. It is
hard to imagine a deeper penetration into the universe than
Rahm's last dive in his plane, or than his inexpressible wordless
selfless line's inscribing the air and dissolving. Any other art may
be permanent. I cannot recall one Rahm sequence. He improvised. If Christo† wraps a building or dyes a harbor, we join his
poignant and fierce awareness that the work will be gone in days.
Rahm's plane shed a ribbon in space, a ribbon whose end unrav-
eled in memory while its beginning unfurled as surprise. He may
have acknowledged that what he did could be called art, but it
would have been, I think, only in the common misusage, which
holds art to be the last extreme of skill. Rahm rode the point of the
line to the possible; he discovered it and wound it down to show.
He made his dazzling probe on the run. "The world is filled, and
filled with the Absolute," Teilhard de Chardin wrote. "To see this is
to be made free."

Reflections and Responses

1. How does Dillard establish a connection between stunt piloting
and artistic performance? Identify the various moments in her
essay when she makes such a connection. What do these moments
have in common? What images do they share?

2. Note that Dillard doesn't wait until the very end of her essay to
introduce Rahm's death. Why do you think she avoids this kind of
climax? What advantage does this give her?

3. "The Stunt Pilot" also appears as an untitled chapter in Dillard's book *The Writing Life*. Why is this an appropriate context for
the essay? What does the essay tell us about expression and composition?

*__Teilhard de Chardin:__ Pierre Teilhard de Chardin (1881–1953), a noted paleontol-
ogist and Catholic priest whose most famous book, *The Phenomenon of Man*,
attempts to bridge the gap between science and religion.

†__Christo:__ A contemporary Bulgarian artist known for staging spectacular environmental effects.

RANDY SHILTS

Talking AIDS to Death

Depending on your point of view, radio and television talk shows can either be the most absorbing material on the air or the most depressing. Defenders of such shows argue that the programs open up previously untapped sources of public opinion, while detractors are quick to point out their circuslike atmosphere. Into this brave new world of free expression stepped a courageous writer fully prepared to educate a largely uninformed public about one of the nation's most controversial topics: AIDS. In this much applauded essay, Shilts recounts — amusingly and frighteningly — his first-hand experiences on America's talk-show and lecture circuit, where he became "an AIDS celebrity": "Never before have I succeeded so well; never before have I failed so miserably."

The recipient of numerous journalism awards, Randy Shilts was the national correspondent of the San Francisco Chronicle *and one of the world's most respected reporters on AIDS. He is the author of several critically acclaimed nonfiction books. His first,* The Mayor of Castro Street: The Life and Times of Harvey Milk *(1982), describes the rise of gay political power in San Francisco. His next two,* And the Band Played On: Politics, People, and the AIDS Epidemic *(1987) and* Conduct Unbecoming: Gays and Lesbians in the U.S. Military *(1993), were national bestsellers. Randy Shilts died of AIDS in 1994. "Talking AIDS to Death" originally appeared in* Esquire *(1989) and was selected by Justin Kaplan for* The Best American Essays 1990.

I'm talking to my friend Kit Herman when I notice a barely perceptible spot on the left side of his face. Slowly, it grows up his cheekbone, down to his chin, and forward to his mouth. He talks on cheerfully, as if nothing is wrong, and I'm amazed that I'm able to smile and chat on, too, as if nothing were there. His eyes become sunken; his hair turns gray; his ear is turning purple now, swelling into a carcinomatous cauliflower, and still we talk on. He's dying in front of me. He'll be dead soon, if nothing is done.

Dead soon, if nothing is done.

"Excuse me, Mr. Shilts, I asked if you are absolutely sure, if you can categorically state that you definitely can *not* get AIDS from a mosquito."

I forget the early-morning nightmare and shift into my canned response. All my responses are canned now. I'm an AIDS talk-show jukebox. Press the button, any button on the AIDS question list, and I have my canned answer ready. Is this Chicago or Detroit?

"Of course you can get AIDS from a mosquito," I begin.

Here, I pause for dramatic effect. In that brief moment, I can almost hear the caller murmur, "I *knew* it."

"If you have unprotected anal intercourse with an infected mosquito, you'll get AIDS," I continue. "Anything short of that and you won't."

The talk-show host likes the answer. All the talk-show hosts like my answers because they're short, punchy, and to the point. Not like those boring doctors with long recitations of scientific studies so overwritten with maybes and qualifiers that they frighten more than they reassure an AIDS-hysteric public. I give good interview, talk-show producers agree. It's amazing, they say, how I always stay so cool and never lose my temper.

"Mr. Shilts, has there ever been a case of anyone getting AIDS from a gay waiter?"

"In San Francisco, I don't think they allow heterosexuals to be waiters. This fact proves absolutely that if you could get AIDS from a gay waiter, all northern California would be dead by now."

I gave that answer once on a Bay Area talk show, and my caller, by the sound of her a little old lady, quicky rejoined: "What if that gay waiter took my salad back into the kitchen and ejaculated into my salad dressing? Couldn't I get AIDS then?"

I didn't have a pat answer for that one, and I still wonder at what this elderly caller thought went on in the kitchens of San Francisco restaurants. Fortunately, this morning's phone-in — in Chicago, it turned out — is not as imaginative.

"You know, your question reminds me of a joke we had in California a couple of years back," I told the caller. "How many heterosexual waiters in San Francisco does it take to screw in a light bulb? The answer is both of them."

The host laughs, the caller is silent. Next comes the obligatory question about whether AIDS can be spread through coughing.

I had written a book to change the world, and here I was on talk shows throughout America, answering questions about mosquitoes and gay waiters.

This wasn't exactly what I had envisioned when I began writing *And the Band Played On.* I had hoped to effect some fundamental changes. I really believed I could alter the performance of the institutions that had allowed AIDS to sweep through America unchecked.

AIDS had spread, my book attested, because politicians, particularly those in charge of federal-level response, had viewed the disease as a political issue, not an issue of public health — they deprived researchers of anything near the resources that were needed to fight it. AIDS had spread because government health officials consistently lied to the American people about the need for more funds, being more concerned with satisfying their political bosses and protecting their own jobs than with telling the truth and protecting the public health. And AIDS had spread because indolent news organizations shunned their responsibility to provide tough, adversarial reportage, instead basing stories largely on the Official Truth of government press releases. The response to AIDS was never even remotely commensurate with the scope of the problem.

I figured the federal government, finally exposed, would stumble over itself to accelerate the pace of AIDS research and put AIDS-prevention programs on an emergency footing. Once publicly embarrassed by the revelations of its years of shameful neglect, the media would launch serious investigative reporting on the epidemic. Health officials would step forward and finally lay bare the truth about how official disregard had cost this country hundreds of thousands of lives. And it would never happen again.

I was stunned by the "success" of my book. I quickly acquired all the trappings of bestsellerdom: *60 Minutes* coverage of my "startling" revelations, a Book of the Month Club contract, a miniseries deal with NBC, translation into six languages, book tours on three continents, featured roles in movie-star-studded AIDS fund-raisers, regular appearances on network news shows, and hefty fees on the college lecture circuit. A central figure in my book became one of *People* magazine's "25 Most Intriguing People of 1987," even though he had been dead for nearly four years, and the *Los Angeles Herald Examiner* pronounced me one of the "in" authors of 1988. The mayor of San Francisco even proclaimed my birthday last year "Randy Shilts Day."

And one warm summer day as I was sunning at a gay resort in the redwoods north of San Francisco, a well-toned, perfectly tanned young man slid into a chaise next to me and offered the ultimate testimony to my fifteen minutes of fame. His dark eyelashes rising and falling shyly, he whispered, "When I saw you on *Good Morning America* a couple weeks ago, I wondered what it would be like to go to bed with you."

"You're the world's first AIDS celebrity," enthused a friend at the World Health Organization, after hearing one of WHO's most eminent AIDS authorities say he would grant me an interview on one condition — that I autograph his copy of my book. "It must be great," he said.

It's not so great.

The bitter irony is, my role as an AIDS celebrity just gives me a more elevated promontory from which to watch the world make the same mistakes in the handling of the AIDS epidemic that I had hoped my work would help to change. When I return from network tapings and celebrity glad-handing, I come back to my home in San Francisco's gay community and see friends dying. The lesions spread from their cheeks to cover their faces, their hair falls out, they die slowly, horribly, and sometimes, suddenly, before anybody has a chance to know they're sick. They die in my arms and in my dreams, and nothing at all has changed.

Never before have I succeeded so well; never before have I failed so miserably.

I gave my first speech on the college lecture circuit at the University of California [at] Los Angeles in January 1988. I told the audience that there were fifty thousand diagnosed AIDS cases in the United States as of that week and that within a few months there would be more people suffering from this deadly disease in the United States than there were Americans killed during the Vietnam War. There were audible gasps. During the question-and-answer session, several students explained that they had heard that the number of AIDS cases in America was leveling off.

In the next speech, at the University of Tennessee, I decided to correct such misapprehension by adding the federal government's projections — the 270,000 expected to be dead or dying from AIDS in 1991, when the disease would kill more people than any single form of cancer, more than car accidents. When I spoke at St. Cloud State University in Minnesota three months later, I noted that the number of American AIDS cases had that week surpassed the Vietnam benchmark. The reaction was more a troubled murmur than a gasp.

By the time I spoke at New York City's New School for Social Research in June and there were sixty-five thousand AIDS cases nationally, the numbers were changing so fast that the constant editing made my notes difficult to read. By then as many as one thousand Americans a week were learning that they, too, had AIDS, or on the average, about one every fourteen minutes. There were new government projections to report, too: by 1993, some 450,000 Americans would be diagnosed with AIDS. In that year, one American will be diagnosed with the disease every thirty-six seconds. Again, I heard the gasps.

For my talk at a hospital administrators' conference in Washington in August, I started using little yellow stick-ons to update the numbers on my outline. That made it easier to read; there were now seventy-two thousand AIDS cases. Probably this month, or next, I'll tell another college audience that the nation's AIDS case load has topped one hundred thousand and there will be gasps again.

The gasps always amaze me. Why are they surprised? In epidemics, people get sick and die. That's what epidemics do to people and that's why epidemics are bad.

When Kit Herman was diagnosed with AIDS on May 13, 1986, his doctor leaned over his hospital bed, took his hand, and assured him, "Don't worry, you're in time for AZT." The drug worked so well that all Kit's friends let themselves think he might make it. And we were bolstered by the National Institutes of Health's assurance that AZT was only the first generation of AIDS drugs, and that the hundreds of millions of federal dollars going into AIDS treatment research meant there would soon be a second and third generation of treatments to sustain life beyond AZT's effectiveness. Surely nothing was more important, considering the federal government's own estimates that between 1 and 1.5 million Americans were infected with the Human Immunodeficiency Virus (HIV), and virtually all would die within the next decade if nothing was done. The new drugs, the NIH assured everyone, were "in the pipeline," and government scientists were working as fast as they possibly could.

Despite my nagging, not one of dozens of public-affairs-show producers chose to look seriously into the development of those long-sought second and third generations of AIDS drugs. In fact, clinical trials of AIDS drugs were hopelessly stalled in the morass of bureaucracy at the NIH, but this story tip never seemed to cut it with producers. Clinical trials were not sexy. Clinical trials were boring.

I made my third *Nightline* appearance in January 1988 because new estimates had been released revealing that one in sixty-one babies born in New York City carried antibodies to the AIDS virus. And the link between those babies and the disease was intravenous drug use by one or both parents. Suddenly, junkies had become the group most likely to catch and spread AIDS through the heterosexual community. Free needles to junkies — now there was a sizzling television topic. I told the show's producers I'd talk about that, but that I was much more interested in the issue of AIDS treatments — which seemed most relevant to the night's program, since Ted Koppel's other guest was Dr. Anthony Fauci, associate NIH director for AIDS, and the Reagan administration's most visible AIDS official.

After fifteen minutes of talk on the ins and outs and pros and cons of free needles for intravenous drug users, I raised the subject of the pressing need for AIDS treatments. Koppel asked Fauci what was happening. The doctor launched into a discussion of treatments "in the pipeline" and how government scientists were working as fast as they possibly could.

I'd heard the same words from NIH officials for three years: drugs were in the pipeline. Maybe it was true, but when were they going to come out of their goddamn pipeline? Before I could formulate a polite retort to Fauci's stall, however, the segment was over, Ted was thanking us, and the red light on the camera had blipped off. Everyone seemed satisfied that the government was doing everything it possibly could to develop AIDS treatments.

Three months later, I was reading a week-old *New York Times* in Kit's room in the AIDS ward at San Francisco General Hospital. It was April, nearly two years after my friend's AIDS diagnosis. AZT had given him two years of nearly perfect health, but now its effect was wearing off, and Kit had suffered his first major AIDS-related infection since his original bout with pneumonia — cryptococcal meningitis. The meningitis could be treated, we all knew, but the discovery of this insidious brain infection meant more diseases were likely to follow. And the long-promised second and third generations of AIDS drugs were still nowhere on the horizon.

While perusing the worn copy of the *Times,* I saw a story about Dr. Fauci's testimony at a congressional hearing. After making Fauci swear an oath to tell the truth, a subcommittee headed by Representative Ted Weiss of New York City asked why it was taking so long to get new AIDS treatments into testing at a time when Congress was putting hundreds of millions of dollars into NIH budgets for just such purposes. At first Fauci talked about unavoidable delays. He claimed government scientists were working as fast as they could. Pressed harder, he finally admitted that the problem stemmed "almost exclusively" from the lack of staffing in his agency. Congress had allocated funds, it was true, but the Reagan administration had gotten around spending the money by stingily refusing to let Fauci hire anybody. Fauci had requested 127 positions to speed the development of AIDS treatments; the administration had granted him 11. And for a year, he had not told anyone. For a year, this spokesman for the public health answered reporters that AIDS drugs were in the pipeline and that government scientists had all the money they needed. It seemed that only when faced with the penalty of perjury would one of the administration's top AIDS officials tell the truth. That was the real story, I thought, but for some reason nobody else had picked up on it.

At the international AIDS conference in Stockholm two months later, the other reporters in "the AIDS pack" congratulated me on my success and asked what I was working on now. I admitted that I was too busy promoting the British and German release of my book to do much writing myself, and next month I had the Australian tour. But if I *were* reporting, I added with a vaguely conspiratorial tone, *I'd* look at the *scandal* in the NIH. Nobody had picked up that *New York Times* story from a few months ago about staffing shortages on AIDS clinical trials. The lives of 1.5 million HIV-infected Americans hung in the balance, and the only way you could get a straight answer out of an administration AIDS official was to put him under oath and make him face the charge of perjury. Where I went to journalism school, *that* was a news story.

One reporter responded to my tip with the question: "But who's going to play *you* in the miniseries?"

A few minutes later, when Dr. Fauci came into the press room, the world's leading AIDS journalists got back to the serious business of transcribing his remarks. Nobody asked him if he was actually telling the truth, or whether they should put him under oath to ensure a candid response to questions about when we'd get AIDS treatments. Most of the subsequent news accounts of Dr. Fauci's comments faithfully reported that many AIDS treatments were in the pipeline. Government scientists, he said once more, were doing all they possibly could.

The producer assured my publisher that Morton Downey, Jr., would be "serious" about AIDS. "He's not going to play games on this issue," the producer said, adding solemnly: "His brother has AIDS. He understands the need for compassion." The abundance of Mr. Downey's compassion was implicit in the night's call-in poll question: "Should all people with AIDS be quarantined?"

Downey's first question to me was, "You *are* a homosexual, aren't you?"

He wasn't ready for my canned answer: "Why do you ask? Do you want a date or something?"

The show shifted into an earnest discussion of quarantine. In his television studio, Clearasil-addled high school students from suburban New Jersey held up MORTON DOWNEY FAN CLUB signs and cheered aggressively when the truculent, chain-smoking host appeared to favor a kind of homespun AIDS Auschwitz. The youths shouted down any audience member who stepped forward to defend the rights of AIDS sufferers, their howls growing particularly vitriolic if the speakers were gay. These kids were the ilk from which Hitler drew his Nazi youth. In the first commercial break, the other guest, an AIDS activist, and I told Downey we would walk off the show if he didn't tone down his gay-baiting rhetoric. Smiling amiably, Downey took a long drag on his cigarette and assured us, "Don't worry, I have a fallback position."

That comment provided one of the most lucid moments in my year as an AIDS celebrity. Downey's "fallback position," it was clear, was the opposite of what he was promoting on the air. Of course, he didn't *really* believe that people with AIDS, people like his brother, should all be locked up. This was merely a deliciously provocative posture to exploit the working-class resentments of people who needed someone to hate. AIDS sufferers and gays would do for this week. Next week, if viewership dropped and Downey needed a new whipping boy, maybe he'd move on to Arabs, maybe Jews. It didn't seem to matter much to him, since he didn't believe what he was saying anyway. For Morton Downey, Jr., talking about AIDS was not an act of conscience; it was a ratings ploy. He knew it, he let his guests know it, his producers certainly knew it, and his television station knew it. The only people left out of the joke were his audience.

The organizers of the Desert AIDS Project had enlisted actor Kirk Douglas and CBS morning anchor Kathleen Sullivan to be honorary cochairs of the Palm Springs fund-raiser. The main events would include a celebrity tennis match pitting Douglas against Mayor Sonny Bono, and a fifteen-hundred-dollar-a-head dinner at which I would receive a Lucite plaque for my contributions to the fight against AIDS. The next morning I would fly to L.A. to speak at still another event, this one with Shirley MacLaine, Valerie Harper, and Susan Dey of *L.A. Law.*

The desert night was exquisite. There were 130 dinner guests, the personification of elegance and confidence, who gathered on a magnificent patio of chocolate-brown Arizona flagstone at the home of one of Palm Springs's most celebrated interior designers. A lot of people had come simply to see what was regarded as one of the most sumptuous dwellings in this sumptuous town.

When I was called to accept my reward, I began with the same lineup of jokes I use on talk shows and on the college lecture circuit. They work every time.

I told the crowd about how you get AIDS from a mosquito.

Kirk Douglas laughed; everybody laughed.

Next, I did the how-many-gay-waiters joke.

Kirk Douglas laughed; everybody laughed.

Then I mentioned the woman who asked whether she could get AIDS from a waiter ejaculating in her salad dressing.

That one always has my college audiences rolling in the aisles, so I paused for the expected hilarity.

But in the utter stillness of the desert night air, all that could be heard was the sound of Kirk Douglas's steel jaw dropping to the magnificent patio of chocolate-brown Arizona flagstone. The rest was silence.

"You've got to remember that most of these people came because they're my clients," the host confided later. "You said that, and all I could think was how I'd have to go back to stitching slip-covers when this was done."

It turned out that there was more to my lead-balloon remark than a misjudged audience. Local AIDS organizers told me that a year earlier, a rumor that one of Palm Spring's most popular restaurants was owned by a homosexual, and that most of its wait-ers were gay, had terrified the elite community. Patronage at the eatery quickly plummeted, and it had nearly gone out of business. Fears that I dismissed as laughable were the genuine concerns of my audience, I realized. My San Francisco joke was a Palm Springs fable.

As I watched the busboys clear the tables later that night, I made a mental note not to tell that joke before dinner again. Never had I seen so many uneaten salads, so much wasted iceberg lettuce.

A friend had just tested antibody positive, and I was doing my best to cheer him up as we ambled down the sidewalk toward a Castro Street restaurant a few blocks from where I live in San Francisco. It seems most of my conversations now have to do with who has tested positive or lucked out and turned up negative, or who is too afraid to be tested. We had parked our car near Coming Home, the local hospice for AIDS patients and others suffering from ter-minal illnesses, and as we stepped around a nondescript, powder-blue van that blocked our path, two men in white uniforms emerged from the hospice's side door. They carried a stretcher, and on the stretcher was a corpse, neatly wrapped in a royal-blue blanket and secured with navy-blue straps. My friend and I stopped walking. The men quickly guided the stretcher into the back of the van, climbed in the front doors, and drove away. We continued our walk but didn't say anything.

I wondered if the corpse was someone I had known. I'd find out Thursday when the weekly gay paper came out. Every week there are at least two pages filled with obituaries of the previous week's departed. Each week, when I turn to those pages, I hold my breath, wondering whose picture I'll see. It's the only way to keep track, what with so many people dying.

Sometimes I wonder if an aberrant mother or two going to mass at the Most Holy Redeemer Church across the street from Coming Home Hospice has ever warned a child, "That's where you'll end up if you don't obey God's law." Or whether some youngster, feeling that first awareness of a different sexuality, has looked at the doorway of this modern charnel house with an awesome, gnawing dread of annihilation.

"Is the limousine here? Where are the dancers?"

The room fell silent. Blake Rothaus had sounded coherent until that moment, but he was near death now and his brain was going. We were gathered around his bed in a small frame house on a dusty street in Oklahoma City. The twenty-four-year-old was frail and connected to life through a web of clear plastic tubing. He stared up at us and seemed to recognize from our looks that he had lapsed into dementia. A friend broke the uncomfortable silence.

"Of course, we all brought our dancing shoes," he said. "Nice fashionable pumps at that. I wouldn't go out without them."

Everyone laughed and Blake Rothaus was lucid again.

Blake had gone to high school in a San Francisco suburb. When he was a sophomore, he told us, he and his best friend sometimes skipped school, sneaking to the city to spend their afternoons in the gay neighborhood around Castro Street.

It's a common sight, suburban teenagers playing hooky on Castro Street. I could easily imagine him standing on a corner not far from my house. But back in 1982, when he was eighteen, I was already writing about a mysterious, unnamed disease that had claimed 330 victims in the United States.

Blake moved back to Oklahoma City with his family after he graduated from high school. When he fell ill with AIDS, he didn't mope. Instead, he started pestering Oklahoma health officials with demands to educate people about this disease and to provide services for the sick. The state health department didn't recoil. At the age of twenty-two, Blake Rothaus had become the one-man nucleus for Oklahoma's first AIDS-patient services. He was the hero of the Sooner State's AIDS movement and something of a local legend.

Though the state had reported only 250 AIDS cases, Oklahoma City had a well-coordinated network of religious leaders, social workers, health-care providers, gay-rights advocates, state legislators, and businessmen, all committed to providing a sane and humane response to this frightening new disease.

"I think it's the old Dust Bowl mentality," suggested one AIDS organizer. "When the hard times come, people pull together."

My past year's travels to twenty-nine states and talks with literally thousands of people have convinced me of one thing about this country and AIDS: most Americans want to do the right thing about this epidemic. Some might worry about mosquitoes and a few may be suspicious of their salad dressing. But beyond these fears is a reservoir of compassion and concern that goes vastly underreported by a media that needs conflict and heartlessness to fashion a good news hook.

In Kalamazoo, Michigan, when I visited my stepmother, I was buttonholed by a dozen middle-aged women who wondered anxiously whether we were any closer to a vaccine or a long-term treatment. One mentioned a hemophiliac nephew. Another had a gay brother in Chicago. A third went to a gay hairdresser who, she quickly added, was one of the finest people you'd ever meet. When I returned to my conservative hometown of Aurora, Illinois, nestled among endless fields of corn and soy, the local health department told me they receive more calls than they know what to do with from women's groups, parishes, and community organizations that want to do something to help. In New Orleans, the archconservative, pronuke, antigay bishop had taken up the founding of an AIDS hospice as a personal mission because, he said, when people are sick, you've got to help them out.

Scientists, reporters, and politicians privately tell me that of course *they* want to do more about AIDS, but they have to think about the Morton Downeys of the world, who argue that too much research or too much news space or too much official sympathy is being meted out to a bunch of miscreants. They do as much as they can, they insist; more would rile the resentments of the masses. So the institutions fumble along, convinced they must pander to the lowest common denominator, while the women and men of America's heartland pull me aside to fret about a dying cousin or coworker and to plead, "When will there be a cure? When will this be over?"

"I think I'll make it through this time," Kit said to me, "but I don't have it in me to go through it again."

We were in room 3 in San Francisco General Hospital's ward 5A, the AIDS ward. The poplar trees outside Kit's window were losing their leaves, and the first winter's chill was settling over the city. I was preparing to leave for my fourth and, I hoped, final media tour, this time for release of the book in paperback and on audiocassette; Kit was preparing to die.

The seizures had started a week earlier, indicating he was suffering either from toxoplasmosis, caused by a gluttonous protozoa that sets up housekeeping in the brain; or perhaps it was a relapse of cryptococcal meningitis; or, another specialist guessed, it could be one of those other nasty brain infections that nobody had seen much of until the past year. Now that AIDS patients were living longer, they fell victim to even more exotic infections than in the early days. But the seizures were only part of it. Kit had slowly been losing the sight in his left eye to a herpes infection. And the Kaposi's sarcoma lesions that had scarred his face were beginning to coat the inside of his lungs. When Kit mentioned he'd like to live until Christmas, the doctors said he might want to consider having an early celebration this year, because he wasn't going to be alive in December.

"I can't take another infection," Kit said.

"What does that mean?"

"Morphine," Kit answered, adding mischievously, "lots of it."

We talked briefly about the mechanics of suicide. We both knew people who'd made a mess of it, and people who had done it right. It was hardly the first time the subject had come up in conversation for either of us. Gay men facing AIDS now exchange formulas for suicide as casually as housewives swap recipes for chocolate-chip cookies.

Kit was released from the hospital a few days later. He had decided to take his life on a Tuesday morning. I had to give my first round of interviews in Los Angeles that day, so I stopped on the way to the airport to say good-bye on Monday. All day Tuesday, while I gave my perfectly formed sound bites in a round of network radio appearances, I wondered: is this the moment he's slipping out of consciousness and into that perfect darkness? When I called that night, it turned out he'd delayed his suicide until Thursday to talk to a few more relatives. I had to give a speech in Portland that day, so on the way to the airport I stopped again. He showed me the amber-brown bottle with the bubble-gum-pink morphine syrup, and we said another good-bye.

The next morning, Kit drank his morphine and fell into a deep sleep. That afternoon, he awoke and drowsily asked what time it was. When told it was five hours later, he murmured, "That's amazing. I should have been dead hours ago."

And then he went back to sleep.

That night, Kit woke up again.

"You know what they say about near-death experiences?" he asked. "Going toward the light?"

Shaking his head, he sighed. "No light. Nothing."

His suicide attempt a failure, Kit decided the timing of his death would now be up to God. I kept up on the bizarre sequence of events by phone and called as soon as I got back to San Francisco. I was going to tell Kit that his theme song should be "Never Can Say Good-by," but then the person on the other end of the phone told me that Kit had lapsed into a coma.

The next morning, he died.

Kit's death was like everything about AIDS — anticlimactic. By the time he actually did die, I was almost beyond feeling.

The next day I flew to Boston for the start of the paperback tour, my heart torn between rage and sorrow. All week, as I was chauffeured to my appearances on *Good Morning America, Larry King Live,* and various CNN shows, I kept thinking, it's all going to break. I'm going to be on a TV show with some officious government health spokesman lying to protect his job, and I'm going to start shouting, "You lying son of a bitch. Don't you know there are people, real people, people I love out there dying?" Or I'll be on a call-in show and another mother will phone about her thirty-seven-year-old son who just died and it will hit me all at once, and I'll start weeping.

But day after day as the tour went on, no matter how many official lies I heard and how many grieving mothers I talked to, the crackup never occurred. All my answers came out rationally in tight little sound bites about institutional barriers to AIDS treatments and projections about 1993 case loads.

By the last day of the tour, when a limousine picked me up at my Beverly Hills hotel for my last round of satellite TV interviews, I knew I had to stop. In a few weeks I'd return to being national correspondent for the *Chronicle*, and it was time to get off the AIDS celebrity circuit, end the interviews and decline the invitations to the star-studded fund-raisers, and get back to work as a newspaper reporter. That afternoon, there was just one last radio interview to a call-in show in the San Fernando Valley, and then it would be over.

The first caller asked why his tax money should go toward funding an AIDS cure when people got the disease through their own misdeeds.

I used my standard jukebox answer about how most cancer cases are linked to people's behavior but that nobody ever suggested we stop trying to find a cure for cancer.

A second caller phoned to ask why her tax money should go to funding an AIDS cure when these people clearly deserved what they got.

I calmly put a new spin on the same answer, saying in America you usually don't sentence people to die for having a different lifestyle from yours.

Then a third caller phoned in to say that he didn't care if all those queers and junkies died, as did a fourth and fifth and sixth caller. By then I was shouting, "You stupid bigot. You just want to kill off everybody you don't like. You goddamn Nazi."

The talk-show host sat in stunned silence. She'd heard I was so *reasonable*. My anger baited the audience further, and the seventh and eighth callers began talking about "you guys," as if only a faggot like myself could give a shit about whether AIDS patients all dropped dead tomorrow.

In their voices, I heard the reporters asking polite questions of NIH officials. Of course, they had to be polite to the government doctors; dying queers weren't anything to lose your temper over. I heard the dissembling NIH researchers go home to their wives at night, complain about the lack of personnel, and shrug; this was just how it was going to have to be for a while. They'd excuse their inaction by telling themselves that if they went public and lost their jobs, worse people would replace them. It was best to go along. But how would they feel if *their* friends, *their* daughters were dying of this disease? Would they be silent — or would they shout? Maybe they'll forgive me for suspecting they believed that ultimately a bunch of fags weren't worth losing a job over. And when I got home, I was going to have to watch my friends get shoved into powder-blue vans, and it wasn't going to change.

The history of the AIDS epidemic, of yesterday and of today, was echoing in the voices of those callers. And I was screaming at them, and the show host just sat there stunned, and I realized I had rendered myself utterly and completely inarticulate.

I stopped, took a deep breath, and returned to compound-complex sentences about the American tradition of compassion and the overriding need to overcome institutional barriers to AIDS treatments.

When I got home to San Francisco that night, I looked over some notes I had taken from a conversation I'd had with Kit during his last stay in the hospital. I was carping about how frustrated I was at the prospect of returning to my reporting job. If an internationally acclaimed best seller hadn't done shit to change the world, what good would mere newspaper stories do?

"The limits of information," Kit said. "There's been a lot written on it."

"Oh," I said.

Kit closed his eyes briefly and faded into sleep while plastic tubes fed him a cornucopia of antibiotics. After five minutes, he stirred, looked up, and added, as if we had never stopped talking, "But you don't really have a choice. You've got to keep on doing it. What else are you going to do?"

Reflections and Responses

1. Note how Shilts interweaves several stories into his essay. How
are these connected? Why do you think he brings his experiences
with his dying friend Kit into this essay? What effect does it have
on your response to the essay?

2. Note the attention Shilts pays to jokes in the essay. What purpose do they serve? To whom are the jokes funny? To whom are
they offensive? What do his jokes tell you about the intended audience for this essay?

3. Consider Shilts's title. How does "talk" figure in the essay? What
expectations does Shilts bring to the various discussion forums in
which he participates? Setting the subject of AIDS aside, what
characteristics of public expression in general does Shilts find disturbing?

ANNE HOLLANDER

Dressed to Thrill

Of all the ways we express ourselves in everyday life, clothing is one of the most noticeable and, to social historians at least, one of the most significant. To Anne Hollander, who has closely studied costume history and design, clothing reveals the image that people want to have of themselves in a particular era. Clothing is thus another "language," communicating the "collective fantasy" of an individual culture. In the following essay, she examines the cool and casual style of the new American androgyny and finds that it mirrors significant changes in our definition of sex roles. Written in 1985, Hollander's essay remains, in its historical survey of American fashions, a relevant and incisive piece of social commentary.

Anne Hollander is an independent scholar and writer living in New York City. She is the author of Seeing Through Clothes *(1978), a study of the clothed figure in art, and* Moving Pictures *(1987), a book about painterly and graphic sources for film.* Sex and Suits, *about the importance of modern masculine tailoring, was published in 1994. Her essays and reviews appear in* The New York Times Magazine, The Times Literary Supplement, The New Republic, Commentary, *and* Raritan. *"Dressed to Thrill" originally appeared in* The New Republic *(1985) and was selected by Elizabeth Hardwick for* The Best American Essays 1986.

When Quentin Bell* applied Veblen's[†] principles of Conspicuous Consumption and Conspicuous Waste to fashion, he added an-

---

*Quentin Bell: British art critic (b. 1910).

[†]Veblen: Thorstein Veblen (1857–1929), influential American economist, whose *The Theory of the Leisure Class* (1899) advanced the idea of "conspicuous consumption" as a psychological need to impress others.

other — Conspicuous Outrage. This one now clearly leads the
other two. In this decade we want the latest trends in appearance to
strain our sense of the suitable and give us a real jolt. The old social
systems that generated a need for conspicuous display have modified enough to dull the chic of straight extravagance: the chic of
shock has continuous vitality. Dramatically perverse sexual signals
are always powerful elements in the modern fashionable vocabulary; and the most sensational component among present trends is
something referred to as androgyny. Many modish women's clothes
imitate what Robert Taylor wore in 1940 publicity stills, and
Michael Jackson's startling feminine beauty challenges public responses from every store window, as well as in many living replicas.

The mode in appearance mirrors collective fantasy, not fundamental aims and beliefs. We are not all really longing for two sexes
in a single body, and the true hermaphrodite still counts as a monster. We are not seeing a complete and free interchange of physical characteristics across the sexual divide. There are no silky false
moustaches or dashing fake goatees finely crafted of imported
sable for the discriminating woman, or luxuriant jaw-length sideburns of the softest bristle sold with moisturizing glue and a designer applicator. Although the new ideal feminine torso has
strong square shoulders, flat hips, and no belly at all, the corresponding ideal male body is certainly not displaying the beauties
of a soft round stomach, flaring hips, full thighs, and delicately
sloping shoulders. On the new woman's ideally athletic shape,
breasts may be large or not — a flat chest is not required; and
below the belt in back, the buttocks may sharply protrude. But no
space remains in front to house a safely cushioned uterus and
ovaries, or even well-upholstered labia: under the lower half of the
new, high-cut minimal swimsuits, there is room only for a clitoris.
Meanwhile the thrilling style of male beauty embodied by Michael
Jackson runs chiefly to unprecedented surface adornment — cosmetics and sequins, jewels and elaborate hair, all the old privileges
once granted to women, to give them every erotic advantage in the
sex wars of the past.

The point about all this is clearly not androgyny at all, but the
idea of detachable pleasure. Each sex is not trying to take up the
fundamental qualities of the other sex, but rather of the other sexuality — the erotic dimension, which can transcend biology and its
attendant social assumptions and institutions. Eroticisim is being

shown to float free of sexual function. Virility is displayed as a capacity for feeling and generating excitement, not for felling trees or enemies and generating children. Femininity has abandoned the old gestures of passivity to take on main force: ravishing female models now stare purposefully into the viewer's eyes instead of flashing provocative glances or gazing remotely away. Erotic attractiveness appears ready to exert its strength in unforeseeable and formerly forbidden ways and places. Recognition is now being given to sexual desire for objects of all kinds once considered unsuitable — some of them inanimate, judging from the seductiveness of most advertising photography.

Homosexual desire is now an acknowledged aspect of common life, deserving of truthful representation in popular culture, not just in coterie vehicles of expression. The aging parents of youthful characters in movie and television dramas are no longer rendered as mentally stuffy and physically withered, but as stunningly attractive sexual beings — legitimate and nonridiculous rivals for the lustful attentions of the young. The curved flanks of travel irons and food processors in Bloomingdale's catalogue make as strong an appeal to erotic desire as the satiny behinds and moist lips of the makeup and underwear models. So do the unfolding petals of lettuces and the rosy flesh of cut tomatoes on TV food commercials. In this general eroticization of the material world, visual culture is openly acknowledging that lust is by nature wayward.

To register as attractive under current assumptions, a female body may now show its affinities not only with delicious objects but with attractive male bodies, without having to relinquish any feminine erotic resources. Male beauty may be enhanced by feminine usages that increase rather than diminish its masculine effect. Men and women may both wear clothes loosely fashioned by designers like Gianni Versace or Issey Miyake to render all bodies attractive whatever their structure, like the drapery of antiquity. In such clothes, sexuality is expressed obliquely in a fluid fabric envelope that follows bodily movement and also forms a graceful counterpoint to the nonchalant postures of modern repose. The aim of such dress is to emphasize the sexiness of a rather generalized sensuality, not of male or female characteristics; and our present sense of personal appearance, like our sense of all material display, shows that we are more interested in generalized sensuality than in anything else. In our multiform culture, it seems to serve as an equalizer.

In fashion, however, pervasive eroticism is still frequently being represented as the perpetual overthrow of all the restrictive categories left over from the last century, a sort of ongoing revolution. We are still pretending to congratulate ourselves on what a long way we have come. The lush men and strong girls now on view in the media may be continuing a long-range trend that began between the World Wars; but there have been significant interruptions and an important shift of tone. Then, too, men had smooth faces, thick, wavy hair and full, pouting lips, and women often wore pants, had shingled hair, and athletic torsos. But the important point in those days was to be as anti-Victorian as possible. The rigid and bearded Victorian male was being eased out of his tight carapace and distancing whiskers; the whole ladylike panoply was being simplified so that the actual woman became apparent to the eye and touch. Much of our present female mannishness and feminized manhood is a nostalgic reference to the effects fashionable for men and women in those pioneering days, rather than a new revolutionary expression of the same authentic kind.

There is obviously more to it all now than there was between the wars. We have already gone through some fake Victorian revivals, both unself-conscious in the 1950s and self-conscious in the sixties and seventies, and lately our sense of all style has become slightly corrupt. Apart from the sexiness of sex, we have discovered the stylishness of style and the fashionableness of fashion. Evolving conventions of dress and sudden revolts from them have both become stylistically forced; there have been heavy quotation marks around almost all conspicuous modes of clothing in the last fifteen or twenty years, as there were not in more hopeful days. Life is now recognized to have a grotesque and inflated media dimension by which ordinary experience is measured, and all fashion has taken to looking over its own shoulder. Our contemporary revolutionary modes are mostly theatrical costumes, since we have now learned to assume that appearances are detachable and interchangeable and only have provisional meanings.

Many of the more extreme new sartorial phenomena display such uncooked incoherence that they fail to represent any main trend in twentieth-century taste except a certain perverse taste for garbage — which is similarly fragmented and inexpressive, even though it can always be sifted and categorized. We have become obsessed with picking over the past instead of plowing it under, where it can do some good. Perversity has moreover been fostered in fashion by its relentless presentation as a form of ongoing public entertainment. The need for constant impact naturally causes originality to get confused with the capacity to cause a sensation; and sensations can always be created, just as in all show business, by the crudest of allusions.

In the twenties, the revolutionary new fashions were much more important but much less brutally intrusive. Photos from the twenties, thirties, and even the very early forties, show the young Tyrone Power and Robert Taylor smiling with scintillating confidence, caressed by soft focus and glittering highlights, and wearing the full-cut, casual topcoats with the collar up that we see in today's ads for women, then as now opened to show the fully-draped trousers, loose sweaters, and long, broad jackets of that time. Then it was an alluringly modern and feminized version of male beauty, freshly suggesting pleasure without violence or loss of decorum, a high level of civilization without any forbidding and tyrannical stiffness or antiquated formality. At the same time, women's fashions were stressing an articulated female shape that sought to be perceived as clearly as the male. Both were the first modern styles to take up the flavor of general physical ease, in timely and pertinent defiance of the social restrictions and symbolic sexual distinctions made by dress in the preceding time. Now, however, those same easy men's clothes are being worn by women; and the honest old figure of freedom seems to be dressed up in the spirit of pastiche. We did come a long way for a while, but then we stopped and went on the stage.

Strong and separate sexual definition in the old Victorian manner tried to forbid the generally erotic and foster the romantic. Against such a background even slightly blurring the definition automatically did the opposite; and so when Victorian women dared adopt any partial assortment of male dress they were always extremely disturbing. They called attention to those aspects of female sexuality that develop in sharp contrast to both female biology and romantic rhetoric. Consequently, when female fashion underwent its great changes early in this century, such aspects were deliberately and vehemently emphasized by a new mobility and quasi-masculine leanness. Women with no plump extensions at all but with obvious and movable legs suddenly made their appearance, occasionally even in trousers. They indicated a mettlesome eagerness for action, even unencumbered amorous action, and great lack of interest in sitting still receiving homage or rocking the cradle. Meanwhile when men adopted the casual suits of modern leisure, they began to suggest a certain new readiness to sit and talk, to listen and laugh at themselves, to dally and tarry rather than couple briskly and straightway depart for work or battle. Men and women visibly desired to rewrite the rules about how the two sexes should express their interest in sex; and the liberated modern ideal was crystallized.

But a sexual ideal of maturity and enlightened savoir faire also informed that period of our imaginative history. In the fantasy of the thirties, manifested in the films of Claudette Colbert, for example, or Gable and Lombard, adult men and women ideally pursued pleasure without sacrificing reason, humor, or courtesy — even in those dramas devoted to the ridiculous. The sexes were still regarded as fundamentally different kinds of being, although the style of their sexuality was reconceived. The aim of amorous life was still to take on the challenging dialectic of the sexes, which alone could yield the fullest kind of sexual pleasure. Erotic feeling was inseparable from dramatic situation.

By those same thirties, modern adult clothing was also a fully developed stylistic achievement. It duly continued to refine, until it finally became unbearably mannered in the first half of the sixties. The famous ensuing sartorial revolution, though perfectly authentic, was also the first to occur in front of the camera — always in the mirror, as it were. And somehow the subsequent two decades have seen a great fragmentation both of fashion and of sexuality.

Extreme imagery, much of it androgynous like Boy George's looks, or the many punk styles and all the raunchier fashion photos, has become quite commonplace; but it has also become progressively remote from most common practice. It offers appearances that we may label "fashion," but that we really know to be media inventions created especially to stun, provoke, and dismay us. At the same time, some very conventional outrageous effects have been revived in the realm of accessible fashion, where there is always room for them. Ordinary outrageousness and perverse daring in dress are the signs of licensed play, never the signal of serious action. They are licitly engaged in by the basically powerless, including clowns and children and other innocuous performers, who are always allowed to make extreme emotional claims that may stir up strong personal responses but have no serious public importance. Women's fashion constantly made use of outrage in this way during the centuries of female powerlessness, and selective borrowing from men was one of its most effective motifs.

After the sixties and before the present menswear mode, the masculine components in women's fashions still made girls look either excitingly shocking or touchingly pathetic. The various neat tuxedos made famous by Yves St. Laurent, for example, were intended to give a woman the look of a depraved youth, a sort of tempting Dorian Gray. The *Annie Hall* clothes swamped the woman in oversized male garments, so that she looked at first like a small child being funny in adult gear, and then like a fragile girl wrapped in a strong man's coat, a combined emblem of bruised innocence and clownishness. These are both familiar "outrageous" devices culled particularly from the theatrical past.

Long before modern fashion took it up, the conventionally outrageous theme of an attractive feminine woman in breeches proved an invariably stimulating refinement in the long history of racy popular art, both for the stage and in print. The most important erotic aim of this theme was never to make a woman actually seem to be a man — looking butch has never been generally attractive — but to make a girl assume the unsettling beauty that dwells in the sexual uncertainty of an adolescent boy. It is an obvious clever move for modern fashionable women to combine the old show-businesslike excitement of the suggestive trousered female with the cultivated self-possession of early twentieth-century menswear — itself already a feminized male style. It suits, especially in the present disintegrated erotic climate that has rendered the purer forms of outrageousness somewhat passé.

Such uses of men's clothes have nothing to do with an impulse toward androgyny. They instead invoke all the old tension between the sexes; and complete drag, whichever sex wears it, also

insists on sexual polarity. Most drag for men veers toward the exaggerated accoutrements of the standard siren; and on the current
screen, *Tootsie* and *Yentl* are both demonstrating how different and
how divided the sexes are.

While the extreme phenomena are getting all the attention,
however, we are acting out quite another forbidden fantasy in our
ordinary lives. The really androgynous realm in personal appearance is that of active sports clothing. The unprecedented appeal of
running gear and gym clothes and all the other garb associated
with strenuous physical effort seems to be offering an alternative
in sexual expression. Beyond the simple pleasures of physical fit-
ness, and the right-minded satisfactions of banishing class difference that were first expressed in the blue-jeans revolution of the
sixties, this version of pastoral suggests a new erotic appeal in the
perceived androgyny of childhood. The short shorts and other in-
genuous bright play clothes in primary colors that now clothe bodies of all sizes and sexes are giving a startling kindergarten cast to
everybody's public looks, especially in summer.

The real excitement of androgynous appearance is again revealed as associated only with extreme youth — apparently the
more extreme the better. The natural androgyny of old age has acquired no appeal. The tendency of male and female bodies to resemble each other in late maturity is still conventionally ridiculous
and deplorable; sportswear on old women looks crisp and convenient, not sexually attractive. But the fresh, unfinished androgyny
of the nursery is evidently a newly expanded arena for sexual
fantasy.

In the unisex look of the ordinary clothing that has become increasingly common in the past two decades, there has been a submerged but unmistakable element of child-worship. This note has
been struck at a great distance from the slick and expensive ambi-
guities of high fashion that include couture children's clothes
aping the vagaries of current adult chic. It resonates instead in the
everyday sexual ambiguity of rough duck or corduroy pants, flan-
nel shirts, T-shirts, sweaters, and sneakers. Any subway car or supermarket is full of people dressed this way. The guises for this
fantasy have extended past play clothes to children's underwear,
the little knitted shirts and briefs that everyone wears at the age of

five. One ubiquitous ad for these even showed a shirtee sliding up to expose an adult breast, to emphasize the sexiness of the fashion; but the breast has been prudently canceled in publicly displayed versions.

Our erotic obsession with children has overt and easily deplored expressions in the media, where steamy twelve-year-old fashion models star in ads and twelve-year-old prostitutes figure in dramas and news stories. The high-fashion modes for children also have the flavor of forced eroticism. Child abuse and kiddy porn are now publicly discussed concerns, ventilated in the righteous spirit of reform; and yet unconscious custom reflects the same preoccupation with the sexual condition of childhood. The androgynous sportswear that was formerly the acceptable everyday dress only of children is now everyone's leisure clothing; its new currency must have more than one meaning.

On the surface, of course, it invokes the straight appeal of the physical life, the rural life, and perhaps even especially the taxing life of the dedicated athlete, which used to include sexual abstinence along with the chance of glory. The world may wish to look as if it were constantly in training to win, or equipped to explore; but there is another condition it is also less obviously longing for — freedom from the strain of fully adult sexuality. These styles of clothing signal a retreat into the unfinished, undefined sexuality of childhood that we are now finding so erotic, and that carries no difficult social or personal responsibilities.

From 1925 to 1965, four-year-old girls and boys could tumble in the sandbox in identical cotton overalls or knitted suits, innocently aping the clothes of skiers, railroadmen, or miners, while their mom wore a dress, hat, and stockings, and their dad a suit, hat, and tie — the modern dress of sexual maturity, also worn by Gable, Lombard, and all the young and glittering Hollywood company. Now the whole family wears sweat suits and overalls and goes bareheaded. Such gear is also designed to encourage the game of dressing up like all the non-amorous and ultraphysical heroes of modern folklore — forest rangers and cowboys, spacemen and frogmen, pilots and motorcyclists, migrant workers and terrorists — that is constantly urged on children. The great masquerade party of the late sixties ostensibly came to an end; but it had irreversibly given to ordinary grownups the right to wear fancy cos-

tumes for fun that was formerly a child's privilege. The traditional
dress of the separate adult sexes is reserved for public appearances, and in general it is now socially correct to express impatience with it. "Informal" is the only proper style in middle-class
social life; and for private leisure, when impulse governs choices,
kids' clothes are the leading one. Apparently the erotic androgynous child is the new forbidden creature of unconscious fantasy,
not only the infantile fashion model or rock star but the ordinary
kid, who has exciting sexual potential hidden under its unsexed
dress-up play clothes.

Fashions of the remote past dealt straightforwardly with the sexuality of children by dressing them just like ordinary adults, suitably
different according to sex. But in Romantic times, children were
perceived to exist in a special condition much purer and closer to
beneficent nature than their elders, requiring clothes that kept
them visibly separate from the complex corruptions of adult society, including full-scale erotic awareness. The habit of putting children in fancy dress began then, too, especially boys. They were
dressed as wee, chubby, and harmless soldiers and sailors, or Turks
and Romans, to emphasize their innocence by contrast. Children's
clothes still differed according to sex — girls had sweet little
chemises and sashes instead of fancy costumes — but their overriding common flavor was one of artlessness.

Later on the Victorians overdid it, and loaded their children
with clothing, but it was still two-sexed and distinctively designed
for them. Finally the enlightened twentieth century invented the
use of mock sportswear for the wiggly little bodies of both boys
and girls. Nevertheless, the costumes now suitable for children on
display still tend toward the Victorian, with a good deal of nostalgic velvet and lace. In line with Romantic views of women, some
feminine styles also used to feature infantine suggestions drawn
from little girls' costumes: the last was the tiny baby dress worn
with big shoes and big hair in the later sixties, just before the erup-
tion of the women's movement. But only since then has a whole
generation of adults felt like dressing up in mock rough gear, like
androgynous children at play, to form a race of apparently presex-
ual but ummistakably erotic beings.

Once again, very pointedly, the clothes for the role are male.

Our modern sense of artlessness seems to prefer the masculine brand; and when we dress our little boys and girls alike to blur their sexuality — or ourselves in imitation of them — that means we dress the girls like the boys, in the manifold costumes celebrating nonsexual physical prowess. At leisure, both men and women prefer to suggest versions of Adam alone in Eden before he knew he had a sex, innocently wearing his primal sweat suit made only of native worth and honor.

The Romantic sense of the child as naturally privileged and instinctively good like Adam seems to stay with us. But we have lately added the belief in a child's potential depravity, which may go unpaid for and unpunished just because of all children's categorical innocence. Perhaps this society abuses its children, and also aggressively dresses them in lipstick and sequins, for the same reason it imitates them — from a helpless envy of what they get away with. The everyday androgynous costume is the suit of diminished erotic responsibility and exemption from adult sexual risk. What it clothes is the child's license to make demands and receive gratification with no risk of dishonor — to be erotic, but to pose as unsexual and therefore unaccountable.

Even more forbidden and outrageous than the sexual child is its near relation, the erotic angel. While the ordinary world is routinely dressing itself and its kids in unisex jeans, it is simultaneously conjuring up mercurial apparitions who offer an enchanting counterpoint to life's mundane transactions. In the rock star form, they embody the opposing fantasy face of the troublesome domestic child or adolescent: the angelic visitor who needs to obey no earthly rules. Funny little E.T. was only one version. The type includes all those supremely compelling creatures who may shine while they stomp and whirl and scream and hum and never suffer the slightest humiliation.

A child, however ideologized, is always real and problematic, but an angel has a fine mythic remoteness however palpable he seems. The opposing kind of androgyny invests him: he exists not before but beyond human sexual life, and he comes as a powerful messenger from spheres where there is no taking or giving in marriage, but where extreme kinds of joy are said to be infinite. Our rock-video beings cultivate the unhuman look of ultimate synthesis: they aim to transcend sexual conflict by becoming fearsome angels, universally stimulating creatures fit for real existence only out of this world. Like all angels, they profoundly excite; but they don't excite desire, even though they do make the air crackle with promise and menace. Their job is to bring the message and then leave, having somehow transformed the world. Michael Jackson reportedly leads a life both angelic and artificially childlike, and he makes his appearance in epiphanic style. David Bowie still appears to be the man who fell to earth, not someone born here. Grace Jones also seems to come from altogether elsewhere. Such idols only function in the sphere of unattainability. While they flourish they remain sojourners, leading lives of vivid otherness in what seems a sexual no man's land.

Angels were in fact once firmly male and uncompromisingly austere. The disturbing sensuality they acquired in the art of later centuries, like that of the luscious angel in Leonardo's *Virgin of the Rocks*, always reads as a feminization — and from this one must conclude that adding feminine elements to the male is what produces androgyny's most intense effects. Almost all our androgynous stars are in fact males in feminized trim; their muscular and crop-haired female counterparts, such as Annie Lennox, are less numerous and have a more limited appeal. The meaning in all our androgyny, both modish and ordinary, still seems to be the same: the male is the primary sex, straightforward, simple, and active. He can be improved and embellished, however, and have and give a better time if he allows himself to be modified by the complexities of female influence.

The process does not work the other way. Elegant women in fashionable menswear expound the same thought, not its opposite: traditional jackets and trousers are austerely beautiful, but they are patently enhanced by high heels, flowing scarves, cosmetics, and earrings. Lisa Lyon, the body builder, has been photographed by Robert Mapplethorpe to show that her excessively developed muscles do not make her mannish but instead have been feminized to go with, not against, her flowered hats and lipstick. Ordinary women wearing men's active gear while wheeling strollers on the street or carrying bags across the parking lot are subduing and adapting harsh male dress to flexible female life and giving it some new scope. Common androgynous costume is always some kind of suit or jumpsuit, or pants, shirt and jacket, not some kind of dress, bodice and skirt, or gown. A hat may go with it, or perhaps a hood or scarf, but not a coif or veil. A few real female skirts (not kilts or Greek evzone skirts) are now being very occasionally and sensationally tried out by some highly visible men — daring designers, media performers and their imitators, fashion models and theirs — but all kinds of pants are being worn by all kinds of women all the time. We can read the message: the male is the first sex, now at last prepared to consider the other one anew, with much fanfare. It is still a case of female sexuality enlightening the straight male world — still the arrival of Eve and all her subsequent business in and beyond the garden — that is being celebrated. The "androgynous" mode for both sexes suggests that the female has come on the scene to educate the male about the imaginative pleasures of sex, signified chiefly by the pleasures of adornment. About its difficulties, summed up by that glaringly absent round belly, she is naturally keeping quiet.

Meanwhile the more glittering versions of modish androgyny continue to reflect what we adore in fantasy. Many of us seem to feel that the most erotic condition of all could not be that of any man or woman, or of any child, or of a human being with two sexes, but that of a very young and effeminate male angel — a new version of art history's lascivious *putto.** Such a being may give and take a guiltless delight, wield limitless sexual power without sexual politics, feel all the pleasures of sex with none of the personal risks, can never grow up, never get wise, and never be old. It is a futureless vision, undoubtedly appropriate to a nuclear age; but if any of us manages to survive, the soft round belly will surely again have its day.

In the meantime, as we approach the end of the century and the millennium, the impulse toward a certain fusion in the habits of the sexes may have a more hopeful meaning. After a hundred years of underground struggle, trousers are no longer male dress sometimes worn by women. They have been successfully feminized

***Putto:** Italian, meaning "boy"; refers here to the little nude boys, often winged, who appear in classical and Renaissance art.

so as to become authentic costume for both sexes, and to regain the authoritative bisexual status the gown once had in the early Middle Ages. This development is clearly not a quick trend but a true change, generations in the making. Male skirts have yet to prove themselves; but men have in fact succeeded in making long-term capital out of the short-lived and now forgotten Peacock Revolution of the late sixties. Whole new ranges of rich color, interesting pattern, texture, and unusual cut have become generally acceptable in male dress since then, and so has a variety of jewelry. The sort of fashionable experiment once associated only with women has become a standard male option. Some new agreement between the sexes may actually be forming, signaled by all these persistent visual projections; but just what that accord will turn out to be it is not safe to predict, nor whether it will continue to civilize us further or only perplex us more.

Reflections and Responses

1. Hollander spends a good portion of her essay surveying a history of clothing styles. Of what importance is that coverage to her essay, which is intended to explain current fashion?

2. Many of Hollander's examples are drawn from the world of media and entertainment. Why do you think this is so? In what ways do celebrities support her argument about sexuality and fashion? Could she have made her case without them?

3. How accurately do you think Hollander predicted in 1985 the fashion trends of the 1990s? Based on her examination, how would you forecast the fashions of the next century?

ALAN M. DERSHOWITZ

Shouting "Fire!"

Artists and performers are not the only ones who explore the boundaries of free expression. Lawyers and judges, too, frequently find themselves struggling to ascertain the limits of free speech. In the following essay, one of America's best-known trial lawyers, Alan M. Dershowitz, takes a close look at one of the most commonly used arguments against free speech, the idea that some speech should be suppressed because it is "just like" falsely shouting fire in a crowded theater. In his investigation into the source of this famous analogy, Dershowitz demonstrates how it has been widely misused and abused by proponents of censorship. Indeed, it was an "inapt analogy even in the context in which it was originally offered." As an expression to suppress expression, the "shouting fire" analogy, Dershowitz maintains, has been "invoked so often, by so many people, in such diverse contexts, that it has become part of our national folk language."

Alan M. Dershowitz is Felix Frankfurter professor of law at Harvard Law School. He is the author of many books, including The Best Defense *(1982),* Taking Liberties *(1988),* Chutzpah *(1991), and* Contrary to Public Opinion *(1992). In addition to his teaching and writing, Professor Dershowitz is an active criminal defense and civil liberties lawyer. "Shouting Fire!" originally appeared in* The Atlantic *(1989) and was selected by Justin Kaplan for* The Best American Essays *1990.*

When the Reverend Jerry Falwell learned that the Supreme Court had reversed his $200,000 judgment against *Hustler* magazine for the emotional distress that he had suffered from an outrageous parody, his response was typical of those who seek to censor speech: "Just as no person may scream 'Fire!' in a crowded theater when there is no fire, and find cover under the First Amendment, likewise, no sleazy merchant like Larry Flynt should be able to use the First Amendment as an excuse for maliciously and dishonestly attacking public figures, as he has so often done."

Justice Oliver Wendell Holmes's classic example of unprotected speech — falsely shouting "Fire!" in a crowded theater — has been invoked so often, by so many people, in such diverse contexts, that it has become part of our national folk language. It has even appeared — most appropriately — in the theater: in Tom Stoppard's play *Rosencrantz and Guildenstern Are Dead* a character shouts at the audience, "Fire!" He then quickly explains: "It's all right — I'm demonstrating the misuse of free speech." Shouting "Fire!" in the theater may well be the only jurisprudential analogy that has assumed the status of a folk argument. A prominent historian recently characterized it as "the most brilliantly persuasive expression that ever came from Holmes' pen." But in spite of its hallowed position in both the jurisprudence of the First Amendment and the arsenal of political discourse, it is and was an inapt analogy, even in the context in which it was originally offered. It has lately become — despite, perhaps even because of, the frequency and promiscuousness of its invocation — little more than a caricature of logical argumentation.

The case that gave rise to the "Fire!"-in-a-crowded-theater analogy, *Schenck* v. *United States,* involved the prosecution of Charles Schenck, who was the general secretary of the Socialist party in Philadelphia, and Elizabeth Baer, who was its recording secretary. In 1917 a jury found Schenck and Baer guilty of attempting to cause insubordination among soldiers who had been drafted to fight in the First World War. They and other party members had circulated leaflets urging draftees not to "submit to intimidation" by fighting in a war being conducted on behalf of "Wall Street's chosen few."

Schenck admitted, and the Court found, that the intent of the pamphlets' "impassioned language" was to "influence" draftees to resist the draft. Interestingly, however, Justice Holmes noted that nothing in the pamphlet suggested that the draftees should use unlawful or violent means to oppose conscription: "In form at least [the pamphlet] confined itself to peaceful measures, such as a petition for the repeal of the act" and an exhortation to exercise "your right to assert your opposition to the draft." Many of its most impassioned words were quoted directly from the Constitution.

Justice Holmes acknowledged that "in many places and in

ordinary times the defendants, in saying all that was said in the circular, would have been within their constitutional rights." "But," he added, "the character of every act depends upon the circumstances in which it is done." And to illustrate that truism he went on to say:

> The most stringent protection of free speech would not protect a man in falsely shouting fire in a theater, and causing a panic. It does not even protect a man from an injunction against uttering words that may have all the effect of force.

Justice Holmes then upheld the convictions in the context of a wartime draft, holding that the pamphlet created "a clear and present danger" of hindering the war effort while our soldiers were fighting for their lives and our liberty.

The example of shouting "Fire!" obviously bore little relationship to the facts of the Schenck case. The Schenck pamphlet contained a substantive political message. It urged its draftee readers to *think* about the message and then — if they so chose — to act on it in a lawful and nonviolent way. The man who shouts "Fire!" in a crowded theater is neither sending a political message nor inviting his listener to think about what he has said and decide what to do in a rational, calculated manner. On the contrary, the message is designed to force action *without* contemplation. The message "Fire!" is directed not to the mind and the conscience of the listener but, rather, to his adrenaline and his feet. It is a stimulus to immediate *action,* not thoughtful reflection. It is — as Justice Holmes recognized in his follow-up sentence — the functional equivalent of "uttering words that may have all the effect of force."

Indeed, in that respect the shout of "Fire!" is not even speech, in any meaningful sense of that term. It is a *clang* sound, the equivalent of setting off a nonverbal alarm. Had Justice Holmes been more honest about his example, he would have said that freedom of speech does not protect a kid who pulls a fire alarm in the absence of a fire. But that obviously would have been irrelevant to the case at hand. The proposition that pulling an alarm is not protected speech certainly leads to the conclusion that shouting the word "fire" is also not protected. But the core analogy is the nonverbal alarm, and the derivative example is the verbal shout. By cleverly substituting the derivative shout for the core alarm, Holmes made it possible to analogize one set of words to another — as he could not have done if he had begun with the self-evident proposition that setting off an alarm bell is not free speech.

The analogy is thus not only inapt but also insulting. Most Americans do not respond to political rhetoric with the same kind of automatic acceptance expected of schoolchildren responding to a fire drill. Not a single recipient of the Schenck pamphlet is known to have changed his mind after reading it. Indeed, one draftee, who appeared as a prosecution witness, was asked whether reading the pamphlet asserting that the draft law was unjust would make him "immediately decide that you must erase that law." Not surprisingly, he replied, "I do my own thinking." A theatergoer would probably not respond similarly if asked how he would react to a shout of "Fire!"

Another important reason why the analogy is inapt is that Holmes emphasizes the factual falsity of the shout "Fire!" The Schenck pamphlet, however, was not factually false. It contained political opinions and ideas about the causes of the war and about appropriate and lawful responses to the draft. As the Supreme Court recently reaffirmed (in *Falwell* v. *Hustler*), "The First Amendment recognizes no such thing as a 'false' idea." Nor does it recognize false opinions about the causes of or cures for war.

A closer analogy to the facts of the Schenck case might have been provided by a person's standing outside a theater, offering the patrons a leaflet advising them that in his opinion the theater was structurally unsafe, and urging them not to enter but to complain to the building inspectors. That analogy, however, would not have served Holmes's argument for punishing Schenck. Holmes needed an analogy that would appear relevant to Schenck's political speech but that would invite the conclusion that censorship was appropriate.

Unsurprisingly, a war-weary nation — in the throes of a know-nothing hysteria over immigrant anarchists and socialists — welcomed the comparison between what was regarded as a seditious political pamphlet and a malicious shout of "Fire!" Ironically, the "Fire!" analogy is nearly all that survives from the Schenck case; the ruling itself is almost certainly not good law. Pamphlets of the kind that resulted in Schenck's imprisonment have been circulated with impunity during subsequent wars.

Over the past several years I have assembled a collection of instance — cases, speeches, arguments — in which proponents of censorship have maintained that the expression at issue is "just like" or "equivalent to" falsely shouting "Fire!" in a crowded theater and ought to be banned, "just as" shouting "Fire!" ought to be banned. The analogy is generally invoked, often with self-satisfaction, as an absolute argument-stopper. It does, after all, claim the high authority of the great Justice Oliver Wendell Holmes. I have rarely heard it invoked in a convincing, or even particularly relevant, way. But that, too, can claim lineage from the great Holmes.

Not unlike Falwell, with his silly comparison between shouting "Fire!" and publishing an offensive parody, courts and commentators have frequently invoked "Fire!" as an analogy to expression that is not an automatic stimulus to panic. A state supreme court held that "Holmes' aphorism . . . applies with equal force to pornography" — in particular to the exhibition of the movie *Carmen Baby* in a drive-in theater in close proximity to highways and homes. Another court analogized "picketing . . . in support of a secondary boycott" to shouting "Fire!" because in both instances "speech and conduct are brigaded." In the famous Skokie case one of the judges argued that allowing Nazis to march through a city where a large number of Holocaust survivors live "just might fall into the same category as one's 'right' to cry fire in a crowded theater."

Outside court the analogies become even more badly stretched. A spokesperson for the New Jersey Sports and Exposition Authority complained that newspaper reports to the effect that a large number of football players had contracted cancer after playing in the Meadowlands — a stadium atop a landfill — were the "journalistic equivalent of shouting fire in a crowded theater." An insect researcher acknowledged that his prediction that a certain amusement park might become roach-infested "may be tantamount to shouting fire in a crowded theater." The philosopher Sidney Hook, in a letter to the *New York Times* bemoaning a Supreme Court decision that required a plaintiff in a defamation action to prove that the offending statement was actually false, argued that the First

Amendment does not give the press carte blanche to accuse innocent persons "anymore than the First Amendment protects the
right of someone falsely to shout fire in a crowded theater."

Some close analogies to shouting "Fire!" or setting off an alarm
are, of course, available: calling in a false bomb threat; dialing
911 and falsely describing an emergency; making a loud, gun-
like sound in the presence of the President; setting off a voice-
activated sprinkler system by falsely shouting "Fire!" In one case in
which the "Fire!" analogy was directly to the point, a creative de-
fendant tried to get around it. The case involved a man who calmly
advised an airline clerk that he was "only here to hijack the plane."
He was charged, in effect, with shouting "Fire!" in a crowded theater, and his rejected defense — as quoted by the court — was as
follows: "If we built fire-proof theaters and let people know about
this, then the shouting of 'Fire!' would not cause panic."

Here are some more-distant but still related examples: the recent incident of the police slaying in which some members of an
onlooking crowd urged a mentally ill vagrant who had taken an officer's gun to shoot the officer; the screaming of racial epithets
during a tense confrontation; shouting down a speaker and pre-
venting him from continuing his speech.

Analogies are, by their nature, matters of degree. Some are
closer to the core example than others. But any attempt to analogize political ideas in a pamphlet, ugly parody in a magazine, offensive movies in a theater, controversial newspaper articles, or
any of the other expressions and actions catalogued above to the
very different act of shouting "Fire!" in a crowded theater is either
self-deceptive or self-serving.

The government does, of course, have some arguably legitimate
bases for suppressing speech which bear no relationship to shouting "Fire!" It may ban the publication of nuclear-weapon codes, of
information about troop movements, and of the identity of undercover agents. It may criminalize extortion threats and conspiratorial agreements. These expressions may lead directly to serious
harm, but the mechanisms of causation are very different from
that at work when an alarm is sounded. One may also argue — less
persuasively, in my view — against protecting certain forms of public obscenity and defamatory statements. Here, too, the mechanisms of causation are very different. None of these exceptions to

the First Amendment's exhortation that the government "shall make no law . . . abridging the freedom of speech, or of the press" is anything like falsely shouting "Fire!" in a crowded theater; they all must be justified on other grounds.

A comedian once told his audience, during the stand-up routine, about the time he was standing around a fire with a crowd of people and got in trouble for yelling "Theater, theater!" That, I think, is about as clever and productive a use as anyone has ever made of Holmes's flawed analogy.

Reflections and Responses

1. Consider Dershowitz's analysis of Justice Holmes's decision in the Schenck case. What does Dershowitz find wrong with Holmes's reasoning? In what ways is Holmes's analogy "flawed"?

2. To what kinds of expression does Dershowitz find Holmes's analogy applicable? Go through Dershowitz's examples of protected and unprotected speech. Why is the "falsely shouting fire" analogy appropriate in some instances and not in others?

3. Consider Dershowitz's anecdote in the last paragraph about the comedian who yells "Theater, theater!" What was the comedian expressing? Why does Dershowitz find this response to Holmes's analogy "clever and productive"?

5

Survival

EDWARD HOAGLAND

Heaven and Nature

Speculation, says Edward Hoagland at the conclusion of this intensely reflective essay, is "a high-risk activity." Since speculation is at the heart of the genre, he might have added that to write essays is essentially to take risks. Intellectual, emotional, and literary security are not attractive goals for personal essayists like Hoagland, whose work often explores the outer edges of personality and social behavior. In "Heaven and Nature," he penetrates territory that most people would prefer to skirt around: the inclination to commit suicide. As usual, his approach is deeply personal and yet remarkably inclusive.

Hoagland, whom John Updike has called "the best essayist" of his generation, is the author of five books of fiction, two travel books, and seven essay collections, including The Courage of Turtles *(1971),* Walking the Dead Diamond River *(1973),* Red Wolves and Black Bears *(1976), and* The Tugman's Passage *(1982). In 1988, he published* Heart's Desire, *a collection of what he considered his best essays from twenty years of writing. Another collection of essays,* Balancing Acts, *appeared in 1992. He is the general editor of the Penguin Nature Library and is a member of the American Academy of Arts and Letters. "Heaven and Nature" originally appeared in* Harper's Magazine *(1988) and was selected by Geoffrey Wolff for* The Best American Essays *1989.*

A friend of mine, a peaceable soul who has been riding the New York subways for thirty years, finds himself stepping back from the tracks once in a while and closing his eyes as the train rolls in. This, he says, is not only to suppress an urge to throw himself in front of it but because every couple of weeks an impulse rises in him to push a stranger onto the tracks, any stranger, thus ending his own life too. He blames this partly on apartment living, "pigeonholes without being able to fly."

It is profoundly startling not to trust oneself after decades of doing so. I don't dare keep ammunition in my country house for a small rifle I bought secondhand two decades ago. The gun had sat in a cupboard in the back room with the original box of .22 bullets under the muzzle all that time, seldom fired except at a few apples hanging in a tree every fall to remind me of my army training near the era of the Korean War, when I'd been considered quite a marksman. When I bought the gun I didn't trust either my professional competence as a writer or my competence as a father as much as I came to, but certainly believed I could keep myself alive. I bought it for protection, and the idea that someday I might be afraid of shooting myself with the gun would have seemed inconceivable — laughable.

One's fifties can be giddy years, as anybody fifty knows. Chest pains, back pains, cancer scares, menopausal or prostate complications are not the least of it, and the fidelities of a lifetime, both personal and professional, may be called into question. Was it a mistake to have stuck so long with one's marriage, and to have stayed with a lackluster well-paying job? (Or *not* to have stayed and stuck?) People not only lose faith in their talents and their dreams or values; some simply tire of them. Grow tired, too, of the smell of fried-chicken grease, once such a delight, and the cold glutinosity of ice cream, the boredom of beer, the stop-go of travel, the hiccups of laughter, and of two rush hours a day, then the languor of weekends, of athletes as well as accountants, and even the frantic birdsong of spring — red-eyed vireos that have been clocked singing twenty-two thousand times in a day. Life is a matter of cultivating the six senses, and an equilibrium with nature and what I think of as its subdivision, human nature, trusting no one completely but almost everyone at least a little; but this is easier said than done.

More than thirty thousand Americans took their own lives last year, men mostly, with the highest rate being among those older than sixty-five. When I asked a friend why three times as many men kill themselves as members of her own sex, she replied with sudden anger, "I'm not going to go into the self-indulgence of men." They won't bend to failure, she said, and want to make themselves memorable. Suicide is an exasperating act as often as it is pitiable. "Committing" suicide is in bad odor in our culture even among those who don't believe that to cash in your chips ahead of time and hand back to God his gifts to you is a blasphemous sin. We the living, in any case, are likely to feel accused by this person who "voted with his feet." It appears to cast a subversive judgment upon the social polity as a whole that what was supposed to work in life — religion, family, friendship, commerce, and industry — did not, and furthermore it frightens the horses in the street, as Shaw's friend Mrs. Patrick Campbell once defined wrongful behavior.

Many suicides inflict outrageous trauma, burning permanent injuries in the minds of their children, though they may have joked beforehand only of "taking a dive." And sometimes the gesture has a peevish or cowardly aspect, or seems to have been senselessly shortsighted as far as an outside observer can tell. There are desperate suicides and crafty suicides, people who do it to cause others trouble and people who do it to save others trouble, deranged exhibitionists who yell from a building ledge and close-mouthed, secretive souls who swim out into the ocean's anonymity. Suicide may in fact be an attempt to escape death, shortcut the dreadful deteriorating processes, abort one's natural trajectory, elude "the ruffian on the stairs," in A. E. Housman's phrase for a cruelly painful, anarchic death — make it neat and not messy. The deed can be grandiose or self-abnegating, vindictive or drably mousy, rationally plotted or plainly insane. People sidle toward death, intent upon outwitting their own bodies' defenses, or they may dramatize the chance to make one last, unambiguous, irrevocable decision, like a captain scuttling his ship — death before dishonor — leaping toward oblivion through a curtain of pain, like a frog going down the throat of a snake. One man I knew hosted a quietly affectionate evening with several unknowing friends on the night before he swallowed too many pills. Another waved an apologetic goodbye to a bystander on a bridge. Seldom shy ordinarily, and rarely considerate, he turned shy and apologetic in the last moment of life. Never physically inclined, he made a great vault toward the ice on the Mississippi.

In the army, we wore dog tags with a notch at one end by which these numbered pieces of metal could be jammed between our teeth, if we lay dead and nameless on a battlefield, for later sorting. As "servicemen" our job would be to kill people who were pointed out to us as enemies, or make "the supreme sacrifice" for a higher good than enjoying the rest of our lives. Life was very much a possession, in other words — not only God's, but the soldier's own to dispose of. Working in an army hospital, I frequently did handle dead bodies, but this never made me feel I would refuse to kill another man whose uniform was pointed out to me as being inimical, or value my life more tremulously and vigilantly. The notion of dying for my country never appealed to me as much as dying free-lance for my ideas (in the unlikely event that I *could* do that), but I was ready. People were taught during the 1940s and 1950s that one should be ready to die for one's beliefs. Heroes were revered because they had deliberately chosen to give up their lives. Life would not be worth living under the tyranny of an invader and Nathan Hale apparently hadn't paused to wonder whether God might not have other uses for him besides being hung. Nor did the pilot Colin Kelly hesitate before plunging his plane into a Japanese battleship, becoming America's first well-publicized hero in World War II.

I've sometimes wondered why people who know that they are terminally ill, or who are headed for suicide, so very seldom have paused to take a bad guy along with them. It is lawless to consider an act of assassination, yet hardly more so, really, than suicide is regarded in some quarters (or death itself, in others). Government bureaucracies, including our own, in their majesty and as the executors of laws, regularly weigh the pros and cons of murdering foreign antagonists. Of course the answer is that most individuals are fortunately more timid as well as humbler in their judgment than government officialdom, but beyond that, when dying or suicidal, they no longer care enough to devote their final energies to doing good works of any kind — Hitler himself in their gunsights they would have passed up. Some suicides become so crushed and despairing that they can't recognize the consequences of anything they do, and it's not primarily vindictiveness that wreaks such havoc upon their survivors but their derangement from ordinary life.

Courting the idea is different from the real impulse. "When he begged for help, we took him and locked him up," another friend of mine says, speaking of her husband. "Not till then. Wishing to be out of the situation you are in — feeling helpless and unable to cope — is not the same as wishing to be dead. If I actually wished to be dead, even my children's welfare would have no meaning."

You might think the ready option of divorce available lately would have cut suicide rates, offering an escape to battered wives, lovelorn husbands, and other people in despair. But it doesn't work that way. When the number of choices people have increases, an entire range of possibilities opens up. Suicide among teenagers has almost quadrupled since 1950, although the standard of comfort that their families enjoy is up. Black Americans, less affluent than white Americans, have had less of a rise in suicides, and the rate among them remains about half of that for whites.

Still, if a fiftyish fellow with fine teeth and a foolproof pension plan, a cottage at the beach and the Fourth of July weekend coming up, kills himself, it seems truculent. We would look at him bafflingly if he told us he no longer likes the Sturm und Drang of banging fireworks.

Then stay at your hideaway! we'd argue with him.

"Big mouths eat little mouths. Nature isn't 'timeless.' Whole lives are squeezed into three months or three days."

What about your marriage?

"She's become more mannish than me. I loved women. I don't believe in marriage between men."

Remarry, then!

"I've gone impotent, and besides, when I see somebody young and pretty I guess I feel like dandling her on my knee."

Marriage is friendship. You can find someone your own age.

"I'm tired of it."

But how about your company? — a widows-and-orphans stock that's on the cutting edge of the silicon frontier? That's interesting.

"I know what wins. It's less and less appetizing."

You're not scared of death anymore?

"It interests me less than it did."

What are you so sick of? The rest of us keep going.

"I'm tired of weathermen and sportscasters on the screen. Of being patient and also of impatience. I'm tired of the president, whoever the president happens to be, and sleeping badly, with forty-eight half-hours in the day — of breaking two eggs every morning and putting sugar on something. I'm tired of the drone of my own voice, but also of us jabbering like parrots at each other — of all our stumpy ways of doing everything."

You're bored with yourself?

"That's an understatement. I'm maybe the least interesting person I know."

But to kill yourself?

"You know, it's a tradition, too," he remarks quietly, not making so bold as to suggest that the tradition is an honorable one, though his tone of voice might be imagined to imply this. "I guess I've always been a latent maverick."

Except in circumstances which are themselves a matter of life and death, I'm reluctant to agree with the idea that suicide is not the result of mental illness. No matter how reasonably the person appears to have examined his options, it goes against the grain of nature for him to destroy himself. And any illness that threatens his life changes a person. Suicidal thinking, if serious, can be a kind of death scare, comparable to suffering a heart attack or undergoing a cancer operation. One survives such a phase both warier and chastened. When — two years ago — I emerged from a bad dip into suicidal speculation, I felt utterly exhausted and yet quite fearless of ordinary dangers, vastly afraid of myself but much less scared of extraneous eventualities. The fact of death may not be tragic; many people die with a bit of a smile that captures their mouths at the last instant, and most people who are revived after a deadly accident are reluctant to be brought to life, resisting resuscitation, and carrying back confusing, beamish, or ecstatic memories. But the same impetuosity that made him throw himself out of the window might have enabled the person to love life all the more if he'd been calibrated somewhat differently at the time of the emergency. Death's edge is so abrupt and near that many people who expect a short and momentary dive may be astounded to find that it is bottomless and change their minds and start to scream when they are only halfway down.

Although my fright at my mind's anarchy superseded my fear of death in the conventional guise of automobile or airplane crashes, heart seizures, and so on, nightmares are more primitive and in my dreams I continued to be scared of a death not sought after — dying from driving too fast and losing control of the car, breaking through thin ice while skating and drowning in the cold, or falling off a cliff. When I am tense and sleeping raggedly, my worst nightmare isn't drawn from anxious prep school memories or my stint in the army or the bad spells of my marriages or any other of adult-hood's vicissitudes. Nothing else from the past half century has the staying power in my mind of the elevated-train rides that my father and I used to take down Third Avenue to the Battery in New York City on Sunday afternoon when I was three or four or five so I could see the fish at the aquarium. We were probably pretty good companions in those years, but the wooden platforms forty feet up shook terribly as trains from both directions pulled in and out. To me they seemed worse than rickety — ready to topple. And the roar was fearful, and the railings left large gaps for a child to fall through, after the steep climb up the slat-sided, windy, shaking stairway from street level. It's a rare dream, but several times a year I still find myself on such a perch, without his company or anybody else's, on a boyish or a grown-up's mission, when the elevated plat-form begins to rattle desperately, seesaw, heel over, and finally come apart, disintegrate, while I cling to struts and trusses.

My father, as he lay dying at home of bowel cancer, used to enjoy watching Tarzan reruns on the children's hour of television. Like a strong green vine, they swung him far away from his deathbed to a world of skinny-dipping and friendly animals and scenic beauty linked to the lost realities of his adolescence in Kansas City. Earlier, when he had still been able to walk without much pain, he'd paced the house for several hours at night, contemplating suicide, I ex-pect, along with other anguishing thoughts, regrets, remem-brances, and yearnings, while the rest of us slept. But he decided to lie down and die the slower way. I don't know how much of that de-cision was for the sake of his wife and children, how much was be-cause he didn't want to be a "quitter," as he sometimes put it, and how much was due to his believing that life belongs to God (which I'm not even sure he did). He was not a churchgoer after his thir-ties. He had belonged to J. P. Morgan's church, St. George's, on Stuyvesant Square — Morgan was a hero of his — but when things went a little wrong for him at the Wall Street law firm he worked for and he changed jobs and moved out to the suburbs, he became a skeptic on religious matters, and gradually, in the absence of faith of that previous kind, he adhered to a determined allegiance to the social order. Wendell Willkie or Dwight D. Eisenhower instead of J. P. Morgan became the sort of hero he admired, and suicide would have seemed an act of insurrection against the laws and conven-tions of the society, internationalist-Republican, that he believed in.

I was never particularly afraid that I might plan a suicide, swallowing a bunch of pills and keeping them down — only of what I think of as being Anna Karenina's kind of death. This most plausible self-killing in all of literature is frightening because it was unwilled, regretted at midpoint, and came as a complete surprise to Anna herself. After rushing impulsively, in great misery, to the Moscow railway station to catch a train, she ended up underneath another one, dismayed, astonished, and trying to climb out from under the wheels even as they crushed her. Many people who briefly verge on suicide undergo a mental somersault for a terrifying interval during which they're upside down, their perspective topsy-turvy, skidding, churning; and this is why I got rid of the bullets for my .22.

Nobody expects to trust his body overmuch after the age of fifty. Incipient cataracts or arthritis, outlandish snores, tooth-grinding, ankles that threaten to turn, are part of the game. But not to trust one's *mind*? That's a surprise. The single attribute that older people were sure to have (we thought as boys) was a stodgy dependability, a steady temperance or caution. Adults might be vain, unimaginative, pompous, and callous, but they did have their affairs tightly in hand. It was not till my thirties that I began to know friends who were in their fifties on equal terms, and I remember being amused, piqued, irritated, and slightly bewildered to learn that some of them still felt as marginal or rebellious or in a quandary about what to do with themselves for the next dozen years as my contemporaries were likely to. That close to retirement, some of them harbored a deep-seated contempt for the organizations they had been working for, ready to walk away from almost everybody they had known and the efforts and expertise of whole decades with very little sentiment. Nor did twenty years of marriage necessarily mean more than two or three — they might be just as ready to walk away from that also, and didn't really register it as twenty years at all. Rather, life could be about to begin all over again. "Bummish" was how one man described himself, with a raffish smile — "Lucky to have a roof over my head" — though he'd just put a child through Yale. He was quitting his job and claimed with exasperation that his wife still cried for her mother in her sleep, as if they'd never been married.

The great English traveler Richard Burton quoted an Arab proverb that speaks for many middle-aged men of the old-fashioned variety: "Conceal thy Tenets, thy Treasure, and thy Traveling." These are serious matters, in other words. People didn't conceal their tenets in order to betray them, but to fight for them more opportunely. And except for kings and princelings, concealing whatever treasure one had went almost without saying. As for travel, a man's travels were also a matter of gravity. Travel was knowledge, ambiguity, dalliances or misalliances, divided loyalty, forbidden thinking; and besides, someday he might need to make a run for it and go to ground someplace where he had made some secret friends. Friends of mine whose husbands or whose wives have died have been quite startled afterward to discover caches of money or traveler's checks concealed around the house, or a bundle of cash in a safe deposit box.

Burton, like any other desert adage-spinner and most individuals over fifty, would have agreed to an addition so obvious that it wasn't included to begin with: "Conceal thy Illnesses." I can remember how urgently my father worried that word would get out, after a preliminary operation for his cancer. He didn't want to be written off, counted out of the running at the corporation he worked for and in other enclaves of competition. Men often compete with one another until the day they die; comradeship consists of rubbing shoulders jocularly with a competitor. As breadwinners, they must be considered fit and sound by friend as well as foe, and so there's lots of truth to the most common answer I heard when asking why three times as many men as women kill themselves: "They keep their troubles to themselves"; "They don't know how to ask for help." Men greet each other with a sock on the arm, women with a hug, and the hug wears better in the long run.

I'm not entirely like that, and I discovered that when I confided something of my perturbation to a woman friend she was likely to keep telephoning me or mailing cheery postcards, whereas a man would usually listen with concern, communicate his sympathy, and maybe intimate that he had pondered the same drastic course of action himself a few years back and would end up respecting my decision either way. Open-mindedness seems an important attribute to a good many men, who pride themselves on being objective, hearing all sides of an issue, on knowing that truth and honesty do not always coincide with social dicta, and who may even cherish a subterranean outlaw streak that, like being ready to

violently defend one's family, reputation, and country, is by tradition male.

Men, being so much freer than women in society, used to feel
they had less of a stake in the maintenance of certain churchly
conventions and enjoyed speaking irreverently about various social truisms, including even the principle that people ought to die
on schedule, not cutting in ahead on their assigned place in line.
Contemporary women, after their triumphant irreverence during
the 1960s and 1970s, cannot be generalized about so easily, however. They turn as skeptical and saturnine as any man. In fact,
women attempt suicide more frequently, but favor pills or other
methods, whereas two-thirds of the men who kill themselves have
used a gun. In 1985, 85 percent of suicides by means of firearms
were done by men. An overdose of medication hasn't the same fi-
nality. It may be reversible if the person is discovered quickly, or
be subject to benign miscalculation to start with. Even if it works,
perhaps it can be fudged by a kindly doctor in the record-keeping.
Like an enigmatic drowning or a single-car accident that baffles
the suspicions of the insurance company, a suicide by drugs can be
a way to avoid making a loud statement, and merely illustrate the
final modesty of a person who didn't wish to ask for too much of
the world's attention.

Unconsummated attempts at suicide can strike the rest of us as
self-pitying and self-aggrandizing, or plaintive plea-bargaining —
"childish," we say, though actually the suicide of children is ghastly
beyond any stunt of self-mutilation an adult may indulge in because of the helplessness that echoes through the act. It would be
hard to define chaos better than as a world where children decide
that they don't want to live.

Love is the solution to all dilemmas, we sometimes hear, and in
those moments when the spirit bathes itself in beneficence and
manages to transcend the static of personalities rubbing fur off of
each other, indeed it is. Without love nothing matters, Paul told
the Corinthians, a mystery which, if true, has no ready Darwinian
explanation. Love without a significant sexual component and for
people who are unrelated to us serves little practical purpose. It
doesn't help us feed our families, win struggles, thrive and prosper. It distracts us from the ordinary business of sizing people up
and making a living, and is not even conducive to intellectual ob-

servation, because instead of seeing them, we see right through them to the bewildered child and dreaming adolescent who inhabited their bodies earlier, the now-tired idealist who fell in love and out of love, got hired and quit, hired and fired, bought cars and wore them out, liked black-eyed Susans, blueberry muffins, and roosters crowing — liked roosters crowing better than skyscrapers but now likes skyscrapers better than roosters crowing. As swift as thought, we select the details that we need to see in order to be able to love them.

Yet at other times we'll dispense with these same poignancies and choose only their grunginess to look at, their pinched mouths and shifty eyes, their thirst for gin at noon and indifference to their kids, their greed for the best tidbit on the buffet table and penchant for poking their penises up the excretory end of other human beings. I tend to gaze quite closely at the faces of priests I meet on the street to see if a lifetime of love has marked them noticeably. Real serenity or asceticism I no longer expect, and I take for granted the beefy calm that frequently goes with Catholic celibacy, but I am watching for the marks of love and often see mere resignation or tenacity.

Many men are romantics, likely to plunge, go for broke, take action in a spirit of exigency rather than waiting for the problem to resolve itself. Then, on the contrary, still as romantics, they may drift into despairing passivity, stare at the TV all day long, and binge with a bottle. Women too may turn frenetic for a while and then throw up their hands; but though they may not seem as grandiosely fanciful and romantic at the outset, they are more often believers — at least I think they tend to believe in God or in humanity, the future, and so on. We have above us the inviting eternity of "the heavens," if we choose to look at it, lying on our backs in the summer grass under starlight, some of which had left its source before mankind became man. But because we live in our heads more than in nature nowadays, even the summer sky is a mine field for people whose memories are mined. With the sky no longer humbling, the sunshine only a sort of convenience, and no godhead located anywhere outside our own heads, every problem may seem insolubly interlocked. When the telephone has become impossible to answer at home, sometimes it finally becomes impossible to stride down the gangplank of a cruise ship in Mombasa too, although no telephones will ring for you there.

But if escapist travel is ruled out in certain emergencies, surely you can *pray*? Pray, yes; but to whom? That requires a bit of preparation. Rarely do people obtain much relief from praying if they haven't stood in line awhile to get a visa. It's an appealing idea that you can just *go*, and in a previous era perhaps you could have, like on an old-fashioned shooting safari. But it's not so simple now. What do you believe in? Whom are you praying to? What are you praying for? There's no crèche on the courthouse lawn; you're not supposed to adhere exactly even to what your parents had believed. Like psychotherapy, praying takes time, even if you know which direction to face when you kneel.

Love is powerfully helpful when the roof falls in — loving other people with a high and hopeful heart and as a kind of prayer. Yet that feat too requires new and sudden insights or long practice. The beatitude of loving strangers as well as friends — loving them on sight with a leap of empathy and intuition — is a form of inspiration, edging, of course, in some cases toward madness, as other states of beatitude can do. But there's no question that a genuine love for the living will stymie suicidal depressions not chemical in origin. Love is an elixir, changing the life of the lover like no other. And many of us have experienced this — a temporary lightening of our leery, prickly disapproval of much of the rest of the world when at a wedding or a funeral of shared emotion, or when we have fallen in love.

Yet the zest for life of those unusual men and women who make a great zealous success of living is due more often in good part to the craftiness and pertinacity with which they manage to overlook the misery of others. You can watch them watch life beat the stuffing out of the faces of their friends and acquaintances, yet they themselves seem to outwit the dense delays of social custom, the tedious tick-tock of bureaucratic obfuscation, accepting loss and age and change and disappointment without suffering punctures in their stomach lining. Breathlessness or strange dull pains from their nether organs don't nonplus them. They fret and doubt in moderation, and love a lobster roast, squeeze lemon juice on living clams on the half shell to prove that the clams are alive, laugh as robins tussle a worm out of the ground or a kitten flees a dog.

Like the problem drinkers, pork eaters, and chain smokers who nevertheless finish out their allotted years, succumbing to a stroke at a nice round biblical age when the best vitamin-eating vegetarian has long since died, their faces become veritable walnuts of fine character, with the same smile lines as the rarer individual whose grin has been affectionate all of his life.

We spend our lives getting to know ourselves, yet wonders never cease. During my adolescent years my states of mind, though undulant, seemed seamless; even when I was unhappy no cracks or fissures made me wonder if I was a danger to myself. My confidence was such that I treaded the slippery lips of waterfalls, fought forest fires, drove ancient cars cross-country night and day, and scratched the necks of menagerie leopards in the course of various adventures which enhanced the joy of being alive. The chemistry of the mind, because unfathomable, is more frightening. In the city, I live on the waterfront and occasionally will notice an agitated-looking figure picking his way along the pilings and string-pieces of the timbered piers nearby, staring at the sliding whorls on the surface of the Hudson as if teetering over an abyss. Our building, across the street, seems imposing from the water and over the years has acted as a magnet for a number of suicides — people who have dreaded the clammy chill, the onerous smothering essential to their first plan. One woman climbed out after jumping in and took the elevator to the roof (my neighbors remember how wringing wet she was) and leapt off, banging window ledges on the way down, and hit with the whap of a sack of potatoes, as others have.

Yet what is more remarkable than that a tiny minority of souls reach a point where they entrust their bodies to the force of gravity is that so few of the rest of us splurge an hour of a summer day gazing at the trees and sky. How many summers do we *have?* One sees prosperous families in the city who keep plants in their apartment windows that have grown so high they block the sunlight and appear to be doing the living for the tenants who are bolted inside. But beauty is nobody's sure salvation: not the beauty of a swimming hole if you get a cramp, and not the beauty of a woman if she doesn't care for you. The swimming hole looks inviting under the blue sky, with its amber bottom, green sedges sticking up in the shallows, and curls of gentle current over a waterlogged basswood tree two feet beneath the surface near the brook that feeds it. Come back at dusk, however, and the pond turns black — as dark as death, or on the contrary, a restful dark, a dark to savor. Take it as you will.

People with sunny natures do seem to live longer than people who are nervous wrecks; yet mankind didn't evolve out of the animal kingdom by being unduly sunny-minded. Life was fearful and phantasmagoric, supernatural and preternatural, as well as encompassing the kind of clockwork regularity of our well-governed day. It had numerous superstitious (from the Latin, "standing over") elements, such as we are likely to catch a whiff of only when we're peering at a dead body. And it was not just our optimism but our pessimistic premonitions, our dark moments as a species, our irrational, frightful speculations, our strange mutations upon the simple theme of love, and our sleepless, obsessive inventiveness — our dread as well as our faith — that made us human beings. Staking one's life on the more general good came to include risking suicide also. Brilliant, fecund people sometimes kill themselves.

"Joy to the world . . . Let heaven and nature sing, and heaven and nature sing. . . Repeat the sounding joy . . ." The famous Christmas carol invokes not only glee but unity: heaven with nature, not always a Christian combination. It's a rapturous hymn, and no one should refuse to surrender to such a pitch of revelation when it comes. But the flip side of rapture can be a riptide of panic, of hysterical gloom. Our faces are not molded as if joy were a preponderant experience. (Nor is a caribou's or a thrush's.) Our faces in repose look stoic or battered, and people of the sunniest temperament sometimes die utterly unstrung, doubting everything they have ever believed in or have done.

Let heaven and nature sing! the hymn proclaims. But *is* there such harmony? Are God and Mother Nature really the same? Are they even compatible? And will we risk burning our wings if we mount high enough to try to see? I've noticed that woods soil in Italy smells the same as woods soil in New England when you pick up a handful of it and enjoy its aromas — but is God there the same? It can be precarious to wonder. I don't rule out suicide as being unthinkable for people who have tried to live full lives, and don't regard it as negating the work and faith and satisfaction and fun and even ecstasy they may have known before. In killing himself a person acknowledges his failures during a time span when perhaps heaven and earth had caught him like a pair of scissors — but not his life span. Man is different from animals in that he speculates, a high-risk activity.

Reflections and Responses

1. Hoagland's position on suicide is noticeably complex. Where do you think he ultimately stands on the issue? Do you think he would say, for example, that individuals have the moral right to take their own lives if they believe it is necessary to do so? Can you identify an instance in the essay in which you can pin down Hoagland's position? If not, why not?

2. Why do you think Hoagland devotes so much attention to the differences between men and women when it comes to suicide? Do you think those differences are significant? Would you say they are natural or cultural?

3. What do you make of the dialogue Hoagland reports on pages 252–253? Do you think it is a transcription of an actual dialogue? If so, who is the person being interviewed? If not, what is Hoagland's purpose in creating it?

NATALIE KUSZ

Vital Signs

Survival has become one of the common themes of our time. Today's essayists seem to be especially candid about personal pain and more willing to disclose the details of illness and injury than were essayists in the past. This literary phenomenon may be stimulated by the public's vast interest in authentic medical case histories and reports, an interest popularly represented by the numerous television hospital shows and Hollywood films based on real cases. In recent literature, one of the most compelling accounts of a brutal accident and subsequent recovery is Natalie Kusz's "Vital Signs." In this moving, five-part narrative essay, Kusz brings us into a world of childhood suffering, where one's life is lived as though "under siege" and where a child must "abide vigorously in each instant."

Kusz (whose last name rhymes with push*) teaches creative writing at Bethel College in St. Paul, Minnesota. In 1989, she received the prestigious Whiting Writers' Award and in 1990 a Christopher Award as well as the General Electric Award for Younger Writers. "Vital Signs" formed part of her autobiographical book,* Road Song *(1990). A winner of a 1991 Pushcart Prize, she is at work on a second book of nonfiction prose. "Vital Signs" originally appeared in* The Threepenny Review *(1989) and was selected by Justin Kaplan for* The Best American Essays *1990.*

I. In Hospital

I was always waking up, in those days, to the smell of gauze soaked with mucus and needing to be changed. Even when I cannot recall what parts of me were bandaged then, I remember vividly that smell, a sort of fecund, salty, warm one like something shut up and kept alive too long in a dead space. Most of the details I remember from that time are smells, and the chancest whiff from the folds of surgical greens or the faint scent of ether on cold fingers can still drag me, reflexively, back to that life, to flux so familiar as to be a constant in itself. Years after Children's Hospital, when I took my own daughter in for stitches in her forehead, and two men unfolded surgical napkins directly under my nose, I embarrassed us all by growing too weak to stand, and had to sit aside by myself until all the work was over.

It seems odd that these smells have power to bring back such horror, when my memories of that time are not, on the whole, dark ones. Certainly I suffered pain, and I knew early a debilitating fear of surgery itself, but the life I measured as months inside and months outside the walls was a good one, and bred in me understandings that I would not relinquish now.

There was a playroom in the children's wing, a wide room full of light, with colored walls and furniture, and carpets on the floor. A wooden kitchen held the corner alongside our infirmary, and my friends and I passed many hours as families, cooking pudding for our dolls before they were due in therapy. Most of the dolls had amputated arms and legs, or had lost their hair to chemotherapy, and when we put on our doctors' clothes we taught them to walk with prostheses, changing their dressings with sterile gloves.

We had school tables, and many books, and an ant farm by the window so we could care for something alive. And overseeing us all was Janine, a pink woman, young even to seven-year-old eyes, with yellow, cloudy hair that I touched when I could. She kept it long, parted in the middle, or pulled back in a ponytail like mine before the accident. My hair had been blond then, and I felt sensitive now about the coarse brown stubble under my bandages. Once, on a thinking day, I told Janine that if I had hair like hers I would braid it and loop the pigtails around my ears. She wore it like that the next day, and every day after for a month.

Within Janine's playroom, we were some of us handicapped, but none disabled, and in time we were each taught to prove this for ourselves. While I poured the flour for new play dough, Janine asked me about my kindergarten teacher: what she had looked like with an eye patch, and if she was missing my same eye. What were the hard parts, Janine said, for a teacher like that? Did I think it was sad for her to miss school sometimes, and did she talk about the hospital? What color was her hair, what sort was her eye patch, and did I remember if she was pretty? What would I be, Janine asked, when I was that age and these surgeries were past? Over the wet salt smell of green dough, I wished to be a doctor with one blue eye, who could talk like this to the sick, who could tell them they were still real. And with her feel for when to stop talking, Janine turned and left me, searching out volunteers to stir up new clay.

She asked a lot of questions, Janine did, and we answered her as we would have answered ourselves, slowly and with purpose. When called to, Janine would even reverse her words, teaching opposite lessons to clear the mist in between; this happened for Thomas and Nick in their wheelchairs, and I grew as much older from watching as they did from being taught. Both boys were eleven, and though I've forgotten their histories, I do remember their natures, the differences that drew them together.

They were roommates and best friends, and their dispositions reverberated within one another, the self-reliant and the needy. Thomas was the small one, the white one, with blue veins in his forehead and pale hair falling forward on one side. He sat always leaning on his elbows, both shoulders pressing up around his ears, and he rested his head to the side when he talked. He depended on Nick, who was tight-shouldered and long, to take charge for him, and he asked for help with his eyes half open, breathing out words through his mouth. And Nick reached the far shelves and brought Thomas books, and proved he could do for them both, never glancing for help at those who stood upright. His skin was darker than Thomas's, and his eyes much lighter, the blue from their centers washing out into the white.

When they played together, those boys, Thomas was the small center of things, the thin planet sunken into his wheelchair, pulling his friend after him. It must not have seemed to Nick that he was being pulled, because he always went immediately to Thomas's aid, never expecting anyone else to notice. Janine, of course, did. When Thomas wanted the television switched, and Nick struggled up to do it, she said, "Nick, would you like me to do that?"

"I can do it," he said.

"But so can I," Janine said, and she strode easily to the television and turned the knob to *Sesame Street*. "Sometimes," she said to

Nick, "you have to let your friends be kind; it makes them feel good." She went back to sit beside Thomas, and she handed him the Erector set. How would he turn the channel, she said, if no one else was here? What could he do by himself? And as the TV went unnoticed, Thomas imagined a machine with gears and little wheels, and Janine said she thought it could work. After that, Thomas was always building, though he still asked for help, and he still got it. Nick never did ask, as long as I knew him, but in time he managed to accept what was offered, and even, in the end, to say thanks.

In this way and in others, Janine encouraged us to change. When we had new ideas, they were outstanding ones, and we could count almost always on her blessing. We planned wheelchair races, and she donated the trophy — bubble-gum ice cream all around. When she caught us blowing up surgical gloves we had found in the trash, she swiped a whole case of them, conjuring a helium bottle besides; that afternoon the playroom smelled of synthetic, powdery rubber, and we fought at the tables over colored markers, racing to decorate the brightest balloon. Janine's was the best — a cigar-smoking man with a four-spiked mohawk — and she handed it down the table to someone's father.

She always welcomed our parents in, so long as they never interfered, and they respected the rule, and acted always unsurprised. When Sheldon's mother arrived one day, she found her son — a four-year-old born with no hands — up to his elbows in orange fingerpaints. She stood for a moment watching, then offered calmly to mix up a new color.

We children enjoyed many moments like these, granted us by adults like Janine and our parents, and these instants of contentment were luxuries we savored, but on which, by necessity, we did not count. I've heard my father, and other immigrant survivors of World War II, speak of behavior peculiar to people under siege, of how they live in terms not of years but of moments, and this was certainly true of our lives. That time was fragmentary, allowing me to remember it now only as a series of flashes, with the most lyrical event likely at any moment to be interrupted. We children were each at the hospital for critical reasons, and a game we planned for one day was likely to be missing one or two players the next, because Charlie hemorrhaged in the night, Sarah was in emergency surgery, or Candice's tubes had pulled out. I myself missed many outings on the lawn because my bone grafts rejected or because my eye grew so infected that I had to be quarantined. At these times, I would watch the others out the closed window, waiting for them to come stand beyond the sterile curtain and shout to me a summary of the afternoon.

In the same way that the future seemed — because it might never arrive — generally less important than did the present, so too was the past less significant. Although each of us children could have recited his own case history by heart, it was rare that any of us required more than a faint sketch of another child's past; we found it both interesting and difficult enough to keep a current daily record of who had been examined, tested, or operated on, and whether it had hurt, and if so, whether they had cried. This last question was always of interest to us, and tears we looked on as marks not of cowards but of heroes, playmates who had endured torture and lived to testify. The older a child was, the greater our reverence when her roommate reported back after an exam; we derived some perverse comfort from the fact that even twelve-year-olds cracked under pressure.

Those of us who did choose to abide vigorously in each instant were able to offer ourselves, during the day, to one another, to uphold that child or parent who began to weaken. If her need was to laugh, we laughed together; if to talk, we listened, and once, I remember, I stood a whole morning by the chair of a fifteen-year-old friend, combing her hair with my fingers, handing her Kleenex and lemon drops, saying nothing. At night, then, we withdrew, became quietly separate, spoke unguardedly with our families. We spent these evening hours regrouping, placing the days into perspective, each of us using our own methods of self-healing. My mother would read to me from the Book of Job, about that faithful and guiltless man who said, "The thing that I so greatly feared has come upon me," and she would grieve, as I learned later, for me and for us all. Or she would sit with me and write letters to our scattered family — my father at work in Alaska, my younger brother and sister with an aunt in Oregon. Of the letters that still exist from that time, all are full of sustenance, of words like "courage" and "honor." It should have sounded ludicrous to hear a seven-year-old speaking such words, but I uttered them without embarrassment, and my parents did not laugh.

For most of us, as people of crisis, it became clear that horror can last only a little while, and then it becomes commonplace. When one cannot be sure that there are many days left, each single day becomes as important as a year, and one does not waste an hour in wishing that that hour was longer, but simply fills it, like a smaller cup, as high as it will go without spilling over. Each moment, to the very ill, seems somehow slowed down and more dense with importance, in the same way that a poem is more compressed than a page of prose, each word carrying more weight than a sentence. And though it is true I learned gentleness, and the spareness of time, this was not the case for everyone there, and in fact there were some who never embraced their mortality.

I first saw Darcy by a window, looking down into her lap, fingering glass beads the same leafy yellow as her skin. She was wearing blue, and her dress shifted under her chin as she looked up, asking me was I a boy, and why was my hair so short. Behind us, our mothers started talking, exchanging histories, imagining a future, and Darcy and I listened, both grown accustomed by now to all this talk of ourselves. Darcy was ten, and she was here for her second attempted kidney transplant, this time with her father as donor. The first try had failed through fault, her mother said, of the surgeons, and Washington State's best lawyer would handle the suit if anything went wrong this time. This threat was spoken loudly and often as long as I knew Darcy, and it was many years before I realized that her parents were afraid, and that they displayed their fear in anger and those thousand sideways glances at their daughter.

As a playmate, Darcy was pleasant, and she and I made ourselves jewelry from glitter and paste, and dressed up as movie stars or as rich women in France. We played out the future as children do, as if it were sure to come and as if, when it did, we would be there. It was a game we all played on the ward, even those sure to die, and it was some time before I knew that to Darcy it was not a game, that she believed it all. We were holding school, and Nick was the teacher, and Darcy was answering that when she grew up she would own a plane, and would give us free rides on the weekends.

"What if," Nick said to her, "what if you die before then?"

NATALIE KUSZ   269

Darcy breathed in and out once, hard, and then she said, "I'm
telling my mother you said that." Then she stood and left the playroom, and did not come back that day. Later, her father complained to Nick's, called him foolish and uncaring, and demanded
that such a thing not happen again.

After that, Darcy came to play less often, and when she did, her
parents looked on, even on days when Janine took us outside to
look at the bay. Darcy grew fretful, and cried a good deal, and took
to feeling superior, even saying that my father didn't love me or he
wouldn't be in Alaska. When I forgave her, it was too late to say so,
because I was gone by then and didn't know how to tell her.

Darcy's absence was a loss, not just to her but to us other children as well. Just as we had no chance to comfort her, to offer our
hands when she was weak, we could not count on her during our
worst times, for she and her family suffered in that peculiar way
that admits no fellowship. I don't remember, if I ever knew, what
became of Darcy, because I came down with chicken pox and was
discharged so as not to jeopardize her transplant. I like to think
she must have lived, it was so important to her, and as I think this,
I hope she did survive, and that one day she grew, as we all did in
some way, to be thankful.

One of my smallest teachers during this time was a leukemia patient, just three years old, who lived down the hall. Because of his
treatments, Samuel had very little hair, and what he did have was
too blond to see. There were always, as I remember, deep moons
under his eyes, but somehow, even to us other children, he was
quite beautiful. His teeth were very tiny in his mouth, and he
chuckled rather than laughed out loud; when he cried, he only
hummed, drawing air in and out his nose, with his eyes squeezed
shut and tears forming in the cracks where there should have been
lashes. Most children's wards have a few favorite patients, and
Samuel was certainly among ours. Those few afternoons when his
parents left the hospital together, they spent twenty minutes, on
their return, visiting every room to find who had taken off with
their son. More often than not, he was strapped to a lap in a
wheelchair, his IV bottle dangling overhead like an antenna, getting motocross rides from an amputee.

Samuel possessed, even for his age, and in spite of the fact that he was so vulnerable, an implicit feeling of security, and it was partly this sense of trust that lent him that dignity I have found in few grown people. His mother, I remember, was usually the one to draw him away from our games when it was time for treatments, and, although he knew what was coming, he never ran from it; when he asked his mother, "Do I have to?" it was not a protest but a question, and when she replied that yes, this was necessary, he would accept her hand and leave the playroom on his feet.

I have heard debate over whether terminally ill children know they are going to die, and I can't, even after knowing Samuel, answer this question. We all, to some extent, knew what death was, simply because each of us had been friends with someone who was gone, and we realized that at some point many of us were likely to die; this likelihood was enough certainty for us, and made the question of time and date too insignificant to ask. I remember the last day I spent with Samuel, how we all invited him for a picnic on the lawn, though he could not eat much. He had had treatments that morning, which made him weak, made his smile very tired, but this was the same vulnerability we had always found charming, and I can't recall anything about that afternoon that seemed unusual. The rest of us could not know that Samuel would die before we woke up next morning, and certainly some things might have been different if we had; but I tend to think we would still have had the picnic, would still have rubbed dandelion petals into our skin, would still have taught Samuel to play slapjack. And, for his part, Samuel would, as he did every day, have bent down to my wrist and traced the moon-shaped scar behind my hand.

II. Attack

Our nearest neighbors through the trees were the Turners, two cabins of cousins whose sons went to my school. Both families had moved here, as we had, from California, escaping the city and everything frightening that lived there. One of the women, Ginny, had a grown son who was comatose now since he was hit on the freeway, and she had come to Alaska to get well from her own mental breakdown, and to keep herself as far away as she could from automobiles.

Brian and Jeff Turner were my best friends then, and we played with our dogs in the cousins' houses or in the wide snowy yard in between. On weekends or days off from school, my parents took us sledding and to the gravel pit with our skates. Sometimes, if the day was long enough, Brian and Jeff and I followed rabbit tracks through the woods, mapping all the new trails we could find, and my mother gave me orders about when to be home. Bears, she said, and we laughed, and said didn't she know they were asleep, and we could all climb trees anyway. We were not afraid, either, when Mom warned of dog packs. Dogs got cabin fever, too, she said, especially in the cold. They ran through the woods, whole crowds of them, looking for someone to gang up on.

That's okay, I told her. We carried pepper in our pockets in case of dogs: sprinkle it on their noses, we thought, and the whole pack would run away.

In December, the day before my birthday, when the light was dim and the days shorter than we had known before, Dad got a break at the union hall, a job at Prudhoe Bay that would save us just in time, before the stove oil ran out and groceries were gone. Mom convinced us children that he was off on a great adventure, that he would see foxes and icebergs, that we could write letters for Christmas and for New Year's, and afford new coats with feathers inside. In this last I was not much interested, because I had my favorite already — a red wool coat that reversed to fake leopard — but I would be glad if this meant we could get back from the pawn shop Dad's concertina, and his second violin, and mine, the half-size with a short bow, and the guitar and mandolin and rifles and pistol that had gone that way one by one. Whether I played each instrument or not, it had been good to have them around, smelling still of campfires and of songfests in the summer.

It was cold after Dad left, cold outside and cold in our house. Ice on the trailer windows grew thick and shaggy, and my sister and I melted handprints in it and licked off our palms. There had been no insulation when the add-on went up, so frost crawled the walls there, too, and Mom had us wear long johns and shoes unless we were in our beds. Brian and Jeff came for my birthday, helped me wish over seven candles, gave me a comb and a mirror. They were good kids, my mother said, polite and with good sense, and she told me that if I came in from school and she was not home, I should take Hobo with me and walk to their house. You're a worry-wart, Mommy, I said. I'm not a baby, you know.

On January 10, only Hobo met me at the bus stop. In the glare from the school bus headlights his blue eye shone brighter than his brown, and he watched until I took the last step to the ground before tackling me in the snow. Most days, Hobo hid in the shadow of the spruce until Mom took my book bag, then he erupted from the dark to charge up behind me, run through my legs and on out the front. It was his favorite trick. I usually lost my balance and ended up sitting in the road with my feet thrown wide out front and steaming dog tongue all over my face.

Hobo ran ahead, then back, brushing snow crystals and fur against my leg. I put a hand on my skin to warm it and dragged nylon ski pants over the road behind me. Mom said to have them along in case the bus broke down, but she knew I would not wear them, could not bear the plastic sounds they made between my thighs.

No light was on in our house.

If Mom had been home, squares of yellow would have shown through the spruce and lit the fog of my breath, turning it bright as I passed through. What light there was now came from the whiteness of snow and from the occasional embers drifting up from our stovepipe. I laid my lunchbox on the top step and pulled at the padlock, slapping a palm on the door and shouting. Hobo jumped away from the noise and ran off, losing himself in darkness and in the faint keening dog sounds going up from over near the Turners' house. I called, "Hobo. Come back here, boy," and took to the path toward Brian's, tossing my ski pants to the storage tent as I passed.

At the property line, Hobo caught up with me and growled, and I fingered his ear, looking where he pointed, seeing nothing ahead there but the high curve and long sides of a quonset hut, the work shed the Turners used also as a fence for one side of their yard. In the fall, Brian and Jeff and I had walked to the back of it, climbing over boxes and tools and parts of old furniture, and we had found in the corner a lemming's nest made from chewed bits of cardboard and paper, packed under the curve of the wall so that shadows hid it from plain sight. We all bent close to hear the scratching, and while Brian held a flashlight I took two sticks and parted the rubbish until we saw the black eyes of a mother lemming and pink naked bodies of five babies. The mother dashed deeper into the pile and we scooped the nesting back, careful not to touch the sucklings for fear that their mama would eat them if they carried scent from our fingers.

The dogs were loud now beyond the quonset, fierce in their howls and sounding many more than just three. Hobo crowded against my legs, and as I walked he hunched in front of me, making me stumble into a drift that filled my boots with snow. I called him a coward and said to quit it, but I held his neck against my thigh, turning the corner into the boys' yard and stopping on the edge. Brian's house was lit in all its windows, Jeff's was dark, and in the yard between them were dogs, new ones I had not seen before, each with its own house and tether. The dogs and their crying filled the yard, and when they saw me they grew wilder, hurling themselves to the ends of their chains, pulling their lips off their teeth. Hobo cowered and ran and I called him with my mouth, but my eyes did not move from in front of me.

There were seven. I knew they were huskies and meant to pull dogsleds, because earlier that winter Brian's grandfather had put on his glasses and shown us a book full of pictures. He had turned the pages with a wet thumb, speaking of trappers and racing people and the ways they taught these dogs to run. They don't feed them much, he said, or they get slow and lose their drive. This was how men traveled before they invented snowmobiles or gasoline.

There was no way to walk around the dogs to the lighted house. The snow had drifted and been piled around the yard in heaps taller than I was, and whatever aisle was left along the sides was narrow and pitted with chain marks where the animals had wandered, dragging their tethers behind. No, I thought, Jeff's house was closest and out of biting range, and someone could, after all, be sitting home in the dark.

My legs were cold. The snow in my boots had packed itself around my ankles and begun to melt, soaking my socks and the felt liners under my heels. I turned toward Jeff's house, chafing my thighs together hard to warm them, and I called cheerfully at the dogs to shut up. Oscar said that if you met a wild animal, even a bear, you had to remember it was more scared than you were.

Don't act afraid, he said, because they can smell fear. Just be loud — stomp your feet, wave your hands — and it will run away without even turning around. I yelled "Shut up" again as I climbed the steps to Jeff's front door, but even I could barely hear myself over the wailing. At the sides of my eyes, the huskies were pieces of smoke tumbling over one another in the dark.

The wood of the door was solid with cold, and even through deerskin mittens it bruised my hands like concrete. I cupped a hand to the window and looked in, but saw only black — black, and the reflection of a lamp in the other cabin behind me. I turned and took the three steps back to the ground; seven more and I was in the aisle between doghouses, stretching my chin far up above the frenzy, thinking hard on other things. This was how we walked in summertime, the boys and I, escaping from bad guys over logs thrown across ditches: step lightly and fast, steady on the hard parts of your soles, arms extended outward, palms down and toward the sound. That ditch, this aisle, was a river, a torrent full of silt that would fill your clothes and pull you down if you missed and fell in. I was halfway across. I pointed my chin toward the house and didn't look down.

On either side, dogs on chains hurled themselves upward, choking themselves to reach me, until their tethers jerked their throats back to earth. I'm not afraid of you, I whispered; this is dumb.

I stepped toward the end of the row and my arms began to drop slowly closer to my body. Inside the mittens, my thumbs were cold, as cold as my thighs, and I curled them in and out again. I was walking past the last dog and I felt brave, and I forgave him and bent to lay my mitten on his head. He surged forward on a chain much longer than I thought, leaping at my face, catching my hair in his mouth, shaking it in his teeth until the skin gave way with a jagged sound. My feet were too slow in my boots, and as I blundered backward they tangled in the chain, burning my legs on metal. I called out at Brian's window, expecting rescue, angry that it did not come, and I beat my arms in front of me, and the dog was back again, pulling me down.

A hole was worn into the snow, and I fit into it, arms and legs drawn up in front of me. The dog snatched and pulled at my mouth, eyes, hair; his breath clouded the air around us, but I did not feel its heat, or smell the blood sinking down between hairs of his muzzle. I watched my mitten come off in his teeth and sail upward, and it seemed unfair then and very sad that one hand should freeze all alone; I lifted the second mitten off and threw it away, then turned my face back again, overtaken suddenly by loneliness. A loud river ran in my ears, dragging me under.

My mother was singing. *Lu-lee, lu-lay, thou little tiny child,* the song to the Christ child, the words she had sung, smoothing my hair, all my life before bed. Over a noise like rushing water I called to her and heard her answer back, Don't worry, just sleep, the ambulance is on its way. I drifted back out and couldn't know then what she prayed, that I would sleep on without waking, that I would die before morning.

She had counted her minutes carefully that afternoon, sure that she would get to town and back, hauling water and mail, with ten minutes to spare before my bus came. But she had forgotten to count one leg of the trip, had skidded up the drive fifteen minutes late, pounding a fist on the horn, calling me home. On the steps, my lunchbox had grown cold enough to burn her hands. She got the water, the groceries, and my brother and sisters inside, gave orders that no one touch the wood stove or open the door, and she left down the trail to Brian's, whistling Hobo in from the trees.

I know from her journal that Mom had been edgy all week about the crazed dog sounds next door. Now the new huskies leaped at her and Hobo rumbled warning from his chest. Through her sunglasses, the dogs were just shapes, indistinct in window light. She tried the dark cabin first, knocking hard on the windows, then turned and moved down the path between doghouses, feeling her way with her feet, kicking out at open mouths. Dark lenses frosted over from her breath, and she moved toward the house and the lights on inside.

"She's not here." Brian's mother held the door open and air clouded inward in waves. Mom stammered out thoughts of bears, wolves, dogs. Ginny grabbed on her coat. She had heard a noise out back earlier — they should check there and then the woods.

No luck behind the cabin and no signs under the trees. Wearing sunglasses and without any flashlight, Mom barely saw even the snow. She circled back and met Ginny under the window light. Mom looked that way and asked about the dogs. "They seem so hungry," she said.

Ginny said, "No. Brian's folks just got them last week, but the

boys play with them all the time." All the same, she and Mom
scanned their eyes over the kennels, looking through and then
over their glasses. Nothing seemed different. "Are you sure she
isn't home?" Ginny said. "Maybe she took a different trail."

Maybe. Running back with Ginny behind her, Mom called my
name until her lungs frosted inside and every breath was a cough.
The three younger children were still the only ones at home, and
Mom handed them their treasure chests, telling them to play on
the bed until she found Natalie. Don't go outside, she said. I'll be
back right soon.

Back at the Turners', Ginny walked one way around the quonset
and Mom the other. Mom sucked air through a mitten, warming
her lungs. While Ginny climbed over deeper snow, she approached the sled dogs from a new angle. In the shadow of one, a
splash of red — the lining of my coat thrown open. "I've found
her," she shouted, and thought as she ran, Oh, thank God. Thank,
thank God.

The husky stopped its howling as Mom bent to drag me out
from the hole. Ginny caught up and seemed to choke. "Is she
alive?" she said.

Mom said, "I think so, but I don't know how." She saw one side
of my face gone, one red cavity with nerves hanging out, scraps of
dead leaves stuck on to the mess. The other eye might be gone,
too; it was hard to tell. Scalp had been torn away from my skull on
that side, and the gashes reached to my forehead, my lips, had left
my nose ripped wide at the nostrils. She tugged my body around
her chest and carried me inside.

III. Vital Signs

I had little knowledge of my mother's experience of the accident
until many months afterward, and even then I heard her story only
after I had told mine, after I had shown how clearly I remembered
the dogs, and their chains, and my own blood on the snow — and
had proven how little it bothered me to recall them. When I said I
had heard her voice, and named for her the songs she had sung to
me then, my mother searched my face, looking into me hard, saying, "I can't believe you remember." She had protected me all

along, she said, from her point of view, not thinking that I might have kept my own, and that mine must be harder to bear. But after she knew all this, Mom felt she owed me a history, and she told it to me then, simply and often, in words that I would draw on long after she was gone.

She said that inside the Turners' cabin, she laid me on Ginny's couch, careful not to jar the bleeding parts of me, expecting me to wake in an instant and scream. But when I did become conscious, it was only for moments, and I was not aware then of my wounds, or of the cabin's warmth, or even of pressure from the fingers of Brian's grandfather, who sat up close and stroked the frozen skin of my hands.

Ginny ordered Brian and Jeff to their room, telling them to stay there until she called them, and then she stood at Mom's shoulder, staring down and swaying on her legs.

Mom looked up through her glasses and said, "Is there a phone to call an ambulance?"

Ginny was shaking. "Only in the front house, kid, and it's locked," she said. "Kathy should be home in a minute, but I'll try to break in." She tugged at the door twice before it opened, and then she went out, leaving my mother to sing German lullabies beside my ear. *When morning comes,* the words ran, *if God wills it, you will wake up once more.* My mother sang the words and breathed on me, hoping I would dream again of summertime, all those bright nights when the music played on outside, when she drew the curtains and sang us to sleep in the trailer. Long years after the accident, when she felt healed again and stronger, Mom described her thoughts to me, and when she did she closed her eyes and sat back, saying, "You can't know how it was to keep singing, to watch air bubble up where a nose should have been, and to pray that each of those breaths was the last one." Many times that night she thought of Job, who also had lived in a spacious, golden land, who had prospered in that place, yet had cried in the end, "The thing that I so greatly feared has come upon me." The words became a chant inside her, filling her head and bringing on black time.

The wait for the ambulance was a long one, and my mother filled the time with her voice, sitting on her heels and singing. She fingered my hair and patted my hands and spoke low words when I called out. Brian's grandfather wept and warmed my fingers in his, and Mom wondered where were my mittens, and how were her other children back home.

Ginny came back and collapsed on a chair, and Kathy, her sister-in-law, hurried in through the door. Ginny began to choke, rocking forward over her knees, telling Kathy the story. Her voice stretched into a wail that rose and fell like music. "It's happening again," she said. "No matter where you go, its always there."

Kathy brought out aspirin, then turned and touched my mother's arm. She said that as soon as Ginny was quiet, she would leave her here and fetch my siblings from the trailer.

"Thank you," Mom told her. "I'll send someone for them as soon as I can." She looked at Ginny then, wishing she had something to give her, some way to make her know that she was not to blame here; but for now Mom felt that Ginny had spoken truth when she said that sorrow followed us everywhere, and there was little else she could add.

The ambulance came, and then everything was movement. I drifted awake for a moment as I was lifted to a stretcher and carried toward the door. I felt myself swaying in air, back and forth and back again. Brian's whisper carried over the other voices in the room, as if blown my way by strong wind. "Natalie's dying," he said; then his words were lost among other sounds, and I faded out again. A month later, when our first-grade class sent me a box full of valentines, Brian's was smaller than the rest, a thick, white heart folded in two. Inside it read, "I love you, Nataly. Pleas dont die." When I saw him again, his eyes seemed very big, and I don't remember that he ever spoke to me anymore.

It was dark inside the ambulance, and seemed even darker to my mother, squinting through fog on her sunglasses. She badgered the medic, begging him to give me a shot for pain. Any minute I would wake up, she said, and I would start to scream. The man kept working, taking my pulse, writing it down, and while he did, he soothed my mother in low tones, explaining to her about physical shock, about the way the mind estranges itself from the body and stands, unblinking and detached, on the outside. "If she does wake up," he said, "she'll feel nothing. She won't even feel afraid." When Mom wrote this in her journal, her voice was filled with wonder, and she asked what greater gift there could be.

At the hospital there were phone calls to be made, and Mom placed them from outside the emergency room. First she called Dick and Esther Conger, two of the only summertime friends who had stayed here over winter. We had met this family on the way up the Alcan, had been attracted to their made-over school bus with its sign, "Destination: Adventure," and to the Alaskan license plates bolted to each bumper. Sometime during the drive up, or during the summer when we shared the same campfires, the children of our families had become interchangeable; Toni and Barry were in the same age group as we were, and discipline and praise were shared equally among us all. It was never shocking to wake up in the morning and find Toni and Barry in one of our beds; we just assumed that the person who belonged there was over sleeping in their bus. Now, as my mother explained the accident to Dick, our friend began to cry, saying, "Oh, Verna. Oh, no," and Esther's voice in the background asked, "What's happened? Let me talk to her." Mom asked the Congers to drive out for my brother and sisters, to watch them until my father came.

Leaning her head to the wall, Mom telephoned a message to the North Slope. She spoke to Dad's boss there, explaining only that "our daughter has been hurt." Just now, she thought, she couldn't tell the whole story again, and besides, the worst "hurt" my father would imagine could not be this bad. The crew boss said a big snowstorm was coming in, but they would try to fly my father out beforehand; if not, they would get him to the radio phone and have him call down. A nurse walked up then and touched Mom's shoulder, saying, "Your daughter is awake, and she's asking for you." A moment before, Mom had been crying, pressing a fist to her teeth, but now she closed up her eyes like a faucet and walked after the nurse, pulling up her chin and breathing deeply in her chest. She had trembled so that she could hardly wipe her glasses, but when she moved through the door and saw the white lights and me lying flat on a table, she was suddenly calm, and the skin grew warmer on her face.

Mom positioned herself in front of my one eye, hoping as she stood there that she wasn't shaking visibly, that her face was not obviously tense. She need not have bothered; as I lay staring right to where my eye veered off, the room was smoky gray, and I was conscious only of a vicious thirst that roughened the edges of my tongue, made them stick to my teeth. I was allowed no water, had become fretful, and when my mother spoke to me, I complained that the rag in my mouth had not been damp enough, and that these people meant to cut my favorite coat off of me. I have to think now that my mother acted courageously, keeping her face smooth, listening to me chatter about school, about the message I had brought from my teacher, that they would skip me to the second grade on Monday. Mom's answers were light, almost vague, and before she left the pre-op room, she told me to listen to the nurses, to let them do all they needed to; they were trying to help me, she said. A little later, after I was wheeled into surgery, a nurse handed her the things they had saved: my black boots and the Alice in Wonderland watch Mom had given me for Christmas.

My mother made more phone calls, to churches in town and to ones in California that we'd left behind, telling the story over again, asking these people to pray. Old friends took on her grief, asking did she need money, telling her to call again when she knew more. These people knew, as my mother did, that money was not so much the question now, but it was something they could offer, and so they did. And for months and years after this they would send cards and letters and candy and flowers and toys, making themselves as present with us as they could. For now, on this first night, they grieved with my mother, and they said to go lie down if she could, they would take over the phones. And each of these people made another call, and another, until, as my mother walked back to the waiting room, she knew she was lifted up by every friend we had ever made.

The Turners had arrived, and for a little while they all sat along the waiting room walls, stuffing fists into their pockets and closing their eyes. None of them wanted to talk about the accident, or to wonder about the progress in surgery, and when my mother said to Kathy, "I just talked to some people in California who would never *believe* the way we live here," her words seemed terribly funny, and started the whole room laughing. It wasn't so much, she said later, that they were forgetting why they were there; in fact, they remembered very well — so well that, compared to that fact, everything else was hilarious. And they could not possibly have continued for as long as they had been, she said, pressing their backs to the walls and waiting. So for hours after Mom's joke, and far into the night, the adults invented names for our kind — "the outhouse set," "the bush league" — and they contributed stories about life in Alaska that would shock most of the people Outside. They joked about Styrofoam outhouse seats — the only kind that did not promote frostbite — about catalogues that no one could afford to buy from, but whose pages served a greater purpose, about the tremendous hardship of washing dishes from melted snow and then tossing the gray water out the door. From time to time, Ginny got up from her seat to walk alone in the hall, but when she came back in she was ready again to laugh.

My father arrived about midnight, dressed in a week's growth of beard and in an army surplus parka and flight pants. Mom met him in the hall and stood looking up; Dad dropped his satchel to the floor, panting, and he watched my mother's face, the eyes behind her glasses. He spoke first, said his was the last plane out in a heavy snowstorm. Then: "How did it happen," he said. "Did she fall out the door?"

My mother waited a beat and looked at him "It wasn't a car accident, Julius," she said. She started telling the story again, and my father looked down then at the blood crusted on her sweater, and he closed his eyes and leaned into the wall. My mother told him, "You can't appreciate how I feel, because you haven't seen her face. But I wish that when you pray you'd ask for her to die soon."

Dad opened his eyes. "That must seem like the best thing to ask," he said. "But we don't make decisions like that on our own. We never have, and we can't start now."

Sometime after two A.M., my three surgeons stepped in. My mother said later that, had they not still worn their surgical greens, she would not have recognized them; during the night she had forgotten their faces.

The men sagged inside their clothes, three sets of shoulders slumped forward under cloth. I was still alive, they said, but only barely, and probably not for long. I had sustained over one hundred lacerations from the shoulders up, and had lost my left cheekbone along with my eye. They'd saved what tissue they could, filling the bulk of the cavity with packings, and what bone fragments they had found were now wired together on the chance that some of them might live.

My father groped for a positive word. "At least she doesn't have brain damage. I heard she was lucid before surgery."

Dr. Butler brushed the surgical cap from his head and held it, twisting it in his hands. His eyes were red as he looked up, explaining as kindly as it seemed he could. A dog's mouth, he said, was filthy, filthier than sewage, and all of that impurity had passed into my body. They had spent four hours just cleaning out the wounds, pulling out dirt and old berry leaves and dog feces. Even with heavy antibiotics, I would likely have massive infections, and they would probably spread into my brain. His voice turned hoarse and he looked across at Dr. Earp, asking the man to continue.

Dr. Earp rubbed hard at the back of his head and spoke softly, working his neck. For now, Dr. Earp said, they had been able to reconstruct the eyelids; that would make the biggest visible difference.

On my parents' first hourly visit to Intensive Care, Mom stopped at the door and put her hand on my father's chest. "No matter how she looks," she said, "don't react. She'll be able to tell what you're thinking."

The nurse at the desk sat under a shaded lamp, the only real light in the room. She stood and whispered that mine was the first bed to the left. "She wakes up for a minute or so at a time," she said. "She's been asking for you."

"First one on the left," my father said after her, a little too loud for that place, and from somewhere inside a great rushing river I heard him and called out. At my bed, Mom watched him as he stood looking down, and when the lines in his face became deeper, she turned from him, pinching his sleeve with her fingers. She walked closer to me and held the bedrail.

IV. The Fear

It had to happen eventually, that I found a mirror and looked in. For the first days after my accident, I had stayed mostly in bed, leaning my bandages back on the pillow and peeling frostbite blisters from my hands. The new skin was pink, and much thinner than the old, as sensitive to touch as the nail beds I uncovered by chewing down to them. I had taken to running two fingers over stitches standing up like razor stubble on my face, then over the cotton that covered the right side and the rest of my head. The whole surgical team came in daily to lift me into a chair and unwind the gauze, releasing into the room a smell like old caves full of bones. And all this time I had never seen myself, never asked what was under there, in the place where my eye belonged.

I had asked my mother once if I would again see out of that eye. It was an hour after my dressings had been changed, and the smell of hot ooze still hovered in my room. Mom stood up and adjusted my bedrail. "Do you want your feet a little higher?" she said. "I can crank them up if you like."

I said, "Mommy, my eye. Will I be able to see from it?"

"Hang on," she said. "I need to use the little girls' room." She started to the door and I screamed after her, "Mommy, you're not answering me." But she was gone, and after that I did not ask.

Later, when the light was out, I lay back and looked far right, then left, concentrating hard, trying to feel the bandaged eye move. I thought I could feel it, rolling up and then down, ceiling to floor, matching its moves with my other eye. Even after I was grown, I could swear that I felt it blink when I pressed my two lids together.

Men from down the hall visited me during the day, rolling in on wheelchairs or walking beside their IV racks. They all wore two sets of pajamas, one wrong way forward so their backsides were covered. The hospital floor was old, its tiles starting to bubble, and the wheels on my friends' IV racks made rumbling sounds as they passed over. If a nurse passed by the door and looked in, the men waved her away, saying, "It's all right, dear. I'm visiting my granddaughter." For a kiss they gave me a sucker and a story about bears, or they carried me to a wheelchair and took me around to visit. In this way, I passed from room to room, brushing at the green curtains between beds, pouring water into plastic glasses, gathering hugs and learning to shake hands in the "cool" way. I signed plaster casts in big red letters, and I visited the baby room, pressing my chin to the glass.

On a day when I felt at my smallest and was in my bed still sleeping, one of my favorite men friends checked out, leaving on my nightstand a gift and a note that said he would miss me. The gift was a music box in pink satin, with a ballerina inside who pirouetted on her toes when I wound the key. And behind her inside the lid, a triangular looking glass not much bigger than she was.

My mother came in behind me as I was staring into the mirror, holding it first from one angle, then from another, and she stood by the bed for a moment, saying nothing. When I turned, she was looking at me with her shoulders forward, and she seemed to be waiting.

"My eye is gone, isn't it?" I said.

She kept looking at me. She said, "Yes it is."

I turned again and lifted the box to my face. "I thought so," I said. "Those dogs were pretty mean."

I didn't understand, or was too small to know, what my mother thought she was protecting me from. It must be something very bad, I thought, for her to avoid every question I asked her. "Mommy," I said once, "I don't *feel* like I'm going to die."

She looked up from her book and the light shone off her glasses. She said, "Oh, no. You're certainly not going to do anything like that."

"Then will I be blind?"

"Well," she said. "You can see now, can't you?" And when I pressed her with more questions, she looked toward the door and said, "Shh. Here comes your lunch tray."

It all made me wonder if my wounds were much worse than everyone said — and of course they were, but there were long years of surgery still ahead, and no one wanted me to feel afraid. I was angry, too — as angry as a seven-year-old can be — that Mom patted my cheek with her palm and said she'd be taking my malemute to the pound before I came home. I stared at her then with my head up and sputtered out a peevish tirade, telling her I didn't hate all dogs, or even most dogs, but just the ones who bit me. It didn't occur to me until my own daughter was seven, the same age I was when I was hurt, that Mom might have been sending my dog away for her own sake.

V. Small Purchase

I have bought a one-eyed fish. As he drifts around the tank near my desk, his skin ripples silver like well-pressed silk, and he moves under the light and hovers with his one bronze eye turned toward me, waiting to be fed. His body is smooth and flat, like a silver dollar but twice the size, and his fins are mottled gold. He is a relative of the piranha, a meat eater with a bold round mouth, but even when the smaller fish challenge him, swishing their tails at his eye, he leaves them alone and swims off. He has not eaten one of them.

I call him Max, because my sister said I should. She did not remind me, when I brought him home, that I had wanted no pets, nothing with a life span shorter than my own, nothing that would die or have to be butchered as soon as I had given it a name. She just looked up with her face very serious as if she knew well how one could become attached to a fish, and she said to me, Max. Yes, that should be his name.

I had told us both, when I bought the aquarium, that fish were low-maintenance animals, without personalities and incapable of friendliness, and if one of them died you just flushed it away and got another. And besides, I said, I needed a fish tank. I had begun to feel stale, inert. I needed the sounds of moving water in my house, and I needed, too, something alive and interesting to stare at when I stopped typing to think of a new sentence.

Last summer, when I was tired and the writing was going badly, I got superstitious about the sea and thought that the lurch and pull of waves would freshen my ears and bring on clean thoughts. So I packed some books and a portable typewriter, drove to Homer on the coast, and rented a cabin near the beach. Something about the place, or its fishy air, or my aloneness in the middle of it worked somehow, and I breathed bigger there in my chest and wrote more clearly on the page. I had forgotten about tides and about the kelp and dried crabs that came in with them, and every morning I shivered into a sweater, put combs in my hair, and walked out to wade and to fill my pockets with what I found. I liked it best when the wind was blowing and the sky was gray, and the sounds of seagulls and my own breathing were carried out with the water.

Kelp pods washed up around my feet, and I stomped on them with tennis shoes to find what was inside. I collected driftwood, and urchins, and tiny pink clam shells dropped by gulls, thin enough to see through and smaller than a thumbnail. When the tide had gone far out, I climbed the bluff back to my cabin and sat writing in front of the window, eating cheese on bread and drinking orange spritzers or tea. The walls and windows there had space in between, and they let in shreds of wind and the arguing of birds and the metal smell of seaweed drying out on the beach. When the tide started back in, I took pen and notebook and sat on a great barnacled rock, letting water creep up and surround me, then jumping to shore just in time. An hour later, the rock would be covered, three feet or more under the gray, and I would know where it lay only because of the froth and swirl of whirlpools just above it.

When I came home I threw my bags on the bed and unfastened them, and a thousand aromas opened up then into my face, drifting out from the folds of my clothes, the seams in my shoes, the pages of my notebook. I had carried them back with me, the smells of wet sand and fish fins, of eagle feathers floating in surf, of candle wax burned at midnight and filled with the empty bodies of moths. I had grieved on the drive home for that place I was leaving, and for the cold wind of that beach, and I had decided that somehow water should move in my house, should rush and bubble in my ears, should bring in the sound of the sea, and the wind and dark currents that move it.

So I bought an aquarium, and fish to go in it, and a water pump strong enough to tumble the surface as it worked. I bought plants for the tank, and waved their smell into the room, and when I thought I was finished I made one more trip to a pet store, just to see what they had.

The shop was a small one, in an old wooden building with low ceilings, and the fish room in back was dark and smelled submarine — humid and slippery and full of live things. All light in the place came from the fish tanks themselves, and the plants inside them absorbed the glow and turned it green, casting it outward to move in shadowed patterns on my skin. When I closed my eyes, the sound was of rivers running out to the coast to be carried away mixed with salt. And the fish inside waved their fins and wandered between the rocks, opening and closing their mouths.

I glanced, but didn't look hard at the larger fish, because I had found already that they were always very expensive. I browsed instead through tetras and guppies, gouramis and cichlids, trying to be satisfied with the small ones, because after all it was just the water and its motion that I really wanted. So when I saw the wide silver fish and a sign that said "$10," I assumed it was a mistake but decided to ask about it while I ordered some neons dipped out. With my neck bent forward, I watched as fifty neons swam fast away from the net that would always catch them anyway. Was that big fish back there really only ten? I said.

The clerk said, "You mean the Matinnis with one eye. He's such a mellow guy."

I swung my head to look at her. One eye?

The woman stared at my face for a moment and opened her mouth. Her cheeks grew pinker, but when she answered me, her voice stayed even. She said, "Yes, his former owners thought he was a piranha and put him in the tank with some. They ate out one eye before anyone could get him back up."

"They go for the eyes so their lunch will quit looking at them," I said. I told the woman I would take the Matinnis. I thought we were a match, I said.

And I was right. As absurd as I felt about my affinity with a one-eyed fish, I found myself watching him for the ways he was like me, and I did find many. Max had already learned, by the time I got him, to hold his body in the water so that whatever he was interested in lay always on the same side of him as his eye. In the same way that I situate myself in movie theaters so that my best friend sits on my right side, Max turns his eye toward the wall of his tank, watching for my arm to move toward the food box. When I drop a worm cube down to him, he shifts his eye up to look at it and then swims at it from the side so he never loses it from vision. If the smaller fish fight, or behave defiantly around him, he turns his dead eye against them and flicks himself away to a far corner of the tank.

I don't know if it is normal to befriend a fish. I think probably not. I do know that as I sit by Max's tank and write, I stop sometimes and look up, and I think then that he looks terribly dashing, swimming around with his bad eye outward, unafraid that something might attack him from his blind side. I buy him special shrimp pellets, and I feed them to him one at a time, careful always to drop them past his good eye. My friends like to feed him, too, and I teach them how, warning them to drop his food where he can see it. Now one of my friends wants to introduce me to his neighbor's one-eyed dog, and another wishes she still had her one-eyed zebra finch so she could give it to me.

That's just what I need, I think — a houseful of blind-sided pets. We could sit around together and play wink-um, wondering was that a wink or just a lid shut down over a dry eyeball. We could fight about who got to sit on whose good side, or we could make jokes about how it takes two of us to look both ways before crossing the street. I laugh, but still I intend to meet the one-eyed dog, to see if he reminds me of Max — or of me. I wonder if he holds himself differently from other dogs, if when he hears a voice he turns his whole body to look.

And I wonder about myself, about what has changed in the world. At first, I wanted fish only for the water they lived in, for the movement it would bring to my house, the dust it would sweep from my brain. I thought of fish as "safe" pets, too boring to demand much attention, soulless by nature and indistinguishable from their peers. Maybe this is true for most of them. But I know that when the smaller fish chase after Max, or push him away from the food, I find myself fiercely angry. I take a vicious pleasure in dropping down shrimp pellets too big and too hard for the small ones to eat, and I find pleasure, too, in the way Max gobbles the food, working it to bits in his mouth. When he is finished, he turns a dead eye to the others and swims away, seeking things more interesting to look at.

Reflections and Responses

1. Consider the narrative structure of Kusz's essay. How does each part fit into the chronology of events? Why do you think Kusz decided not to follow a strict chronological pattern?

2. What kinds of things does seven-year-old Natalie learn in the hospital? Can you find any connections between what she learned then and what she appears to know now as a writer? Can you detect any connections, that is, between her experiences and her impulse to write?

3. What is the significance of part five, "Small Purchase," to Kusz's theme? Why does she want the fish? How is the fish connected with the act of writing?

LEONARD KRIEGEL

Falling into Life

Acts of survival sometimes require spiritual as well as physical therapy. In "Falling into Life" a noted essayist, permanently crippled by polio from the age of twelve, recalls the rigors of his rehabilitation and how they taught him lifelong lessons for survival. The most important thing he had to learn was the one lesson he dreaded most: how to fall down. No matter how hard he tried, he wasn't able to let go. At last his therapist convinced him that "learning to fall was learning the most essential of American lessons: how to turn incapacity into capacity." Now in middle age, having long ago mastered the art of "falling into life," he realizes he must learn new survival skills along with another kind of falling.

Kriegel lives and writes in New York City. The author of seven books, the most recent of which is a collection of personal essays, Falling into Life, *he has been the recipient of both Guggenheim and Rockefeller fellowships as well as a number of other awards. His essays and stories have appeared in a wide variety of literary quarterlies and national periodicals, including* Harper's, The New York Times Magazine, The American Scholar, Partisan Review, *and* The Sewanee Review. *His books include a memoir,* Notes for the Two-Dollar Window *(1976), and a novel,* Quitting Time *(1982). "Falling Into Life" originally appeared in* The American Scholar *(1988) and was selected by Geoffrey Wolff for* The Best American Essays 1989.

It is not the actual death a man is doomed to die but the deaths his imagination anticipates that claim attention as one grows older. We are constantly being reminded that the prospect of death forcefully concentrates the mind. While that may be so, it is not a prospect that does very much else for the imagination — other than to make one aware of its limitations and imbalances.

Over the past five years, as I have moved into the solidity of middle age, my own most formidable imaginative limitation has turned out to be a surprising need for symmetry. I am possessed by a peculiar passion: I want to believe that my life has been balanced out. And because I once had to learn to fall in order to keep that life mine, I now seem to have convinced myself that I must also learn to fall into death.

Falling into life wasn't easy, and I suspect that is why I hunger for such awkward symmetry today. Having lost the use of my legs during the polio epidemic that swept across the eastern United States during the summer of 1944, I was soon immersed in a process of rehabilitation that was, at least when looked at in retrospect, as much spiritual as physical.

That was a full decade before the discovery of the Salk vaccine ended polio's reign as the disease most dreaded by America's parents and their children. Treatment of the disease had been standardized by 1944: following the initial onslaught of the virus, patients were kept in isolation for a period of ten days to two weeks. Following that, orthodox medical opinion was content to subject patients to as much heat as they could stand. Stiff paralyzed limbs were swathed in heated, coarse woolen towels known as "hot packs." (The towels were that same greenish brown as blankets issued to American GIs, and they reinforced a boy's sense of being at war.) As soon as the hot packs had baked enough pain and stiffness out of a patient's body so that he could be moved on and off a stretcher, the treatment was ended, and the patient faced a series of daily immersions in a heated pool.

I would ultimately spend two full years at the appropriately named New York State Reconstruction Home in West Haverstraw. But what I remember most vividly about the first three months of my stay there was being submerged in a hot pool six times a day, for periods of between fifteen and twenty minutes. I would lie on a stainless steel slab, my face alone out of water, while the wet heat rolled against my dead legs and the physical therapist was at my side working at a series of manipulations intended to bring my useless muscles back to health.

Each immersion was a baptism by fire in the water. While my

mind pitched and reeled with memories of the "normal" boy I had been a few weeks earlier, I would close my eyes and focus not, as my therapist urged, on bringing dead legs back to life but on my strange fall from the childhood grace of the physical. Like all eleven-year-old boys, I had spent a good deal of time thinking about my body. Before the attack of the virus, however, I thought about it only in connection with my own lunge toward adolescence. Never before had my body seemed an object in itself. Now it was. And like the twenty-one other boys in the ward — all of us between the ages of nine and twelve — I sensed I would never move beyond the fall from grace, even as I played with memories of the way I once had been.

Each time I was removed from the hot water and placed on a stretcher by the side of the pool, there to await the next immersion, I was fed salt tablets. These were simply intended to make up for the sweat we lost, but salt tablets seemed to me the cruelest confirmation of my new status as spiritual debtor. Even today, more than four decades later, I still shiver at the mere thought of those salt tablets. Sometimes the hospital orderly would literally have to pry my mouth open to force me to swallow them. I dreaded the nausea the taste of salt inspired in me. Each time I was resubmerged in the hot pool, I would grit my teeth — not from the flush of heat sweeping over my body but from the thought of what I would have to face when I would again be taken out of the water. To be an eater of salt was far more humiliating than to endure pain. Nor was I alone in feeling this way. After lights-out had quieted the ward, we boys would furtively whisper from cubicle to cubicle of how we dreaded being forced to swallow salt tablets. It was that, rather than the pain we endured, that anchored our sense of loss and dread.

Any recovery of muscle use in a polio patient usually took place within three months of the disease's onset. We all knew that. But as time passed, every boy in the ward learned to recite stories of those who, like Lazarus, had witnessed their own bodily resurrection. Having fallen from physical grace, we also chose to fall away from the reality in front of us. Our therapists were skilled and dedicated, but they weren't wonder-working saints. Paralyzed legs and arms rarely responded to their manipulations. We could not admit to ourselves, or to them, that we were permanently crippled. But each of us knew without knowing that his future was tied to the body that floated on the stainless steel slab.

We sweated out the hot pool and we choked on the salt tablets, and through it all we looked forward to the promise of rehabilitation. For, once the stiffness and pain had been baked and boiled out of us, we would no longer be eaters of salt. We would not be what we once had been, but at least we would be candidates for re-entry into the world, admittedly made over to face its demands encased in leather and steel.

I suppose we might have been told that our fall from grace was permanent. But I am still grateful that no one — neither doctors nor nurses nor therapists, not even that sadistic orderly, himself a former polio patient, who limped through our lives and through our pain like some vengeful presence — told me that my chances of regaining the use of my legs were nonexistent. Like every other boy in the ward, I organized my needs around whatever illusions were available. And the illusion I needed above any other was that one morning I would simply wake up and rediscover the "normal" boy of memory, once again playing baseball in French Charley's Field in Bronx Park rather than roaming the fields of his own imagination. At the age of eleven, I needed to weather reality, not face it. And to this very day, I silently thank those who were concerned enough about me, or indifferent enough to my fate, not to tell me what they knew.

Like most boys, sick or well, I was an adaptable creature — and rehabilitation demanded adaptability. The fall from bodily grace transformed each of us into acolytes of the possible, pragmatic Americans for whom survival was method and strategy. We would learn, during our days in the New York State Reconstruction Home, to confront the world that was. We would learn to survive the way we were, with whatever the virus had left intact.

I had fallen away from the body's prowess, but I was being led toward a life measured by different standards. Even as I fantasized about the past, it disappeared. Rehabilitation, I was to learn, was ahistorical, a future devoid of any significant claim on the past. Rehabilitation was a thief's primer of compensation and deception: its purpose was to teach one how to steal a touch of the normal from an existence that would be striking in its abnormality.

When I think back to those two years in the ward, the boy who made his rehabilitation most memorable was Joey Tomashevski. Joey was the son of an upstate dairy farmer, a Polish immigrant who had come to America before the Depression and whose English was even poorer than the English of my own shtetl-bred father. The virus had left both of Joey's arms so lifeless and atrophied that I could circle where his bicep should have been with pinky and thumb and still stick the forefinger of my own hand through. And yet, Joey assumed that he would make do with whatever had been left him. He accepted without question the task of making his toes and feet over into fingers and hands. With lifeless arms encased in a canvas sling that looked like the breadbasket a European peasant might carry to market, Joey would sit up in bed and demonstrate how he could maneuver fork and spoon with his toes.

I would never have dreamed of placing such confidence in my fingers, let alone my toes. I found, as most of the other boys in the ward did, Joey's unabashed pride in the flexibility and control with which he could maneuver a forkful of mashed potatoes into his mouth a continuous indictment of my sense of the world's natural order. We boys with dead legs would gather round his bed in our wheelchairs and silently watch Joey display his dexterity with a vanity so open and naked that it seemed an invitation to being struck down yet again. But Joey's was a vanity already tested by experience. For he was more than willing to accept whatever challenges the virus threw his way. For the sake of demonstrating his skill to us, he kicked a basketball from the auditorium stage through the hoop attached to a balcony some fifty feet away. When one of our number derisively called him lucky, he proceeded to kick five of seven more balls through that same hoop.

I suspect that Joey's pride in his ability to compensate for what had been taken away from him irritated me, because I knew that, before I could pursue my own rehabilitation with such singular passion, I had to surrender myself to what was being demanded of me. And that meant I had to learn to fall. It meant that I had to learn, as Joey Tomashevski had already learned, how to transform absence into opportunity. Even though I still lacked Joey's instinctive willingness to live with the legacy of the virus, I found myself being overhauled, re-created in much the same way as a car engine is rebuilt. Nine months after I arrived in the ward, a few weeks before my twelfth birthday, I was fitted for double long-legged braces bound together by a steel pelvic band circling my waist. Lifeless or not, my legs were precisely measured, the steel carefully molded to form, screws and locks and leather joined to one another for my customized benefit alone. It was technology that would hold me up — another offering on the altar of compensation. "You get what you give," said Jackie Lyons, my closest friend in the ward. For he, too, was now a novitiate of the possible. He, too, now had to learn how to choose the road back.

Falling into life was not a metaphor; it was real, a process learned only through doing, the way a baby learns to crawl, to stand, and then to walk. After the steel bands around calves and thighs and pelvis had been covered over by the rich-smelling leather, after the braces had been precisely fitted to allow my fear-ridden imagination the surety of their holding presence, I was pulled to my feet. For the first time in ten months, I stood. Two middle-aged craftsmen, the hospital bracemakers who worked in a machine shop deep in the basement, held me in place as my therapist wedged two wooden crutches beneath my shoulders.

They stepped back, first making certain that my grip on the crutches was firm. Filled with pride in their technological prowess, the three of them stood in front of me, admiring their skill. Had I been created in the laboratory of Mary Shelley's Dr. Frankenstein, I could not have felt myself any more of the creature of scientific pride. I stood on the braces, crutches beneath my shoulders slanting outward like twin towers of Pisa. I flushed, swallowed hard, struggled to keep from crying, struggled not to be overwhelmed by my fear of falling.

My future had arrived. The leather had been fitted, the screws had been turned to the precise millimeter, the locks at the knees and the bushings at the ankles had been properly tested and retested. That very afternoon I was taken for the first time to a cavernous room filled with barbells and Indian clubs and crutches and walkers. I would spend an hour each day there for the next six months. In the rehab room, I would learn how to mount two large wooden steps made to the exact measure of a New York City bus's. I would swing on parallel bars from one side to the other, my arms learning how they would have to hurl me through the world. I balanced Indian clubs like a circus juggler because my therapist in-

sisted it would help my coordination. And I was expected to learn
to fall.

I was a dutiful patient. I did as I was told because I could see no
advantage to doing anything else. I hungered for the approval of
those in authority — doctors, nurses, therapists, the two bracemakers. Again and again, my therapist demonstrated how I was to
throw my legs from the hip. Again and again, I did as I was told.
Grabbing the banister with my left hand, I threw my leg from the
hip while pushing off my right crutch. Like some baby elephant
(despite the sweat lost in the heated pool, the months of inactivity
in bed had fattened me up considerably), I dangled from side to
side on the parallel bars. Grunting with effort, I did everything demanded of me. I did it with an unabashed eagerness to please
those who had power over my life. I wanted to put myself at risk. I
wanted to do whatever was supposed to be "good" for me. I believed as absolutely as I have ever believed in anything that rehabilitation would finally placate the hunger of the virus.

But when my therapist commanded me to fall, I cringed. For the
prospect of falling terrified me. Every afternoon, as I worked
through my prescribed activities, I prayed that I would be able to
fall when the session ended. Falling was the most essential "good"
of all the "goods" held out for my consideration by my therapist. I
believed that. I believed it so intensely that the belief itself was
painful. Everything else asked of me was given — and given gladly.
I mounted the bus stairs, pushed across the parallel bars until my
arms ached with the effort, allowed the medicine ball to pummel
me, flailed away at the empty air with my fists because my therapist
wanted me to rid myself of the tension within. The slightest sign of
approval from those in authority was enough to make me puff with
pleasure. Other boys in the ward might not have taken rehabilitation seriously, but I was an eager servant cringing before the
promise of approval.

Only I couldn't fall. As each session ended, I would be led to the
mats that took up a full third of the huge room. "It's time," the
therapist would say. Dutifully, I would follow her, step after step.
Just as dutifully, I would stand on the edge of those two-inch-thick
mats, staring down at them until I could feel my body quiver. "All
you have to do is let go," my therapist assured me. "The other boys
do it. Just let go and fall."

But the prospect of letting go was precisely what terrified me. That the other boys in the ward had no trouble in falling added to my shame and terror. I didn't need my therapist to tell me the two-inch-thick mats would keep me from hurting myself. I knew there was virtually no chance of injury when I fell, but that knowledge simply made me more ashamed of a cowardice that was as monumental as it was unexplainable. Had it been able to rid me of my sense of my own cowardice, I would happily have settled for bodily harm. But I was being asked to surrender myself to the emptiness of space, to let go and crash down to the mats below, to feel myself suspended in air when nothing stood between me and the vacuum of the world. *That* was the prospect that overwhelmed me. *That* was what left me sweating with rage and humiliation. The contempt I felt was for my own weakness.

I tried to justify what I sensed could never be justified. Why should I be expected to throw myself into emptiness? Was this sullen terror the price of compensation, the badge of normality? Maybe my refusal to fall embodied some deeper thrust than I could then understand. Maybe I had unconsciously seized upon some fundamental resistance to the forces that threatened to overwhelm me. What did it matter that the ground was covered by the thick mats? The tremors I feared were in my heart and soul.

Shame plagued me — and shame is the older brother to disease. Flushing with shame, I would stare down at the mats. I could feel myself wanting to cry out. But I shriveled at the thought of calling more attention to my cowardice. I would finally hear myself whisper, "I'm sorry. But I can't. I can't let go."

Formless emptiness. A rush of air through which I would plummet toward obliteration. As my "normal" past grew more and more distant, I reached for it more and more desperately, recalling it like some movie whose plot has long since been forgotten but whose scenes continue to comfort through images disconnected from anything but themselves. I remembered that there had been a time when the prospect of falling evoked not terror but joy: football games on the rain-softened autumn turf of Mosholu Parkway, belly-flopping on an American Flyer down its snow-covered slopes in winter, rolling with a pack of friends down one of the steep hills in Bronx Park. Free falls from the past, testifying not to a loss of the self but to an absence of barriers.

My therapist pleaded, ridiculed, cajoled, threatened, bullied. I was sighed over and railed at. But I couldn't let go and fall. I couldn't sell my terror off so cheaply. Ashamed as I was, I wouldn't allow myself to be bullied out of terror.

A month passed — a month of struggle between me and my therapist. Daily excursions to the rehab room, daily practice runs through the future that was awaiting me. The daily humiliation of discovering that one's own fear had been transformed into a public issue, a subject of discussion among the other boys in the ward, seemed unending.

And then, terror simply evaporated. It was as if I had served enough time in that prison. I was ready to move on. One Tuesday afternoon, as my session ended, the therapist walked resignedly alongside me toward the mats. "All right, Leonard. It's time again. All you have to do is let go and fall." Again, I stood above the mats. Only this time, it was as if something beyond my control or understanding had decided to let my body's fall from grace take me down for good. I was not seized by the usual paroxysm of fear. I didn't feel myself break out in a terrified sweat. It was over.

I don't mean that I suddenly felt myself spring into courage. That wasn't what happened at all. The truth was I had simply been worn down into letting go, like a boxer in whose eyes one recognizes not the flicker of defeat — that issue never having been in doubt — but the acceptance of defeat. Letting go no longer held my imagination captive. I found myself quite suddenly faced with a necessary fall — a fall into life.

So it was that I stood above the mat and heard myself sigh and then felt myself let go, dropping through the quiet air, crutches slipping off to the sides. What I didn't feel this time was the threat of my body slipping into emptiness, so mummified by the terror before it that the touch of air pre-empted even death. I dropped. I did not crash. I dropped. I did not collapse. I dropped. I did not plummet. I felt myself enveloped by a curiously gentle moment in my life. In that sliver of time before I hit the mat, I was kissed by space.

My body absorbed the slight shock and I rolled onto my back, braced legs swinging like unguided missiles into the free air, crutches dropping away to the sides. Even as I fell through the air, I could sense the shame and fear drain from my soul, and I knew that my sense of my own cowardice would soon follow. In falling, I had given myself a new start, a new life.

"That's it!" my therapist triumphantly shouted. "You let go! And there it is!"

You let go! And there it is! Yes, and you discover not terror but the only self you are going to be allowed to claim anyhow. You fall free, and then you learn that those padded mats hold not courage but the unclaimed self. And if it turned out to be not the most difficult of tasks, did that make my sense of jubilation any less?

From that moment, I gloried in my ability to fall. Falling became an end in itself. I lost sight of what my therapist had desperately been trying to demonstrate for me — that there was a purpose in learning how to fall. For she wanted to teach me through the fall what I would have to face in the future. She wanted to give me a wholeness I could not give myself. For she knew that mine would be a future so different from what confronts the "normal" that I had to learn to fall into life in order not to be overwhelmed.

From that day, she urged me to practice falling as if I were a religious disciple being urged by a master to practice spiritual discipline. Letting go meant allowing my body to float into space, to turn at the direction of the fall and follow the urgings of emptiness. For her, learning to fall was learning the most essential of American lessons: how to turn incapacity into capacity.

"You were afraid of hurting yourself," she explained to me. "But that's the beauty of it. When you let go, you can't hurt yourself."

An echo of the streets and playgrounds I called home until I met the virus. American slogans: go with the flow, roll with the punch, slide with the threat until it is no longer a threat. They were simply slogans, and they were all intended to create strength from weakness, a veritable world's fair of compensation.

I returned to the city a year later. By that time, I was a willing convert, one who now secretly enjoyed demonstrating his ability to fall. I enjoyed the surprise that would greet me as I got to my feet, unscathed and undamaged. However perverse it may seem, I felt a certain pleasure when, as I walked with a friend, I felt a crutch slip out of my grasp. Watching the thrust of concern darken his features, I felt myself in control of my own capacity. For falling had become the way my body sought out its proper home. It was an earthbound body, and mine would be an earthbound life. My quest would be for the solid ground beneath me. Falling with confidence, I fell away from terror and fear.

Of course, some falls took me unawares, and I found myself letting go too late or too early. Bruised in ego and sometimes in body, I would pull myself to my feet to consider what had gone wrong. Yet I was essentially untroubled. Such defeats were part of the game, even when they confined me to bed for a day or two afterward. I was an accountant of pain, and sometimes heavier payment was demanded. In my mid-thirties, I walked my two-year-old son's babysitter home, tripped on the curbstone, and broke my wrist. At forty-eight, an awkward fall triggered by a carelessly unlocked brace sent me smashing against the bathtub and into surgery for a broken femur. It took four months for me to learn to walk on the crutches all over again. But I learned. I already knew how to fall.

I knew such accidents could be handled. After all, pain was not synonymous with mortality. In fact, pain was insurance against an excessive consciousness of mortality. Pain might validate the specific moment in time, but it didn't have very much to do with the future. I did not yet believe that falling into life had anything to do with falling into death. It was simply a way for me to exercise control over my own existence.

It seems to me today that, when I first let my body fall to those mats, I was somehow giving myself the endurance I would need to survive in this world. In a curious way, falling became a way of celebrating what I had lost. My legs were lifeless, useless, but their loss had created a dancing image in whose shadowy gyrations I recognized a strange but potentially interesting new self. I would survive. I knew that now. I could let go, I could fall, and, best of all, I could get up.

To create an independent self, a man had to rid himself of both the myths that nurtured him and the myths that held him back. Learning to fall had been the first lesson in how I yet might live successfully as a cripple. Even disease had its inviolate principles. I understood that the most dangerous threat to the sense of self I needed was an inflated belief in my own capacity. Falling rid a man of excess baggage; it taught him how each of us is dependent on balance.

But what really gave falling legitimacy was the knowledge that I could get to my feet again. That was what taught me the rules of survival. As long as I could pick myself up and stand on my own two feet, brace-bound and crutch-propped as I was, the fall testified to my ability to live in the here and now, to stake my claim as an American who had turned incapacity into capacity. For such a man, falling might well be considered the language of everyday achievement.

But the day came, as I knew it must come, when I could no longer pick myself up. It was then that my passion for symmetry in endings began. On that day, spurred on by another fall, I found myself spinning into the inevitable future.

The day was actually a rainy night in November of 1983. I had just finished teaching at the City College Center for Worker Education, an off-campus degree program for working adults, and had joined some friends for dinner. All of us, I remember, were in a jovial, celebratory mood, although I no longer remember what it was we were celebrating. Perhaps it was simply the satisfaction of being good friends and colleagues at dinner together.

We ate in a Spanish restaurant on Fourteenth Street in Manhattan. It was a dinner that took on, for me at least, the intensity of a time that would assume greater and greater significance as I grew older, one of those watershed moments writers are so fond of. In the dark, rain-swept New York night, change and possibility seemed to drift like a thick fog all around us.

Our mood was still convivial when we left the restaurant around eleven. The rain had slackened off to a soft drizzle and the street glistened beneath the play of light on the wet black creosote. At night, rain in the city has a way of transforming proportion into optimism. The five of us stood around on the slicked-down sidewalk, none of us willing to be the first to break the richness of the mood by leaving.

Suddenly, the crutch in my left hand began to slip out from under me, slowly, almost deliberately, as if the crutch had a mind of its own and had not yet made the commitment that would send me down. Apparently, I had hit a slick patch of city sidewalk, some nub of concrete worn smooth as medieval stone by thousands of shoppers and panhandlers and tourists and students who daily pounded the bargain hustlings of Fourteenth Street.

Instinctively, I at first tried to fight the fall, to seek for balance by pushing off from the crutch in my right hand. But as I recognized that the fall was inevitable, I simply went slack — and for the thousandth time my body sought vindication in its ability to let go and drop. These good friends had seen me fall before. They knew my childish vanities, understood that I still thought of falling as a way to demonstrate my control of the traps and uncertainties that lay in wait for us all.

Thirty-eight years earlier, I had discovered that I could fall into life simply by letting go. Now I made a different discovery — that I could no longer get to my feet by myself. I hit the wet ground and quickly turned over and pushed up, trying to use one of the crutches as a prop to boost myself to my feet, as I had been taught to do as a boy of twelve.

But try as hard as I could, I couldn't get to my feet. It wasn't that I lacked physical strength. I knew that my arms were as powerful as ever as I pushed down on the wet concrete. It had nothing to do with the fact that the street was wet, as my friends insisted later. No, it had to do with a subtle, if mysterious, change in my own sense of rhythm and balance. My body had decided — *and decided on its own, autonomously* — that the moment had come for me to face the question of endings. It was the body that chose its time of recognition.

It was, it seems to me now, a distinctively American moment. It left me pondering limitations and endings and summations. It left me with the curiously buoyant sense that mortality had quite suddenly made itself a felt presence rather than the rhetorical strategy used by the poets and novelists I taught to my students. This was what writers had in mind when they spoke of the truly common fate, this sense of ending coming to one unbidden. This had brought with it my impassioned quest for symmetry. As I lay on the wet ground — no more than a minute or two — all I could think of was how much I wanted my life to balance out. It was as if I were staring into a future in which time itself had evaporated.

Here was a clear, simple perception, and there was nothing mystical about it. There are limitations we recognize and those that recognize us. My friends, who had nervously been standing around while I tried to get to my feet, finally asked if they could help me up. "You'll have to," I said. "I can't get up any other way."

Two of them pulled me to my feet while another jammed the crutches beneath my arms, as the therapist and the two bracemakers had done almost four decades earlier. When I was standing, they proceeded to joke about my sudden incapacity in that age-old way men of all ages have, as if words might codify loss and change and time's betrayal. I joined in the joking. But what I really wanted was to go home and contemplate this latest fall in the privacy of my apartment. The implications were clear: I would never again be an eater of salt, I would also never again get to my feet on my own. A part of my life had ended. But that didn't depress me. In fact, I felt almost as exhilarated as I had thirty-eight years earlier, when my body surrendered to the need to let go and I fell into life.

Almost four years have passed since I fell on the wet sidewalk of Fourteenth Street. I suppose it wasn't a particularly memorable fall. It wasn't even particularly significant to anyone who had not once fallen into life. But it was inevitable, the first time I had let go into a time when it would no longer even be necessary to let go.

It was a fall that left me with the knowledge that I could no longer pick myself up. That meant I now needed the help of others as I had not needed their help before. It was fall that left me burning with this strange passion for symmetry, this desire to balance my existence out. When the day comes, I want to be able to fall into my death as nakedly as I once had to fall into my life.

Do not misunderstand me. I am not seeking a way out of mortality, for I believe in nothing more strongly than I believe in the permanency of endings. I am not looking for a way out of this life, a life I continue to find immensely enjoyable — even if I can no longer pull myself to my own two feet. Of course, a good deal in my life has changed. For one thing, I am increasingly impatient with those who claim to have no use for endings of any sort. I am also increasingly embarrassed by the thought of the harshly critical adolescent I was, self-righteously convinced that the only way for a man to go to his end was by kicking and screaming.

But these are, I suppose, the kinds of changes any man or woman of forty or fifty would feel. Middle-aged skepticism is as natural as adolescent acne. In my clearer, less passionate moments, I can even laugh at my need for symmetry in beginnings and endings as well as my desire to see my own eventual death as a line running parallel to my life. Even in mathematics, let alone life, symmetry is sometimes too neat, too closed off from the way things actually work. After all, it took me a full month before I could bring myself to let go and fall into life.

I no longer talk about how one can seize a doctrine of compensation from disease. I don't talk about it, but it still haunts me. In my heart, I believe it offers a man the only philosophy by which he can actually live. It is the only philosophy that strips away both spiritual mumbo jumbo and the procrustean weight of existential anxiety. In the final analysis, a man really is what a man does.

Believing as I do, I wonder why I so often find myself trying to frame a perspective that will prove adequate to a proper sense of ending. Perhaps that is why I find myself sitting in a bar with a friend, trying to explain to him all that I have learned from falling. "There must be a time," I hear myself tell him, "when a man has the right to stop thinking about falling."

"Sure," my friend laughs. "Four seconds before he dies."

Reflections and Responses

1. Consider the many connotations of the word "fall." How many different senses of the word can you find in Kriegel's essay?

2. How does Kriegel establish a spiritual context for his rehabilitation? What terms and images throughout the essay lend a religious coloring to his experiences?

3. Several times in his essay Kriegel refers to skills that seem particularly "American." What does he mean by this? Why do you think he introduces the idea at all? What is especially "American" about his experiences?

GRETEL EHRLICH

Spring

"Recuperation is like spring," writes Gretel Ehrlich in a lyrical essay that sensitively charts the changes both within a Wyoming season and a woman's psyche. A model of the modern reflective essay, her meditation on her slow recovery from pneumonia and the death of a young rancher branches out into thoughts about time and space, sex and death, dream and reality, cosmology and Jurassic landscapes. As she considers the way life and thought move between the linear and the circular, particle and wave, she shapes her essay accordingly, at some moments pursuing a narrative, at others following the trail of an image: "In March I'm ramshackle, weak in the knees, giddy, dazzled by broken-backed clouds, the passing of Halley's comet, the on-and-off strobe of sun."

Ehrlich is the author of The Solace of Open Spaces *(1985),* Wyoming Stories *(1986),* Heart Mountain *(1988), and* Islands, the Universe, Home *(1991). Her essays have appeared in* Harper's, The Atlantic, Time, *the* New York Times, *and many other national periodicals. She divides her time between the central coast of California and Wyoming. "Spring" originally appeared in* Antaeus *(1986) and was selected by Gay Talese for* The Best American Essays *1987.*

We have a nine-acre lake on our ranch and a warm spring that feeds it all winter. By mid-March the lake ice begins to melt where the spring feeds in, and every year the same pair of mallards come ahead of the others and wait. Though there is very little open water they seem content. They glide back and forth through a thin estuary, brushing watercress with their elegant folded wings, then tip end-up to eat and, after, clamber onto the lip of ice that retreats, hardens forward, and retreats again.

Mornings, a transparent pane of ice lies over the meltwater. I peer through and see some kind of waterbug — perhaps a leech — paddling like a sea turtle between green ladders of lakeweed. Cattails and sweetgrass from the previous summer are bone dry, marked with black mold spots, and bend like elbows into the ice. They are swords that cut away the hard tenancy of winter. At the wide end a mat of dead waterplants has rolled back into a thick, impregnable breakwater. Near it, bubbles trapped under the ice are lenses focused straight up to catch the coming season.

It's spring again and I wasn't finished with winter. That's what I said at the end of summer too. I stood on the twenty-foot-high haystack and yelled "No!" as the first snow fell. We had been up since four in the morning picking the last bales of hay from the oatfield by hand, slipping under the weight of them in the mud, and by the time we finished the stack, six inches of snow had fallen.

It's spring but I was still cataloguing the different kinds of snow: snow that falls dry but is rained on; snow that melts down into hard crusts; wind-driven snow that looks blue; powder snow on hardpack on powder — a Linzertorte of snow. I look up. The troposphere is the seven-to-ten-mile-wide sleeve of air out of which all our weather shakes. A bank of clouds drives in from the south. Where in it, I wonder, does a snowflake take on its thumbprint uniqueness? Inside the cloud where schools of flakes are flung this way and that like schools of fish? What gives the snowflake its needle, plate, column, branching shapes — the battering wind or the dust particles around which water vapor clings?

Near town the river ice breaks up and lies stacked in industrial-sized hunks — big as railway cars — on the banks, and is flecked black by wheeling hurricanes of newly plowed topsoil. That's how I feel when winter breaks up inside me: heavy, onerous, upended, inert against the flow of water. I had thought about ice during the cold months too. How it is movement betrayed, water seized in the moment of falling. In November, ice thickened over the lake like a cataract, and from the air looked like a Cyclops, one bad eye. Under its milky spans over irrigation ditches, the sound of water running south was muffled. One solitary spire of ice hung noiselessly against dark rock at the Falls as if mocking or mirroring the broom-tail comet on the horizon. Then, in February, I tried for words not about ice, but words hacked from it — the ice at the end of the mind, so to speak — and failed.

Those were winter things and now it is spring, though one name can't describe what, in Wyoming, is a three-part affair: false spring, the vernal equinox, and the spring when flowers come and the grass grows.

Spring means restlessness. The physicist I've been talking to all winter says if I look more widely, deeply, and microscopically all at once I might see how springlike the whole cosmos is. What I see as order and stillness — the robust, time-bound determinacy of my life — is really a mirage suspended above chaos. "There's a lot of random jiggling going on all the time, everywhere," he tells me. Winter's tight sky hovers. Under it, the hayfields are green, then white, then green growing under white. The confinement I've felt since November resembles the confinement of subatomic particles, I'm told. A natural velocity finally shows itself. The particle moves; it becomes a wave.

The sap rises in trees and in me and the hard knot of perseverance I cultivated to meet winter dissipates; I walk away from the obsidian of bitter nights. Now, when snow comes, it is wet and heavy, but the air it traverses feels light. I sleep less and dream not of human entanglements, but of animals I've never seen: a caterpillar fat as a man's thumb, made of linked silver tubes, has two heads — one human, one a butterfly's.

Last spring at this time I was coming out of a bout with pneumonia. I went to bed on January first and didn't get up until the end of February. Winter was a cocoon in which my gagging, basso cough shook the dark figures at the end of my bed. Had I read too much Hemingway? Or was I dying? I'd lie on my stomach and look out. Nothing close up interested me. All engagements of mind — the circumlocutions of love interests and internal gossip — appeared false. Only my body was true. And my body was trying to close down, go out the window without me.

I saw things out there. Our ranch faces south down a long treeless valley whose vanishing point is two gray hills, folded one in front of the other like two hands, and after that — space, cerulean air, clouds like pleated skirts, and red mesas standing up like breaching whales in a valley three thousand feet below. Afternoons, our young horses played, rearing up on back legs and pawing oh so carefully at each other, reaching around, ears flat back, nipping manes and withers. One of those times their falsetto squeals looped across the pasture and hung on frozen currents of air. But when I tried to ingest their sounds of delight, I found my lungs had no air.

It was thirty-five below zero that night. Our plumbing froze, and because I was very weak my husband had to bundle me up and help me to the outhouse. Nothing close at hand seemed to register with me: neither the cold nor the semicoziness of an uninsulated house. But the stars were lurid. For a while I thought I saw the horses, dead now, and eating each other, and spinning round and round in the ice of the air.

My scientist friends talk with relish about how insignificant we humans are when placed against the time-scale of geology and the cosmos. I had heard it a hundred times, but never felt it truly. As I lay in bed, the black room was a screen through which some part of my body traveled, leaving the rest behind. I thought I was a sun flying over a barge whose iron holds soaked me up until I became rust floating on a bright river.

A ferocious loneliness took hold of me. I felt spring-inspired desire, a sense of trajectory, but no interception was in sight. In fact, I wanted none. My body was a parenthetical dash laid against a landscape so spacious it defied space as we know it — space as a membrane — and curved out of time. That night a luscious, creamy fog rolled in, like a roll of fat, hugging me, but it was snow.

Recuperation is like spring: dormancy and vitality collide. In any year I'm like a bear, a partial hibernator. During January thaws I stick my nose out and peruse the frozen desolation as if reading a book whose language I don't know. In March I'm ramshackle, weak in the knees, giddy, dazzled by broken-backed clouds, the passing of Halley's comet, the on-and-off strobe of sun. Like a sheepherder I X out each calendar day as if time were a forest through which I could clear-cut a way to the future. My physicist friend straightens me out on this point too. The notion of "time passing," like a train through a landscape, is an illusion, he says. I hold the Big Ben clock taken from a dead sheepherder's wagon and look at it. The clock measures intervals of time, not the speed of time, and the calendar is a scaffolding we hang as if time were rushing water we could harness. Time-bound, I hinge myself to a linear bias — cause and effect all laid out in a neat row — and in this we learn two things: blame and shame.

Julius Caesar had a sense of humor about time. The Roman

calendar with its calends, nones, and ides — counting days — changed according to who was in power. Caesar serendipitously added days, changed the names of certain months, and when he was through, the calendar was so skewed that January fell in autumn.

Einsteinian time is too big for even Julius Caesar to touch. It stretches and shrinks and dilates. In fact, it is the antithesis of the mechanistic concept we've imposed on it. Time, indecipherable from space, is not one thing but an infinity of space-times, overlapping, interfering, wavelike. There is no future that is not now, no past that is not now. Time includes every moment.

It's the ides of March today.

I've walked to a hill a mile from the house. It's not really a hill but a mountain slope that heaves up, turns sideways, and comes down again, straight down to a foot-wide creek. Everything I can see from here used to be a flatland covered with shallow water. "Used to be" means several hundred million years ago, and the land itself was not really "here" at all, but part of a continent floating near Bermuda. On top is a fin of rock, a marine deposition created during Jurassic times by small waves moving in and out slapping the shore.

I've come here for peace and quiet and to see what's going on in this secluded valley, away from ranch work and sorting corrals, but what I get is a slap on the ass by a prehistoric wave, gains and losses in altitude and aridity, outcrops of mud composed of rotting volcanic ash that fell continuously for ten thousand years a hundred million years ago. The soils are a geologic flag — red, white, green, and gray. On one side of the hill, mountain mahogany gives off a scent like orange blossoms; on the other, colonies of sagebrush root wide in ground the color of Spanish roof tiles. And it still looks like the ocean to me. "How much truth can a man stand, sitting by the ocean, all that perpetual motion," Mose Allison, the jazz singer, sings.

The wind picks up and blusters. Its fat underbelly scrapes the uneven ground, twisting like taffy toward me, slips up over the mountain, and showers out across the Great Plains. The sea smell it carried all the way from Seattle has long since been absorbed by pink gruss — the rotting granite that spills down the slopes of the Rockies. Somewhere over the Midwest the wind slows, tangling in the hair of hardwood forests, and finally drops into the corridors of the cities, past Manhattan's World Trade Center, ripping free again as it crosses the Atlantic's green swell.

Spring jitterbugs inside me. Spring *is* wind, symphonic and billowing. A dark cloud pops like a blood blister over me, letting hail down. It comes on a piece of wind that seems to have widened the sky, comes so the birds have something to fly on.

A message reports to my brain but I can't believe my eyes. The sheet of wind had a hole in it: an eagle just fell out of the sky. It fell as if down the chute of a troubled airplane. Landed, falling to one side as if a leg were broken. I was standing on the hill overlooking the narrow valley that had been a seashore 170 million years ago, whose sides had lifted like a medic's litter to catch up this eagle now.

She hops and flaps seven feet of wing and closes them down and sways. She had come down (on purpose?) near a dead fawn whose carcass had recently been feasted upon. When I walked closer, all I could see of the animal was a ribcage rubbed red with fine tissue and the decapitated head lying peacefully against sagebrush, eyes closed.

At twenty yards the eagle opened her wings halfway and rose up, her whole back lengthening and growing stiff. At forty feet she looked as big as a small person. She craned her neck, first to one side, then the other, and stared hard. She's giving me the eagle eye, I thought.

Friends who have investigated eagles' nests have literally feared for their lives. It's not that they were in danger of being pecked to death but, rather, grabbed. An eagle's talons are a powerful jaw. Their grip is so strong the talons can slice down through flesh to bone in one motion.

But I had come close only to see what was wrong, to see what I could do. An eagle with a bum leg will starve to death. Was it broken, bruised, or sprained? How could I get close enough to know? I approached again. She hopped up in the air, dashing the critical distance between us with her great wings. Best to leave her alone, I decided. My husband dragged a road-killed deer up the mountain slope so she could eat, and I brought a bucket of water. Then we turned toward home.

A golden eagle is not golden but black with yellow spots on the neck and wings. Looking at her, I had wondered how feathers came to be, how their construction — the rachis, vane, and quill — is unlike anything else in nature.

Birds are glorified flying lizards. The remarkable feathers that, positioned together, are like hundreds of smaller wings, evolved from reptilian scales. Ancestral birds had thirteen pairs of cone-shaped teeth that grew in separate sockets like a snake's, rounded ribs, and bony tails. Archaeopteryx was half bird, half dinosaur who glided instead of flying; ichthyornis was a fish-bird, a relative of the pelican; diatryma was a giant, seven feet tall with a huge beak and wings so absurdly small they must have been useless, though later the wingbone sprouted from them. *Aquila chrysaëtos,* the modern golden eagle, has seven thousand contour feathers, no teeth, and weighs about eight pounds.

I think about the eagle. How big she was, how each time she spread her wings it was like a thought stretching between two seasons.

Back at the house I relax with a beer. At 5:03 the vernal equinox occurs. I go outside and stand in the middle of a hayfield with my eyes closed. The universe is restless but I want to feel celestial equipoise: twelve hours of daylight, twelve of dark, and the earth ramrod straight on its axis. In celebration I straighten my posture in an effort to resist the magnetic tilt back into dormancy, spiritual and emotional reticence. Far to the south I imagine the equatorial sash, now nose to nose with the sun, sizzling like a piece of bacon, then the earth slowly tilting again.

In the morning I walk up to the valley again. I glass both hillsides, back and forth through the sagebrush, but the eagle isn't there. The hindquarters of the road-killed deer have been eaten. Coyote tracks circle the carcass. Did they have eagle for dinner too?

Afternoon. I return. Far up on the opposite hill I see her, flapping and hopping to the top. When I stop, she stops and turns her head. Her neck is the plumbline on which earth revolves. Even at two hundred yards, I can feel her binocular vision zeroing in; I can feel the heat of her stare.

Later, I look through my binoculars at all sorts of things. I'm seeing the world with an eagle eye. I glass the crescent moon. How jaded I've become, taking the moon at face value only, forgetting the charcoal, shaded backside, as if it weren't there at all.

That night I dream about two moons. One is pink and spins fast;

the other is an eagle's head, farther away and spinning in the opposite direction. Slowly, both moons descend and then it is day.

At first light I clamber up the hill. Now the dead deer my husband brought is only a hoop of ribs, two forelegs, and hair. The
eagle is not here or along the creek or on either hill. I go to the
hill and sit. After a long time an eagle careens out from the narrow
slit of the red-walled canyon whose creek drains into this valley.
Surely it's the same bird. She flies by. I can hear the bone-creak
and whoosh of air under her wings. She cocks her head and looks
at me. I smile. What is a smile to her? Now she is not so much flying as lifting above the planet, far from me.

Late March. The emerald of the hayfields brightens. A flock of
gray-capped rosy finches who overwintered here swarms a leafless
apple tree, then falls from the smooth boughs like cut grass. The
tree was planted by the Texan who homesteaded this ranch. As I
walk past, one of the boughs, shaped like an undulating dragon,
splits off from the trunk and falls.

Space is an arena in which the rowdy particles that are the building blocks of life perform their antics. All spring, things fall; the
general law of increasing disorder is on the take. I try to think of
what it is to be a cause without an effect, an effect without a cause.
To abandon time-bound thinking, the use of tenses, the tempo-
rally related emotions of impatience, expectation, hope, and fear.
But I can't. I go to the edge of the lake and watch the ducks. Like
them, my thinking rises and falls on the same water.

Another day. Sometimes when I'm feeling small-minded I take a
plane ride over Wyoming. As we take off I feel the plane's resistance to accepting air under its wings. Is this how an eagle feels?
Ernst Mach's* principle tells me that an object's resistance against
being accelerated is not the intrinsic property of matter, but a
measure of its interaction with the universe; that matter has inertia
only because it exists in relation to other matter.

Airborne, then, I'm not aloof but in relation to everything —
like Wallace Stevens's floating eagle for whom the whole, intricate
Alps is a nest. We fly southeast from Heart Mountain across the Big
Horn River, over the long red wall where Butch Cassidy trailed
stolen horses, across the high plains to Laramie. Coming home

---

***Ernst Mach**: Austrian physicist and philosopher (1838–1916).

the next day, we hit clouds. Turbulence, like many forms of trouble, cannot always be seen. We bounce so hard my arms sail helplessly above my head. In evolution, wingbones became arms and hands; perhaps I'm de-evolving.

From ten thousand feet I can see that spring is only half here: the southern part of the state is white, the northern half is green. Land is also time. The greening of time is a clock whose hands are blades of grass moving vertically, up through the fringe of numbers, spreading across the middle of the face, sinking again as the sun moves from one horizon to the other. Time doesn't go anywhere; the shadow of the plane, my shadow, moves across it.

To sit on a plane is to sit on the edge of sleep where the mind's forge brightens into incongruities. Down there I see disparate wholenesses strung together and the string dissolving. Mountains run like rivers; I fly through waves and waves of chiaroscuro light. The land looks bare but is articulate. The body of the plane is my body, pressing into spring, pressing matter into relation with matter. Is it even necessary to say the obvious? That spring brings on surges of desire? From this disinterested height I say out loud what Saint Augustine wrote: "My love is my weight. Because of it I move."

Directly below us now is the fine old Wyoming ranch where Joel, Mart, Dave, Hughy, and I have moved thousands of head of cattle. Joel's father, Smokey, was one of two brothers who put the outfit together. They worked hard, lived frugally, and even after Fred died, Smokey did not marry until his late fifties. As testimony to a long bachelorhood, there is no kitchen in the main house. The cookhouse stands separate from all the other buildings. In back is a bedroom and bath, which have housed a list of itinerant cooks ten pages long.

Over the years I've helped during roundup and branding. We'd rise at four. Smokey, now in his eighties, cooked flapjacks and boiled coffee on the wood cookstove. There was a long table. Joel and Smokey always sat at one end. They were lookalikes, both skin-and-bones tall with tipped-up dark eyes set in narrow faces. Stern and vigilant, Smokey once threw a young hired hand out of the cookhouse because he hadn't grained his saddle horse after a long day's ride. "On this outfit we take care of our animals first," he said. "Then if there's time, we eat."

Even in his early twenties, Joel had his father's dignity and razor-sharp wit. They both wore white Stetsons identically shaped. Only their hands were different: Joel had eight fingers and one thumb — the other he lost while roping.

Eight summers ago my parents visited their ranch. We ate a hearty meal of homemade whiskey left over from Prohibition days, steaks cut from an Angus bull, four kinds of vegetables, water-melon, ice cream, and pie. Despite a thirteen-year difference in our ages, Smokey wanted Joel and me to marry. As we rose from the meal, he shook my father's hand. "I guess you'll be my son's fa-ther-in-law," he said. That was news to all of us. Joel's face turned crimson. My father threw me an astonished look, cleared his throat, and thanked his host for the fine meal.

One night Joel did come to my house and asked me if I would take him into my bed. It was a gentlemanly proposition — doffed hat, moist eyes, a smile almost grimacing with loneliness. "You're an older woman. Think of all you could teach me," he said jauntily, but with a blush. He stood ramrod straight waiting for an answer. My silence turned him away like a rolling wave and he drove to the home ranch, spread out across the Emblem Bench thirty-five miles away.

The night Joel died I was staying at a writer's farm in Missouri. I had fallen asleep early, then awakened suddenly, feeling claustro-phobic. I jumped out of bed and stood in the dark. I wanted to get out of there, drive home to Wyoming, and I didn't know why. Fi-nally, at seven in the morning, I was able to sleep. I dreamed about a bird landing, then lifting out of a tree along a river bank. That was the night Joel's pickup rolled. He was found five hours after the accident occurred — just about daylight — and died on the way to the hospital.

Now I'm sitting on a fin of Gypsum Springs rock looking west. The sun is setting. What I see are three gray cloud towers letting rain down at the horizon. The sky behind these massifs is gilded gold, and long fingers of land — benches where the Hunt Oil Compa-ny's Charolais cattle graze — are pink. Somewhere over Joel's grave the sky is bright. The road where he died shines like a dash in a Paul Klee painting. Over my head, it is still winter: snow so dry it feels like Styrofoam when squeezed together, tumbles into my lap. I think about flying and falling. The place in the sky where the eagle fell is dark, as if its shadow had burned into the backdrop of rock — Hiroshima style. Why does a wounded eagle get well and fly away; why do the head wounds of a young man cut him down? Useless questions.

Sex and death are the riddles thrown into the hopper, thrown down on the planet like hailstones. Where one hits the earth, it makes a crater and melts, perhaps a seed germinates, perhaps not. If I dice life down into atoms, the trajectories I find are so wild, so random, anything could happen: life or nonlife. But once we have a body, who can give it up easily? Our own or others'? We check our clocks and build our beautiful narratives, under which indeterminacy seethes.

Sometimes, lying in bed, I feel like a flounder with its two eyes on one side pointing upward into nothingness. The casings of thought rattle. Then I realize there are no casings at all. Is it possible that the mind, like space, is finite, but has no boundaries, no center or edge? I sit cross-legged on old blankets. My bare feet strain against the crotch of my knees. Time is between my toes, it seems. Just as morning comes and the indigo lifts, the leaflessness of the old apple tree looks ornate. Nothing in this world is plain.

"Every atom in your body was once inside a star," another physicist says, but he's only trying to humor me. Not all atoms in all kinds of matter are shared. But who wouldn't find that idea appealing? Outside, shadows trade places with a sliver of sun that trades places with shadow. Finally the lake ice goes and the water — pale and slate blue — wears its coat of diamonds all day. The mallards number twenty-six pairs now. They nest on two tiny islands and squabble amicably among themselves. A Pacific storm blows in from the south like a jibsail reaching far out, backhanding me with a gust of something tropical. It snows into my mouth, between my breasts, against my shins. Spring teaches me what space and time teach me: that I am a random multiple; that the many fit together like waves; that my swell is a collision of particles. Spring is a kind of music, a seething minor, a twelve-tone scale. Even the odd harmonies amassed only lift up to dissolve.

Spring passes harder and harder and is feral. The first thunder cracks the sky into a larger domain. Sap rises in obdurateness. For the first time in seven months, rain slants down in a slow pavane —

sharp but soft — like desire, like the laying on of hands. I drive the
highway that crosses the wild-horse range. Near Emblem I watch a
black studhorse trot across the range all alone. He travels north,
then turns in my direction as if trotting to me. Now, when I dream
of Joel, he is riding that horse and he knows he is dead. One night
he rides to my house, all smiles and shyness. I let him in.

Reflections and Responses

1. What does the author's physicist friend contribute to the essay?
How does particle physics enter into Ehrlich's thinking? Would you
say that she is scientific or nonscientific in her approach to nature?

2. Of what significance to Ehrlich's theme is the eagle with the
"bum leg"? Consider carefully the passage in which she describes
the eagle. What thoughts does the incident prompt? Why is it important that the eagle is hurt?

3. Much of Ehrlich's essay deals with time. Aside from her philosophical reflections on the subject, how does she mark the passage
of time in the essay? Can you reconstruct her chronological outline? What is the time of the essay's opening, and how does it proceed? Of what importance is Wyoming's "three-part" spring to her
structure?

JOY WILLIAMS

The Killing Game

In today's world, survival is a theme that includes all of nature, not merely human life. When the following angry attack on hunting originally appeared in a popular men's magazine, the editors were deluged with equally angry letters from hundreds of subscribers. As you read the essay, you'll see at once why it enraged hunters and hunting advocates. Williams did not choose to write a calm, composed, and gently persuasive critique of hunting but went all out in a savage and often sarcastic attack on American hunters, a group she considers "overequipped . . . insatiable, malevolent, and vain."

Williams is the author of three novels and two collections of stories, Taking Care *(1982) and* Escapes *(1989), as well as a 1987 history and guide to the Florida Keys. Her nonfiction includes articles on sharks, James Dean, the environment, and the electric chair. In 1993 she received the Strauss Living Award from the American Academy of Arts and Letters. "The Killing Game" originally appeared in* Esquire *(1990) and was selected by Joyce Carol Oates for* The Best American Essays 1991.

Death and suffering are a big part of hunting. A big part. Not that you'd ever know it by hearing hunters talk. They tend to downplay the killing part. To kill is to put to death, extinguish, nullify, cancel, destroy. But from the hunter's point of view, it's just a tiny part of the experience. *The kill is the least important part of the hunt,* they often say, or, *Killing involves only a split second of the innumerable hours we spend surrounded by and observing nature . . .* For the animal, of course, the killing part is of considerable more importance. José Ortega y Gasset, in *Meditations on Hunting,* wrote, *Death is a sign of re-*

ality in hunting. One does not hunt in order to kill; on the contrary, one kills in order to have hunted. This is the sort of intellectual blather that the "thinking" hunter holds dear. The conservation editor of *Field & Stream,* George Reiger, recently paraphrased this sentiment by saying, *We kill to hunt, and not the other way around,* thereby making it truly fatuous. A hunter in West Virginia, one Mr. Bill Neal, blazed through this philosophical fog by explaining why he blows the toes off tree raccoons so that they will fall down and be torn apart by his dogs. *That's the best part of it. It's not any fun just shooting them.*

Instead of monitoring animals — many animals in managed areas are tagged, tattooed, and wear radio transmitters — wildlife managers should start hanging telemetry gear around hunters' necks to study their attitudes and listen to their conversations. It would be grisly listening, but it would tune out for good the *suffering as sacrament* and *spiritual experience* blather that some hunting apologists employ. *The unease with which the good hunter inflicts death is an unease not merely with his conscience but with affirming his animality in the midst of his struggles toward humanity and clarity,* Holmes Rolston III drones on in his book *Environmental Ethics.*

There is a formula to this in literature — someone the protagonist loves has just died, so he goes out and kills an animal. This makes him feel better. But it's kind of a sad feeling-better. He gets to relate to Death and Nature in this way. Somewhat. But not really. Death is still a mystery. Well, it's hard to explain. It's sort of a semireligious thing. . . Killing and affirming, affirming and killing, it's just the cross the "good" hunter must bear. The bad hunter just has to deal with postkill letdown.

Many are the hunter's specious arguments. Less semireligious but a long-standing favorite with them is the vegetarian approach: you eat meat, don't you? If you say no, they feel they've got you — you're just a vegetarian attempting to impose your weird views on others. If you say yes, they accuse you of being hypocritical, of allowing your genial A&P butcher to stand between you and reality. The fact is, the chief attraction of hunting is the pursuit and murder of animals — the meat-eating aspect of it is trivial. If the hunter chooses to be *ethical* about it, he might cook his kill, but the meat of most animals is discarded. Dead bear can even be dangerous! A bear's heavy hide must be skinned at once to prevent meat spoilage. With effort, a hunter can make okay chili, *something to keep in mind*, a sports rag says, *if you take two skinny spring bears.*

As for subsistence hunting, please . . . Granted that there might be one "good" hunter out there who conducts the kill as spiritual exercise and two others who are atavistic enough to want to supplement their Chicken McNuggets with venison, most hunters hunt for the hell of it.

For hunters, hunting is fun. Recreation is play. Hunting is recreation. Hunters kill for play, for entertainment. They kill for the thrill of it, to make an animal "theirs." (The Gandhian doctrine of nonpossession has never been a big hit with hunters.) The animal becomes the property of the hunter by its death. Alive, the beast belongs only to itself. This is unacceptable to the hunter. *He's yours . . . He's mine . . . I decided to . . . I decided not to . . . I debated shooting it, then I decided to let it live . . .* Hunters like beautiful creatures. A "beautiful" deer, elk, bear, cougar, bighorn sheep. A "beautiful" goose or mallard. Of course, they don't stay "beautiful" for long, particularly the birds. Many birds become rags in the air, shredded, blown to bits. *Keep shooting till they drop!* Hunters get a thrill out of seeing a plummeting bird, out of seeing it crumple and fall. *The big pheasant folded in classic fashion.* They get a kick out of "collecting" new species. *Why not add a unique harlequin duck to your collection?* Swan hunting is satisfying. *I let loose a three-inch Magnum. The large bird only flinched with my first shot and began to gain altitude. I frantically ejected the round, chambered another, and dropped the swan with my second shot. After retrieving the bird I was amazed by its size. The swan's six-foot wingspan, huge body, and long neck made it an impressive trophy.* Hunters like big animals, trophy animals. A "trophy" usually means that the hunter doesn't deign to eat it. Maybe he skins it or mounts it. Maybe he takes a picture. *We took pictures, we took pictures.* Maybe he just looks at it for a while. The disposition of the "experience" is up to the hunter. He's entitled to do whatever he wishes with the damn thing. It's dead.

Hunters like categories they can tailor to their needs. There are the "good" animals — deer, elk, bear, moose — which are allowed to exist for the hunter's pleasure. Then there are the "bad" animals, the vermin, varmints, and "nuisance" animals, the rabbits and raccoons and coyotes and beavers and badgers, which are discouraged to exist. The hunter can have fun killing them, but the pleasure is diminished because the animals aren't "magnificent."

Then there are the predators. These can be killed any time, because, hunters argue, they're predators, for godssakes.

Many people in South Dakota want to exterminate the red fox because it preys upon some of the ducks and pheasant they want to hunt and kill each year. They found that after they killed the wolves and coyotes, they had more foxes than they wanted. The ring-necked pheasant is South Dakota's state bird. No matter that it was imported from Asia specifically to be "harvested" for sport, it's South Dakota's state bird and they're proud of it. A group called Pheasants Unlimited gave some tips on how to hunt foxes. *Place a small amount of larvicide* [a grain fumigant] *on a rag and chuck it down the hole . . . The first pup generally comes out in fifteen minutes . . . Use a .22 to dispatch him . . . Remove each pup shot from the hole. Following gassing, set traps for the old fox who will return later in the evening . . .* Poisoning, shooting, trapping — they make up a sort of sportsman's triathlon.

In the hunting magazines, hunters freely admit the pleasure of killing to one another. *Undeniable pleasure radiated from her smile. The excitement of shooting the bear had Barb talking a mile a minute.* But in public, most hunters are becoming a little wary about raving on as to how much fun it is to kill things. Hunters have a tendency to call large animals by cute names —"bruins" and "muleys," "berry-fed blackies" and "handsome cusses" and "big guys," thereby implying a balanced jolly game of mutual satisfaction between the hunter and the hunted —*Bam, bam, bam, I get to shoot you and you get to be dead.* More often, though, when dealing with the nonhunting public, a drier, businesslike tone is employed. Animals become a "resource" that must be "utilized." Hunting becomes "a legitimate use of the resource." Animals become a product like wool or lumber or a crop like fruit or corn that must be "collected" or "taken" or "harvested." Hunters love to use the word *legitimate.* (Oddly, Tolstoy referred to hunting as "evil legitimized.") *A legitimate use, a legitimate form of recreation, a legitimate escape, a legitimate pursuit.* It's a word they trust will slam the door on discourse. Hunters are increasingly relying upon their spokesmen and supporters, state and federal game managers and wildlife officials, to employ the drone of a solemn bureaucratic language and toss around a lot of questionable statistics to assure the nonhunting public (93 percent!) that there's nothing to worry about. The pogrom is under control.

The mass murder and manipulation of wild animals is just another business. Hunters are a tiny minority, and it's crucial to them that the millions of people who don't hunt not be awakened from their long sleep and become antihunting. Nonhunters are okay. Dweeby, probably, but okay. A hunter *can respect the rights* of a nonhunter. It's the "antis" he despises, those *misguided, emotional, not-in-possession-of-the-facts, uninformed zealots who don't understand nature . . . Those dime-store ecologists cloaked in ignorance and spurred by emotion . . . Those doggy-woggy types, who under the guise of being environmentalists and conservationists are working to deprive him of his precious right to kill.* (Sometimes it's just a *right*; sometimes it's a *God-given* right.) Antis can be scorned, but nonhunters must be pacified, and this is where the number crunching of wildlife biologists and the scripts of *professional resource managers* come in. Leave it to the professionals. They know what numbers are the good numbers. Utah determined that there were six hundred sandhill cranes in the state, so permits were issued to shoot one hundred of them. Don't want to have too many sandhill cranes. California wildlife officials reported "sufficient numbers" of mountain lions to "justify" renewed hunting, even though it doesn't take a rocket scientist to know the animal is extremely rare. (It's always a dark day for hunters when an animal is adjudged *rare*. How can its numbers be "controlled" through hunting if it scarcely exists?) A recent citizens' referendum prohibits the hunting of the mountain lion in perpetuity — not that the lions aren't killed anyway, in California and all over the West, hundreds of them annually by the government as part of the scandalous Animal Damage Control Program. Oh, to be the lucky hunter who gets to be an official government hunter and can legitimately kill animals his buddies aren't supposed to! Montana officials, led by K. L. Cool, that state's wildlife director, have definite ideas on the number of buffalo they feel can be tolerated. Zero is the number. Yellowstone National Park is the only place in America where bison exist, having been annihilated everywhere else. In the winter of 1988, nearly six hundred buffalo wandered out of the north boundary of the park and into Montana, where they were immediately shot at point-blank range by lottery-winning hunters. It was easy. And it was obvious from a video taken on one of the blow-away-the-bison days that the hunters had a heck of a good time. The buffalo, Cool says, threaten ranchers' livelihoods by doing damage to property — by which he means, I guess, that they eat the grass. Montana wants zero buffalos; it also wants zero wolves.

Large predators — including grizzlies, cougars, and wolves — are often the most "beautiful," the smartest and wildest animals of all. The gray wolf is both a supreme predator and an endangered species, and since the Supreme Court recently affirmed that ranchers have no constitutional right to kill endangered predators — apparently some God-given rights are not constitutional ones — this makes the wolf a more or less lucky dog. But not for long. A small population of gray wolves has recently established itself in northwestern Montana, primarily in Glacier National Park, and there is a plan, long a dream of conservationists, to "reintroduce" the wolf to Yellowstone. But to please ranchers and hunters, part of the plan would involve immediately removing the wolf from the endangered-species list. Beyond the park's boundaries, he could be hunted as a "game animal" or exterminated as a "pest." (Hunters kill to hunt, remember, except when they're hunting to kill.) The area of Yellowstone where the wolf would be restored is the same mountain and high-plateau country that is abandoned in winter by most animals, including the aforementioned luckless bison. Part of the plan, too, is compensation to ranchers if any of their far-ranging livestock is killed by a wolf. It's a real industry out there, apparently, killing and controlling and getting compensated for losing something under the Big Sky.

Wolves gotta eat — a fact that disturbs hunters. Jack Atcheson, an outfitter in Butte, said, *Some wolves are fine if there is control. But there never will be control. The wolf-control plan provided by the Fish and Wildlife Service speaks only of protecting domestic livestock. There is no plan to protect wildlife . . . There are no surplus deer or elk in Montana . . . Their numbers are carefully managed. With uncontrolled wolf populations, a lot of people will have to give up hunting just to feed wolves. Will you give up your elk permit for a wolf?*

It won't be long before hunters start demanding compensation for animals they aren't able to shoot.

Hunters believe that wild animals exist only to satisfy their wish to kill them. And it's so easy to kill them! The weaponry available is staggering, and the equipment and gear limitless. *The demand for big boomers has never been greater than right now,* Outdoor Life *crows, and the makers of rifles and cartridges are responding to the craze with a variety of light artillery that is virtually unprecedented in the history of sporting arms* . . . Hunters use grossly overpowered shotguns and rifles and compound bows. They rely on four-wheel-drive vehicles and three-wheel ATVs and airplanes . . . *He was interesting, the only moving, living creature on that limitless white expanse. I slipped a cartridge into the barrel of my rifle and threw the safety off* . . . They use snowmobiles to run down elk, and dogs to run down and tree cougars. It's easy to shoot an animal out of a tree. It's virtually impossible to miss a moose, a conspicuous and placid animal of steady habits . . . *I took a deep breath and pulled the trigger. The bull dropped. I looked at my watch: 8:22. The big guy was early. Mike started whooping and hollering and I joined him. I never realized how big a moose was until this one was on the ground. We took pictures* . . . Hunters shoot animals when they're resting . . . *Mike selected a deer, settled down to a steady rest, and fired. The buck was his when he squeezed the trigger. John decided to take the other buck, which had jumped up to its feet. The deer hadn't seen us and was confused by the shot echoing about in the valley. John took careful aim, fired, and took the buck. The hunt was over.* . . . And they shoot them when they're eating . . . *The bruin ambled up the stream, checking gravel bars and backwaters for fish. Finally he plopped down on the bank to eat. Quickly, I tiptoed into range* . . . They use decoys and calls . . . *The six-point gave me a cold-eyed glare from ninety steps away. I hit him with a 130-grain Sierra boat-tail handload. The bull went down hard. Our hunt was over.* . . . They use sex lures . . . *The big buck raised its nose to the air, curled back its lips, and tested the scent of the doe's urine. I held my breath, fought back the shivers, and jerked off a shot. The 180-grain spire-point bullet caught the buck high on the back behind the shoulder and put it down. It didn't get up* . . . They use walkie-talkies, binoculars, scopes . . . *With my 308 Browning BLR, I steadied the 9X cross hairs on the front of the bear's massive shoulders and squeezed. The bear cartwheeled backward for fifty yards* . . . *The second Federal Premium 165-grain bullet found its mark. Another shot anchored the bear for good* . . . They bait deer with corn. They spread popcorn on golf courses for Canada geese and they douse meat baits with fry grease and honey for bears . . . *Make the baiting site redolent of inner-city doughnut shops.* They use blinds and tree stands and mobile stands. They go out in groups, in gangs, and

employ "pushes" and "drives." So many methods are effective. So
few rules apply. It's fun! . . . *We kept on repelling the swarms of birds as
they came in looking for shelter from that big ocean wind, emptying our
shell belts* . . . A species can, in the vernacular, be *pressured by hunting* (which means that killing them has decimated them), but that
just increases the fun, the *challenge.* There is practically no criticism of conduct within the ranks . . . *It's mostly a matter of opinion
and how hunters have been brought up to hunt* . . . Although a recent
editorial in *Ducks Unlimited* magazine did venture to primly suggest
that one should *not fall victim to greed-induced stress through piggish
competition with others.*

But hunters are piggy. They just can't seem to help it. They're
overequipped . . . insatiable, malevolent, and vain. They maim and
mutilate and despoil. And for the most part, they're inept. Grossly
inept.

Camouflaged toilet paper is a must for the modern hunter,
along with his Bronco and his beer. Too many hunters taking a
dump in the woods with their roll of Charmin beside them were
mistaken for white-tailed deer and shot. Hunters get excited.
They'll shoot anything — the pallid ass of another sportsman or
even themselves. A Long Island man died last year when his shotgun went off as he clubbed a wounded deer with the butt. Hunters
get mad. They get restless and want to fire! They want to use those
assault rifles and see foamy blood on the ferns. Wounded animals
can travel for miles in fear and pain before they collapse. Count-
less gut-shot deer — *if you hear a sudden, squashy thump, the animal
has probably been hit in the abdomen* — are "lost" each year. "Poorly
placed shots" are frequent, and injured animals are seldom
tracked, because most hunters never learned how to track. The
majority of hunters will shoot at anything with four legs during
deer season and anything with wings during duck season. Hunters
try to nail running animals and distant birds. They become so
overeager, so *aroused,* that they misidentify and misjudge, spraying
their "game" with shots but failing to bring it down.

The fact is, hunters' lack of skill is a big, big problem. And
nowhere is the problem worse than in the new glamour recreation, bow hunting. These guys are elitists. They doll themselves
up in camouflage, paint their faces black, and climb up into tree
stands from which they attempt the penetration of deer, elk, and

turkeys with modern, multiblade, broadhead arrows shot from sophisticated, easy-to-draw compound bows. This "primitive" way of
hunting appeals to many, and even the nonhunter may feel that it's
a "fairer" method, requiring more strength and skill, but bow
hunting is the cruelest, most wanton form of wildlife disposal of
all. Studies conducted by state fish and wildlife departments repeatedly show that bow hunters wound and fail to retrieve as many
animals as they kill. An animal that flees, wounded by an arrow,
will most assuredly die of the wound, but it will be days before he
does. Even with a "good" hit, the time elapsed between the strike
and death is exceedingly long. *The rule of thumb has long been that we
should wait thirty to forty-five minutes on heart and lung hits, an hour or
more on a suspected liver hit, eight to twelve hours on paunch hits, and
that we should follow immediately on hindquarter and other muscle-only
hits, to keep the wound open and bleeding,* is the advice in the magazine *Fins and Feathers.* What the hunter does as he hangs around
waiting for his animal to finish with its terrified running and dying
hasn't been studied — maybe he puts on more makeup, maybe he
has a highball.

Wildlife agencies promote and encourage bow hunting by per-
mitting earlier and longer seasons, even though they are well
aware that, in their words, *crippling is a by-product of the sport,* making archers pretty sloppy for elitists. The broadhead arrow is a very
inefficient killing tool. Bow hunters are trying to deal with this
problem with the suggestion that they use poison pods. These poi-
soned arrows are illegal in all states except Mississippi *(Ah'm gonna
get ma deer even if ah just nick the little bastard),* but they're widely
used anyway. You wouldn't want that deer to suffer, would you?

The mystique of the efficacy and decency of the bow hunter is as
much an illusion as the perception that a waterfowler is a refined
and thoughtful fellow, a *romantic aesthete,* as Vance Bourjaily put it,
equipped with his faithful Labs and a love for solitude and wild
places. More sentimental drivel has been written about bird shooting than any other type of hunting. It's a soul-wrenching pursuit,
apparently, the execution of birds in flight. Ducks Unlimited — an
organization that has managed to put a spin on the word *conservation* for years — works hard to project the idea that duck hunters
are blue bloods and that duck stamps with their pretty pictures are

responsible for saving all the saved puddles in North America. *Sportsman's conservation* is a contradiction in terms (We protect things now so that we can kill them later) and is broadly interpreted (Don't kill them all, just kill most of them). A hunter is a conservationist in the same way a farmer or a rancher is: he's not. Like the rancher who kills everything that's not stock on his (and the public's) land, and the farmer who scorns wildlife because "they don't pay their freight," the hunter uses nature by destroying its parts, mastering it by simplifying it through death.

George ("We kill to hunt and not the other way around") Reiger, the conservationist-hunter's spokesman (he's the best they've got, apparently), said that the "dedicated" waterfowler will shoot other game "of course," but *we do so much in the same spirit of the lyrics, that when we're not near the girl we love, we love the girl we're near.* (Duck hunters practice tough love.) The fact is, far from being a "romantic aesthete," the waterfowler is the most avaricious of all hunters . . . *That's when Scott suggested the friendly wager on who would take the most birds . . .* and the most resistant to minimum ecological decency. Millions of birds that managed to elude shotgun blasts were dying each year from ingesting the lead shot that rained down in the wetlands. Year after year, birds perished from feeding on spent lead, but hunters were "reluctant" to switch to steel. They worried that it would impair their shooting, and ammunition manufacturers said a changeover would be "expensive." State and federal officials had to weigh the poisoning against these considerations. It took forever, this weighing, but now steel-shot loads are required almost everywhere, having been judged "more than adequate" to bring down the birds. This is not to say, of course, that most duck hunters use steel shot almost everywhere. They're traditionalists and don't care for all the new, pesky rules. Oh, for the golden age of waterfowling, when a man could measure a good day's shooting by the pickup load. But those days are gone. Fall is a melancholy time, all right.

Spectacular abuses occur wherever geese congregate, Shooting Sportsman notes quietly, something that the more cultivated Ducks Unlimited would hesitate to admit. Waterfowl populations are plummeting and waterfowl hunters are out of control. "Supervised" hunts are hardly distinguished from unsupervised ones. A biologist with the Department of the Interior who observed a hunt at Sand Lake in

South Dakota said, *Hunters repeatedly shot over the line at incoming flights where there was no possible chance of retrieving. Time and time again I was shocked at the behavior of hunters. I heard them laugh at the plight of dazed cripples that stumbled about. I saw them striking the heads of retrieved cripples against fence posts.* In the South, wood ducks return to their roosts after sunset when shooting hours are closed. Hunters find this an excellent time to shoot them. Dennis Anderson, an outdoors writer, said, *Roost shooters just fire at the birds as fast as they can, trying to drop as many as they can. Then they grab what birds they can find. The birds they can't find in the dark, they leave behind.*

Carnage and waste are the rules in bird hunting, even during legal seasons and open hours. Thousands of wounded ducks and geese are not retrieved, left to rot in the marshes and fields . . . *When I asked Wanda where hers had fallen, she wasn't sure.* Cripples, and there are many cripples made in this pastime, are still able to run and hide, eluding the hunter even if he's willing to spend time searching for them, which he usually isn't . . . *It's one thing to run down a cripple in a picked bean field or a pasture, and quite another to watch a wing-tipped bird drop into a huge block of switch grass.* Oh nasty, nasty switch grass. A downed bird becomes invisible on the ground and is practically unfindable without a good dog, and few "water-fowlers" have them these days. They're hard to train — usually a professional has to do it — and most hunters can't be bothered. Birds are easy to tumble . . . *Canada geese — blues and snows — can all take a good amount of shot. Brant are easily called and decoyed and come down easily. Ruffed grouse are hard to hit but easy to kill. Sharptails are harder to kill but easier to hit* . . . It's just a nuisance to recover them. But it's fun, fun, fun swatting them down . . . *There's distinct pleasure in watching a flock work to a good friend's gun.*

Teal, the smallest of common ducks, are really easy to kill. Hunters in the South used to *practice* on teal in September, prior to the "serious" waterfowl season. But the birds were so diminutive and the limit so low (four a day) that many hunters felt it hardly worth going out and getting bit by mosquitoes to kill them. Enough did, however, brave the bugs and manage to "harvest" 165,000 of the little migrating birds in Louisiana in 1987 alone. *Shooting is usually best on opening day. By the second day you can sometimes detect a decline in local teal numbers. Areas may deteriorate to virtu-*

ally no action by the third day . . . The area *deteriorates.* When a flock is
wiped out, the skies are empty. *No action.*

Teal declined more sharply than any duck species except mallard last year; this baffles hunters. Hunters and their procurers —
wildlife agencies — will *never* admit that hunting is responsible for
the decimation of a species. John Turner, head of the federal Fish
and Wildlife Service, delivers the familiar and litanic line. Hunting
is not the problem. *Pollution* is the problem. *Pesticides, urbanization,
deforestation, hazardous waste,* and *wetlands destruction* are the problem. And drought! There's been a big drought! Antis should devote their energies to solving these problems if they care about
wildlife, and leave the hunters alone. While the Fish and Wildlife
Service is busily conducting experiments in cause and effect, like
releasing mallard ducklings on a wetland sprayed with the insecti-
cide ethyl parathion (they died — it was known they would, but
you can never have enough studies that show guns aren't a duck's
only problem), hunters are killing some 200 million birds and animals each year. But these deaths are incidental to the problem, according to Turner. A factor, perhaps, but a *minor* one. Ducks
Unlimited says the problem isn't hunting, it's *low recruitment* on the
part of the birds. To the hunter, *birth* in the animal kingdom is *recruitment.* They wouldn't want to use an emotional, sentimental
word like *birth.* The black duck, a very "popular" duck in the
Northeast, so "popular," in fact, that game agencies felt that
hunters couldn't be asked to refrain from shooting it, is scarce
and getting scarcer. Nevertheless, it's still being hunted. *A number
of studies are currently under way in an attempt to discover why black
ducks are disappearing, Sports Afield* reports. Black ducks are disappearing because they've been shot out, their elimination being a
dreadful example of game management, and managers who are
loath to "displease" hunters. The skies — *flyways* — of America
have been divided into four administrative regions, and the states,
advised by a federal government coordinator, have to agree on
policies.

There's always a lot of squabbling that goes on in flyway meetings — lots of complaints about short-stopping, for example.
Short-stopping is the deliberate holding of birds in a state, often
by feeding them in wildlife refuges, so that their southern migration is slowed or stopped. Hunters in the North get to kill more

than hunters in the South. This isn't fair. Hunters demand equity in opportunities to kill.

Wildlife managers hate closing the season on anything. Closing the season on a species would indicate a certain amount of *mis*management and misjudgment at the very least — a certain reliance on overly optimistic winter counts, a certain overappeasement of hunters who would be "upset" if they couldn't kill their favorite thing. And worse, closing a season would be considered victory for the antis. Bird-hunting "rules" are very complicated, but they all encourage killing. There are shortened seasons and split seasons and special seasons for "underutilized" birds. (Teal were very recently considered "underutilized.") The limit on coots is fifteen a day — shooting them, it's easy! They don't fly high — giving the hunter something to do while he waits in the blind. Some species are "protected," but bear in mind that hunters begin blasting away one half hour before sunrise and that most hunters can't identify a bird in the air even in broad daylight. Some of them can't identify birds in hand either, and even if they can (*#%*! I got me a canvasback, that duck's frigging protected . . .*), they are likely to bury unpopular or "trash" ducks so that they can continue to hunt the ones they "love."

Game "professionals," in thrall to hunters' "needs," will not stop managing bird populations until they've doled out the final duck (*I didn't get my limit but I bagged the last one, by golly . . .*). The Fish and Wildlife Service services legal hunters as busily as any madam, but it is powerless in tempering the lusts of the illegal ones. Illegal kill is a monumental problem in the not-so-wonderful world of waterfowl. Excesses have always pervaded the "sport," and bird shooters have historically been the slobs and profligates of hunting. *Doing away with hunting would do away with a vital cultural and historical aspect of American life,* John Turner claims. So, do away with it. Do away with those who have already done away with so much. Do away with them before the birds they have pursued so relentlessly and for so long drop into extinction, sink, in the poet Wallace Stevens's words, "downward to darkness on extended wings."

"Quality" hunting is as rare as the Florida panther. What you've got is a bunch of guys driving over the plains, up the mountains, and through the woods with their stupid tag that cost them a couple of bucks and immense coolers full of beer and body parts.

There's a price tag on the right to destroy living creatures for play, but it's not much. *A big-game hunting license is the greatest deal going since the Homestead Act,* Ted Kerasote writes in *Sports Afield. In many states residents can hunt big game for more than a month for about $20.* It's cheaper than taking the little woman out to lunch. It's cheap all right, and it's because killing animals is considered *recreation* and is underwritten by state and federal funds. In Florida, state moneys are routinely spent on "youth hunts," in which kids are guided to shoot deer from stands in wildlife-management areas. The organizers of these events say that these staged hunts *help youth to understand man's role in the ecosystem.* (Drop a doe and take your place in the ecological community, son . . .)

Hunters claim (they don't actually believe it but they've learned to say it) that they're doing nonhunters a favor, for if they didn't *use* wild animals, wild animals would be useless. They believe that they're just *helping Mother Nature control populations (you wouldn't want those deer to die of starvation, would you?).* They claim that their tiny fees provide *all* Americans with wild lands and animals. (People who don't hunt get to enjoy animals all year round while hunters get to enjoy them only during hunting season . . .) Ducks Unlimited feels that it, in particular, is a selfless provider and environmental champion. Although members spend most of their money lobbying for hunters and raising ducks in pens to release later over shooting fields, they do save some wetlands, mostly by persuading farmers not to fill them in. *See that little pothole there the ducks like? Well, I'm gonna plant more soybeans there if you don't pay me not to . . .* Hunters claim many nonsensical things, but the most nonsensical of all is that they *pay their own way.* They do not pay their own way. They *do* pay into a perverse wildlife-management system that manipulates "stocks" and "herds" and "flocks" for hunters' killing pleasure, but these fees in no way cover the cost of highly questionable ecological practices. For some spare change . . . *the greatest deal going* . . . hunters can hunt on public land — national parks, state forests — preserves for hunters! — which the nonhunting and antihunting public pay for. (Access to private lands is becoming increasingly difficult for them, as experience has taught people that hunters are obnoxious.) Hunters kill on millions of acres of land all over America that are maintained with general taxpayer revenue, but the most shocking, really twisted subsidization takes place on national wildlife refuges. Nowhere is the arrogance and the insidiousness of this small, aggressive minority more clearly demonstrated. Nowhere is the murder of animals, the manipulation of language, and the distortion of public intent more flagrant. The public perceives national wildlife refuges as safe havens, as sanctuaries for animals. And why wouldn't they? The word *refuge* of course *means* shelter from danger and distress. But the dweeby nonhunting public — they tend to be so literal. The word has been reinterpreted by management over time and now hunters are invited into more than half of the country's more than 440 wildlife "sanctuaries" each year to bang them up and kill more than half a million animals. This is called *wildlife-oriented recreation.* Hunters think of this as being no less than their due, claiming that refuge lands were purchased with duck stamps *(. . . our duck stamps paid for it . . . our duck stamps paid for it . . .).* Hunters equate those stupid stamps with the mystic, multiplying power of the Lord's loaves and fishes, but of 90 million acres in the Wildlife Refuge System, only 3 million were bought with hunting-stamp revenue. Most wildlife "restoration" programs in the states are translated into clearing land to increase deer habitats (so that too many deer will require hunting . . . you wouldn't want them to die of starvation, would you?) and trapping animals for restocking and study (so hunters can shoot more of them). Fish and game agencies hustle hunting — instead of conserving wildlife, they're killing it. It's time for them to get in the business of protecting and preserving wildlife and creating balanced ecological systems instead of pimping for hunters who want their deer/duck/pheasant/turkey — animals stocked to be shot.

Hunters' self-serving arguments and lies are becoming more preposterous as nonhunters awake from their long, albeit troubled, sleep. Sport hunting is immoral; it should be made illegal. Hunters are persecutors of nature who should be prosecuted. They wield a disruptive power out of all proportion to their numbers, and pandering to their interests — the special interests of a group that just wants to kill things — is mad. It's preposterous that every year less than 7 percent of the population turns the skies into shooting galleries and the woods and fields into abattoirs. It's time to stop actively supporting and passively allowing hunting, and time to stigmatize it. It's time to stop being conned and cowed by hunters, time to stop pampering and coddling them, time to get them off the government's duck-and-deer dole, time to stop thinking of wild animals as "resources" and "game," and start thinking of them as sentient beings that deserve our wonder and respect, time to stop allowing hunting to be creditable by calling it "sport" and "recreation." Hunters make wildlife *dead, dead, dead.* It's time to wake up to this indisputable fact. As for the hunters, it's long past check-out time.

Reflections and Responses

1. In her sixth paragraph, Williams introduces the following quotes: *"He's yours . . . He's mine . . . I decided to . . . I decided not to . . . I debated shooting it, then I decided to let it live . . ."* Who is supposedly saying these things? What point is Williams making about hunters?

2. Williams criticizes not only the morality of hunting but the "manipulation of language" by "hunting apologists." To what extent does she focus her argument on language? What aspects of the pro-hunting language does she most dislike? What euphemisms does she satirize? Do you think she criticizes this language fairly? Explain.

3. Go through the essay systematically and list the pro-hunting arguments Williams introduces. How many can you identify? How do you think she handles them? For example, do you agree with her refutation of the position that people who eat meat are hypocritical in their criticism of hunters?

6

Journeys

JAMAICA KINCAID

On Seeing England
for the First Time

One of the most sinister sides of imperialism is the way it promotes the ruling nation's culture and rejects the colony's. The effect of this on an impressionable young person is vividly described in Jamaica Kincaid's sensitive and angry autobiographical essay about growing up in Antigua with the dark shadow of England continually looming over her. England and a reverence for things English invaded every aspect of her daily life and education. Yet it was not until adulthood that she finally journeyed to England and really saw it for the first time. "The space between the idea of something and its reality," Kincaid writes, "is always wide and deep and dark." The real England she finally sees is far different from the other England, whose maps and history she was made to memorize as a schoolgirl in Antigua.

Kincaid is the author of At the Bottom of the River *(1983),* Annie John *(1985),* A Small Place *(1988), and* Lucy *(1990). A staff writer for* The New Yorker, *her stories and essays have also appeared in* Rolling Stone, Paris Review, *and other literary periodicals. She was born in Antigua and currently lives in Vermont. "On Seeing England for the First Time" originally appeared in* Transition *(1991) and was selected by Susan Sontag for* The Best American Essays *1992.*

When I saw England for the first time, I was a child in school sitting at a desk. The England I was looking at was laid out on a map gently, beautifully, delicately, a very special jewel; it lay on a bed of sky blue — the background of the map — its yellow form mysterious, because though it looked like a leg of mutton, it could not really look like anything so familiar as a leg of mutton because it was England — with shadings of pink and green, unlike any shad-

ings of pink and green I had seen before, squiggly veins of red running in every direction. England was a special jewel all right, and
only special people got to wear it. The people who got to wear England were English people. They wore it well and they wore it everywhere: in jungles, in deserts, on plains, on top of the highest
mountains, on all the oceans, on all the seas, in places where they
were not welcome, in places they should not have been. When my
teacher had pinned this map up on the blackboard, she said, "This
is England" — and she said it with authority, seriousness, and adoration, and we all sat up. It was as if she had said, "This is
Jerusalem, the place you will go to when you die but only if you
have been good." We understood then — we were meant to understand then — that England was to be our source of myth and the
source from which we got our sense of reality, our sense of what
was meaningful, our sense of what was meaningless — and much
about our own lives and much about the very idea of us headed
that last list.

At the time I was a child sitting at my desk seeing England for
the first time, I was already very familiar with the greatness of it.
Each morning before I left for school, I ate a breakfast of half a
grapefruit, an egg, bread and butter and a slice of cheese, and a
cup of cocoa; or half a grapefruit, a bowl of oat porridge, bread
and butter and a slice of cheese, and a cup of cocoa. The can of
cocoa was often left on the table in front of me. It had written on it
the name of the company, the year the company was established,
and the words "Made in England." Those words, "Made in England," were written on the box the oats came in too. They would
also have been written on the box the shoes I was wearing came in;
a bolt of gray linen cloth lying on the shelf of a store from which
my mother had bought three yards to make the uniform that I was
wearing had written along its edge those three words. The shoes I
wore were made in England; so were my socks and cotton under-
garments and the satin ribbons I wore tied at the end of two plaits
of my hair. My father, who might have sat next to me at breakfast,
was a carpenter and cabinet maker. The shoes he wore to work
would have been made in England, as were his khaki shirt and
trousers, his underpants and undershirt, his socks and brown felt
hat. Felt was not the proper material from which a hat that was expected to provide shade from the hot sun should be made, but my

father must have seen and admired a picture of an Englishman
wearing such a hat in England, and this picture that he saw must
have been so compelling that it caused him to wear the wrong hat
for a hot climate most of his long life. And this hat — a brown felt
hat — became so central to his character that it was the first thing
he put on in the morning as he stepped out of bed and the last
thing he took off before he stepped back into bed at night. As we
sat at breakfast a car might go by. The car, a Hillman or a Zephyr,
was made in England. The very idea of the meal itself, breakfast,
and its substantial quality and quantity was an idea from England;
we somehow knew that in England they began the day with this
meal called breakfast and a proper breakfast was a big breakfast.
No one I knew liked eating so much food so early in the day; it
made us feel sleepy, tired. But this breakfast business was Made in
England like almost everything else that surrounded us, the exceptions being the sea, the sky, and the air we breathed.

At the time I saw this map — seeing England for the first time —
I did not say to myself, "Ah, so that's what it looks like," because
there was no longing in me to put a shape to those three words
that ran through every part of my life, no matter how small; for me
to have had such a longing would have meant that I lived in a certain atmosphere, an atmosphere in which those three words were
felt as a burden. But I did not live in such an atmosphere. My father's brown felt hat would develop a hole in its crown, the lining
would separate from the hat itself, and six weeks before he
thought that he could not be seen wearing it — he was a very vain
man — he would order another hat from England. And my
mother taught me to eat my food in the English way: the knife in
the right hand, the fork in the left, my elbows held still close to my
side, the food carefully balanced on my fork and then brought up
to my mouth. When I had finally mastered it, I overheard her saying to a friend, "Did you see how nicely she can eat?" But I knew
then that I enjoyed my food more when I ate it with my bare
hands, and I continued to do so when she wasn't looking. And
when my teacher showed us the map, she asked us to study it carefully, because no test we would ever take would be complete without this statement: "Draw a map of England."

I did not know then that the statement "Draw a map of England" was something far worse than a declaration of war, for in fact

a flat-out declaration of war would have put me on alert, and again in fact, there was no need for war — I had long ago been conquered. I did not know then that this statement was part of a process that would result in my erasure, not my physical erasure, but my erasure all the same. I did not know then that this statement was meant to make me feel in awe and small whenever I heard the word "England": awe at its existence, small because I was not from it. I did not know very much of anything then — certainly not what a blessing it was that I was unable to draw a map of England correctly.

After that there were many times of seeing England for the first time. I saw England in history. I knew the names of all the kings of England. I knew the names of their children, their wives, their disappointments, their triumphs, the names of people who betrayed them, I knew the dates on which they were born and the dates they died. I knew their conquests and was made to feel glad if I figured in them; I knew their defeats. I knew the details of the year 1066 (the Battle of Hastings, the end of the reign of the Anglo-Saxon kings) before I knew the details of the year 1832 (the year slavery was abolished). It wasn't as bad as I make it sound now; it was worse. I did like so much hearing again and again how Alfred the Great, traveling in disguise, had been left to watch cakes, and because he wasn't used to this the cakes got burned, and Alfred burned his hands pulling them out of the fire, and the woman who had left him to watch the cakes screamed at him. I loved King Alfred. My grandfather was named after him; his son, my uncle, was named after King Alfred; my brother is named after King Alfred. And so there are three people in my family named after a man they have never met, a man who died over ten centuries ago. The first view I got of England then was not unlike the first view received by the person who named my grandfather.

This view, though — the naming of the kings, their deeds, their disappointments — was the vivid view, the forceful view. There were other views, subtler ones, softer, almost not there — but these were the ones that made the most lasting impression on me, these were the ones that made me really feel like nothing. "When morning touched the sky" was one phrase, for no morning touched the sky where I lived. The mornings where I lived came on abruptly, with a shock of heat and loud noises. "Evening approaches" was another, but the evenings where I lived did not approach; in fact, I had no evening — I had night and I had day and they came and went in a mechanical way: on, off; on, off. And then there were gentle mountains and low blue skies and moors over which people took walks for nothing but pleasure, when where I lived a walk was an act of labor, a burden, something only death or the automobile could relieve. And there were things that a small turn of a head could convey — entire worlds, whole lives would depend on this thing, a certain turn of a head. Everyday life could be quite tiring, more tiring than anything I was told not to do. I was told not to gossip, but they did that all the time. And they ate so much food, violating another of those rules they taught me: do not indulge in gluttony. And the foods they ate actually: if only sometime I could eat cold cuts after theater, cold cuts of lamb and mint sauce, and Yorkshire pudding and scones, and clotted cream, and sausages that came from upcountry (imagine, "up-country"). And having troubling thoughts at twilight, a good time to have troubling thoughts, apparently; and servants who stole and left in the middle of a crisis, who were born with a limp or some other kind of deformity, not nourished properly in their mother's womb (that last part I figured out for myself; the point was, oh to have an untrustworthy servant); and wonderful cobbled streets onto which solid front doors opened; and people whose eyes were blue and who had fair skins and who smelled only of lavender, or sometimes sweet pea or primrose. And those flowers with those names: delphiniums, foxgloves, tulips, daffodils, floribunda, peonies; in bloom, a striking display, being cut and placed in large glass bowls, crystal, decorating rooms so large twenty families the size of mine could fit in comfortably but used only for passing through. And the weather was so remarkable because the rain fell gently always, only occasionally in deep gusts, and it colored the air various shades of gray, each an appealing shade for a dress to be worn when a portrait was being painted; and when it rained at twilight, wonderful things happened: people bumped into each other unexpectedly and that would lead to all sorts of turns of events — a plot, the mere weather caused plots. I saw that people rushed: they rushed to catch trains, they rushed toward each other and away from each other; they rushed and rushed and rushed. That word: rushed! I did not know what it was to do that. It was too hot to do that, and so I came to envy people who would rush, even though it had no meaning to me to do such a thing. But there they are again. They loved their children; their children were sent to their own rooms as a punishment, rooms larger than my entire house. They were special, everything about them said so, even their clothes; their clothes rustled, swished, soothed. The world was theirs, not mine; everything told me so.

If now as I speak of all this I give the impression of someone on the outside looking in, nose pressed up against a glass window, that is wrong. My nose was pressed up against a glass window all right, but there was an iron vise at the back of my neck forcing my head to stay in place. To avert my gaze was to fall back into something from which I had been rescued, a hole filled with nothing, and that was the word for everything about me, nothing. The reality of my life was conquests, subjugation, humiliation, enforced amnesia. I was forced to forget. Just for instance, this: I lived in a part of St. John's, Antigua, called Ovals. Ovals was made up of five streets, each of them named after a famous English seaman — to be quite frank, an officially sanctioned criminal: Rodney Street (after George Rodney), Nelson Street (after Horatio Nelson), Drake Street (after Francis Drake), Hood Street, and Hawkins Street (after John Hawkins). But John Hawkins was knighted after a trip he made to Africa, opening up a new trade, the slave trade. He was then entitled to wear as his crest a Negro bound with a cord. Every single person living on Hawkins Street was descended from a slave. John Hawkins's ship, the one in which he transported the people he had bought and kidnapped, was called *The Jesus*. He later became the treasurer of the Royal Navy and rear admiral.

Again, the reality of my life, the life I led at the time I was being shown these views of England for the first time, for the second time, for the one-hundred-millionth time, was this: the sun shone with what sometimes seemed to be a deliberate cruelty; we must have done something to deserve that. My dresses did not rustle in the evening air as I strolled to the theater (I had no evening, I had no theater; my dresses were made of a cheap cotton, the weave of which would give way after not too many washings). I got up in the morning, I did my chores (fetched water from the public pipe for my mother, swept the yard), I washed myself, I went to a woman to have my hair combed freshly every day (because before we were allowed into our classroom our teachers would inspect us, and children who had not bathed that day, or had dirt under their fingernails, or whose hair had not been combed anew that day, might not be allowed to attend class). I ate that breakfast. I walked to school. At school we gathered in an auditorium and sang a hymn, "All Things Bright and Beautiful," and looking down on us as we sang were portraits of the Queen of England and her husband; they wore jewels and medals and they smiled. I was a Brownie. At each meeting we would form a little group around a flagpole, and after raising the Union Jack, we would say, "I promise to do my best, to do my duty to God and the Queen, to help other people every day and obey the scouts' law."

Who were these people and why had I never seen them, I mean really seen them, in the place where they lived? I had never been to England. No one I knew had ever been to England, or I should say, no one I knew had ever been and returned to tell me about it. All the people I knew who had gone to England had stayed there. Sometimes they left behind them their small children, never to see them again. England! I had seen England's representatives. I had seen the governor general at the public grounds at a ceremony celebrating the Queen's birthday. I had seen an old princess and I had seen a young princess. They had both been extremely not beautiful, but who of us would have told them that? I had never seen England, really seen it, I had only met a representative, seen a picture, read books, memorized its history. I had never set foot, my own foot, in it.

The space between the idea of something and its reality is always wide and deep and dark. The longer they are kept apart — idea of thing, reality of thing — the wider the width, the deeper the depth, the thicker and darker the darkness. This space starts out empty, there is nothing in it, but it rapidly becomes filled up with obsession or desire or hatred or love — sometimes all of these things, sometimes some of these things, sometimes only one of these things. The existence of the world as I came to know it was a result of this: idea of thing over here, reality of thing way, way over there. There was Christopher Columbus, an unlikable man, an unpleasant man, a liar (and so, of course, a thief) surrounded by maps and schemes and plans, and there was the reality on the other side of that width, that depth, that darkness. He became obsessed, he became filled with desire, the hatred came later, love was never a part of it. Eventually, his idea met the longed-for reality. That the idea of something and its reality are often two completely different things is something no one ever remembers; and so when they meet and find that they are not compatible, the weaker of the two, idea or reality, dies. That idea Christopher Columbus had was more powerful than the reality he met, and so the reality he met died.

And so finally, when I was a grown-up woman, the mother of two children, the wife of someone, a person who resides in a powerful country that takes up more than its fair share of a continent, the owner of a house with many rooms in it and of two automobiles, with the desire and will (which I very much act upon) to take from the world more than I give back to it, more than I deserve, more than I need, finally then, I saw England, the real England, not a picture, not a painting, not through a story in a book, but England, for the first time. In me, the space between the idea of it and its reality had become filled with hatred, and so when at last I saw it I wanted to take it into my hands and tear it into little pieces and then crumble it up as if it were clay, child's clay. That was impossible, and so I could only indulge in not-favorable opinions.

There were monuments everywhere; they commemorated victories, battles fought between them and the people who lived across the sea from them, all vile people, fought over which of them would have dominion over the people who looked like me. The monuments were useless to them now, people sat on them and ate their lunch. They were like markers on an old useless trail, like a piece of old string tied to a finger to jog the memory, like old decoration in an old house, dirty, useless, in the way. Their skins were so pale, it made them look so fragile, so weak, so ugly. What if I had the power to simply banish them from their land, send boat after boatload of them on a voyage that in fact had no destination, force them to live in a place where the sun's presence was a constant? This would rid them of their pale complexion and make them look more like me, make them look more like the people I love and treasure and hold dear, and more like the people who occupy the near and far reaches of my imagination, my history, my geography, and reduce them and everything they have ever known to figurines as evidence that I was in divine favor, what if all this was in my power? Could I resist it? No one ever has.

And they were rude, they were rude to each other. They didn't like each other very much. They didn't like each other in the way they didn't like me, and it occurred to me that their dislike for me was one of the few things they agreed on.

I was on a train in England with a friend, an English woman. Before we were in England she liked me very much. In England she didn't like me at all. She didn't like the claim I said I had on England, she didn't like the views I had of England. I didn't like England, she didn't like England, but she didn't like me not liking it too. She said, "I want to show you my England, I want to show you the England that I know and love." I had told her many times before that I knew England and I didn't want to love it anyway. She no longer lived in England; it was her own country, but it had not been kind to her, so she left. On the train, the conductor was rude to her; she asked something, and he responded in a rude way. She became ashamed. She was ashamed at the way he treated her; she was ashamed at the way he behaved. "This is the new England," she said. But I liked the conductor being rude; his behavior seemed quite appropriate. Earlier this had happened: we had gone to a store to buy a shirt for my husband; it was meant to be a special present, a special shirt to wear on special occasions. This was a store where the Prince of Wales has his shirts made, but the shirts sold in this store are beautiful all the same. I found a shirt I thought my husband would like and I wanted to buy him a tie to go with it. When I couldn't decide which one to choose, the salesman showed me a new set. He was very pleased with these, he said, because they bore the crest of the Prince of Wales, and the Prince of Wales had never allowed his crest to decorate an article of clothing before. There was something in the way he said it; his tone was slavish, reverential, awed. It made me feel angry; I wanted to hit him. I didn't do that. I said, my husband and I hate princes, my husband would never wear anything that had a prince's anything on it. My friend stiffened. The salesman stiffened. They both drew themselves in, away from me. My friend told me that the prince was a symbol of her Englishness, and I could see that I had caused offense. I looked at her. She was an English person, the sort of English person I used to know at home, the sort who was nobody in England but somebody when they came to live among the people like me. There were many people I could have seen England with; that I was seeing it with this particular person, a person who reminded me of the people who showed me England long ago as I sat in church or at my desk, made me feel silent and afraid, for I wondered if, all these years of our friendship, I had had a friend or had been in the thrall of a racial memory.

I went to Bath — we, my friend and I, did this, but though we were together, I was no longer with her. The landscape was almost as familiar as my own hand, but I had never been in this place before, so how could that be again? And the streets of Bath were familiar, too, but I had never walked on them before. It was all those years of reading, starting with Roman Britain. Why did I have to know about Roman Britain? It was of no real use to me, a person living on a hot, drought-ridden island, and it is of no use to me now, and yet my head is filled with this nonsense, Roman Britain. In Bath, I drank tea in a room I had read about in a novel written in the eighteenth century. In this very same room, young women wearing those dresses that rustled and so on danced and flirted and sometimes disgraced themselves with young men, soldiers, sailors, who were on their way to Bristol or someplace like that, so many places like that where so many adventures, the outcome of which was not good for me, began. Bristol, England. A sentence that began "That night the ship sailed from Bristol, England" would end not so good for me. And then I was driving through the countryside in an English motorcar, on narrow winding roads, and they were so familiar, though I had never been on them before; and through little villages the names of which I somehow knew so well though I had never been there before. And the countryside did have all those hedges and hedges, fields hedged in. I was marveling at all the toil of it, the planting of the hedges to begin with and then the care of it, all that clipping, year after year of clipping, and I wondered at the lives of the people who would have to do this, because wherever I see and feel the hands that hold up the world, I see and feel myself and all the people who look like me. And I said, "Those hedges" and my friend said that someone, a woman named Mrs. Rothchild, worried that the hedges weren't being taken care of properly; the farmers couldn't afford or find the help to keep up the hedges, and often they replaced them with wire fencing. I might have said to that, well if Mrs. Rothchild doesn't like the wire fencing, why doesn't she take care of the hedges herself, but I didn't. And then in those fields that were now hemmed in by wire fencing that a privileged woman didn't like was planted a vile yellow flowering bush that produced an oil, and my friend said that Mrs. Rothchild didn't like this either; it ruined the English countryside, it ruined the traditional look of the English countryside.

It was not at that moment that I wished every sentence, everything I knew, that began with England would end with "and then it all died; we don't know how, it just all died." At that moment, I was thinking, who are these people who forced me to think of them all the time, who forced me to think that the world I knew was incomplete, or without substance, or did not measure up because it was not England; that I was incomplete, or without substance, and did not measure up because I was not English. Who were these people? The person sitting next to me couldn't give me a clue; no one person could. In any case, if I had said to her, I find England ugly, I hate England; the weather is like a jail sentence, the English are a very ugly people, the food in England is like a jail sentence, the hair of English people is so straight, so dead looking, the English have an unbearable smell so different from the smell of people I know, real people of course, she would have said that I was a person full of prejudice. Apart from the fact that it is I — that is, the people who look like me — who made her aware of the unpleasantness of such a thing, the idea of such a thing, prejudice, she would have been only partly right, sort of right: I may be capable of prejudice, but my prejudices have no weight to them, my prejudices have no force behind them, my prejudices remain opinions, my prejudices remain my personal opinion. And a great feeling of rage and disappointment came over me as I looked at England, my head full of personal opinions that could not have public, my public, approval. The people I come from are powerless to do evil on grand scale.

The moment I wished every sentence, everything I knew, that began with England would end with "and then it all died, we don't know how, it just all died" was when I saw the white cliffs of Dover. I had sung hymns and recited poems that were about a longing to see the white cliffs of Dover again. At the time I sang the hymns and recited the poems, I could really long to see them again because I had never seen them at all, nor had anyone around me at the time. But there we were, groups of people longing for something we had never seen. And so there they were, the white cliffs, but they were not that pearly majestic thing I used to sing about, that thing that created such a feeling in these people that when they died in the place where I lived they had themselves buried facing a direction that would allow them to see the white cliffs of Dover when they were resurrected, as surely they would be. The white cliffs of Dover, when finally I saw them, were cliffs, but they were not white; you would only call them that if the word "white" meant something special to you; they were dirty and they were steep; they were so steep, the correct height from which all my views of England, starting with the map before me in my classroom and ending with the trip I had just taken, should jump and die and disappear forever.

Reflections and Responses

1. Note that Kincaid opens her essay with various images of England. What do these images have in common? How do they reflect colonialism? How do they reflect literature? Why do you think Kincaid begins by placing the images in the context of a classroom?

2. Consider Kincaid's account of her father's hat. In what ways does the "brown felt hat" represent England? How does Kincaid view the hat?

3. When Kincaid finally visits England, what aspects of the country does she dislike the most? What does she mean when she says toward the end of her essay that "I may be capable of prejudice, but my prejudices have no weight to them"? Do you find her opinions prejudiced? In your opinion has she or has she not "prejudged" England?

BARRY LOPEZ

The Stone Horse

Great works of art do not always hang in museums, accessible to anyone who cares to see them. When Barry Lopez wanted to see a mysterious stone horse carved perhaps some four hundred years ago by the Quechan people, his journey took him far off the beaten track. What he finds in the deserts of southern California near the Mexican border is the kind of large ground carving (an intaglio) that some think was intended as a sign to extraterrestrials. But, upon seeing the horse, Lopez does not believe it was "meant to be seen by gods in the sky above" nor does he think it can even be properly appreciated by an aerial photograph. How we see this work of art, Lopez suggests, is as important as what we see. And how we see it requires the journey to it.

One of America's most distinguished nonfiction writers, Lopez is the author of Arctic Dreams, *which won the National Book Award in 1986, and* Of Wolves and Men, *which won the John Burroughs Medal in 1979. His other publications include* Winter Count *(1981),* Crossing Open Ground *(1988),* Coyote Love *(1989), and* The Rediscovery of North America *(1990). He received an award for fiction from the Friends of American Writers in 1982 and the Award in Literature from the American Academy and Institute of Arts and Letters in 1986. "The Stone Horse" originally appeared in* Antaeus *(1986) and was selected by Gay Talese for* The Best American Essays 1987.

I

The deserts of southern California, the high, relatively cooler and wetter Mojave and the hotter, dryer Sonoran to the south of it, carry the signatures of many cultures. Prehistoric rock drawings in the Mojave's Coso Range, probably the greatest concentration of petroglyphs in North America, are at least three thousand years old. Big-game-hunting cultures that flourished six or seven thousand years before that are known from broken spear tips, choppers, and burins left scattered along the shores of great Pleistocene lakes, long since evaporated. Weapons and tools discovered at China Lake may be thirty thousand years old; and worked stone from a quarry in the Calico Mountains is, some argue, evidence that human beings were here more than 200,000 years ago.

Because of the long-term stability of such arid environments, much of this prehistoric stone evidence still lies exposed on the ground, accessible to anyone who passes by — the studious, the acquisitive, the indifferent, the merely curious. Archaeologists do not agree on the sequence of cultural history beyond about twelve thousand years ago, but it is clear that these broken bits of chalcedony, chert, and obsidian, like the animal drawings and geometric designs etched on walls of basalt throughout the desert, anchor the earliest threads of human history, the first record of human endeavor here.

Western man did not enter the California desert until the end of the eighteenth century, 250 years after Coronado brought his soldiers into the Zuni pueblos in a bewildered search for the cities of Cibola. The earliest appraisals of the land were cursory, hurried. People traveled *through* it, en route to Santa Fe or the California coastal settlements. Only miners tarried. In 1823 what had been Spain's became Mexico's, and in 1848 what had been Mexico's became America's; but the bare, jagged mountains and dry lake beds, the vast and uniform plains of creosote bush and yucca plants, remained as obscure as the northern Sudan until the end of the nineteenth century.

Before 1940 the tangible evidence of twentieth-century man's passage here consisted of very little — the hard tracery of travel corridors; the widely scattered, relatively insignificant evidence of mining operations; and the fair expanse of irrigated fields at the desert's periphery. In the space of a hundred years or so the wagon roads were paved, railroads were laid down, and canals and high-tension lines were built to bring water and electricity across the desert to Los Angeles from the Colorado River. The dark mouths of gold, talc, and tin mines yawned from the bony flanks of

desert ranges. Dust-encrusted chemical plants stood at work on
the lonely edges of dry lake beds. And crops of grapes, lettuce,
dates, alfalfa, and cotton covered the Coachella and Imperial valleys, north and south of the Salton Sea, and the Palo Verde Valley
along the Colorado.

These developments proceeded with little or no awareness of
earlier human occupations by cultures that preceded those of the
historic Indians — the Mojave, the Chemehuevi, the Quechan.
(Extensive irrigation began actually to change the climate of the
Sonoran Desert, and human settlements, the railroads, and farming introduced many new, successful plants into the region.)

During World War II, the American military moved into the
desert in great force, to train troops and to test equipment. They
found the clear weather conducive to year-round flying, the dry air
and isolation very attractive. After the war, a complex of training
grounds, storage facilities, and gunnery and test ranges was permanently settled on more than three million acres of military
reservations. Few perceived the extent or significance of the destruction of the aboriginal sites that took place during tank maneuvers and bombing runs or in the laying out of highways,
railroads, mining districts, and irrigated fields. The few who intu-
ited that something like an American Dordogne Valley lay exposed
here were (only) amateur archaeologists; even they reasoned that
the desert was too vast for any of this to matter.

After World War II, people began moving out of the crowded
Los Angeles basin into homes in Lucerne, Apple, and Antelope
valleys in the western Mojave. They emigrated as well to a stretch
of resort land at the foot of the San Jacinto Mountains that included Palm Springs, and farther out to old railroad and military
towns like Twentynine Palms and Barstow. People also began exploring the desert, at first in military-surplus jeeps and then with a
variety of all-terrain and off-road vehicles that became available in
the 1960s. By the mid-1970s, the number of people using such vehicles for desert recreation had increased exponentially. Most
came and went in innocent curiosity; the few who didn't wreaked a
havoc all out of proportion to their numbers. The disturbance of
previously isolated archaeological sites increased by an order of
magnitude. Many sites were vandalized before archaeologists,
themselves late to the desert, had any firm grasp of the bounds of

human history in the desert. It was as though in the same moment an Aztec library had been discovered intact various lacunae had begun to appear.

The vandalism was of three sorts: the general disturbance usually caused by souvenir hunters and by the curious and the oblivious; the wholesale stripping of a place by professional thieves for black-market sale and trade; and outright destruction, in which vehicles were actually used to ram and trench an area. By 1980, the Bureau of Land Management estimated that probably 35 percent of the archaeological sites in the desert had been vandalized. The destruction at some places by rifles and shotguns, or by power winches mounted on vehicles, was, if one cared for history, demoralizing to behold.

In spite of public education, land closures, and stricter law enforcement in recent years, the BLM estimates that, annually, about 1 percent of the archaeological record in the desert continues to be destroyed or stolen.

II

A BLM archaeologist told me, with understandable reluctance, where to find the intaglio. I spread my Automobile Club of Southern California map of Imperial County out on his desk, and he traced the route with a pink felt-tip pen. The line crossed Interstate 8 and then turned west along the Mexican border.

"You can't drive any farther than about here," he said, marking a small X. "There's boulders in the wash. You walk up past them."

On a separate piece of paper he drew a route in a smaller scale that would take me up the arroyo to a certain point where I was to cross back east, to another arroyo. At its head, on higher ground just to the north, I would find the horse.

"It's tough to spot unless you know it's there. Once you pick it up . . ." He shook his head slowly, in a gesture of wonder at its existence.

I waited until I held his eye. I assured him I would not tell anyone else how to get there. He looked at me with stoical despair, like a man who had been robbed twice, whose belief in human beings was offered without conviction.

I did not go until the following day because I wanted to see it at dawn. I ate breakfast at four A.M. in El Centro and then drove

south. The route was easy to follow, though the last section of road
proved difficult, broken and drifted over with sand in some spots.
I came to the barricade of boulders and parked. It was light
enough by then to find my way over the ground with little trouble.
The contours of the landscape were stark, without any masking
vegetation. I worried only about rattlesnakes.

I traversed the stone plain as directed, but, in spite of the frankness of the land, I came on the horse unawares. In the first moment of recognition I was without feeling. I recalled later being
startled, and that I held my breath. It was laid out on the ground
with its head to the east, three times life size. As I took in its outline I felt a growing concentration of all my senses, as though my
attentiveness to the pale rose color of the morning sky and other
peripheral images had now ceased to be important. I was aware
that I was straining for sound in the windless air, and I felt the uneven pressure of the earth hard against my feet. The horse, out-
lined in a standing profile on the dark ground, was as vivid before
me as a bed of tulips.

I've come upon animals suddenly before, and felt a similar tension, a precipitate heightening of the senses. And I have felt the inexplicable but sharply boosted intensity of a wild moment in the
bush, where it is not until some minutes later that you discover the
source of electricity — the warm remains of a grizzly bear kill, or
the still moist tracks of a wolverine.

But this was slightly different. I felt I had stepped into an unoc-
cupied corridor. I had no familiar sense of history, the temporal
structure in which to think: this horse was made by Quechan people three hundred years ago. I felt instead a headlong rush of images: people hunting wild horses with spears on the Pleistocene
veld of southern California; Cortés riding across the causeway into
Montezuma's Tenochtitlán; a short-legged Comanche, astride his
horse like some sort of ferret, slashing through cavalry lines of
young men who rode like farmers; a hoof exploding past my face
one morning in a corral in Wyoming. These images had the weight
and silence of stone.

When I released my breath, the images softened. My initial feeling, of facing a wild animal in a remote region, was replaced with a
calm sense of antiquity. It was then that I became conscious, like
an ordinary tourist, of what was before me, and thought: this horse

was probably laid out by Quechan people. But when? I wondered. The first horses they saw, I knew, might have been those that came north from Mexico in 1692 with Father Eusebio Kino. But Cocopa people, I recalled, also came this far north on occasion, to fight with their neighbors, the Quechan. And *they* could have seen horses with Melchior Díaz, at the mouth of the Colorado River in the fall of 1540. So, it could be four hundred years old. (No one in fact knows.)

I still had not moved. I took my eyes off the horse for a moment to look south over the desert plain into Mexico, to look east past its head at the brightening sunrise, to situate myself. Then, finally, I brought my trailing foot slowly forward and stood erect. Sunlight was running like a thin sheet of water over the stony ground and it threw the horse into relief. It looked as though no hand had ever disturbed the stones that gave it its form.

The horse had been brought to life on ground called desert pavement, a tight, flat matrix of small cobbles blasted smooth by sand-laden winds. The uniform, monochromatic blackness of the stones, a patina of iron and magnesium oxides called desert varnish, is caused by long-term exposure to the sun. To make this type of low-relief ground glyph, or intaglio, the artist either selectively turns individual stones over to their lighter side or removes areas of stone to expose the lighter soil underneath, creating a negative image. This horse, about eighteen feet from brow to rump and eight feet from withers to hoof, had been made in the latter way, and its outline was bermed at certain points with low ridges of stone a few inches high to enhance its three-dimensional qualities. (The left side of the horse was in full profile; each leg was extended at 90 degrees to the body and fully visible, as though seen in three-quarter profile.)

I was not eager to move. The moment I did I would be back in the flow of time, the horse no longer quivering in the same way before me. I did not want to feel again the sequence of quotidian events — to be drawn off into deliberation and analysis. A human being, a four-footed animal, the open land. That was all that was present — and a "thoughtless" understanding of the very old desires bearing on this particular animal: to hunt it, to render it, to fathom it, to subjugate it, to honor it, to take it as a companion.

What finally made me move was the light. The sun now filled the

shallow basin of the horse's body. The weighted line of the stone
berm created the illusion of a mane and the distinctive roundness
of an equine belly. The change in definition impelled me. I moved
to the left, circling past its rump, to see how the light might flesh
the horse out from various points of view. I circled it completely
before squatting on my haunches. Ten or fifteen minutes later I
chose another view. The third time I moved, to a point near the
rear hooves, I spotted a stone tool at my feet. I stared at it a long
while, more in awe than disbelief, before reaching out to pick it
up. I turned it over in my left palm and took it between my fingers
to feel its cutting edge. It is always difficult, especially with something so portable, to rechannel the desire to steal.

I spent several hours with the horse. As I changed positions and
as the angle of the light continued to change I noticed a number
of things. The angle at which the pastern carried the hoof away
from the ankle was perfect. Also, stones had been placed within
the image to suggest at precisely the right spot the left shoulder
above the foreleg. The line that joined thigh and hock was similarly accurate. The muzzle alone seemed distorted — but perhaps
these stones had been moved by a later hand. It was an admirably
accurate representation, but not what a breeder would call perfect
conformation. There was the suggestion of a bowed neck and an
undershot jaw, and the tail, as full as a winter coyote's, did not appear to be precisely to scale.

The more I thought about it, the more I felt I was looking at an
individual horse, a unique combination of generic and specific detail. It was easy to imagine one of Kino's horses as a model, or a
horse that ran off from one of Coronado's columns. What kind of
horses would these have been? I wondered. In the sixteenth century the most sought-after horses in Europe were Spanish, the off-
spring of Arabian stock and Barbary horses that the Moors
brought to Iberia and bred to the older, eastern European strains
brought in by the Romans. The model for this horse, I speculated,
could easily have been a palomino, or a descendant of horses
trained for lion hunting in North Africa.

A few generations ago, cowboys, cavalry quartermasters, and
draymen would have taken this horse before me under consideration and not let up their scrutiny until they had its heritage fixed
to their satisfaction. Today, the distinction between draft and har-

ness horses is arcane knowledge, and no image may come to mind for a blue roan or a claybank horse. The loss of such refinement in everyday conversation leaves me unsettled. People praise the Eskimo's ability to distinguish among forty types of snow but forget the skill of others who routinely differentiate between overo and tobiano pintos. Such distinctions are made for the same reason. You have to do it to be able to talk clearly about the world.

For parts of two years I worked as a horse wrangler and packer in Wyoming. It is dim knowledge now; I would have to think to remember if a buckskin was a kind of dun horse. And I couldn't throw a double-diamond hitch over a set of panniers — the packer's basic tie-down — without guidance. As I squatted there in the desert, however, these more personal memories seemed tenuous in comparison with the sweep of this animal in human time. My memories had no depth. I thought of the Hittite cavalry riding against the Syrians 3,500 years ago. And the first of the Chinese emperors, Ch'in Shih Huang, buried in Shensi Province in 210 B.C. with thousands of life-size horses and soldiers, a terra-cotta guardian army. What could I know of what was in the mind of whoever made this horse? Was there some racial memory of it as an animal that had once fed the artist's ancestors and then disappeared from North America? And then returned in this strange alliance with another race of men?

Certainly, whoever it was, the artist had observed the animal very closely. Certainly the animal's speed had impressed him. Among the first things the Quechan would have learned from an encounter with Kino's horses was that their own long-distance runners — men who could run down mule deer — were no match for this animal.

From where I squatted I could look far out over the Mexican plain. Juan Bautista de Anza passed this way in 1774, extending El Camino Real into Alta California from Sinaloa. He was followed by others, all of them astride the magical horse; *gente de razón*, the people of reason, coming into the country of *los primitivos*. The horse, like the stone animals of Egypt, urged these memories upon me. And as I drew them up from some forgotten corner of my mind — huge horses carved in the white chalk downs of southern England by an Iron Age people; Spanish horses rearing and wheeling in fear before alligators in Florida — the images seemed tethered before me. With this sense of proportion, a memory of my own — the morning I almost lost my face to a horse's hoof — now had somewhere to fit.

I rose up and began to walk slowly around the horse again. I had taken the first long measure of it and was now looking for a way to depart, a new angle of light, a fading of the image itself before the rising sun, that would break its hold on me. As I circled, feeling both heady and serene at the encounter, I realized again how strangely vivid it was. It had been created on a barren bajada between two arroyos, as nondescript a place as one could imagine. The only plant life here was a few wands of ocotillo cactus. The ground beneath my shoes was so hard it wouldn't take the print of a heavy animal even after a rain. The only sounds I heard here were the voices of quail.

The archaeologist had been correct. For all its forcefulness, the horse is inconspicuous. If you don't care to see it you can walk right past it. That pleases him, I think. Unmarked on this bleak shoulder of the plain, the site signals to no one; so he wants no protective fences here, no informative plaque, to act as beacons. He would rather take a chance that no motorcyclist, no aimless wanderer with a flair for violence and a depth of ignorance, will ever find his way here.

The archaeologist had given me something before I left his office that now seemed peculiar — an aerial photograph of the horse. It is widely believed that an aerial view of an intaglio provides a fair and accurate depiction. It does not. In the photograph the horse looks somewhat crudely constructed; from the ground it appears far more deftly rendered. The photograph is of a single moment, and in that split second the horse seems vaguely impotent. I watched light pool in the intaglio at dawn; I imagine you could watch it withdraw at dusk and sense the same animation I did. In those prolonged moments its shape and so, too, its general character changed — noticeably. The living quality of the image, its immediacy to the eye, was brought out by the light-in-time, not, at least here, in the camera's frozen instant.

Intaglios, I thought, were never meant to be seen by gods in the sky above. They were meant to be seen by people on the ground, over a long period of shifting light. This could even be true of the huge figures on the Plain of Nazca in Peru, where people could

walk for the length of a day beside them. It is our own impatience
that leads us to think otherwise.

This process of abstraction, almost unintentional, drew me
gradually away from the horse. I came to a position of attention at
the edge of the sphere of its influence. With a slight bow I paid my
respects to the horse, its maker, and the history of us all, and departed.

III

A short distance away I stopped the car in the middle of the
road to make a few notes. I could not write down what I was thinking when I was with the horse. It would have seemed disrespectful,
and it would have required another kind of attention. So now I patiently drained my memory of the details it had fastened itself
upon. The road I'd stopped on was adjacent to the All American
Canal, the major source of water for the Imperial and Coachella
valleys. The water flowed west placidly. A disjointed flock of coots,
small, dark birds with white bills, was paddling against the current,
foraging in the rushes.

I was peripherally aware of the birds as I wrote, the only movement in the desert, and of a series of sounds from a village a half-
mile away. The first sounds from this collection of ramshackle
houses in a grove of cottonwoods were the distracted dawn voices
of dogs. I heard them intermingled with the cries of a rooster.
Later, the high-pitched voices of children calling out to each other
came disembodied through the dry desert air. Now, a little after
seven, I could hear someone practicing on the trumpet, the same
rough phrases played over and over. I suddenly remembered how
as children we had tried to get the rhythm of a galloping horse
with hands against our thighs, or by fluttering our tongues against
the roofs of our mouths.

After the trumpet, the impatient calls of adults summoning children. Sunday morning. Wood smoke hung like a lens in the trees.
The first car starts — a cold eight-cylinder engine, of Chrysler ex-
traction perhaps, goosed to life, then throttled back to murmur
through dual mufflers, the obbligato music of a shade-tree mechanic. The rote bark of mongrel dogs at dawn, the jagged out-
cries of men and women, an engine coming to life. Like a
thousand villages from West Virginia to Guadalajara.

I finished my notes — where was I going to find a description of the horses that came north with the conquistadors? Did their manes come forward prominently over the brow, like this one's, like the forelocks of Blackfeet and Assiniboin men in nineteenth-century paintings? I set the notes on the seat beside me.

The road followed the canal for a while and then arced north, toward Interstate 8. It was slow driving and I fell to thinking how the desert had changed since Anza had come through. New plants and animals — the MacDougall cottonwood, the English house sparrow, the chukar from India — have about them now the air of the native-born. Of the native species, some — no one knows how many — are extinct. The populations of many others, especially the animals, have been sharply reduced. The idea of a desert impoverished by agricultural poisons and varmint hunters, by off-road vehicles and military operations, did not seem as disturbing to me, however, as this other horror, now that I had been those hours with the horse. The vandals, the few who crowbar rock art off the desert's walls, who dig up graves, who punish the ground that holds intaglios, are people who devour history. Their self-centered scorn, their disrespect for ideas and images beyond their ken, create the awful atmosphere of loose ends in which totalitarianism thrives, in which the past is merely curious or wrong.

I thought about the horse sitting out there on the unprotected plain. I enumerated its qualities in my mind until a sense of its vulnerability receded and it became an anchor for something else. I remembered that history, a history like this one, which ran deeper than Mexico, deeper than the Spanish, was a kind of medicine. It permitted the great breadth of human expression to reverberate, and it did not urge you to locate its apotheosis in the present.

Each of us, individuals and civilizations, has been held upside down like Achilles in the River Styx. The artist mixing his colors in the dim light of Altamira; an Egyptian ruler lying still now, wrapped in his byssus,* stored against time in a pyramid; the faded Dorset culture of the Arctic; the Hmong and Samburu and Walbiri of historic time; the modern nations. This great, imperfect stretch of human expression is the clarification and encourage-

---

*byssus: Ancient cloth.

ment, the urging and the reminder, we call history. And it is inscribed everywhere in the face of the land, from the mountain
passes of the Himalayas to a nameless bajada in the California
desert.

Small birds rose up in the road ahead, startled, and flew off. I
prayed no infidel would ever find that horse.

Reflections and Responses

1. Lopez divides his essay into three parts. How does each of these
parts differ? What purpose does each serve?

2. Examine Lopez's choice of words. When does he introduce
technical terms into the essay? Go through the essay and identify
the various technical terms. From what diverse disciplines are they
drawn? How do these terms affect your response to both the author and his subject?

3. When this essay originally appeared, it included no photographs of the carving. Why do you think that decision was made?
What distortions would photography introduce? What would a
photograph *not* be able to show us? What is Lopez's attitude toward photography in this instance?

ELEANOR MUNRO

On the Pilgrim's Path to Lourdes

A pilgrim is a traveler with a sacred destination. Today, even though most travelers are largely tourists—visiting sites simply to see them—many people still make pilgrimages for spiritual purposes. In the following essay, Eleanor Munro visits one of the world's most popular sacred sites, the small town of Lourdes in southwestern France. Between February 11 and July 16, 1858, a fourteen-year old peasant girl of Lourdes, Bernadette Soubirous, reported a series of visions in which she was visited by the Blessed Virgin Mary. Though regarded skeptically by many prominent Catholics, Bernadette's visions possessed enormous popular appeal and were eventually accorded papal approval. The shrine at Lourdes, with its underground spring, has become a world-famous religious site, where millions of people gather in processions each summer. Many of these pilgrims come to Lourdes hoping that their illnesses and disabilities will be cured by the waters of its miraculous fountain. For Munro, the experience is compelling: "I was transfixed at Lourdes because through those imprisoning bodies, some entangled yet separate will *to continue living had glinted out with shocking immediacy—the same I had witnessed elsewhere in travels to other pilgrimage sites."*

An art critic and writer, Munro publishes essays and commentary in many national journals, including the New York Times, Art in America, *and* The New Republic. *She has written, among other books,* Originals: American Women Artists, *(1979)* On Glory Roads: A Pilgrim's Book about Pilgrimage *(1987), and* Memoir of a Modernist's Daughter *(1988). "On the Pilgrim's Path to Lourdes" originally appeared in the* San Francisco Examiner and Chronicle *(1987) and was selected by Annie Dillard for* The Best American Essays 1988.

Among sacred pilgrimage sites of the world — far-off snowy peaks on which gods are thought to dance, thronged temples by the

Ganges, gold-domed cathedrals or humble country altars — the French shrine of Lourdes in its gloomy mountain setting may be one of the most instructive.

That is to say, if you look beyond the blatant commercialism of the new town and steep yourself instead in the geography, architecture and massed population of the sacred precinct, you may gain an inkling of the meaning of this ancient and universal human practice. For pilgrimage is an enterprise of deep antiquity and powerful psychological appeal, and its associated rites are much the same across all religions, and the same today as in the past.

When a pilgrim arrives at his destination (it can as well be a natural feature, rock, tree or riverbank as a man-made church or temple), he invariably can be seen walking a circular path around or in it, often following the clockwise course of the sun. If by night, he will carry a candle or torch, which, multiplied many times in many hands, becomes a galaxy of stars turning slowly in darkness. The metaphor holds. In these circumambulations, the pilgrim imitates the flight of the stars and planets, which orbit the celestial pole, disappearing and reappearing in a harmonic order we on earth find both beautiful and eternal. So the pilgrim enacts the answer to his longing for immortality.

Indeed, the folklore that has grown up around Lourdes describes its location at "the confluence of seven valleys"— seven being one of those immemorial mystical numbers in scripture and myth referring to the visible planets, the outermost travelers of the solar system. Mystical Lourdes thus is identified as its axis.

Legend in this case enhances geography. Actual Lourdes lies betwixt gorges and bare cliffs, where icy torrents off the high slopes collide in a perpetual tumult of white water, ethereal rainbows and ghostly low-hanging clouds.

A hundred years ago, when its modern history began, Lourdes was no more than a scatter of wretched stone huts wedged along a couple of crooked climbing streets. Perched on an overhanging rock stood the town jail. In one of those freezing dwellings lived a poor miller, sometimes resident in the jail, and his wife and children, all of them suffering from hunger and ill health.

It was a bitter February day in 1858 when Bernadette, the eldest child, went with her sister to the riverbank to gather kindling. And there, as she later recalled with the help of her confessor and other priests of the region, "I heard a noise like a gust of wind. I saw the trees were not swaying. I heard the same noise again. As I lifted my head and looked at the grotto, I saw a lady in white. Fear took hold of me. My hand shook."

What she reported seeing in an "aureole of sunlight" was a woman who much resembled a statue of the Madonna in a church nearby, save that instead of treading on a snake as the plaster woman did, the Beautiful Lady wore on each foot a yellow rose.

Not till her third visit did the Lady explain who she was, adding, "I cannot promise to make you happy in this world, but in *the other.*" A skeptic may suppose Bernadette's life history shaped her visions, for she had twice been sent as a boarder to another village, once in infancy and later as a hired shepherdess, where she enjoyed milk and bread in abundance offered by a warm-hearted foster mother. In any case, at her ninth appearance, the Lady spoke words both motherly and rural: "Go drink and wash at the fountain. Eat the grass you will find there."

So strange a suggestion led Bernadette to tear hungrily at the grass by the cliff and so to widen the opening over an underground spring which today, some 125 years later, is the most famous water source in the Western world. Over four million pilgrims visit it each summer, and it has become the nexus of a vast ecclesiastical, touristic and economic bureaucracy.

For the Beautiful Lady, who in the end identified herself in terms Bernadette said she had never heard before — "I am the Immaculate Conception"— asked that a chapel be built by the spring and pilgrims attend it "in procession." And so it was done, and so they do, but not by miracle alone.

Four years before the visions, in 1854, the Pope, against stiff opposition from within the church but in response to a centuries-long groundswell of popular faith, had announced the dogma of the Immaculate Conception of the Virgin. Bernadette's visions, tailored and broadcast by her confessors, brought that arcane dogma down to earth and gave it sentimental color.

She herself died at thirty-six, a reclusive nun, leaving only a modest disclaimer: "The Blessed Lady used me. I am nothing without her." In 1925, she was beatified and, eight years later, on the Feast Day of the Immaculate Conception, canonized. The Vatican still maintains a stiffish attitude toward the occasional reported cures at the place, but pastors from all over Europe shepherd their charges there, often in special railroad cars fitted out as hospitals. Even if the cures are dubious or short-lasting, the patients return home, sometimes to institutions that are their lifelong homes, lifted in mind and heart by the experience.

The modern commercial town of Lourdes offers hotels and boarding houses great and small — some four hundred of them — wax museums, audio-visual instructional parlors and shops where you can pick up a cuckoo clock, pine candy, a skein of Pyrenees wool, a set of cowbells, color prints of the Angelus and all sizes of plastic Virgin-shaped water bottles.

Near the sacred precinct stands the Hospice of Our Lady of Seven Sorrows, where bedridden pilgrims are tenderly housed and fed before and after their ritual visit to the shrine. The order was started four years after the visions were officially accepted, by Marie St. Frai, a mountain woman with a mission toward the terminally ill. Her nuns still wear black in bereavement. But the rule of the order is *allegresse,* lightness of heart, and so these sisters' spirit seems to be.

I asked one of them, Sister Stanislaw, a dainty young person with dancing eyes, how she came to the order. She grew up in a secular, bourgeois home, in which she danced and partied and wore pretty clothes. But, she said, "I loved the poor and I followed the thread to the end. When I came into the order, I shut the door behind me. And ever since, it's as if I were in heaven."

The mystical center or axis of heavenly Lourdes is the place by the riverbank where Bernadette knelt to tear at the grass. There bubbles the famous spring, its open mouth protected by plate glass. Its waters are piped off into twice-seven tubs in as many little cold bathrooms where volunteer attendants convey the suffering hopeful. Alternately, in the open air is a row of bright copper taps, through which water is constantly drawn off into gallon tanks, thermoses and bottles to be carried to Christian homes around the world.

Behind that place of holy power, the ground rises sharply toward the cliff top, where great trees fill with mountain wind, bending half-over under the scudding clouds. At the axial summit stands the basilica, a neo-Gothic concoction like a Disneyland castle. In the sanctuary's mosaic-adorned dome, a smiling teenage Bernadette in a golden crown holds out thin arms to her petitioners.

At four each afternoon and again at eight in the evening, a procession takes place in Lourdes. The pilgrims form rows, six abreast, some walking but most wheeled by attendants in chairs or litters.

The lines, also guided by ecclesiastics in full regalia, move gravely, in perfect order, along the base of the cliff beside the spring and the water taps, then out along a wide, tree-shaded alley leading toward the commercial town, where they turn as if in orbit to return toward the basilica and begin again.

I stood there one afternoon watching and asking myself what the meaning was of what I saw.

I was standing as if on a shore while toward me flowed faces by the six, by the twelve, by the hundred — peasant faces and faces suggestive of high station, such a host of sufferers I couldn't have imagined without being there. I even wished for the power of a Homer to help me describe that tremendous host — thick fingers twisted in blankets or splayed upon them, wasted flesh gray as cement, cheeks and noses sharp as cut stone, black brows bristling over sunken eyes; polio-afflicted children in their mothers' arms; a handsome woman whose well-combed hair framed frantic, maniacal eyes; men with barrel chests and legs like rolled towels, stretching anguished faces back toward the spring even after their litters had been wheeled on past.

Look, these shapes on their beds seemed to be saying to the clouds — Look on us: *your handiwork.*

There were still more painful cases to come, reaching with hands flailing like flags run off their pulleys, crossing themselves with the heels of those flapping hands. There were beings without legs or arms at all, with swollen heads too heavy to lift, or shaped like turnips.

The procession moved to amplified music, minor-keyed folk songs, plaintive chants, wistful children's choirs, until at last, inevitably, came the cry from loudspeakers all along the way: *Lord . . . heal us.*

That evening I stood on the balcony of my hotel looking down on thousands of little lights turning in rainy darkness, asking myself whether it was morbidity that had kept me fixed to the sight of so many individuals there in extremes of deformity and fear. But I thought it was not.

I was transfixed at Lourdes because through those imprisoning bodies, some entangled yet separate *will* to continue living had glinted out with shocking immediacy — the same I had witnessed elsewhere in travels to other pilgrimage sites.

In India, you see human suffering in the open, unapologetically displayed, considered an inevitable feature of the material world. Hindu religious practice helps you overlook immediate pain and dwell instead on vast metaphysical abstractions. Western religious thought focuses on the narrower, more piercing mystery of human consciousness in an inhuman world. And every single person who walked or was rolled before my eyes at Lourdes was like a plumb-weight pulling the cords of a whole belief system into alignment.

I went down to the shrine where the lights were still turning among the trees and took a flame from a taper in the hand of a country woman with averted eyes and heavy facial hair who, when I thanked her, replied in the deep stoic timbre of a hermaphrodite.

There came into my mind then the well-known words *Eppur si muove:* And still it moves. That there exists some natural law or force that binds such pilgrims into their passionate faith and labor seems to me as unarguable — yet still as mysterious — as was, to Galileo, the turning of the earth around the sun.

Reflections and Responses

1. Munro begins by saying that the site at Lourdes may be one of the world's "most instructive" pilgrimage sites. Why? What does she find especially instructive about her visit? Does she learn anything at Lourdes? What is her attitude toward Bernadette's visions, for example?

2. Why is it necessary for Munro to "look beyond the blatant commercialism of the new town"? If she hadn't overlooked this aspect

of Lourdes, what might her essay have been like? At what moments does her essay read like a travel essay for prospective tourists?

3. Consider the "metaphor" Munro introduces in her third paragraph. What is the metaphor, i.e., what two things are being compared? How does the metaphor reflect Munro's attitude toward pilgrimages? How does the metaphor resurface in the essay?

MARY HOOD

Why Stop?

English literature's most famous pilgrimage remains, of course, the fictional one undertaken at daybreak on April 17, 1387, when twenty-nine pilgrims set out from the Tabard Inn to visit the shrine of St. Thomas à Becket in Canterbury. It was spring and—as Chaucer's Middle English would have it—"Than longen folk to goon on pilgrimages . . . The blisful holy martir for to seke." Today, as Mary Hood suggests, our pilgrimages are more likely to wend toward Graceland in search of a different sort of shrine and spiritual experience. In "Why Stop?" she examines the human urge to travel to out-of-the-way places to see some special sight—a marker, monument, museum, mausoleum, or memorial—that has become interesting simply "because it's there": "The brochures and one's neighbors and coworkers label this sort a 'must see' for no other reason than that many have seen it." The "shrine" may be "the world's largest concrete buffalo," a "forty-foot-tall fiberglass pheasant," or a historical plaque in Texas marking the spot where O. Henry picked up his mail. Whatever and wherever the sight, why indeed do we stop to look?

Hood is the author of a novel, Familiar Heat *(1994), and two volumes of short stories,* How Far She Went *(1984) and* And Venus Is Blue *(1986). She has published essays and nonfiction in such periodicals as* Harper's Magazine, North American Review, The Gettysburg Review, *and* Art & Antiques. *"Why Stop?" originally appeared in* The Gettysburg Review *(1988) and was selected by Geoffrey Wolff for* The Best American Essays *1989.*

Si monumentum requiris, circumspice.
        —Wren

There is an essential human ichor of awe, an instinct for reverence, a gracious sap which rises in us seasonally and flowers into
devotions and wreaths. "Than longen folk to goon on pilgrimages." Goon indeed. Every sap has its sucker. SEE THE CONTINENTAL
DIVIDE IN ACTION, the billboard in the Rockies invites. The parking
lot is not empty. (When one sparrow decides to bathe, they all
splash in.) Yet whether we queue up at the thronged-in-August,
hell-hot gates of Graceland, candle and rose in hand, "the blisful
holy martir for to seke," or shiver alone on the wintry bleak summit
of the Kill Devil Hills contemplating the Wright brothers, who may
have climbed the dune as we did but found quite another way
down, it is all one expression of the wayfaring urge, now sublime,
now ridiculous, which must not be confused with religious piety —
whose zeal seeks the soul's perpetuation in a timeless future;
homage, on the other hand, cherishes endurance of mortal report — fame — and acknowledges the past's claims upon us. We
raise memorials against oblivion, not death. Death is, to the makers of monuments and pilgrimages, but one more occasion.

Apparently, any occasion will do. Near Jamestown, North
Dakota, broods the world's largest concrete buffalo (three stories).
South Dakota, not to be outdone, has erected a forty-foot-tall fiberglass pheasant. Although these monuments of civic pride stand in
somewhat out-of-the-way places, seekers find them, eager to feel
themselves dwarfed in the sweep of those great manmade shadows. The mood is festive, more aw shucks than awe. Yet even when
a monument may have originally honored some historic glory beyond its place and pile, it can ultimately win its own fame as a land-
mark which travelers seek, not for the spirit of its intention or any
love of history, but for itself alone, *because it's there*. The brochures
and one's neighbors and coworkers label this sort a "must see" for
no other reason than that many have seen it. Such a pilgrimage
risks devolving into merest tourism. Still, if touring — travel for curiosity and recreation — is reverence's lowest expression, at worst
a Pavlovian response to report of marvel or infamy, at least it is
motion, and at best it offers some poignancy, if not poetry, to be
recollected in whatever tranquillity the post-vacation letdown af-
fords. At times we are moved only to laughter on the scene, out of

embarrassment, perhaps, at our being there at all, yet who would willingly miss an Alabama meteorite as long as it first missed us? Is not the Cardiff giant*— ten and a half feet of midwestern gypsum sleeping in a Cooperstown museum — more popular now in his exposure to ridicule than ever he was when first exposed to light?

"Was this here then?" asks a child at the top of the San Jacinto monument in Texas, staring down at the curried swale where Sam Houston, that tough old bird, caught his worm by rising early. Tourists are all children at history's knee, begging for some snatch of song or scrap of idea to play with. Though all the world's a stage, we prefer the sideshow. "'I know not,' said Rasselas[†], 'what pleasure the sight of the catacombs can afford; but since nothing else is offered, I am resolved to view them, and shall place this with many other things which I have done because I would do something.'"

Even now, in Providence, lines are forming to view the root of the apple tree which consumed Roger Williams in his grave. They say it curved around his skull, grew straight down his spine, branched for arms and legs, and turned up at his feet. "I'll believe that when I see it," we scoff, already loading the camera and car, keen to meddle ourselves in legend; like so many Mandevilles and Marco Polos, we'll bring home proof in our trunk. In Kodachrome: WE WERE THERE.

"Fame is proof that people are gullible," Emerson warns all pilgrims. But what cynic could fail to share the curator's pride in the key exhibit of the Jimmy Rodgers Museum in Mississippi, The Singing Brakeman's simple iron bedstead: "Over a hundred years old so far at least." For the small toll of admission we may wander around for hours, studying the trainman's guitar, signal flags, oilcan, cap, his wife's red dress, and the ordinary postal scale with which he weighed his replies to fan mail. We walk out into the present tense as though waking from a tender dream. And though roadside museums can offer the traveler the greatest opportunity for disappointment or suffocation, there yet remain these sur-

---

*Cardiff giant:** A well-known American hoax: the fake prehistoric man "discovered" in 1869 can now be seen in a New York museum.

†Rasselas:** The main character of Samuel Johnson's 1759 moral fable. *The History of Rasselas. Prince of Abyssinia.*

prises and satisfactions, reminders that the quotidian has its
charms and adventures.

LOOK WHAT'S HIDING
IN YOUR CUPBOARD!

urges an enthusiast's placard in the rice museum in Crowley,
Louisiana. At an Arcadian shrine a candid *genius loci** has scrawled
this *caveat*:

> Yes we have
> mosquitoes we
> don't give re-
> funds.

Sometimes the spirit of a place "gives out glory, sometimes its
little light must be sought to be seen," Eudora Welty notes of her
own sorties down byroads. And sometimes, "generations have
trod, have trod, have trod," as at San Juan Capistrano, where the
returning swallows gull the punctual busloads in, to squint
through lenses at those twittering walls and then further stretch
their credulity and legs in the SACRED GIFT SHOP, whose harried
clerks are more expert at making change than small talk.

Disappointment, from time to time, plagues every pilgrim. The
shrine may be closed for the afternoon, or the week, or the duration. Roads and rivers may have altered course and given the lie to
the sincerest maps. Rustic parlors suffer urbane renewals and portraits enjoy retouchings with a glossy wink toward beauty rather
than authenticity. Mice and moss invade and creep. The arbors
sag. The cobbles sleep under layers of asphalt. The jambs and sills
of a birthplace may glower too low to have ever framed our heroes.
Legend lengthens stature until truth cannot keep up. Doubts
creep in with the unforecast rains. The winds and attendants may
be contrary. One's will, or train, or diligence may falter. In short,
"I have not the memory of Chinon," as Henry James sighs on his
little tour in France, "I have only the regret." The most eagerly anticipated romantic tumults can eventuate as mere drips; honey-
mooners have been stranded high and dry at Niagara when for
reasons of civil engineering the falls are shut down as though a tap

---

***genius loci**: Latin, a local genius.

had been turned. Authorized biographies and lyrical guidebooks may prove fiction or trumpery, and the reality leaves us unabashed and cold. "If the house is small the tablet is very big," Henry James observes on that same tour, when viewing the birthplace of Lamartine*. We may either give up the hunt or become stoics. "Do I fail to find in the place to which I go the things that were reported to me? . . . I do not regret my pains," shrugs Montaigne. "I have learned that what was told me was not there."

If you seek a monument, look around, Sir Christopher Wren[†] advises us from his grave. Even the most cursory glance around harvests treasures of homage. We honor Liberty, Justice, and the Boll Weevil with shrines of perpetual glory. We similarly remind the world of the site of the birth of the first English child in America, and upon the National Honor Roll list the date of the first live birth in an airplane. Lest we forget, earmuffs were patented in 1877, and the ball-point pen is having its centenary. There is a museum for moonshiners in Georgia and one for sponge divers in Florida. Besides labor, we celebrate rest: the hammock in South Carolina, rock skipping in Michigan and California.

When it seems as though no one else will, we honor ourselves. There was a ton or so of granite ordered carved and shipped south, the story goes, by a homesick native son relocated in the Midwest. When the shoulder-high marker arrived by freight on the L&N rail, was no one left alive in his native place to know and honor the man's beau geste? Did his patriotic love go unclaimed? Or was it simply too daunting a task, too monumental a labor in horse-and-buggy days, easier to offload it and set it there rather than try to trundle it over land to its intended homesite? Gentle mystery surrounds it even today. It stands facing west behind the superannuated Holly Springs depot — trains don't stop there anymore, and the kudzu gropes yearly nearer — in Cherokee County, Georgia. Its journey over, it has for almost a century announced to the setting sun:

---

*Lamartine: Alphonse de Lamartine, the French poet, writer, and statesman (1790–1869).

[†]Sir Christopher Wren: Famous English architect (1632–1723) who built St. Paul's Cathedral and many other notable London churches.

Birthplace of
Julian M. Hughes
Feby. 3. 1860.

HERE EARLY ONE MORN I WAS BORN.
AMONG THE HILLS AND MIDST THE
CHARMS OF LOVELY CHEROKEE
IN DEAR OLD GEORGIA SO SWEET TO ME.

Mr. Hughes is famous for his having been born, if not for his poem. But perhaps the most cherished and lively posterities are reserved to fortune's children who have surprised and surpassed local custom in martyrdom for love. Every hamlet has its lovers' leap, or lane, or oak; its Frankie and Johnnie; its Helen or Romeo; the Hatfields and McCoys even tried for a second Troy. When Longfellow invented Evangeline and Gabriel, he could not have imagined that Dolores Del Rio would pose for the statue, or that it would be erected facing Bayou Teche a few paces from where the actual Evangeline (Emmeline Labiche) lies buried in the church-yard. The real story is sadder than poetry. (Isn't that what lovers always learn?) And then there is that bull moose in New England who became enthralled with a dairy cow; in all weathers he guarded her — lovelorn, dignified, loyal — the very exemplar of Longfellow's "affection that hopes, and endures, and is patient"; and didn't the country lanes clog with the traffic of pilgrims who wanted to pay their respects to that enchanted fool?

That nine days' wonder brought out the best in us; we didn't seek to disillusion the moose, or ride by to jeer at his amazing valentine. We cheered. But if fame can elicit the finest of our instincts, it can also draw forth the worst. Milton calls the fever for fame the "last infirmity of noble mind." And it is true that a man who will not take the slightest steps to alter his pace of living to prevent illness will run long risks to assure remembrance; in fact, he may be stimulated by the notion of death, though not craving its early sting — "Fame is the spur" — to raise advertisements to it thereafter. Didn't Cheops close the temples and exhaust four hundred thousand Egyptians in his service annually for a decade, merely to construct the smooth approaches to his future tomb? The pyramid itself required twenty years more to build. Cheops must have been as shrewd as he was determined, to know to begin early and live long, to keep alert till that bed was made, when so many could have rested if he'd slept sooner.

According to Herodotus*, one wall of the tomb bears a grudging inscription complaining how much garlic, onions, and radishes the slaves on that project consumed. Cheops's expenses, beyond greengroceries and even with forced labor, were so staggering that he ordered his daughter into a brothel to procure by her own industry "a certain sum — how much I cannot say, for I was not told"— the historian modestly confesses. By her monumental exertions the daughter — who had begun to lust for a pyramid of her own — exacted from each client not only her father's levied tribute but also the gift of a building stone for herself. Thus, one by one she laid the foundations, 150 feet along each side, of her own tomb. The work was completed in her lifetime, or as the perpetual-care salesmen call it nowadays, "pre-need." Is there something as interesting as radishes, onions, and garlic inscribed on her death chamber? Herodotus does not mention it.

Fashions in tombs and inscriptions — and in monuments and literature — have changed over time. Yet from the beginning, we can be sure, there were both events and ways to remember. "Before the music, there were drums," Eudora Welty reminds us, in "Some Notes on River Country." Before there were alphabets and tools to carve them, there were the mute stones, to be shouldered upright, single, slow-weathering, massive, or accreted, toss on toss, into sun-bleached cairns. The stones are all that last long, say the Cheyenne. "When people pass and remember, they bring stones," Paco explains in Harriet Doerr's novel, *Stones for Ibarra*, voicing the primitive principle of reverence and respect which allows the most awful historic catastrophe to be witnessed in human perspective and sympathy, and claimed on a personal level. It is no longer a vainglorious and Kilroy boast of "I was there." It becomes rather a humble gesture of inclusion, present tense, a comprehension and admission of decent and deep kinship. According to myth, Fame is the last child of Mother Earth, brought forth in anguish at the deaths of her sons. Whether we chase it in granite or sandstone or marble, fame is the quarry. *Quisque Ibarra lapidenda est*, we might say; every Ibarra must have its stones. Considered in this way, remembrance is an act of mercy, as is burying the dead.

***Herodotus:** Ancient Greek historian (c.484–425 BC) noted for his history of the Persian Wars.

Monumental fashions ever change, reflecting the tastes — now sober, now giddy — of the era. Sir Christopher Wren, rebuilding St. Paul's after the Great Fire, got the dead back on their feet, preferring his nobles upright rather than reclining upon stone biers, under their own effigies, guarded by fabulous beasts and antic angels. Vengeances and jests abound; in Paris, Napoleon's eternal couch is so framed that all who approach must bow. Emerson's marker is an elephantine and unpolished hunk of pinkish rock; Thoreau's, in the same Massachusetts cemetery, is a plain tablet, ankle-high, announcing simply HENRY. The Victorians had, perhaps, the most generally elaborate funerary furnishings since the Chinese emperors and the pharaohs. No expense nor word nor feeling was spared; if there lacked wit, in these public performances and reminders, there was not room for it. Handkerchiefs were larger then, also.

But even before Victoria's reign and storm of tears, perhaps since the beginning of messages on stone, a certain uncandor has canted the proceedings. *Cum grano salis** ought to be the motto of the churchyard pilgrim, and the statue gazer and battlefield stalker. "In lapidary inscriptions a man is not upon oath," Samuel Johnson cautions. All the sweet old protocols and decorums of hero-making and worship failed in the aftershock of World War I. Literature and the survivors have been dusting off the fallout ever since. While valor had its finest hour, glory had its worst. On Peace Day, 1919, Virginia Woolf wrote, "I can't help listening to speaking as though it were writing and thus the flowers, which [were] brandished now and again, look terribly artificial. . . . A melancholy thing to see the incurable soldiers lying in bed at the Star and Garter with their backs to us, smoking cigarettes and waiting for the noise to be over."

There have been wars since, never a day in this century when there was not armed conflict somewhere on earth, but in the English-speaking world, stone has latterly learned a new bluntness and integrity, as has literature, and — intermittently — politics. That frankness achieves as well as honors heroic moments, as though truth and emotion finally have found a lasting, living style. The minimalist tendency to offer the anguished facts and allow the seeker to supply the emotional caption has culminated in a stark

*Cum grano salis: Latin, with a grain of salt.

and dark modern monument, the Vietnam Veterans Memorial, a black wall furnished with no rhetoric, simply the names and dates, row on row, achieving, below ground level, the monitory and pathetic impact of that archaic epitaph on a Greek clifftop: *When my ship sank, the others sailed on.*

Perhaps the pendulum is already swinging back, and our memorials, unsparing and spare, will once again costume themselves to honor the drama of history. If old ways may return, new ways might also be discovered to make some statement mocking transience. Already, for a price, one may have one's ashes rocketed into space, to be outward bound forever, or till the stars fail. That's about as far as any pilgrim can go: *Hic jacet** for speed readers; "urn buriall" at the velocity of light.

On earth, in pioneer days, it was unusual to have surveyors at one's beck and call; landowners did their best to locate and abide by the boundaries and landmarks mentioned in their grant deeds. To assure that the bounds, once agreed upon, wouldn't alter, the settler would take his sons — to whom the land would pass at his death — and stand them at the corners of the lots and sections, near some memorable natural marker, or if none existed, a stone hauled in on a leather sling behind an ox; the child was beaten and left there alone all day, to watch and absorb his surroundings. No water, no food. The ordeal was repeated, day by day, corner by corner. It was a common enough practice to have a name: "beating the bounds." That purpose was to engrave, by suffering and privation and the child's eager willingness to please his elders, the exact location of the corners and lines upon the youth's impressionable memory. He would indelibly have a mental map of what was his to claim. He would know his limits. He would be able to recognize, in all weathers and seasons — for after the boundaries were learned, they were patrolled from time to time, to check for incursion or erosion — what was rightfully his to cherish, and how precious it was, for it had been both earned, and learned, by blood.

Pilgrims make the same journeys and suffer similar ordeals, though the boundaries are less clear, and larger, and the patrols longer. We find out by patience and witness who we are, where we belong, how much we hold in common with the rest of humanity. Sometimes there is but a rubble; at other times incised and magnificent stones speak to us, invite us to stop and look around.

*__Hic jacet__: Latin, Here lies; traditional words on a tombstone.

Sometimes we must suffer to find it; at other times we lose our way, confuse one place for another, or miss our exit. We must try again. "Have I left anything behind me unseen? I go back to see it; it is always in my way," says Montaigne, who knew the joys of taken pains.

There is a directory published by Lone Star Legends — you may purchase it in the gift shop at the Alamo — which advertises that near Cotulla, Texas, twenty-five miles southeast of farm/market road 468 on private property — GATES LOCKED, we are warned — there is a historical marker celebrating the fact that "O. Henry came to Fort Ewell for his mail." Who would not detour many anxious miles over washboard or desolate roads to relish that or any such legend in cast bronze in its own natural context? However, the editors of the directory point out on the back cover, "This book is published so that you can read the inscriptions on 2,850 Texas roadside historical markers without having to stop. You will not only save time but also be rewarded with knowledge." The guidebook — a menu of morsels to whet any pilgrim's appetite — is poignantly titled *Why Stop?*

Why stop? As Satchmo* answered, when asked to define jazz, if you've gotta ask, you're never gonna know.

Reflections and Responses

1. Note the source of Hood's title. Why do you think she chose this as the title for her essay? How is she using the phrase? What does she mean by the quotation from Louis Armstrong in the final paragraph?

2. How does Hood use the lines from Chaucer's *Canterbury Tales* in her opening paragraph? What central image does Chaucer provide her? What does she mean by "Goon indeed"? How many literary references can you find in the essay?

3. How would you describe Hood's attitude toward the landmarks that figure in her essay? Is her attitude reverential? Satirical? What do you find complex about her position? Why do we stop?

*Satchmo:** Nickname of famous jazz trumpeter and bandleader, Louis Armstrong (1900–1971).

STEPHEN JAY GOULD

Counters and Cable Cars

Stephen Jay Gould visited San Francisco in the fall of 1989, just before the Great Earthquake of October 17. While there, he was impressed as always by the things that make San Francisco so genuinely pleasurable. As he thought about his experiences—both as a paleontologist and essayist—he realized how much of his affection for the city depends upon our deep-seated need for authenticity. As he thrills to his cable car's descent down Russian Hill, Gould poses a central question that all serious travelers should consider: "As I ride, I ponder a psychological puzzle that has long intrigued me: why does authenticity—as a purely conceptual theme—exert such a hold upon us?" "Counters and Cable Cars" offers an equally intriguing answer to that question.

One of our most highly acclaimed essayists and scientists, Gould teaches biology, geology, and the history of science at Harvard University. He is the author of many complete works of nonfiction, including Ontogeny and Phylogeny *(1977),* The Mismeasure of Man *(1982),* Wonderful Life *(1989), and six collections of essays:* Ever Since Darwin *(1977),* The Panda's Thumb *(1980),* Hen's Teeth and Horse's Toes *(1983),* The Flamingo's Smile *(1985),* An Urchin in the Storm *(1987), and* Bully for Brontosaurus *(1991). A MacArthur Prize Fellow, he writes a monthly scientific essay for* Natural History *magazine and is a regular contributor to* The New York Review of Books, *where he frequently writes about two of his favorite subjects, biology and baseball. "Counters and Cable Cars" originally appeared in* Natural History *(1990) and was selected by Joyce Carol Oates for* The Best American Essays 1991.

San Francisco, October 11, 1989

In a distinctive linguistic regionalism, New Yorkers like me stand "on line," while the rest of the nation waits patiently "in line." Actually, I spend a good part of my life trying to avoid that particular activity altogether, no matter what preposition it may bear. I am a firm supporter of the Yogi Berra principle regarding once fashionable restaurants: "No one goes there anymore; it's too crowded."

Consequently, in San Francisco this morning, I awoke before sunrise in order to get my breakfast of Sears's famous eighteen pancakes (marvel not, they're very small) before the morning crush of more amenable hours rendered the restaurant uninhabitable on Berra's maxim. Then out the door by 7:30 to the cable car stop at Union Square for a ride that thrills me no less in middle life than on my first trip as a boy. What moment in public transportation could possibly surpass that final steep descent down Russian Hill? (For a distant second and third in America, I nominate the Saint Charles streetcar of New Orleans, last of the old-time trolley lines, as it passes by the antebellum houses of the garden district; and the Staten Island Ferry, only a nickel in my youth and the world's most distinguished cheap date, as it skirts the Statue of Liberty by moonlight.) I travel during the last minutes of comfort and accessibility. By 9 A.M., long lines of tourists will form and no one will want to ride anymore.

We paleontologists are driven, almost by professional definition, to an abiding respect for items and institutions that have prevailed and prospered with integrity in an unending sea of change (although I trust that we can also welcome, even foster, intellectual innovation). I love Sears restaurant with its familiar, uniformly excellent, and utterly nonyuppie breakfast menu. And I adore those Victorian cars with their wooden seats and their distinctive sounds — the two-clang signal to move, the hum of the cable perpetually running underground, the grasp of the grip as it takes hold to pull the passive car along.

As I ride, I ponder a psychological puzzle that has long intrigued me: why does authenticity — as a purely conceptual theme — exert such a hold upon us? An identical restaurant with the same food, newly built in the San Francisco segment of a Great Cities Theme Park, would supply me with nothing but calories; a perfect replica of a cable car, following an even hillier route in Disneyland, would be a silly bauble.

Authenticity has many guises, each contributing something essential to our calm satisfaction with the truly genuine. Authenticity of *object* fascinates me most deeply because its pull is entirely abstract and conceptual. The art of replica making has reached such sophistication that only the most astute professional can now tell the difference between, say, a genuine dinosaur skeleton and a well-made cast. The real and the replica are effectively alike in all but our abstract knowledge of authenticity, yet we feel awe in the presence of bone once truly clothed in dinosaur flesh and mere interest in fiberglass of identical appearance.

If I may repeat, because it touched me so deeply, a story on this subject told once before in this forum (November 1984). A group of blind visitors met with the director of the Air and Space Museum in Washington to discuss greater accessibility, especially of the large objects hanging from the ceiling of the great atrium and perceptible only by sight. The director asked his guests whether a scale model of Lindbergh's *Spirit of St. Louis,* mounted and fully touchable, might alleviate the frustration of nonaccess to the real McCoy. The visitors replied that such a solution would be most welcome, but only if the model was placed directly beneath the invisible original. Simple knowledge of the imperceptible presence of authenticity can move us to tears.

We also respect an authenticity of *place.* Genuine objects out of context and milieu may foster intrigue, but rarely inspiration. London Bridge dismantled and reassembled in America becomes a mere curiosity. I love to watch giraffes in zoo cages, but their jerky, yet somehow graceful, progress over the African veld provokes a more satisfying feeling of awe.

Yet, until today, I had not appreciated the power of a third authenticity, that of *use.* Genuine objects in their proper place can be devalued by altered use — particularly when our avid appetite for casual and ephemeral leisure overwhelms an original use in the honorable world of daily work.

Lord knows, being one myself, I have no right to complain about tourists mobbing cable cars. Visitors have an inalienable right to reach Fisherman's Wharf and Ghirardelli Square by any legal means sanctioned and maintained by the city of San Francisco. Still, I love to ride incognito to 7:30 A.M. with native San

Franciscans using the cable car as a public conveyance to their place of work — Asian students embarking on their way to school as the car skirts by Chinatown; smartly dressed executives with their monthly transit passes.

But I write this essay because I experienced a different, unanticipated, and most pleasant example of authenticity of use in Sears this morning. (I could not have asked for a better context. The Bay Area, this week, is experiencing a bonanza in authenticity of place — as the Oakland A's and the San Francisco Giants prepare for the first single-area World Series since 1956, when the seventh and last "subway series" of ten glorious childhood years in New York, 1947 to 1956, produced Don Larsen's perfect game and the revenge of my beloved Yankees for their only defeat, the year before, by the Dodgers in their true home in Brooklyn. Think what we would lose if, in deference to October weather and a misplaced sense of even opportunity, the World Series moved from the home cities of full-season drama to some neutral turf in balmy Miami or New Orleans.)

I have always gone to Sears with other people and sat at a table. This time I went alone and ate at the counter. I had not known that the counter is a domain of regulars, native San Franciscans on their way to work. One man gets up and says to the waitress, "Real good, maybe I'll come back again sometime." "He's in here every morning," whispers the waitress to me. Another man takes the empty seat, saying "Hi, honey" to the woman on the next stool. "You're pretty early today," she replies. "The works!" he says as the waitress passes by. "You got it," she replies. A few minutes later, she returns with a plate of pancakes and a dish of scrambled eggs. But first she slides the eggs off the plate onto a napkin, blotting away the butter. "No good for him," she explains. He begins a discussion on the relative merits of cloth napkins and paper towels in such an enterprise. Good fellowship in authenticity of use; people taking care of each other in small ways of enduring significance.

As I present talks on evolutionary subjects all around America, I can be sure of certain questions following any speech: Where is human evolution going? What about genetic engineering? Are blacks really better at basketball? (Both the dumb and the profound share this character of inevitability.) High on the list of these perennial inquiries, I must rank the ecological question, usually asked with compassion but sometimes with pugnacity: Why do we need to save all these species anyway?

I know the conventional answers rooted in practicality. I even believe in them: you never know what medical or agricultural use might emerge from species currently unknown or ignored; beneficial diversity of gene pools in cultivated species can often be fostered by interbreeding with wild relatives; interconnectedness of ecological webs may lead to dire and unintended consequences for "valued" species when "insignificant" creatures are rubbed out. Still, I prefer to answer with an ethical, more accurately a viscerally aesthetic, statement espoused by nearly all evolutionary biologists as a virtual psychic necessity for wanting to enter the field in the first place: we relish diversity; we love every slightly different way, every nuance of form and behavior; and we know that the loss of a significant fraction of this gorgeous variety will quench our senses and our satisfactions for any future worth contemplating in human terms (potential recovery of diversity several million years down the road is too abstract and conjectural for this legitimately selfish argument). What in the world could possibly be more magnificent than the fact that beetle anatomy presents itself in more than half a million separate packages called species?

I have always been especially wary of "soft" and overly pat analogies between biological evolution and human cultural change. (Some comparisons are apt and informative, for all modes of change must hold features in common; but the mechanisms of biological evolution and cultural change are so different that close analogies usually confuse far more than they enlighten.) Nonetheless, aesthetic statements may claim a more legitimate universality, especially when an overt form rather than the underlying mechanism of production becomes the subject of our consideration. If you feel aesthetic pleasure in proportions set by the "golden section," then you may gain similar satisfaction from a nautilus shell or a Greek building despite their maximally different methods and causes of construction. I do, therefore, feel justified in writing an essay on the moral and aesthetic value of diversity both in natural and in human works — and in trying to link the genesis and defense of diversity with various meanings of authenticity. (In addition, *Natural History* has been breaking ground within its genre for many years by including the diversity of human works under its mantle, and by recognizing that the life of modern cities belongs as firmly to natural history as the overphotographed and overromanticized ways of the few human groups still living as hunters and gatherers in pristine habitats.)

(Finally, if I may make a terrible confession for a working biologist and a natural historian: I grew up on the streets of New York, and I suppose that one never loses a primary affection for things first familiar — call it authenticity of place if you wish. I do think that America's southwestern desert, in the four corners region around Monument Valley, is the most sublime spot on earth. But when I crave diversity rather than majesty, I choose cities and the products of human labor, as they resist conformity and embody authenticity of object, place, and use. My motto must be the couplet of Milton's "L'Allegro" and "Il Penseroso"— from the happy rather than the pensive side: "Towered cities please us then/And the busy hum of men." Several years ago I visited India on a trip sponsored by Harvard's natural history museum. My colleagues delighted in arising at 4 A.M., piling into a bus, driving to a nature reserve, and trying to spot the dot of a tiger at some absurd distance, rendered only slightly more interesting by binoculars. I yearned to be let off the bus alone in the middle of any bazaar in any town.)

Natural diversity exists at several levels. Variety permeates any nonclonal population from within. Even our tightest genealogical groups contain fat people and thin people, tall and short. The primal folk wisdom of the ages proclaims the enormous differences in temperament among siblings of a single family. But the greatest dollop of natural diversity arises from our geographical divisions — the differences from place to place as we adapt to varying environments and accumulate our distinctiveness by limited contact with other regions. If all species, like rats and pigeons, lived all over the world, our planet would contain but a tiny fraction of its actual diversity.

I therefore tend to revel most in the distinctive diversity of geographical regions when I contemplate the aesthetic pleasure of differences. Since I am most drawn to human works, I find my greatest joy in learning to recognize local accents, regional customs of greeting and dining, styles of architecture linked to distinctive times and places. I also, at least in my head if not often enough in overt action, think of myself as a watchdog for the preservation of this fragile variety and an implacable foe of standardization and homogenization.

I recognize, of course, that official programs of urban layout and road building must produce more elements of commonality than a strict aesthetic of maximal diversity might welcome. After all, criteria of design have a universality that becomes more and more pressing at upper limits of size and speed. If you have to move a certain number of cars through a given region at a stated speed, the road can't meander along the riverbanks or run through the main streets of old market towns. Public buildings and city street grids beg for an optimal efficiency that imposes some acceptable degree of uniformity.

But the sacred task of regionalism must be to fill in the spaces between with a riotous diversity of distinctive local traditions — preferably of productive work, not only of leisure. With this model of a potentially standardized framework for roads and public spaces filled in, softened, and humanized by local products made by local people for local purposes — authenticity of object, place, and use — I think that I can finally articulate why I love the Sears counter and the cable cars in the early morning. They embody all the authenticities, but they also welcome the respectful stranger. (Again, nature and human life jibe in obedience to basic principles of structural organization. Ecological rules and principles — flow of energy across tophic levels, webs of interaction that define the "balance of nature" — have generality corresponding to permissible uniformity in the framework of public space. But local diversity prevails because different organisms embody the rules from place to place — lions or tigers or bears as predictable carnivores of three separate continents — just as uniquely local businesses should fill the slots within a more uniform framework.)

I also now understand, with an intellectual argument to back a previous feeling, what I find so troubling about the drive for standardization, on either vernacular (McDonald's) or boutique levels (Ghirardelli Square or Harborside or Quincy Market or how can you tell which is where when all have their gourmet chocolate chip cookie cart and their Crabtree Evelyn soap store). I cannot object to the homogenization per se, for I accept such uniformity in the essential framework of public spaces. But McDonald's introduces standardization at the wrong level, for it usurps the smaller spaces of immediate and daily use, the places that cry out for local distinction and its attendant sense of community. McDonald's is a flock of pigeons ordering all endemic birds to the block, a horde of rats wiping out all the mice, gerbils, hamsters, chinchillas, squirrels, beavers, and capybaras. The Mom-and-Pop chain stores of Phoenix and Tucson are almost a cruel joke, a contradiction in terms.

I grew up in Queens, next to a fine establishment called the T-Bone Diner (it is still there, *mirabile dictu*)*. The contrast between railroad-car-style diners of my youth and McDonald's of my midlife brings us to the heart of the dilemma. Diners were manufactured in a few standardized sizes and shapes — many by the Worcester Car Company in my adopted state — and then shipped to their prospective homes. Owners then took their standard issue and proceeded to cultivate the distinctness that defines this precious item of American culture: menus abounding with local products and suited to the skills and tastes of owners; waiters and waitresses with a flair for uniqueness, even eccentricity, of verve, sassiness, or simple friendliness; above all, a regular clientele forged into a community of common care. McDonald's works in precisely the opposite way and becomes perverse in its incongruity. It enters the small-scale domain of appropriate uniqueness within the interstices of an allowable uniform framework. It even occupies spaces of widely differing designs, placements, and previous uses. It then forges this diversity into a crushing uniformity that permits not a millimeter of variation in the width of a fry from Oakland to Ogunquit.

But we are not defeated. Uniqueness has a habit of crawling back in and around the uniformities of central planning. Uniqueness also has staying power against all the practical odds of commercial culture because authenticities speak to the human soul. Many of those old diners are still flourishing in New England. I am at least a semiregular at one of the finest. On my last visit, the counter lady pointed to a jar with dollar bills. A regular customer, she told me, had a sick child in need of an operation, and everyone was kicking in, if only as a symbol of support and community. No one even mentioned the jar to casual customers on that particular morning; but I was simply told to contribute. No pleas, no harangues, no explanations beyond the simple facts of the case. Our

*__mirabile dictu:__ Latin, wonderful to relate.

communities are many, overlapping, and of various strengths. I am proud to be part of this aggregate, forged to a coherent species by a common place of local integrity. So long as these tiny communities continue to form in the interstices of conformity, I will remain optimistic about the power of diversity. And I will remember Elijah's discovery during his flight from Jezebel (1 Kings 19:11–12): "After the wind an earthquake. . . . And after the earthquake a fire. . . . And after the fire a still, small voice."

Postscript: As the dateline indicates, I wrote this essay just a week before the great San Francisco earthquake of October 17. This violently altered circumstance has converted my closing line into an utterance that, if intended after the fact rather than written unwittingly before, might seem overly pointed, if not verging on cruel. In using Elijah to reemphasize my central contrast between small-scale, local, and distinctive diversity (the "still, small voice") and global effects (well represented by general catastrophes), I was, I freely confess, also trying to make a small joke about San Francisco as the location of my essay — for the 1906 earthquake did wreak its main destruction with a tremor followed by fire.

Little did I know that my attempt at humor would soon be turned so sour by nature. I could, of course, just change the ending, sink this postscript, and fudge a fine fit with history — the virtue of working with a magazine's three-month, rather than a newspaper's one-day, lead time. But I would rather show what I wrote originally — appropriate at its moment, but not a week later — as a testimony to nature's continuing power over our fortunes, and as a working example of another theme so often addressed in this series: the quirky role of unique historical events both in nature and in human life.

The earthquake has also illuminated several other points that I raised about authenticity and local diversity. The World Series, although delayed, was not moved to neutral turf but was played by honoring baseball's powerful tradition for authenticity of place, despite the practical difficulties. My line about "people taking care of each other in small ways of enduring significance," although meant only as a comment about the Sears counter, soon extended to the whole region. Every fire or flood provokes endless rumination and pious commentary about why we seem to need disaster to bring out the best in us. But clichés are hackneyed because they are true; and the framework of this essay does put a different twist upon a commonplace: just as McDonald's marks the dark side by bringing the allowable conformity of large-scale public space into the inappropriate arena of local distinctiveness, human kindness after disaster, on the bright side, has a precisely opposite effect, for it promotes the usual caring of small and local communities to the large and overt domain of anonymity and callousness. Now how can this still, small voice be heard and felt at all scales all the time?

Reflections and Responses

1. Consider Gould's title. What do counters and cable cars have in common? Why do they appeal to Gould as a tourist? Why do they appeal to Gould as a paleontologist?

2. What connection does Gould find between counters, cable cars, and the preservation of species? What have aesthetic questions to do with ecological ones? In what way is authenticity related to diversity?

3. Note the several parenthetical interruptions in Gould's essay. Note, too, his decision to include a postscript about the earthquake. In what way can these compositional decisions be defended on grounds of authenticity?

7

Americana

JOHN UPDIKE

The Mystery of Mickey Mouse

The cartoon mouse was even a mystery to his creator, Walt Disney, who said: "Sometimes I've tried to figure out why Mickey appealed to the whole world. Everybody's tried to figure it out. So far as I know, nobody has." One of the more recent attempts to penetrate the mystery of Mickey Mouse's universal appeal also happens to be one of the most insightful and eloquent. In John Updike's perceptive analysis of this durable American icon, we find a Mickey Mouse we may never have noticed before—full of "black blood," a character with "soul." For Updike, Mickey is a great symbol of America: "He is America as it feels to itself—plucky, put-on, inventive, good-natured, game." In an essay that can function as a model of popular culture analysis, Updike not only helps explain Mickey's irresistible attraction but also helps us understand the broader meaning of any icon.

Updike was born in 1932 in Shillington, Pennsylvania. After graduation from Harvard in 1954 and a year at an English art school, he worked for the New Yorker's *"Talk of the Town" department for two years. Since 1957 he has lived in Massachusetts as a freelance writer. A novelist, poet, essayist, and reviewer, Updike is one of the nation's most distinguished authors. His fiction has won the Pulitzer Prize, the National Book Award, the American Book Award, and the National Book Critics Circle Award. He has published thirty-six books and collections; his most recent novel—his sixteenth—is* Brazil *(1993). "The Mystery of Mickey Mouse" originally appeared in* Art and Antiques *(1991) and was selected by Susan Sontag for* The Best American Essays *1992.*

It's all in the ears. When Mickey Mouse was born, in 1927, the world of early cartoon animation was filled with two-legged zoomorphic humanoids, whose strange half-black faces were distinguished one from another chiefly by the ears. Felix the Cat had pointed triangular ears and Oswald the Rabbit—Walt Disney's first successful cartoon creation, which he abandoned when his New York distributor, Charles Mintz, attempted to swindle him— had long floppy ears, with a few notches in the end to suggest fur. Disney's Oswald films, and the Alice animations that preceded them, had mice in them, with linear limbs, wiry tails, and ears that are oblong, not yet round. On the way back to California from New York by train, having left Oswald enmeshed for good in the machinations of Mr. Mintz, Walt and his wife Lillian invented an- other character based — the genesis legend claims — on the tame field mice that used to wander into Disney's old studio in Kansas City. His first thought was to call the mouse Mortimer; Lillian pro- posed instead the less pretentious name Mickey. Somewhere be- tween Chicago and Los Angeles, the young couple concocted the plot of Mickey's first cartoon short, *Plane Crazy,* costarring Minnie and capitalizing on 1927's Lindbergh craze. The next short pro- duced by Disney's fledgling studio — which included, besides himself and Lillian, his brother Roy and his old Kansas City asso- ciate Ub Iwerks — was *Gallopin' Gaucho,* and introduced a fat and wicked cat who did not yet wear the prosthesis that would give him his name of Pegleg Pete. The third short, *Steamboat Willie,* in- corporated that brand-new novelty a sound track, and was re- leased first, in 1928. Mickey Mouse entered history, as the most persistent and pervasive figment of American popular culture in this century.

His ears are two solid black circles, no matter the angle at which he holds his head. Three-dimensional images of Mickey Mouse — toy dolls, or the papier-mâché heads the grotesque Disneyland Mickeys wear — make us uneasy, since the ears inevitably exist edgewise as well as frontally. These ears properly belong not to three-dimensional space but to an ideal realm of notation, of sym- bolization, of cartoon resilience and indestructibility. In drawings, when Mickey is in profile, one ear is at the back of his head like a spherical ponytail, or like a secondary bubble in a computer-gen- erated Mandelbrot set. We accept it, as we accepted Li'l Abner's hair always being parted on the side facing the viewer. A surreal optical consistency is part of the cartoon world, halfway between our world and the plane of pure signs, of alphabets and trade- marks.

In the sixty-four years since Mickey Mouse's image was promulgated, the ears, though a bit more organically irregular and flexible than the classic 1930s appendages, have not been essentially modified. Many other modifications have, however, overtaken that first crude cartoon, born of an era of starker stylizations. White gloves, like the gloves worn in minstrel shows, appeared after those first, to cover the black hands. The infantile bare chest and shorts with two buttons were phased out in the forties. The eyes have undergone a number of changes, most drastically in the late thirties, when, some historians mistakenly claim, they acquired pupils. Not so: the old eyes, the black oblongs that acquired a nick of reflection in the sides, *were* the pupils; the eye whites filled the entire space beneath Mickey's cap of black, its widow's peak marking the division between these enormous oculi. This can be seen clearly in the face of the classic Minnie; when she bats her eyelids, their lashed shades cover over the full width of what might be thought to be her brow. But all the old animated animals were built this way from Felix the Cat on; Felix had lower lids, and the Mickey of *Plane Crazy* also. So it was an evolutionary misstep that, beginning in 1938, replaced the shiny black pupils with entire oval eyes, containing pupils of their own. No such mutation has overtaken Pluto, Goofy, or Donald Duck. The change brought Mickey closer to us humans, but also took away something of his vitality, his alertness, his bugeyed cartoon readiness for adventure. It made him less abstract, less iconic, more merely cute and dwarfish. The original Mickey, as he scuttles and bounces through those early animated shorts, was angular and wiry, with much of the impudence and desperation of a true rodent. He was gradually rounded to the proportions of a child, a regression sealed by his fifties manifestation as the genius of the children's television show *The Mickey Mouse Club,* with its live Mouseketeers. Most of the artists who depict Mickey today, though too young to have grown up, as I did, with his old form, have instinctively reverted to it; it is the barechested basic Mickey, with his yellow shoes and oval buttons on his shorts, who is the icon, beside whom his modified later version is a mere mousy trousered pipsqueak.

His first, iconic manifestation had something of Chaplin to it; he was the little guy, just over the border of the respectable. His circular ears, like two minimal cents, bespeak the smallest economic unit, the overlookable democratic man. His name has passed into the language as a byword for the small, the weak — a "Mickey Mouse operation" means an undercapitalized company or minor surgery. Children of my generation — wearing our Mickey Mouse watches, prying pennies from our Mickey Mouse piggy banks (I won one in a third-grade spelling bee, my first intellectual triumph), following his running combat with Pegleg Pete in the daily funnies, going to the local movie-house movies every Saturday afternoon and cheering when his smiling visage burst onto the screen to introduce a cartoon — felt Mickey was one of us, a bridge to the adult world of which Donald Duck was, for all of his childish sailor suit, an irascible, tyrannical member. Mickey didn't seek trouble, and he didn't complain; he rolled with the punches, and surprised himself as much as us when, as in *The Little Tailor,* he showed warrior resourcefulness and won, once again, a blushing kiss from dear, all but identical Minnie. His minimal, decent nature meant that he would yield, in the Disney animated cartoons, the starring role to combative, sputtering Donald Duck and even to Goofy, with his "gawshes" and Gary Cooper–like gawkiness. But for an occasional comeback like the "Sorcerer's Apprentice" episode of *Fantasia,* and last year's rather souped-up *The Prince and the Pauper,* Mickey was through as a star by 1940. But as with Marilyn Monroe when her career was over, his life as an icon gathered strength. The American that is not symbolized by that imperial Yankee Uncle Sam is symbolized by Mickey Mouse. He is America as it feels to itself — plucky, put-on, inventive, resilient, good-natured, game.

Like America, Mickey has a lot of black blood. This fact was revealed to me in conversation by Saul Steinberg, who, in attempting to depict the racially mixed reality of New York streets for the supersensitive and race-blind *New Yorker* of the sixties and seventies, hit upon scribbling numerous Mickeys as a way of representing what was jauntily and scruffily and unignorably there. From just the way Mickey swings along in his classic, trademark pose, one three-fingered gloved hand held on high, he is jiving. Along with round black ears and yellow shoes, Mickey has soul. Looking back to such early animations as the early Looney Tunes' Bosko and Honey series (1930–36) and the Arab figures in Disney's own *Mickey in Arabia* of 1932, we see that blacks were drawn much like cartoon animals, with round button noses and great white eyes creating the double arch of the curious peaked skullcaps. Cartoon characters' rubberiness, their jazziness, their cheerful buoyance and idleness, all chimed with popular images of African Americans, earlier embodied in minstrel shows and in Joel Chandler Harris's tales of Uncle Remus, which Disney was to make into an animated feature, *Song of the South*, in 1946.

Up to 1950, animated cartoons, like films in general, contained caricatures of blacks that would be unacceptable now; in fact, *Song of the South* raised objections from the NAACP when it was released. In recent reissues of *Fantasia*, two Nubian centaurettes and a pickaninny centaurette who shines the others' hooves have been edited out. Not even the superb crows section of *Dumbo* would be made now. But there is a sense in which all animated cartoon characters are more or less black. Steven Spielberg's hectic tribute to animation, *Who Framed Roger Rabbit?*, has them all, from the singing trees of Silly Symphonies to Daffy Duck and Woody Woodpecker, living in a Los Angeles ghetto, Toonville. As blacks were second-class citizens with entertaining qualities, so the animated shorts were second-class movies, with unreal actors who mocked and illuminated from underneath the real world, the live-actor cinema. Of course, even in a ghetto there are class distinctions. Porky Pig and Bugs Bunny have homes that they tend and defend, whereas Mickey started out, like those other raffish stick figures and dancing blots from the twenties, as a free spirit, a wanderer. As Richard Schickel has pointed out, "The locales of his adventures throughout the 1930s ranged from the South Seas to the Alps to the deserts of Africa. He was, at various times, a gaucho, teamster, explorer, swimmer, cowboy, fireman, convict, pioneer, taxi driver, castaway, fisherman, cyclist, Arab, football player, inventor, jockey, storekeeper, camper, sailor, Gulliver, boxer," and so forth. He was, in short, a rootless vaudevillian who would play any part that the bosses at Disney Studios assigned him. And though the comic strip, which still persists, has fitted him with all of a white man's household comforts and headaches, it is as an unencumbered drifter whistling along on the road of hard knocks, ready for whatever adventure waits at the next turning, that he lives in our minds.

Cartoon characters have soul as Carl Jung defined it in his *Archetypes and the Collective Unconscious:* "soul is a life-giving demon who plays his elfin game above and below human existence." Without the "leaping and twinkling of the soul," Jung says, "man would rot away in his greatest passion, idleness." The Mickey Mouse of the thirties shorts was a whirlwind of activity, with a host of unsuspected skills and a reluctant heroism that rose to every occasion. Like Chaplin and Douglas Fairbanks and Fred Astaire, he acted out our fantasies of endless nimbleness, of perfect weightlessness. Yet withal, there was nothing aggressive or self-promoting about him, as there was about Popeye. Disney, interviewed in the thirties, said, "Sometimes I've tried to figure out why Mickey appealed to the whole world. Everybody's tried to figure it out. So far as I know, nobody has. He's a pretty nice fellow who never does anybody any harm, who gets into scrapes through no fault of his own, but always manages to come up grinning." This was perhaps Disney's image of himself: for twenty years he did Mickey's voice in the films, and would often say, "There's a lot of the Mouse in me." Mickey was a character created with his own pen, and nurtured on Disney's memories of his mouse-ridden Kansas City studio and of the Missouri farm where his struggling father tried for a time to make a living. Walt's humble, scrambling beginnings remained embodied in the mouse, whom the Nazis, in a fury against the Mickey-inspired Allied legions (the Allied code word on D-Day was "Mickey Mouse"), called "the most miserable ideal ever revealed . . . mice are dirty."

But was Disney, like Mickey, just "a pretty nice fellow"? He was until crossed in his driving perfectionism, his Napoleonic capacity to marshal men and take risks in the service of an artistic and entrepreneurial vision. He was one of those great Americans, like Edison and Henry Ford, who invented themselves in terms of a new technology. The technology — in Disney's case, film animation — would have been there anyway, but only a few driven men seized the full possibilities and made empires. In the dozen years between *Steamboat Willie* and *Fantasia,* the Disney studios took the art of animation to heights of ambition and accomplishment it would never have reached otherwise, and Disney's personal zeal was the animating force. He created an empire of the mind, and its emperor was Mickey Mouse.

The thirties were Mickey's conquering decade. His image circled the globe. In Africa, tribesmen painfully had tiny mosaic Mickey Mouses inset into their front teeth, and a South African tribe refused to buy soap unless the cakes were embossed with Mickey's image, and a revolt of some native bearers was quelled when the safari masters projected some Mickey Mouse cartoons for them. Nor were the high and mighty immune to Mickey's elemental appeal — King George V and Franklin Roosevelt insisted that all film showings they attended include a dose of Mickey Mouse. But other popular phantoms, like Felix the Cat, have faded, where Mickey has settled into the national collective consciousness. The television program revived him for my children's generation, and the theme parks make him live for my grandchildren's. Yet survival cannot be imposed through weight of publicity; Mickey's persistence springs from something unhyped, something timeless in the image that has allowed it to pass in status from a fad to an icon.

To take a bite out of our imaginations, an icon must be simple. The ears, the wiggly tail, the red shorts, give us a Mickey. Donald Duck and Goofy, Bugs Bunny and Woody Woodpecker are inextricably bound up with the draftsmanship of the artists who make them move and squawk, but Mickey floats free. It was Claes Oldenburg's pop art that first alerted me to the fact that Mickey Mouse had passed out of the realm of commercially generated image into that of artifact. A new Disney gadget, advertised on television, is a camera-like box that spouts bubbles when a key is turned; the key consists of three circles, two mounted on a larger one, and the image is unmistakably Mickey. Like yin and yang, like the Christian cross and the star of Israel, Mickey can be seen everywhere — a sign, a rune, a hieroglyphic trace of a secret power, an electricity we want to plug into. Like totem poles, like African masks, Mickey stands at that intersection of abstraction and representation where magic connects.

Usually cartoon figures do not age, and yet their audience does age, as generation succeeds generation, so that a weight of allusion and sentimental reference increases. To the movie audiences of the early thirties, Mickey Mouse was a piping-voiced live wire, the latest thing in entertainment; by the time of *Fantasia* he was already a sentimental figure, welcomed back. *The Mickey Mouse Club,* with its slightly melancholy pack leader, Jimmie Dodd, created a Mickey more removed and marginal than in his first incarnation. The generation that watched it grew up into the rebels of the sixties, to whom Mickey became camp, a symbol of U.S. cultural fast food, with a touch of the old rodent raffishness. Politically, Walt, stung by the studio strike of 1940, moved to the right, but Mickey remains one of the thirties proletariat, not uncomfortable in the cartoon-rickety, cheerfully verminous crash pads of the counter-culture. At the Florida and California theme parks, Mickey manifests himself as a short real person wearing an awkward giant head, costumed as a ringmaster; he is in danger, in these nineties, of seeming not merely venerable kitsch but part of the great trash problem, one more piece of visual litter being moved back and forth by the bulldozers of consumerism.

But never fear, his basic goodness will shine through. Beyond recall, perhaps, is the simple love felt by us of the generation that grew up with him. He was five years my senior and felt like a playmate. I remember crying when the local newspaper, cutting down its comic pages to help us win World War II, eliminated the Mickey Mouse strip. I was old enough, nine or ten, to write an angry letter to the editor. In fact, the strips had been eliminated by the votes of a readership poll, and my indignation and sorrow stemmed from my incredulous realization that not everybody loved Mickey Mouse as I did. In an account of my boyhood written over thirty years ago, "The Dogwood Tree," I find these sentences concerning another boy, a rival: "When we both collected Big Little Books, he outbid me for my supreme find (in the attic of a third boy), the first Mickey Mouse. I can still see that book. I wanted it so badly, its paper tan with age and its drawings done in Disney's primitive style, when Mickey's black chest is naked like a child's and his eyes are two nicked oblongs." And I once tried to write a short story called "A Sensation of Mickey Mouse," trying to superimpose on adult experience, as a shiver-inducing revenant, that indescribable childhood sensation — a rubbery taste, a licorice smell, a feeling of supernatural clarity and close-in excitation that Mickey Mouse gave me, and gives me, much dimmed by the years, still. He is a "genius" in the primary dictionary sense of "an attendant spirit," with his vulnerable bare black chest, his touchingly big yellow shoes, the mysterious place at the back of his shorts where his tail came out, the little cleft cushion of a tongue, red as a valentine and glossy as candy, always peeping through the catenary curves of his undiscourageable smile. Not to mention his ears.

Reflections and Responses

1. Why do you think Updike begins by considering Mickey Mouse's ears? What is the effect of his opening sentence? Why are the ears so important in understanding the phenomenon of Mickey Mouse?

2. "Like America," Updike writes, "Mickey has a lot of black blood." What does Updike mean by this? What evidence does he introduce to support this observation? How does his vocabulary reinforce this contention?

3. Updike uses the term "icon" throughout his essay, though he never explicitly defines it. Given the way he uses the word in context, what do you think he means by the word? Are Bugs Bunny and Daffy Duck also icons? Given Updike's sense of the word, explain why or why not.

SUE HUBBELL

The Vicksburg Ghost

When Elvis Presley died in 1977, "his likeness," Sue Hubbell reminds us, "was more widely reproduced than any other save that of Mickey Mouse." Since then, the iconography has grown even more phenomenal; not only is Elvis a constant tabloid feature but his career has even—despite a great deal of controversy—been commemorated with a postage stamp. In the following essay, Hubbell investigates one of the most bizarre aspects of what seems to be an unending Presley craze—the "King's" frequent sightings. Hubbell tracks down a woman from Vicksburg, Michigan, who claimed she saw Elvis in the checkout line of her local supermarket. Hubbell's trip to Vicksburg to learn the full story of this encounter takes her into the heart of a peculiar American darkness.

A noted essayist and nonfiction writer, Hubbell is the author of A Country Year *(1986),* Book of Bees *(1988), and* Broadsides from the Other Orders *(1993). She writes occasional pieces for* The New Yorker, *the* New York Times, *and* Smithsonian Magazine. *She lives in Washington, D.C., and in the Ozarks of southern Missouri, where she runs a commercial bee farm. "The Vicksburg Ghost" originally appeared in* The New Yorker *(1989) and was selected by Justin Kaplan for* The Best American Essays *1990.*

> The human predicament is typically so complex that it is not altogether clear which lies are vital and what truths beg for discovery.
> — "Vital Lies, Simple Truths: The Psychology of Self-Deception," by Daniel Goleman

I guess most people found it hard to believe that Elvis Presley didn't die after all but instead is alive and well and shopping at

Felpausch's Supermarket, in Vicksburg, Michigan. I know I did
when I read about it in the *New York Times* last fall. The *Times* wasn't
on record as saying "The King Lives," or anything like that, but it
did report that a Vicksburg woman named Louise Welling had said
she'd seen him the year before, in the supermarket's checkout line.
Her sighting encouraged Elvins everywhere, many of whom believe that Presley faked his death. It also added an extra fillip to
Elvismania, which is part nostalgia and part industry, the industry
part consisting of the production of Elvis memorabilia, books, articles, tours, and prime-time TV "docudramas." Fans have made pe-
riodic demands for an Elvis postage stamp, and a multimedia
musical. *Elvis: A Rockin' Remembrance,* had an off-Broadway run this
summer.

Promotion was what made Elvis Presley. In 1977, the year of his
death, his likeness was more widely reproduced than any other
save that of Mickey Mouse, and it has been reported that the news
of his demise was greeted by one cynic with the words "Good career move!" According to Albert Goldman, the biographer who
tells this story, Presley was by then a porky, aging, drug-befuddled
Las Vegas entertainer and was getting to be a hard personality to
promote. The Presley image shorn of the troublesome real man
was easier to market. For example, after the King's death, Presley's
manager, Colonel Thomas A. Parker, contracted with a vineyard in
Paw Paw, Michigan — a town not far from Vicksburg — to produce
a wine called Always Elvis. Its label bears a head shot of the entertainer, in a high-collared spangled white shirt, singing into a hand-
held microphone. Colonel Parker's own four-stanza poem appears
on the back of the bottle. Goldman has computed that the poem
earned Parker $28,000 in royalties, "making him, line for line, the
best-paid poet in the world." Although the wine is no longer produced, I was able to find a dusty old bottle in my local liquor store.
In the interests of journalism, I sampled it. It was an adequate
companion to the poem, which closes with the couplet

> We will play your songs from day to day
> For you really never went away.

In its year-end double issue, *People* ran a story featuring recent
photographs of Elvis purportedly taken by readers around the
country, each picture as vague and tantalizing as snapshots of the
Loch Ness monster. While debate mounted over whether or not

Elvis Presley was still alive, I got stuck back there in the part of the *Times* story which said that he was shopping at Felpausch's. By the latter part of the 1950s, when Elvis arrived to sweep away the dreariness of the Eisenhower years, I was too old to respond to the Dionysian sexual appeal that he had for his teenage maenads; consequently, I was also unmoved by retro-Elvis. But I did grow up near Vicksburg. My family lived in Kalamazoo, a bigger town (in which Elvis was also said to have appeared) twelve miles to the north, and we spent our summers at a lake near Vicksburg. My widowed mother now lives at the lake the year round, and when I visit her I often shop at Felpausch's myself. I know Vicksburg tolerably well, so when I read the account in the *Times* I strongly suspected that the reporter had been snookered by a group of the guys over at Mar-Jo's Café on Main Street, half a block from Felpausch's, which is on Prairie Street, the town's other commercial thoroughfare. Last June, while I was visiting my mother, I decided to drive into Vicksburg and find out what I could about the Elvis Presley story.

Vicksburg is a pretty village of two thousand people, more or less. A hundred and fifty years ago, when it was first settled by white people, the land was prairie and oak forest. James Fenimore Cooper, who lived for a time in the nearby town of Schoolcraft, wrote about the area in his book *Oak Openings*. It is in southern Michigan, where the winters are long and gray, and even the earliest settlers complained of the ferocity of the summertime mosquitoes. Vicksburg's one-block commercial section has been spruced up in recent years. There are beds of petunias at the curb edges, and new facades on the nineteenth-century buildings. The carefully maintained Victorian houses on the side streets are shaded by maples big enough to make you think elm. A paper mill, built near a dam that the eponymous John Vickers constructed on Portage Creek for his flour mill, has long provided employment for the local people, but today the village has become something of a bedroom community for commuters to Kalamazoo. Still, it seems very like the place I knew when I used to come to band concerts on Wednesday evenings at the corner of Main and Prairie during the summers of the 1930s and 1940s. The band concerts are a thing of the past, but there are other homegrown entertainments, such as one going on the week I was there — the annual

Vicksburg Old Car Festival, which is run by Skip Knowles, a local insurance man. The festival has a fifties theme, and last year, inspired by the commotion that Louise Welling's sighting of Elvis had produced, Knowles added an Elvis-look-alike contest to the roster of events. Knowles has his office in a storefront on Main Street that used to be Matz's Confectionery, where I first discovered lime phosphates (known locally as "green rivers").

And the teenagers are still bored. While I was in the library going through back issues of local newspapers, two high school girls introduced themselves to me, saying that they had lived in Vicksburg all their lives and would be happy to talk to me about it. I asked them what they thought about Elvis Presley. They smiled patronizingly and informed me that no one they knew paid any attention to him. "But *everything* just stands still in Vicksburg," one of them confided. "We go to Kalamazoo on Saturday nights. I can't wait to get out of here and go to college."

Mar-Jo's has stayed the same, too. It has been in the same place for forty years. It was named after Marge Leitner and her partner, Josephine, whose last name no one at the café can remember. It is your basic tan place: tan floor, tan walls, tan tables, tan counter. The sign taped to the cash register was new to me. It said:

> THIS IS NOT
> BURGER KING
> YOU GET IT
> MY WAY
> OR YOU DON'T
> GET IT
> AT ALL

But the men having coffee together at the big round table near the front windows could have been the same ones sitting there the last time I was in, which was a couple of years ago.

"How's you-know-who?" gray crew cut asks feed-store cap. "Don't see her anymore."

The others guffaw, and one says, "He's taken her clothes."

"What clothes?" feed-store cap shoots back. A ripple of caffeine-fueled laughter circles the table.

Shirley White, a small, wiry woman, has been a waitress at Mar-

Jo's for eleven years. Her hair is dark and tightly curled. She is efficient and cheerful. She knows virtually all her customers by name
and how they like their coffee, and she banters with all of them. She
gets to work at 4:45 every morning, so she is usually way ahead of
the best of the town wits, giving as good as she gets. The coffee-club
boys once arranged the kind of prank on her that made me suspect
them of the Elvis Presley caper. One of the regulars was a big man
whom she could deftly unsettle with a clever phrase or two. His in-
variable riposte was a mumbled "Paybacks are hell." A few years
ago, he was on vacation in Florida when her birthday came around,
and she had nearly forgotten about him. Mar-Jo's was jammed that
day, and no one would tell her why. "Just as I was busiest, this really
big monkey walked in," she told me. "At least, it was a big guy
dressed in a monkey costume, and he kept following me around,
getting in my way. I was real embarrassed, and everyone kept laughing. Then a messenger handed me something called an Ape-O-
Gram. It had just three words: 'Paybacks are hell.'"

Nearly all the coffee drinkers thought that the Elvis Presley
sighting was as funny as the Ape-O-Gram, but no one would own
up to having had a hand in making up the story. Louise Welling, it
seemed, was a real person, and well known in town. She lived to
the east, a few miles outside the village, they told me. "She's different, that's for sure," one of the coffee drinkers said. "No one believes her about Elvis Presley, but we all enjoyed it. Kind of put
Vicksburg on the map. Isn't it funny? Elvis Presley wasn't even a
very good singer. But I don't think Louise thinks it's funny." They
referred me to a woman in town who knew Louise Welling better
than they did and lived not far from her.

I went over to see the woman, who had an office in town, and
talked to her with the understanding that her name would not be
used. "Yes," she said. "I guess you could say that Louise is different.
Her whole family is different, except for her husband, who works
at General Motors. He's real quiet. But she's not crazy or anything.
In fact, I think she's real bright. I don't know what to make of her
claim that she saw Elvis Presley. She was a big Elvis fan from way
back, but she doesn't bring him up or talk about this stuff unless
someone asks her. She's a kind woman. She's reliable, too, and I
wouldn't hesitate to call her if I had trouble. I'm afraid that after
the story came out a lot of people played jokes on her. Made Elvis

phone calls. Sent her Elvis letters. I'm pretty sure she's not in it for money. She just seems to think it's an interesting story, and it makes her mad when people don't believe her. Of course, none of us do. I don't know anyone in this town who thinks she really saw Elvis Presley. She was furious with the Vicksburg newspaper because they wouldn't run her story."

It seemed odd to me that the *Vicksburg Commercial* had not used Louise Welling's story — a story that had made the *New York Times* — so I called up Jackie Lawrence, the owner of the *Commercial,* and asked her to meet me for lunch at Mar-Jo's. Jackie Lawrence, a former nurse, is a big woman with curly brown hair, and she smiles a lot when she talks about Vicksburg, her adopted town. There are, she said, perhaps a dozen loyal Elvis fans in town — people who make pilgrimages to Graceland and would *like* to believe Louise Welling even if they don't.

We studied the daily specials, which were posted on the wall, and I decided to order Ken's Homemade Goulash. Next to the list of specials were snapshots of Ken Fowler, a cheerful young man with a fine brushy mustache, who bought Mar-Jo's two years ago and does a lot of the café's cooking. Shortly after he bought the place, he had a birthday, and the regulars, the waitresses, and Ken's wife conspired to bring in a belly dancer. The event was captured on film, and the posted snapshots show Ken, in apparent embarrassment, on a chair in one corner of the café, surrounded by laughing customers as a woman in gold draperies writhes in front of him.

Jackie Lawrence told me that she remembered Louise Welling coming into the newspaper office, which is a few doors down from Mar-Jo's, in March 1988, six months after the sighting at Felpausch's. At the time of her visit, Mrs. Welling knew that her story would soon be printed nationally, in the *Weekly World News* — and so it was, three months later. (According to Jim Leggett, who is the dean of freelance tabloid photojournalists and once schemed to drill a hole in Howard Hughes's coffin in order to photograph his face, the *Weekly World News* is not exactly esteemed in the trade. "It prints the flotsam left by the better tabloids," he told me.) Mrs. Welling had wanted the *Commercial* to run her story first, Lawrence said. "She stood right by my desk, trying to tell me all about it. I said to her, 'I'm sorry, I don't have time for this,' and showed her out the door. And if she came in again, I'd say the same thing."

There was only one mention in the *Commercial* of the stir caused by Louise Welling's encounter with Elvis. The winner of Skip Knowles's 1988 Elvis-look-alike contest, a truck driver named Ray Kajkowski, came into the newspaper office a few days after the event to ask for prints of any pictures that might have been taken. While he was there, he kissed Jean Delahanty, one of the *Commercial*'s reporters, and she wrote a column about it, which concluded, "Some days are better than others!"

There is no chamber of commerce, as such, in Vicksburg. The town doesn't need one; it has Skip Knowles. I had telephoned Knowles before coming to Vicksburg. "Give me a jingle when you get in," he said. "Maybe we can do lunch." He is a handsome, trim, dark-haired man, and at our lunch a gold chain showed through the open collar of his shirt. There was another gold chain around his wrist. He was born in Atchison, Kansas, he told me, but spent his teenage years — from 1962 to 1968 — near Detroit, where he developed a passion for cars and for cruising, that cool, arm-on-the-window, slow patrolling of city streets which was favored by the young in those days. His dark eyes sparkled at the memory.

"We had what we called the Woodward Timing Association," he said. "It was made up of the guys that cruised Woodward Avenue. The Elias Big Boy at Thirteen Mile Road and Woodward was the place we'd go. But you know how the grass is always greener somewhere else? Well, my ultimate dream was to cruise the Sunset Strip. It wasn't until I got married, in 1969, and went out to California that I got to do that. And I talked to those guys cruising the Strip, and you know what they told me? It was *their* dream to cruise Woodward." He shook his head and laughed. "My wife and I still cruise when we go to a city." He hoped the local people had got cruising down pat for this year's festival, he said, handing me a packet of publicity material and a schedule of festival events. "I had to *teach* them how to cruise last year, which was the first time we closed off the streets for it."

The second annual Elvis-look-alike contest would be held at 9 P.M. Saturday over on Prairie Street, in the parking lot of the Filling Station, a fast-food restaurant across the street from Felpausch's. Skip Knowles knew a good thing when he had it. Before last summer, he said, the festival had been drawing several thousand people, but each year he had had more trouble getting good publicity. "I can't understand the way they handled the Elvis business over at Felpausch's," he told me. "They even refused an interview with the *New York Times*. But I decided to play it for whatever it was worth."

After the first Elvis-look-alike contest, Knowles received a lot of calls from Louise Welling, who wanted to talk about Elvis Presley with him. "I put her off," he said. "She's *really* different. I think she really believes Presley never died." He also received other phone calls and visits. When his secretary told him last fall that a reporter from the *Times* was in his outer office waiting to talk to him, he thought it was just a hoax — a joke like the ones dreamed up at Mar-Jo's. But when he came out the man introduced himself as the paper's Chicago bureau chief and interviewed him about the Elvis contest. Then a producer from Charles Kuralt's show, *Sunday Morning*, called and said he was interested in doing a segment for the show on the impact of the Elvis sighting in Vicksburg, and would anything be going on in Vicksburg around Thanksgiving time? "I told him, 'Look, I'll do *anything* to get you here,'" Knowles recalled. "'If you want me to rent Cadillac limos and parade them up and down Main Street for you to film, I'll get them.' But the TV people never came."

I decided that it was time to talk to Louise Welling herself. I couldn't make an appointment with her by telephone because she had recently obtained an unlisted number, but one midweek morning I took a chance on finding her at home and drove out to see her. The Wellings live in the country, in a modest splitlevel house on non-split-level terrain; this is the sandy, flat part of Michigan, too far south for the ice-age glaciers to have sculpted it. Mrs. Welling sometimes works as a babysitter, but this morning she was home, along with four of her five children — all of them grown — and Nathan, her four-year-old grandson. Mrs. Welling is a heavyset woman with closely cropped dark hair and a pleasant face. Her eyes stay sad when she smiles. She touched my arm frequently as we talked, and often interrupted herself to digress as she told me her story. She said that she grew up in Kalamazoo and for a time attended St. Mary's, a Catholic grammar school there. When she turned sixteen, she was given a special present — a ticket to a Presley concert in Detroit. "Somehow, the fellow who took tickets didn't take mine, so after the first show I was able to move up, and I sat in front during the second," she said. "And then, toward the end, Elvis got down on his knee right in front of me and spread his arms wide open. Well, you can imagine what *that* would be like for a sixteen-year-old girl." Her voice trailed off, and she fell silent, smiling.

I asked her if she had continued to follow his career.

"When I got married, I started having children, and I never thought much about Elvis," she said. "After all, I had problems of my own." But then, in 1973, she saw a notice in a throwaway shopping newspaper from Galesburg, a nearby town, saying that Presley would be in Kalamazoo and, although he would not be performing, would stay at the Columbia Hotel there.

"I didn't try to get in touch with him," Mrs. Welling said, adding, with a womanly smile, "I had a husband, and you know how that is." Three years later, however, Presley appeared in concert in Kalamazoo, and she sent flowers to him at the Columbia Hotel, because she assumed that he would be staying there again. She went to the concert, too, and as she remembers it, Elvis announced in the course of it that he had a relative living in Vicksburg. "He said he liked this area," she recalled. "Kalamazoo is a peaceful place. He'd like that. And I think he's living at the Columbia right now, under another name. But they won't admit it there. Every time I call, I get a runaround. You know what I think? I think he has become an undercover agent. He was interested in that sort of thing."

"What year was it that you saw him in concert in Detroit?" I asked. I had read somewhere that Presley had not started touring outside the South until 1956.

"Oh, I don't remember," Mrs. Welling said, "I'm fifty-one now, and I just had turned sixteen — you figure it out."

The arithmetic doesn't work out — nor, for someone who grew up in Kalamazoo, does the Columbia Hotel. The Columbia had its days of glory between the First World War and Prohibition, and it was growing seedy by the forties, when I used to ride by it on my way to school. Its decline continued after I left Kalamazoo, until — according to Dan Carter, one of the partners in a development company that remodeled the hotel to create an office complex called Columbia Plaza — it became "a fleabag flophouse and, for a while, a brothel." Carter also told me that in the mid-eighties a rumor arose that Elvis Presley was living there, behind the grand pink double doors on the mezzanine, which open into what was once a ballroom. The doors have been locked for years — the empty ballroom, its paint peeling, belongs to the man who owns Bimbo's Pizza on the floor below — but that didn't deter Elvins here and abroad from making pilgrimages to Columbia Plaza. "You'd hear foreign voices out in the hallway almost every day," he said. "Then there was a visit from some people from Graceland — at least, they told us they were from Graceland, and they looked the part — who came by to see if we were making any money off this." They weren't, he said, and today the building's management denies that Elvis Presley, under any name, lives anywhere on the premises.

Mrs. Welling's next good look at Elvis Presley came at Felpausch's in September, 1987. There had been, she told me, earlier hints. In 1979, she had seen a man in the back of the county sheriff's car when the police came to her house to check on the family's dog, which had nipped a jogger. "The man in the back seat was all slouched down, and he didn't look well," she said. "I'm sure it was Elvis." A few years later, black limousines began to appear occasionally on the road where she lives. "Now, who around here would have a limo?" she asked. Then she began seeing a man she believes was Elvis in disguise. "He looked real fake," she recalled. "He was wearing new bib overalls, an Amish hat, and a beard that didn't look real. I talked to a woman who had seen the same man, and she said he sometimes wore a false nose. Now, why does he have to bother with disguises? Why couldn't he have said that he needed a rest, and gone off to some island to get better?"

A note of exasperation had crept into Mrs. Welling's voice. She showed me a cassette that she said contained a tape that Presley made after he was supposed to have died; in it, she said, he explained why he had faked his death. But when she played it the sound was blurred and rumbly, and I couldn't make out the words. The tape had been issued in 1988, to accompany a book by a woman — with whom Mrs. Welling has corresponded — who put forward the theory that the body buried as Presley's was not his own. The book and another by the same author, which Welling said was a fictional account of a rock star who fakes his death, were lovingly inscribed ("It's hard to take the heat") to Mrs. Welling.

Here is what Mrs. Welling said happened to her in September

1987. She had just been to eleven o'clock Sunday Mass at St. Martin's Church. With grandson Nathan, she stopped at Felpausch's to pick up a few groceries. Having just celebrated one publicly accepted miracle, she saw nothing strange in the private miracle at the supermarket.

"The store was just about deserted," she said. "There wasn't even anyone at the checkout register when I went in. But back in the aisles I felt and heard someone behind me. It must have been Elvis. I didn't turn around, though. And then, when I got up to the checkout, a girl was there waiting on Elvis. He seemed kind of nervous. He was wearing a white motorcycle suit and carrying a helmet. He bought something little — fuses, I think, not groceries. I was so startled I just looked at him. I knew it was Elvis. When you see someone, you know who he is. I didn't say anything, because I'm kind of shy and I don't speak to people unless they speak first. After I paid for the groceries, I went out to the parking lot, but no one was there."

I asked Mrs. Welling if she had told anyone at the time what she had seen. She replied that she had told no one except the author of the Elvis-isn't-dead book, who was "very supportive." After that, she and her daughter Linda started seeing Elvis in Kalamazoo — once at a Burger King, once at the Crossroads Shopping Mall, and once driving a red Ferrari. And she said that just recently, while she was babysitting and filling her time by listening to the police scanner, she heard a man's voice ask, "Can you give me a time for the return of Elvis?" and heard Presley reply, "I'm here now."

I asked her what her family thought about her experiences. Linda, a pale, blond woman who was sitting off to one side in a dining alcove smoking cigarettes while I talked to her mother, was obviously a believer, and occasionally she interjected reports of various Elvis contacts of her own. "But *my* mother thinks it's all nutty," Mrs. Welling said, laughing. "She says I should forget about it. My husband doesn't say much — he's real quiet — but he knows I'm not crazy."

It wasn't until the spring of 1988, Mrs. Welling said, that she started getting in touch with the media. She claims that she didn't bother talking to the people at the Vicksburg newspaper (although Jackie Lawrence remembers otherwise), because "it wasn't an important newspaper." Instead, she tried to tell her story to the

Kalamazoo Gazette and people at the television station there. No one would take her seriously — except, of course, the author of the Elvis book. After Mrs. Welling had written to her and talked to her on the telephone, a writer for the *Weekly World News* phoned for an interview. Mrs. Welling asked him how he knew about her, but he declined to reveal his sources. In early May, the tabloid prepared the ground for Mrs. Welling's story by running one that took note of the rumor that Presley was living in Columbia Plaza, and gave Mrs. Welling's friend a nice plug for her book. Shortly after that, the syndicated columnist Bob Greene gave the rumor a push. By that time, the *Kalamazoo Gazette* realized that it could no longer ignore Mrs. Welling's phone calls, and in its May 15 issue Tom Haroldson, a staff writer, wrote a front-page story headlined "'Elvis Alive' in Kalamazoo, Say Area Woman and News Tabloid." That was the beginning of Mrs. Welling's fame, but it was not until June 28 that the *Weekly World News* told her whole story. In thousands of supermarkets, the issue appeared with a big front-page picture of Mrs. Welling and a headline in type an inch and a half high proclaiming, "I've Seen Elvis in the Flesh!" The story began to be picked up by newspapers around the country as a brightener to the increasingly monotonous accounts of the preconvention presidential campaigns. CBS investigated it for possible production on *60 Minutes*. Radio stations from coast to coast and as far away as Australia called to interview Louise Welling and anyone else they could find. Kalamazoo's mayor, Edward Annen, reacted to all this by announcing to a *Gazette* reporter, "I've told them that everyone knows this is where he lives and that they should send their residents here to spend tourist dollars to find him."

Funny signs sprouted throughout Kalamazoo and Vicksburg in places of commerce. A rival market of Felpausch's posted one that said, "Jimmy Hoffa Shops Here." A dentist boasted, "Elvis Has His Teeth Cleaned Here." At Mar-Jo's, the sign read, "Elvis Eats Our Meatloaf." The folks at Felpausch's, however, were not amused. Cecil Bagwell, then the store's manager, told the *Gazette*, "The cashier who supposedly checked out Elvis that day cannot remember anything about it," and characterized Mrs. Welling as "an Elvis fanatic." Bagwell no longer works at Felpausch's, but I spoke with Jack Mayhew, the assistant manager, who scowled when I brought up the subject. "I won't comment," he said, adding, nonetheless,

"We've never given the story to anyone, and we're not going to. All I'll say is that the woman is totally —" and he rotated an extended finger beside his head.

Before I left Mrs. Welling that morning, I asked her why she thought it was that *she* had seen Elvis, when others had not — did not even believe her.

"I don't know, but the Lord does," she answered. "I'm a religious woman, and when things like this happen — that we don't understand — it just proves that the Lord has a plan."

The next day, a friend who had heard about my investigations telephoned to tell me that there had been an Elvis sighting just a week or so earlier, in Kalamazoo, at the delivery bay of the Fader Construction Company, which is owned by her family. She hadn't seen the man herself, she said, but the women in the office had insisted that the truck driver making the delivery was Elvis Presley. I suspected that it might have been Ray Kajkowski, winner of the Elvis-look-alike contest and kisser of Jean Delahanty. This turned out to be true. On Friday evening, at a runthrough for the Old Car Festival's cruising event, I was introduced to Kajkowski by Skip Knowles, and Kajkowski confirmed that he had made quite a stir while delivering a shipment of concrete forms to Fader. He gave me his card — he has apparently made a second career for himself as an Elvis impersonator at parties and night clubs — and then he whipped out a pair of mirrored sunglasses, put them on, and kissed me, too. "Young, old, fat, skinny, black, white, good looking, not so good looking, I kiss them all," he said. "I'm a pretty affectionate fellow. I was raised in a family that hugged a lot."

Ray Kajkowski lives in Gobles, not far from Vicksburg. At forty-one, he is thick-featured, a bit on the heavy side, and looks like — well, he looks like Elvis Presley. He has big sideburns and dyed black hair, which he wears in a pompadour. He went down to Graceland recently with his wife and his two teenage sons to study the Presley scene and recalls that while he was in the mansion's poolroom a couple came in and the wife took one look at him and collapsed on the floor in a faint.

"When I was growing up, I felt like an outsider," he told me. "I didn't think I was as good as other people, because my dad wasn't a doctor or a lawyer. We were just common folks. I knew about Elvis even when I was a little kid. I didn't pay much attention, though, except that some of my buddies had pictures of Elvis, so we'd trade those to our older sisters and their friends for baseball cards." He laughed.

"I felt like we were invaded when the Beatles came over," he continued. By that time—1963—he was at Central High School in Kalamazoo, and had begun to appreciate Presley's music and to defend it against foreign stars. "I mean, Elvis was a small-town boy who made good. He was just ordinary, and, sure, he made some mistakes, just like me or you or any of us. But he went from zero to sixty. He had charisma with a capital C, and somehow people still know it."

After Presley's death, Kajkowski said, he felt sad and started reading about Elvis and studying his old movies. "Then, in September or October 1987, right around then, I was at a 1950s dance in Gobles. My hair was different then, and I had a beard, but there was a fifty-dollar prize for the best Elvis imitator. Fifty bucks sounded pretty good to me, and I watched this one guy do an imitation, and he didn't move or anything, and I thought to myself, I can do better than that, so I got up and entered and won, beard and all. After that, I shaved off my beard, dyed my hair, and started building my act. I do lip-synch to Elvis tapes. I've got three suits now, one black, one white, one blue. My wife does my setups for me and runs the strobe lights. Evenings when we don't have anything else to do, we sit around and make scarves for me to give away. I cut them, and she hems them. When I'm performing, I sweat real easy, and I mop off the sweat with the scarves and throw them out to the gals. They go crazy over them. And the gals proposition me. They don't make it easy. Sometimes they rub up against me, and when I kiss them they stick their tongues halfway down my throat. Once, I went over to shake the guys' hands, because I figured it was better to have them on my side. But one big guy wouldn't shake my hand, and later he came over and grabbed me like a grizzly bear and told me to quit it. 'You don't sound like Elvis Presley. You don't look like Elvis Presley. Stop it.' I told him, 'Hey, it's all lip-synch! It's just an act! It's entertainment!' But I try to keep it under control. My wife's the woman I have to go home with after the act."

I asked Kajkowski if he had ever been in Felpausch's. As a truck driver, he said, he had made deliveries there; occasionally, he even shopped there. But although he owned a motorcycle, he said, he rarely drove it, and he never wore a white motorcycle suit.

I asked him what he made of Mrs. Welling's story.

"Well," he said thoughtfully, "when someone puts another person at the center of their life, they read about him, they think about him, I'm not surprised that he becomes real for that person."

Saturday night at nine o'clock Louise Welling is standing next to me in the Filling Station's parking lot — it is built on the site of John Vickers's flour mill — in a crowd that has just seen prizes awarded in the fifties dance concert and is waiting for the beginning of the second annual Elvis-look-alike contest. She is neatly dressed in a blue-and-white checked overblouse and dark pants. Her hair is fluffed up, and she is wearing pretty pink lipstick. She invited me to come to the contest, and told me that although many of the entrants in such affairs didn't come close to Elvis she was hoping that this one would draw the real Elvis Presley out from hiding. "If he came to me in the past, I believe he'll come again," she said. "I hope it will be before I die. If he comes, I'm going to grab him and hold on to him and ask him why he couldn't just be honest about needing to get away for a rest. Why couldn't he just tell the truth? Look at all the trouble he's caused those who love him."

Earlier in the day, I stopped in at Mar-Jo's for coffee. There were lots of extra visitors in the café. Ken Fowler had turned on the radio to WHEZ, a Kalamazoo station, which was broadcasting live from out on the street, acting as the festival's musical host. Rock music filled the café. Patrons were beating time on their knees, and the waitresses had begun to boogie up and down behind the counter. I asked one of them — a girl named Laurie, who was decked out fifties style with a white floaty scarf around her ponytail — what she made of Mrs. Welling's story. "I think it's kind of fun," she said. "I haven't met the lady, but, you know, maybe she's right. After all, if Elvis Presley never died he has to be someplace."

Mrs. Welling is subdued as she stands next to me, but all attention — scanning the people, anticipatory. We are at the very back of the good-natured crowd, which has enjoyed the nostalgia, the slick cars, the dances, the poodle skirts, and the ponytails. She spots Kajkowski and says to me that he's not Elvis but "so far he's the only one here who even looks anything like him."

Skip Knowles is up on the stage, in charge of what has turned out to be a successful event. There have been record-breaking crowds. Six hundred and fifty cars were entered. He has had plenty of media coverage, and he seems to be having a very good time. He calls for the Elvis contest to begin. Ray Kajkowski's act is so good now that he has no competition — he is the only one to enter. I watch him play the crowd. He had told me, "When I first started, I really liked the attention, but now it's just fun to do the show, and, yeah, I do get caught up in it. I like the holding power I have over people. I know how it is to feel left out, so I play to everyone. But I like people in their mid-thirties or older best. I don't like to entertain for these kids in their twenties. The gals back off when I try to drape a scarf around them. I think that's an insult." Now he is dancing around the edge of the crowd, reaching out to kiss the women, who respond to him with delight and good humor, and then he launches into what Mrs. Welling tells me is "You're a Devil in Disguise." I look at her, and she seems near tears. Her shoulders slump. "I don't like to watch," she says softly, and walks away to gather her family together for the trip home.

On my own way home, on the morning after the festival, I made one final stop in Vicksburg, on the south side of town, at what is left of Fraser's Grove. For about forty years — up until the early 1920s — Fraser's Grove was one of this country's premier spiritualist centers. In 1883, Mrs. John Fraser, the wife of a well-to-do Vicksburg merchant, turned the twenty-acre woodland into a camp and gathering place for mediums, believers in mediums, and the curious. She had been inspired by a lecture on spiritualism given in a hall on Prairie Street by one Mrs. R. S. Lily, of Cassadaga, New York, a town in the spiritually fervent "burned-over" district of that state. In the years that followed, Mrs. Fraser became a national figure in séance circles, and another resident of Vicksburg, C. E. Dent, was elected president of something called the Mediums' Protection Union. A group calling itself the Vicksburg Spiritualists was formed shortly after Mrs. Lily's visit, and it met each Sunday. Its Ladies' Auxiliary held monthly chicken dinners (fifteen cents a plate, two for a quarter). On summer Sunday afternoons, people from around this country and abroad packed the campground at Fraser's Grove to talk of materialization and reincarnation and watch mediums go into trances to contact the dead. According to a

1909 issue of the *Vicksburg Commercial,* they debated subjects such as "Is the planet on which we live approaching final destruction, or is it becoming more permanent?" (A follow-up article reports that the Spiritualists opted for permanency.)

Trees still stand in much of Fraser's Grove, although some of them have been cut down to make room for a small housing development. The campground itself has been taken over by the Christian Tabernacle, which makes use of the old camp buildings. Tazzie, my German shepherd, was with me, and I parked at the edge of the grove to let her out for a run before we drove onto the interstate highway. We headed down a dim path, where events passing strange are said to have taken place. The grove produced no Elvis, no John Vickers, not even a phantom band concert or the apparition of Mr. Matz — no spirits at all. But Tazzie did scare up a rabbit, and the oaks were still there, and, untamed through a hundred and fifty generations, so were the mosquitoes.

Reflections and Responses

1. Why does Hubbell travel to Vicksburg to investigate the Elvis sighting? What is her interest in Elvis? How does her motivation for writing the essay affect her coverage of the event?

2. Hubbell cites a *New York Times* story as her first source of information about the Elvis sighting. What other sources does she use? How do these different sources suggest different attitudes toward the incident? In what ways does Hubbell's story differ from all the others?

3. After reading the essay, reconsider the epigraph by Daniel Goleman. Why is it appropriate? How does it suggest Hubbell's perspective on the incident she investigates?

GERALD EARLY

Life with Daughters: Watching the Miss America Pageant

Why would the annual Miss America pageant be so fascinating to an African-American college professor and literary intellectual? What does the contest say about our culture and its racial values? In the following essay, Gerald Early confesses to something few intellectuals would admit—that, in "a perverse way," he enjoys watching the Miss America pageant every year with his wife and daughters. The contest, he acknowledges with some embarrassment, has even become a household tradition. Early's reflections on this "cultural rite" take him into both public and personal territory as he considers the contest's influence on both black and white America as well as its impact on his own family relationships.

Early teaches at Washington University in St. Louis. He is the author of Tuxedo Junction: Essays on American Culture *(1989) and* The Culture of Bruising: Prizefighting, Literature, and Modern American Culture *(1991). He is the editor of* My Soul's High Song: The Collected Writings of Countee Cullen *(1991), the two-volume* Speech and Power: The African-American Essay, from Polemic to Pulpit *(1992), and* Lure and Loathing: Essays on Race, Identity, and the Ambivalence of Assimilation *(1993). His latest book,* Daughters, *is about his experiences as a father. "Life with Daughters: Watching the Miss America Pageant" originally appeared in* The Kenyon Review *(1990) and was selected by Joyce Carol Oates for* The Best American Essays 1991. *The notes included in this essay are Gerald Early's.*

The theater is an expression of our dream life — of our unconscious aspirations.

> — David Mamet, "A Tradition of the Theater as Art," *Writing in Restaurants*

Aunt Hester went out one night, — where or for what I do not know, — and happened to be absent when her my master desired her presence.

> — Frederick Douglass, *Narrative of the Life of Frederick Douglass*

Adults, older girls, shops, magazines, newspapers, window signs — all the world had agreed that a blue-eyed, yellow-haired, pink-skinned doll was what every child treasured.

> — Toni Morrison, *The Bluest Eye*

It is now fast becoming a tradition, if one can use that word to describe a habit about which I still feel a certain amount of shame-facedness, for our household to watch the Miss America contest on television every year. The source of my embarrassment is that this program remains, despite its attempts in recent years to modernize its frightfully antique quality of "women on parade," a kind of maddeningly barbarous example of the persistent hard, crass urge to sell: from the plugs for the sponsor that are made a part of the script (that being an antique of fifties and sixties television; the show does not remember its history as much as it seems bent on repeating it) to the constant references to the success of some of the previous contestants and the reminders that this is some sort of scholarship competition; the program has all the cheap earnestness of a social uplift project being played as a musical revue in Las Vegas. Paradoxically, it wishes to convince the public that it is a common entertainment while simultaneously wishing to convey that it is more than mere entertainment. The Miss America pageant is the worst sort of "Americanism," the soft smile of sex and the hard sell of toothpaste and hair dye ads wrapped in the dreamy ideological gauze of "making it through one's own effort." In a perverse way, I like the show; it is the only live television left other than sports, news broadcasts, performing arts awards programs, and speeches by the president. I miss live TV. It was the closest thing to theater for the masses. And the Miss America contest is, as it has been for some time, the most perfectly rendered theater in our culture, for it so perfectly captures what we yearn for: a low-class ritual, a polished restatement of vulgarity, that wants to open the door to high-class respectability by way of plain middle-class anxiety and ambition. Am I doing all right? the contestants seem to ask in a kind of reassuring, if numbed, way. The contest brings together all the American classes in a showbiz spectacle of classlessness and tastelessness.

My wife has been interested in the Miss America contest since childhood, and so I ascribe her uninterrupted engagement with America's cultural passage into fall (Miss America, like college and pro football, signifies for us as a nation, the end of summer; the contest was invented, back in 1921, by Atlantic City merchants to prolong the summer season past Labor Day) as something mystically and uniquely female. She, as a black woman, had a long-standing quarrel with the contest until Vanessa Williams was chosen the first black Miss America, in September 1983. Somehow she felt vindicated by Williams for all those years as a black girl in Dallas, Texas, watching white women win the crown and thumb their noses at her, at her blackness, at her straightened hair, her thick lips, her wide nose. She played with white Barbie dolls as a little girl and had, I suppose, a "natural" or at least an understandable and predictable interest in seeing the National White Barbie Doll chosen every year because for such a long time, of course, the Miss America contest, with few exceptions, was a totemic preoccupation with and representation of a particularly stilted form of patriarchal white supremacy. In short, it was a national white doll contest. And well we know that every black girl growing up in the fifties and early sixties, had her peculiar love-hate affair with white dolls, with mythicized white femininity. I am reminded of this historical instance: everyone knows that in the Brown versus Topeka Board of Education case (the case that resulted in the Supreme Court decision to integrate public schools) part of the sociological evidence used by the plaintiffs to show the psychological damage suffered by blacks because of Jim Crow was an account by Kenneth Clarke of how, when offered a choice between a black doll and a white doll, little black girls invariably chose the white doll because they thought it "prettier."

On the front page of the January 6, 1962, *Pittsburgh Courier,* a black weekly, is a picture of a hospitalized black girl named Connie Smith holding a white doll sent to her by Attorney General Robert Kennedy. Something had occurred between 1954, when the Supreme Court made its decision, and 1962 which made it impossible for Kennedy to send the girl a black doll, and this impossibility was to signal, ironically, that the terms of segregation and the terms of racial integration, the very icon of them, were to be exactly the same. Kennedy could not send the girl a black doll as it would have implied, in the age of integration, that he was, in effect, sending her a Jim Crow toy, a toy that would emphasize the girl's race. In the early sixties such a gesture would have been considered condescending. To give the black girl a white doll in the early sixties was to mainstream the black girl into the culture, to say that she was worthy of the same kind of doll that a white girl would have. But how can it be that conservatism and liberalism, segregation and integration could produce, fantastically, the same results, the identical iconography: a black girl hugging a white doll because everyone thinks it is best for her to have it? How can it be that at one time the white doll is the sign of the black girl's rejection and inferiority and fewer than ten years later it is the sign of her acceptance and redemption? Those who are knowledgeable about certain aspects of the black mind or the collective black consciousness realize, of course, that the issues of segregation and integration, of conservatism and liberalism, of acceptance and rejection, of redemption and inferiority, are all restatements of the same immovable and relentless reality of the meaning of American blackness; that this is all a matter of the harrowing and compelling intensity that is called, quaintly, race pride. And in this context, the issue of white dolls, this fetishization of young white feminine beauty, and the complexity of black girlhood becomes an unresolved theme stated in a strident key. Blacks have preached for a long time about how to heal their daughters of whiteness: in the November 1908 issue of *The Colored American Magazine*, E. A. Johnson wrote an article entitled, "Negro Dolls for Negro Babies," in which he said, "I am convinced that one of the best ways to teach Negro children to respect their own color would be to see to it that the children be given colored dolls to play with. . . . To give a Negro child a white doll means to create in it a prejudice against its own color, which will cling to it through life" (583). Lots of black people believed this and, for all I know, probably still do, as race pride, or the lack thereof, burns and crackles like a current through most African-American public and private discourse. Besides, it is no easy matter to wish white dolls away.

A few years ago I was thumbing through an album of old family photographs and saw one of me and my oldest sister taken when I was four and she was nine. It struck me, transfixed me really, as it was a color photo and most of the old family pictures taken when I was a boy were black and white because my mother could not afford to have color pictures developed. We, my sister and I, are sitting on an old stuffed blue chair and she is holding a white doll in her hand, displaying it for the picture. I remember the occasion very well as my sister was to be confirmed in our small, all-black Episcopal church that day and she was, naturally, proud of the moment and wanted to share it with her favorite toy. That, I remembered, was why these were color pictures. It was a very special day for the family, a day my mother wanted to celebrate by taking very special pictures. My mother is a very dark woman who has a great deal of race pride and often speaks about my sisters having black dolls. I was surprised, in looking at the picture recently, that they ever owned a white one, that, indeed, a white one had been a favorite.

My wife grew up — enjoyed the primary years of black girlhood so to speak — during the years 1954 through 1962; she was about five or six years younger than my older sister. She lived in a southern state or a state that was a reasonable facsimile of a southern state. She remembers that signs for colored and white bathrooms and water fountains persisted well into the mid-sixties in Texas. She remembers also Phyllis George, the Miss America from Denton, Texas, who went on to become a television personality for several years. She has always been very interested in George's career and she has always disliked her. "She sounds just like a white girl from Texas," my wife likes to say, always reminding me that while both blacks and whites in Texas have accents, they do not sound alike. George won the contest in 1971, my wife's freshman year at the University of Pennsylvania and around the time she began to wear an Afro, a popular hairstyle for young black women in the days of "our terrible blackness" or "our black terribleness." It was a year fraught with complex passages into black womanhood for her. To think that a white woman from Texas should win the Miss America title that year! For my wife, the years of watching the Miss America contest were nothing more, in some sense continue to be nothing more, than an expression of anger made all the worse by the very unconscious or semi-conscious nature of it. But if the anger has been persistent, so has her enormous capacity to "take it"; for in all these years it has never occurred to her to refuse because, like the black girl being offered the white doll, like all black folk being offered white gifts, she has absolutely no idea how that is done and she is not naive enough to think that a simple refusal would be an act of empowerment. Empowerment comes only through making demands of our bogeymen, not by trying to convince ourselves we are not tormented. Yet, paradoxically, among blacks there is the bitter hope that a simplistic race pride will save us, a creed that masks its complex contradictions beneath lapping waves of bourgeois optimism and bourgeois anguish; for race pride clings to the opposing notions that the great hope (but secret fear) of an African-American future is, first, that blacks will always remain black and, second, that the great fear (but secret hope) of an African-American future is that blacks will not always remain black but evolve into something else. Race pride, which at its most insistent, argues that blackness is everything, becomes, in its attempt to be the psychological quest for sanity, a form of dementia that exists as a response to that form of white dementia that says blackness is nothing. Existing as it does as a reactive force battling against a white preemptive presumption, race pride begins to take on the vices of an unthinking dogma and the virtues of a disciplined religious faith, all in the same instance. With so much at stake, race pride becomes both the act of making a virtue of a necessity and making a necessity of a virtue and, finally, making a profound and touching absurdity of both virtue and necessity. In some ways my wife learned her lessons well in her youth: she never buys our daughters white dolls.

My daughters, Linnet, age ten, and Rosalind, age seven, have become staunch fans of beauty contests in the last three years. In that time they have watched, in their entirety, several Miss America pageants, one Miss Black America contest, and one Miss USA. At first, I ascribed this to the same impulse that made my wife interested in such events when she was little: something secretly female just as an interest in professional sports might be ascribed to something peculiarly male. Probably it is a sort of resentment that black girls harbor toward these contests. But that could not really be the case with my daughters. After all they have seen several black contestants in these contests and have even seen black winners. They also have black dolls.

Back in the fall of 1983 when Vanessa Williams became Miss America, we, as a family, had our picture taken with her when she visited Saint Louis. We went, my wife and I, to celebrate the grand moment when white American popular culture decided to embrace black women as something other than sexual subversives or as fat, kindly maids cleaning up and caring for white families. We had our own, well, royalty, and royal origins mean a great deal to people who have been denied their myths and their right to human blood. White women reformers may be ready to scrap the Miss America contest. (And the contest has certainly responded to the criticism it has been subjected to in recent years by muting some of the fleshier aspects of the program while, in its attempts to be even more the anxiety-ridden middle-class dream-wish, emphasizing more and more the magic of education and scholarly attainments.) It is now the contest that signifies the quest for professionalism among bourgeois women, and the first achievement of the professional career is to win something in a competition. But if there is a movement afoot to bring down the curtain finally on Miss America, my wife wants no part of it: "Whites always want to reform and end things when black people start getting on the gravy train they've been enjoying for years. What harm does the Miss America contest do?" None, I suppose, especially since black women have been winning lately.

Linnet and Rosalind were too young when we met Vanessa Williams to recall anything about the pictures, but they are amazed to see themselves in a bright, color Polaroid picture with a famous person, being part of an event which does not strike a chord in their consciousness, because they cannot remember being alive when it happened. I often wonder if they attach any significance to the pictures at all. They think Vanessa is very pretty, prettier than their mother, but they attach no significance to being pretty, that is to say, no real value; they would not admire someone simply because he or she was good-looking. They think Williams is beautiful, but they do not wish that she was their mother. And this issue of being beautiful is not to be taken lightly in the life of a black girl. About two years ago Linnet started coming home from school wishing aloud that her hair was long and blond so that she could fling it about, the way she saw many of her white classmates doing. As she attends a school that is more than 90 percent white, it seemed inevitable to my wife that one of our daughters would become sensitive about her appearance. At this time Linnet's hair was not straightened and she wore it in braids. Oddly, despite the fact that she wanted a different hairstyle that would permit her hair to "blow in the wind," so to speak, she vehemently opposed having it straightened, although my wife has straightened hair, after having worn an Afro for several years. I am not sure why Linnet did not want her hair straightened; perhaps, after seeing her teenage cousin have her hair straightened on several occasions, the process of hair straightening seemed distasteful or disheartening or frightening. Actually, I do not think Linnet wanted to change her hair to be beautiful; she wanted to be like everyone else. But perhaps this is simply wishful thinking here or playing with words because Linnet must have felt her difference as being a kind of ugliness. Yet she is not a girl who is subject to illusion. Once, about a year earlier, when she had had a particularly rough day in school, I told her, in a father's patronizing way with a daughter, that I thought she was the most beautiful girl in the world. She looked at me strangely when I said that and then replied matter-of-factly: "I don't think I'm beautiful at all. I think I'm just ordinary. There is nothing wrong with that, is there, Daddy? Just to be ordinary?" "Are you unhappy to be ordinary?" I asked. She thought for a moment, then said quietly and finally, "No. Are you?"

Hair straightening, therefore, was not an option and would not have been even if Linnet had wanted it, because my wife was opposed to having Linnet's hair straightened at her age. At first, Linnet began going to school with her hair unbraided. Unfortunately, this turned out to be a disastrous hairdo as her hair shrank during the course of a day to a tangled mess. Finally, my wife decided to have both Linnet and Rosalind get short Afro haircuts. Ostensibly, this was to ease the problem of taking swim lessons during the summer. In reality, it was to end Linnet's wishes for a white hairstyle by, in effect, foreclosing any possibility that she could remotely capture such a look. Rosalind's hair was cut so that Linnet would not feel that she was being singled out. (Alas, the trials of both being both the second and the younger child!) At first, the haircuts caused many problems in school. Some of the children — both black and white — made fun of them. Brillo heads, they were called, and fungus and Afro heads. One group of black girls at school refused to play with Linnet. "You look so ugly with that short hair," they would say. "Why don't you wear your hair straight like your mom? Your mom's hair is so pretty." Then, for the first time, the girls were called niggers by a white child on their school bus, although I think neither the child nor my daughters completely understood the gravity of that obscenity. People in supermarkets would refer to them as boys unless they were wearing dresses. Both girls went through a period when they suffered most acutely from that particularly American disease, that particularly African-American disease, the conjunction of oppression and exhibitionistic desire: self-consciousness. They thought about their hair all the time. My wife called the parents of the children who teased them. The teasing stopped for the most part, although a few of the black girls remained so persistent that the white school counselor suggested that Linnet and Rosalind's hair be straightened. "I'm white," he said, "and maybe I shouldn't get into this, but they might feel more comfortable if they wore a different hairstyle." My wife angrily rejected that bit of advice. She had them wear dresses more often to make them look unmistakably like girls, although she refused out of hand my suggestion of having their ears pierced. She is convinced that pierced ears are just a form of mutilation, primitive tattooing or scarring, passing itself off as something fashionable. Eventually, the girls became used to their hair. Now, after more than a year, they hardly think about it and even if Linnet wears a sweat suit or jeans, no one thinks she is a boy because she is budding breasts. Poor Rosalind still suffers on occasion in supermarkets because she shows no outward signs of sexual maturity. Once, while watching Linnet look at her mother's very long and silken, straight hair, the hair that the other black girls at school admire, always calling it "pretty," I asked her if she would like to have hers straightened.

"Not now," she said. "Maybe when I'm older. It'll be something different."

"Do you think you will like it?" I asked.

"Maybe," she said.

And in that "maybe," so calmly and evenly uttered, rests the complex contradictions, the uneasy tentative negotiations of that which cannot be compromised yet can never be realized in this flawed world as an ideal; there is, in that "maybe," the epistemology of race pride for black American women so paradoxically symbolized by their straightened hair. In the February, 1939, issue of the *Atlantic Monthly,* a black woman named Kimbal Goffman (possibly a pseudonym) wrote an essay entitled "Black Pride" in which she accused blacks of being ashamed of their heritage and, even more damningly in some of her barbs obviously aimed at black women, of their looks:

> . . . why are so many manufacturers becoming rich through the manufacture of bleaching preparations? Why are hair-straightening combs found in nearly every Negro home? Why is the following remark made so often to a newborn baby, when grandma or auntie visits it for the first time? "Tell Mother she must pinch your nose every morning. If she doesn't, you're gonna have a sure 'nough darky nose."

According to Goffman, blacks do not exploit what society has given them; they are simply ashamed to have what they have, tainted as it is with being associated with a degraded people, and long to be white or to have possessions that would accrue a kind of white status. In the essay, blacks in general receive their share of criticism but only black women are criticized in a gender-specific way that their neurotic sense of inferiority concerning physical appearance is a particularly dangerous form of reactionism as it stigmatizes each new generation. According to Goffman, it is black women, because they are mothers, who perpetuate their sense of inferiority by passing it on to their children. In this largely DuBoisian argument, Goffman advises, "Originality is the backbone of all progress." And, in this sense, originality means understanding blackness as something uncontrolled or uninfluenced by what whites say it is. This is the idealism of race pride that demands both purity and parity. Exactly one year later, in the February, 1940, issue of *The Brown American Magazine,* a black publication published in Philadelphia, Lillian Franklin McCall wrote an article about the history of black women beauty shop owners and entrepreneurs entitled "Appointment at Seven." The opening paragraph is filled with dollar signs:

> The business of straightening milady's insistent curls tinkles cash registers in the country to the tune of two million and a half dollars a year. And that covers merely the semimonthly session with the hairdresser for the estimated four million of Eve's sepia adult daughters by national census. Today there is a growing trend to top off the regular, "Shampoo and wave", with a facial; and, perhaps, a manicure. New oil treatments and rinses prove a lure, too, so milady finds her beauty budget stepped

up from approximately $39 yearly for an average $1.25 or $1.50 "hair-do", to $52.00 per year if she adds a facial to the beauty rite, and $10 more, for the manicure.

In a Booker T. Washington-tone, McCall goes on to describe how the establishment of a black beauty culture serves as a source of empowerment for black women:

> Brown business it is, in all its magnitude for Miss Brown America receives her treatments from the hands of Negro beauticians and her hair preparations and skin creams come, usually from Negro laboratories.

She then tells the reader that leading companies in this field were founded by black women: Madam C. J. Walker, Mrs. Annie Turbo Malone, Madame Sara Spencer Washington. And one is struck by the absences that this essay evokes, not only in comparison to Goffman's piece but also to Elsie Johnson McDougald's major manifesto on black women, "The Task of Negro Womanhood," that appeared in Alain Locke's seminal 1925 anthology of African-American thought, *The New Negro*. In McDougald's piece, which outlines all the economic status and achievements of black women at the time, there is absolutely no mention of black beauty culture, no mention of Madame C. J. Walker, although her newspaper ads were among the biggest in black newspapers nationwide during the twenties. (And why did McDougald not mention black women's beauty workers and business people-culture along with the nurses, domestics, clerks, and teachers she discusses at length? It can scarcely be because she, as a trained and experienced writer on black sociological matters, did not think of it.*) It is not simply

---

*Richard Wright tells a story in his 1956 account of the Bandung conference entitled *The Color Curtain* that emphasizes the absence of the black woman. He relates how a white woman journalist knocks upon his hotel room door during the course of the conference and confides the strange behavior of her roommate — a black woman journalist from Boston. Her roommate walks around in the middle of the night and the white woman often covertly spies her in "a dark corner of the room . . . bent over a tiny blue light, a very low and a very blue flame. . . . It seemed like she was combing her hair, but I wasn't sure. Her right arm was moving and now and then she would look over her shoulder toward my bed. . . ." The white woman thinks that the black woman is practicing voodoo. But Wright soon explains that the black woman is simply straightening her hair:

"But why would she straighten her hair? Her hair seems all right?" [the white woman journalist asks].

"Her hair is all right. But it's not straight. It's kinky. But she does not want you, a white woman, to see her when she straightens her hair. She would feel embarrassed —"

"Why?"

money or black woman's industry or endeavor that makes the black woman present or a presence; it is beauty culture generally which finally brings her into being, and specifically, her presence is generated by her hair. What, for one black woman writer, Goffman, is an absence and thus a sign of degradation, is for another a presence and a sign of economic possibilities inherent in feminine aesthetics.

What did I see as a boy when I passed the large black beauty shop on Broad and South Streets in Philadelphia where the name of its owner, Adele Reese, commanded such respect or provoked such jealousy? What did I see there but a long row of black women dressed immaculately in white tunics, washing and styling the hair of other black women. That was a sign of what culture, of what set of politics? The sheen of those straightened heads, the entire enterprise of the making of black feminine beauty: was it an enactment of a degradation inspirited by a bitter inferiority or was it a womanly laying on of hands where black women were, in their way, helping themselves to live through and transcend their degradation? As a boy, I used to watch and wonder as my mother straightened my sisters' hair every Saturday night for church on Sunday morning. Under a low flame on the stove, the hot comb would glow dully; from an opened jar of Apex bergamont hair oil or Dixie Peach, my mother would extract blobs and place them on the back of one hand, deftly applying the oil to strands of my sisters' hair with the other. And the strange talk about a "light press" or a "heavy press" or a "close press" to get the edges and the ends;

"Because you were born with straight hair, and she wants to look as much like you as possible. . . ."

The woman stared at me, then clapped her hands to her eyes and exclaimed: "Oh!"

I leaned back and thought: here in Asia, where everybody was dark, that poor American Negro woman was worried about the hair she was born with. Here, where practically nobody was white, her hair would have been acceptable; no one would have found her "inferior" because her hair was kinky; on the contrary, the Indonesians would perhaps have found her different and charming.

The conversation continues with an account of the black woman's secretive skin lightening treatments. What is revealing in this dialogue which takes on both political and psychoanalytic proportions is the utter absence of the black woman's voice, her presence. She is simply the dark, neurotic ghost that flits in the other room while the black male and the white female, both in the same room, one with dispassionate curtness and the other with sentimentalized guilt, consider the illness that is enacted before them as a kind of bad theater. Once again, the psychopathology of the black American is symbolized by the black woman's straightened hair, by her beauty culture.

the concern about the hair "going back" if caught in the rain. Going back where, I wondered. To Africa? To the bush? And the constant worry and vigil about burning, getting too close to the scalp. I can remember hearing my sisters' hair sizzle and crackle as the comb passed through with a kind of pungent smell of actually burning hair. And I, like an intentional moth, with lonely narrow arcs, hovered near this flame of femininity with a fascinated impertinence. Had I witnessed the debilitating nullity of absence or was it the affirmation of an inescapable presence? Had I witnessed a mutilation or a rite of devotion? Black women's hair is, I decided even as a boy, unintelligible. And now I wonder, is the acceptance of the reigns of black women as Miss America a sign that black beauty has become part of the mainstream culture? Is the black woman now truly a presence?

We, I and my wife and our daughters, sat together and watched the latest Miss America contest. We did what we usually do. We ate popcorn. We laughed at all the talent numbers, particularly the ones when the contestants were opera singers or dancers. We laughed when the girls tried to answer grand social questions — such as "How can we inspire children to achieve and stay in school?" or "How can we address the problem of mainstreaming physically disadvantaged people?" in thirty seconds. In fact, as Rosalind told me after the show, the main reason my daughters watch the Miss America pageant is that "it's funny." My daughters laugh because they cannot understand why the women are doing what they are doing, why they are trying so hard to please, to be pleasing. This must certainly be a refreshing bit of sanity, as the only proper response for such a contest is simply to dismiss it as hilarious; this grandiose version of an elocution, charm school, dance and music recital, which is not a revelation of talent but a reaffirmation of bourgeois cultural conditioning. And this bit of sanity on my daughters' part may prove hopeful for our future, for our American future, for our African-American future, if black girls are, unlike my wife when she was young, no longer angry. When it was announced that Miss Missouri, Debbye Turner, the third black to be Miss America, was the winner, my children were indifferent. It hardly mattered to them who won, and a black woman's victory meant no more than if any other contestant had prevailed. "She's pretty," Linnet said. She won two dollars in a bet with my wife who did not think it possible that another black Miss America would be chosen. "Vanessa screwed up for the whole race," she told me once. "It's the race burden, the sins of the one become the original sins of us all." Linnet said simply, "She'll win because she is the best." Meritocracy is still a valid concept with the young.

For me, it was almost to be expected that Miss Turner would win. First she received more pre-contest publicity than any other contestant in recent years with the possible exception of the black woman who was chosen Miss Mississippi a few years ago. Second, after the reign of Vanessa Williams, one would think that the Miss America powers-that-be very much wanted to have another black win and have a successful reign so that the contest itself could prove both its good faith (to blacks) and forestall criticism from white feminists and liberals (who are always put in a difficult position when the object of their disapproval is a black woman). As with the selection of Williams, the contest gained a veneer of postmodernist social and political relevance not only by selecting a black again but by having an Asian, a kidney donor, and a hearing impaired woman among the top ten finalists. This all smacks of affirmative action or the let's-play-fair-with-the-underrepresented doctrine which, as Miss Virginia pointed out after the contest, smacks of politics. But the point she missed, of course, is the point that all people who oppose affirmative action miss. The selection process for the Miss America contest has always been political. Back in the days when only white college women, whose main interest in most instances was a degree in MRS, could win, the contest was indeed just as poltiical as it is now, a clear ideological bow to both patriarchal ideals and racism. It is simply a matter of which politics you prefer, and while no politics are perfect, some are clearly better than others. But in America, it must be added, the doctrine of fair play should not even be graced with such a sophisticated term as *political*. It is more our small-town, bourgeois Christian, muscular myth of ethical rectitude, the tremendous need Americans feel to be decent. So Miss Turner is intended to be both the supersession of Vanessa Williams — a religious vet student whose ambitions are properly, well, postmodernist Victorianism, preach do-goodism, evoke the name of God whenever you speak of your ambitions, and live with smug humility — and the redemption of the image of black women in American popular culture since the Miss America contest is one of the few vehicles of display and competition for women in popular culture.

And if my daughters have come to one profound penetration of this cultural rite, it is that the contest ought to be laughed at in some ways, as most of the manifestations of popular culture ought to be for being the shoddy illusions that they are. For one always ought to laugh at someone or a group of someones who are trying to convince you that nothing is something — and that is not really the same as someone trying to convince you that you can have something for nothing, because in the popular culture business, the price for nothing is the same as the price for something; this "nothing is something" is, in fact, in most cases, what the merchandising of popular culture is all about. (But as Mother reminded me as a boy: nothing is nothing and something is something. Accept no substitutes!) For my children, the contest can be laughed at because it is so completely meaningless to them; they know it is an illusion despite its veneer as a competition. And it is that magical word, *competition,* that is used over and over again all night long by the host and hostesses of the Miss America show (a contest, like most others these days, from the SATs to professional sports, that is made up of a series of competitions within the framework of larger competitions in such a pyramid that the entire structure of the outside world, for the bourgeois mind, is a frightful maze, a strangulating skein of competitions) that is the touchstone of reality, the momentous signifier, that the sponsors of the pageant hope will give this extravaganza new significance and new life. For everything that we feel is important now is a matter of competition, beating out someone else for a prize, for some cheap prestige, a moment of notice before descending to cipherhood again; competition ranging from high culture (literary prizes, which seem to be awarded every day in the week, and classical musical competitions for every instrument in a symphony orchestra, because of course for high culture one can never have enough art) to mid-culture (the entire phenomenon of American education, from academic honors to entrance requirements to enter prestigious schools because, of course, for the middle class one can never have enough education or enough professionalism) to low culture (playing the lottery and various forms of gambling because, of course, for the lower class one can never hope enough for money). And the more stringent and compulsively expressed the competition is (and the Miss America contest has reached a new height of hysteria in both the stridency and compulsion of the competition), the more legitimate and noteworthy it is.

Everyone in our culture wants to win a prize. Perhaps that is the grand lesson we have taken with us from kindergarten in the age of the perversions of Dewey-style education: everyone gets a ribbon, and praise becomes a meaningless narcotic to soothe egoistic distemper. And in our bourgeois coming-of-age, we simply crave more and more ribbons and praise, the attainment of which becomes all the more delightful and satisfying if they are gotten at someone else's expense. Competition, therefore, becomes in the end a kind of laissez-faire psychotherapy that structures and orders our impossible rages of ambition, our rages to be noticed. But competition does not produce better people (a myth we have swallowed whole); it does not even produce better candidates, it simply produces more desperately grasping competitors. The "quality" of the average Miss America contestant is not significantly better now than it was twenty-five years ago, although the desires of today's contestants may meet with our approval (who could possibly disapprove of a black woman who wishes to be a vet in this day of careerism as the expression of independence and political empowerment), but then the women of twenty-five years ago wanted what their audiences approved of as well. That is not necessarily an advance or progress; that is simply a recognition that we are all bound by the mood and temper of our time. So, in this vast competition, this fierce theatrical warfare where all the women are supposed to love their neighbor while they wish to beat her brains out, this warfare so pointedly exposed before the nation, what we have chosen is, not the Royal American Daughter (although the contest's preoccupation with the terminology of aristocracy mirrors the public's need for such a person as the American princess), but rather the Cosmopolitan Girl. As the magazine ad states*

> Can a girl be too Busy? I'm taking seventeen units at Princeton, pushing on with my career during vacations and school breaks, study singing and dancing when I can, try never to lose track of my five closest chums, steal the time for Michael Jackson and Thomas Hardy, work for

---

*Jacques Barzun. "Culture High and Dry." *The Culture We Deserve* (Middletown, Conn.: Wesleyan University Press, 1989).

an anti-drug program for kids and, of yes, I hang out with three horses, three cats, two birds and my dog Jack. My favorite magazine says "too busy" just means you don't want to miss anything . . . I love that magazine. I guess you can say I'm That Cosmopolitan Girl.

When one reads about these women in the Miss America contest, that is precisely what they sound like: The Cosmopolitan Girl who knows how to have serious fun and she has virtually nothing with which to claim our attention except a moralistic bourgeois diligence. To use a twenties term: she sounds "swell." She is an amalgam of both lead characters portrayed by Patty Duke on her old TV show: the studious, serious kid and the "typical" wacky but good-hearted suburban teenager or, to borrow Ann Douglas's concept, she is the Teen Angel: the bourgeois girl who can do everything, is completely self-absorbed with her leisure, and has a heart of gold. Once again, with the Miss America contest, we have America's vehement preoccupation with innocence, with its inability to deal with the darkness of youth, the darkness of its own uselessly expressed ambition, the dark complexity of its own simplistic morality of sunshine and success, the darkness, righteous rage, and bitter depth of its own daughters. Once again, when the new Miss America, victorious and smiling, walks down the runway, we know that runway, that victory march, to be the American catwalk of supreme bourgeois self-consciousness and supreme illusion. We are still being told that nothing is something.

Nonetheless, the fact that Miss Turner won struck both my wife and me as important, as something important for the race. We laughed during the contest, but we did not laugh when she was chosen. We wanted her to win very much; it is impossible to escape that need to see the race uplifted, to thumb your nose at whites in a competition. It is impossible for blacks not to want to see their black daughters elevated to the platforms where white women are. Perhaps this tainted desire, an echoing "Ballad of the Brown Girl" that resounds in the unconscious psyche of all black people, is the unity of feeling which is the only race pride blacks have ever had since they became Americans; for race pride for the African-American, finally, is something that can only be understood as existing on the edge of tragedy and history and is, finally, that which binds both together to make the African-American the darkly and richly complicated person he or she is. In the end, both black women magazine writers quoted earlier were right: race pride is transcending your degradation while learning to live in it and with it. To paraphrase an idea of Dorothy Sayers, race pride must teach blacks that they are not to be saved *from* degradation but saved *in* it.

A few days after the contest I watched both my daughters playing Barbies as they call it. They squat on the floor on their knees moving their dolls around through an imaginary town and in imaginary houses. I decided to join them and squatted down too, asking them the rules of their game which they patiently explained as though they did not mind having me, the strange adult, invade their children's world. I told them it was hard for me to squat and asked if I could simply sit down, but they said that one always plays Barbies while squatting. It was a rule that had to be obeyed. As they went along, explaining relationships among their myriad dolls and the several landscapes, as complicated a genealogy as anything Faulkner ever dreamed up, a theater as vast as the entire girlhood of the world, they told me that one particular black Ken doll and one particular black Barbie doll were married and that the dolls had a child. Then Rosalind held up a white doll that someone, probably a grandparent, had given them (my wife is fairly strict on the point of our daughters not having white dolls, but I guess a few have slipped through), explaining that this doll was the daughter of the black Ken and Barbie.

"But," I said, "how could two black dolls have a white daughter?"

"Oh," said Rosalind, looking at me as if I were an object deserving of only her indulgent pity, "we're not racial. That's old-fashioned. Don't you think so, Daddy? Aren't you tired of all that racial stuff?"

Bowing to that wisdom which, it is said, is the only kind that will lead us to Christ and to ourselves, I decided to get up and leave them to their play. My knees had begun to hurt and I realized, painfully, that I was much too old, much too at peace with stiffness and inflexibility, for children's games.

Reflections and Responses

1. Why is Early somewhat embarrassed about his interest in the Miss America pageant? What aspects of the contest disconcert him? Do you feel that his embarrassment is justified?

2. Note the theme of "dolls" in the essay. In what ways are they important to his topic? Of what significance is the white doll that Robert Kennedy gave to a black child? How do dolls surface in both aspects of his essay — the personal and the public?

3. Consider Early's position on his subject. Do you think his attitude toward the pageant and the issue of female beauty is free of bias or do you think he brings a specifically male perspective to the topic?

JACOB COHEN

Yes, Oswald Alone Killed Kennedy

Public personalities, John Updike reminds us in his essay on Mickey Mouse, are most likely to be transformed into cultural icons only after they die. We have only to observe the careers of such celebrities as Marilyn Monroe and Elvis Presley or such public figures as Abraham Lincoln and John F. Kennedy. Kennedy is a good case in point; a president elected by one of the narrowest margins in American history, he struggled hard to earn popular approval. Yet after his assassination in Dallas, he became—almost overnight—one of our most loved and esteemed presidents. Kennedy's death not only elevated him to a martyr's stature, it spawned an entire assassination industry: Since the event, over two thousand books have been published on the subject and not a November 22 goes by without several television "specials" honoring the occasion by featuring yet another "theory" of what happened that day in Dallas. Almost all of these theories, of course, elaborate some version of conspiracy. One of the most recent and most publicized accounts of the assassination is Oliver Stone's three-hour 1991 film, JFK. *The movie received an enormous amount of media attention and incited a flurry of articles attacking or defending the conspiracy theory. One of these responses came from Jacob Cohen, a scholar who for thirty years has seriously studied every facet of the assassination. In the following essay, he systematically reviews and assails every argument raised by the conspiracists.*

Cohen is chairman of the American Studies Department at Brandeis University. He has written widely about allegations of government conspiracy throughout American history. "Yes, Oswald Alone Killed Kennedy" originally appeared in Commentary *(1992) and was selected by Joseph Epstein for* The Best American Essays 1993.

Even the strongest supporters of *JFK*, Oliver Stone's notorious film on the assassination of President John F. Kennedy, concede that it is deceptive: fabricated footage gussied up as documentary fact; fictional characters and scenes offered as proof of perfidy; paranoid insinuations about the conscious involvement of the highest officials in the land; outright lies. Yet to an extraordinary number of often intelligent people, these characterizations seem utterly beside the point. "Don't trust anyone who says the movie is hogwash," writes a *Newsweek* critic, David Ansen, "and don't trust the movie either . . . [it] is a remarkable, a necessary, provocation." "One of the worst great movies ever made," declaims Norman Mailer. One wonders: how false, fanciful, and downright mendacious does a work purporting to portray and interpret historical events need to be before it is not just chided but discounted, disqualified, disgraced?

Those who defend the film's meta-purposes seem confident that if not all, then some and *certainly at least one* of its basal assertions of fact reflect what actually happened in Dallas: more than one person fired at the President. And if there was more than one gunman, there is *prima facie** evidence of a consiracy of some sort or another.

Having spent a considerable part of my life over the last three decades studying and discussing the Kennedy assassination, I can testify to the tenacity of that basal assertion. Challenging the notion of multiple gunmen has become tantamount to suggesting that it was the United States which attacked Japan in 1941, Poland which attacked Germany in 1939. And yet, I will contend that for anyone who has seriously studied the original Warren Report on the assassination (and not just had it read to him by its critics); has gone over the materials produced in the reconsideration of that Report by the House of Representatives in 1977–78; and has familiarized himself with the many scientific studies over the years, including three separate reviews of the medical material, which have examined the testable bases of the single-assassin theory — to anyone who has done all this, the notion of multiple gunmen, on which nearly every conspiracy theory extant rests, is a demonstra-

---

***prima facie:** Latin, at first view; immediately clear. In law refers to evidence sufficient to establish a fact.

ble chimera. And if there was one and only one assassin, and if that assassin was Lee Harvey Oswald, then nearly every insinuation in *JFK,* and in the mountain of conspiracy literature which it summarizes, collapses.

II

The case for multiple assassins consists of four lines of argument: (1) there was not enough time for a single gunman to have done what the Warren Commission alleges Oswald did; (2) compelling eyewitness, photographic, and earwitness testimony place a second gunman on the fabled grassy knoll; (3) the evidence of Kennedy's wounds and the reaction of his body to the shots establishes the presence of assassins other than on the knoll; and (4) the so-called single-bullet theory, popularly known as the magic-bullet theory, the indispensable prerequisite of the notion that there was only one assassin, is a palpable absurdity.

These arguments are mutually reinforcing, but it is fair to say if any of them holds water, the single-assassin theory would be untenable. However, as we shall see, all four are baseless.

Consider the issue of timing. Repeatedly, like a mantra, *JFK,* and the critics it mimics, declare that the famous Zapruder film (a home movie taken of the assassination by a Dallas manufacturer, Abraham Zapruder) "established three shots in 5.6 seconds" and that such a feat would stretch the capacity of the most expert rifleman, and undoubtedly was beyond Oswald and his gun. In interviews and speeches Oliver Stone frequently refers to "the 5.6-second Zapruder film," as if that were all there was to it, 5.6 seconds, and many commentators on *JFK* dutifully repeat these data, usually in the movie's own tone of outraged incredulity.

Yet: (1) the Zapruder film, which is 30 seconds long in toto, firmly established only the final and unmistakable shot to Kennedy's head. (2) Even assuming that two hits occurred 5.6 seconds apart, nothing in Zapruder indicates that a possible third shot, which missed, had to have come *between* the two hits. The Warren Commission concluded only that there were probably three shots and that *the two hits,* not the three shots, came within 5.6 seconds of each other. The miss could have come first, or last, though it probably came first. That means the gunman had more than eight seconds to shoot, and more than five seconds — ample time — between the two hits. (3) Even if the miss had come between the two hits, there would still have been 2.8 seconds to fire and refire — enough time even for an amateur used to handling guns, like Oswald. Stone and/or his advisers know this, as does everyone who has studied the case.

Were there shots from the grassy knoll by another assassin? Allegedly, eyewitness, photographic, and earwitness testimony placed a second gunman there. The knoll, I would remind the reader, was in front and to the right of the President's car when he was first struck, and directly to his right when he was fatally shot in the head. The Warren Commission placed the lone gunman above and behind the President in the Texas Book Depository building.

Surely, the most significant eye- and earwitnesses to the assassination were Abraham Zapruder himself and his secretary, Marilyn Sitzman, who was standing next to him as he took his famous home movie. The two of them were on the knoll, on a three-foot-high concrete pedestal overlooking the scene and directly overlooking the entire area behind a five-foot wooden fence at the top of the knoll from behind which, Stone and the other conspiracists say, an assassin shot at and killed the President.

But here is a point omitted by Stone and the conspiracists: Zapruder and Sitzman were within 50 feet, above, slightly *behind,* and in clear line of sight of the alleged assassin and (in Stone's recreation) his alleged "spotter." Fifty feet is ten feet less than the distance between home plate and the mound. Understand: Zapruder and Sitzman were on the mound facing the batter, as it were, and Stone would have us believe that they did not happen to hear or see two assassins to their right front halfway down the third base line, firing two explosive shots. They simply failed to glance that way during the shooting or to notice the gunman while he waited for the President to arrive.

Zapruder is now dead, but Sitzman was interviewed for a sensational five-part documentary produced by the Arts and Entertainment (A&E) Network on cable TV. Somehow, the interviewer did not ask her whether she noticed a man shooting the President just to her right front.

Those who have seen the A&E documentary will recall the gripping analysis of a black-and-white Polaroid snapshot of the knoll which was taken by one Mary Moorman just before the fatal head shot. In that picture, we are told, one may now see the clear image of "the badge man," a man in uniform, who, allegedly, fired at the

President from the knoll. Yet while that image may leap out at the consultants to the A&E documentary, it was not clear to the panel of photographic experts who, in 1977, perused it for the House Assassinations Committee.

Of course, those experts were not privy to the blown-up, "colorized" enhancements of the photo developed by the A&E consultants, who claim to see in the photo not only a man (nothing remarkable in that, it's a free country and people were allowed to roam about the knoll) but a hatless man in uniform. They even claim to be able to see the label on his shirt and, "perhaps," a gun. Well, if "badge man" is an assassin, he fired from a spot right next to, at most fifteen feet below and to the right of, Zapruder and Sitzman. Again, they did not notice.

There are other pictures of the knoll — twenty-two persons were taking pictures in Dealey Plaza, the assassination site, that afternoon — and several are of the knoll at the time of the shooting. Over the years conspiracists have discerned in these pictures riflemen and rifles, only to have photographic expertise reveal the illusions created by light and shadow.

For example, in one set of photos purporting to show a rifleman in "the classic firing position," the rifleman, to be actual, would need to have been floating in the air nine feet above the ground. Another rifle, supposedly visible in Zapruder frame 413, turned out to be a small branch in a bush in front of the fence, and the head behind that bush, the one with a "tennis hat" on, would have to be the size of a lemon in order to have been where the critics say it is.

Notwithstanding Stone's insinuations, no one saw a gun on the knoll, though it would have been in the clear line of sight of hundreds of the 692 people who have been identified in Dealey Plaza. No one: not one of the eighteen people on the railroad bridge who, looking up Elm Street at the approaching President, could easily have spotted a gun about a hundred feet in front of them and slightly to their left; no one in the plaza, neither Zapruder nor Sitzman, who were on the knoll; none of the hundreds who, we presume, were following the presidential limousine with their eyes and need only have raised their gaze a few degrees to have seen the gun; not Lee Bowers, who surveyed the scene from a tower behind the alleged assassins; no one in the presidential caravan, including Secret Service men whom film and photos show scanning the surrounding scene. (Were they ordered not to see anything? Have they remained silent to this day about those criminal orders?) On the other hand, six people saw the rifle *inside* the sixth-floor, southeast corner window of the Book Depository: Oswald's rifle, the one that fired all the bullets that were recovered. Two people actually saw the rifle as it was fired, and two of them identified Oswald in a police lineup.

Those who have seen the Stone film, or the A&E documentary, or are familiar with the conspiracy literature, may now protest vehemently: what about Jean Hill, the woman in the Stone film who fervently claims she saw a "gunman" running? What about the others who swear passionately that the shots came from the knoll? What about the many, like A. J. Holland, who saw gunsmoke on the knoll, and the sheer weight of earwitness testimony that the shots came from the knoll? What about the deaf mute who for twenty-eight years has been trying to get someone to understand his signing message that, a few minutes before the assassination, from a distance of over a hundred yards, he saw men walking with rifles near the knoll?

And what about the lady who now claims to be the "babushka lady" visible in photos of the plaza, and who says she will go to her death believing there was a gunman on the knoll? And what of Gordon Arnold, who claims, after more than a quarter century of silence, that he filmed the assassination from in front of the fence on the knoll, that he sensed bullets whizzing past his ear, and that after the shooting a man with "dirty hands," in a uniform, came up to him, weeping, and threw him to the ground, physically forcing him to relinquish the incriminating film? Arnold's is one of several stories by people who claim they were roughed up and threatened because they had seen inadmissible things. Stone graphically depicts these alleged brutalities and the reign of terror which insiders to the assassination have been enduring.

Here are the answers. Jean Hill said she "saw a man running," not from the knoll but from the Depository. Stone has Hill say that the man was a "gunman." But a gunman, presumably, is a man holding a gun. Hill did not say that she saw a gun. It is possible that, as many witnesses do, she has fused two disparate facts — the President is shot, a man is running — and created the saga she has made a career of telling?

Holland, who is the only one to say he saw a man with a subma-chine gun stand up in the back of the President's limousine, claims also to have seen smoke over the knoll. Others, too, saw smoke, and identified it with a shot. The Stone film shows a considerable puff of smoke wafting above the knoll, pretty much as Holland de-scribed it. But modern weapons do not make big puffs of smoke. Hot steam pipes do produce such cumulus effects, and there were hot steam pipes at the top of the knoll where the smoke was seen.

Beverly Oliver, the woman who claims to be the "babushka lady," not only swears "to her death" that the shots came from the knoll (although she saw no gun), but she also identifies herself as having been a nightclub singer in a club next to Jack Ruby's and has said that when Ruby, Oswald's eventual assassin, introduced her there to Oswald they casually identified themselves as "CIA agents." She says, too, that in 1968 she met for two hours with Richard Nixon, whom she ties to the killing. Stone knows all this detail, but omits much of it in order to create the character of a sympathetic night-club singer terrified to tell the world about her certain knowledge of links between Oswald and Ruby. (No persuasive links between the two have ever been established.)

Was Gordon Arnold there? He does not appear in photos, though some find him in the Moorman photo right next to "badge man." (Apparently Arnold did not notice the "badge man" shoot-ing the President.) As for the story that he was brutalized and his film removed — it is interesting that no one brutalized or even spoke to Zapruder and Sitzman, or removed them from the pivotal perch from which they filmed the assassination and, presumably, saw the assassins. And as for the deaf mute, whose twenty-eight years of silent frustration were ended when A&E finally found someone to read his signs and put him on television, is it indeco-rous to suggest that his story sounds like a routine on *Saturday Night Live*?

Stone and others would have us believe that on the knoll that day there was a platoon of conspirators, incognito, surveying every person's eyes, entering minds and cameras, knowing infallibly who had incriminating evidence and who did not. Like Santa Claus, they knew who had been bad or good, and they brutalized only those who saw or photographed the bad thing. And these people, in fear and trembling, agreed to be silent. Now, nearly three decades later, these same victims have agreed to take their ten minutes in the spotlight at the invitation of A&E and Oliver Stone.

And the earwitnesses? Undeniably, several people thought shots came from the knoll, said so freely to the Warren Commission, the FBI, the Secret Service, and the Dallas police, and were reported as having said so. Fourteen years later, in 1977, at the request of the House Assassinations Committee, a panel of acoustical scientists and psychologists examined all the earwitness evidence and then correlated it with observations they made at Dealey Plaza when rifles were test-fired from the knoll and the Book Depository. They discovered that of 178 earwitness accounts which they sampled, 132 thought there were three shots, 149 thought there were three or fewer. Six people thought there were four shots; one thought there were five, and one, Jean Hill, heard six. (Six is the number that Stone, and most conspiracists, say were fired.)

With regard to the source of the shots: 49 of the 178 thought it was the Depository, 21 thought it was the knoll, 30 gave other sources, 78 did not know. Crucially, however, only 4 of the 178 thought shots came from more than one direction. Since we know that at least some shots came from the Depository — the rifle, Oswald's, which fired all the recovered bullets and shells was found there, and six people saw a rifle in the window — shots would have needed to have come from two directions if there were also shots from the knoll. The panel concluded:

> It is hard to believe a rifle was fired from the knoll. . . . [D]espite the various sources of confusion in the locus of any single shot, a second shot from a different location should be distinctive and different enough to cause more than four witnesses to report multiple origins for the shots.*

---

*One further comment on the matter of earwitness testimony. The House Assassinations Committee in 1979 concluded that a tape recording of police communications at the time of the assassination registered four, not three, shots, and specifically, three shots from the Depository and one from the knoll. Solely on the basis of that piece of evidence, the Committee decided that an unseen gunman shot an (unrecovered) bullet, and missed. In 1982 the National Academy of Science asked a blue ribbon panel of physicists and acoustical experts to review the recording and the accompanying studies which had persuaded the House Committee that there was a gunman on the knoll. The panel concluded unanimously and vigorously that the alleged sounds on the tape could not have been made at the time of the shooting, and also scoffed at the calculations and methodology of the House consultants.

According to *JFK*, there were ten to twelve assassins, firing six shots from three directions. No one heard it that way; no one. Nor do the conspiracists answer this question: if the idea (as Stone suggests) was to frame Oswald for having fired three shots, why fire six? Did the Conspiracy expect that no one would notice?

To take the full measure of what Stone and the others are suggesting, we must remember that this ingenious plot *intended* that the assassins on the knoll be invisible and escape unnoticed. But how could they have known where spectators would be, where cameras would be? Just behind the fence was a public parking lot, filled with cars. Anyone could have gone to retrieve his car at any time. And why does Stone not show us the (inevitably hilarious) planning session where it was decided that a feigned epileptic fit fifteen minutes before the shooting to distract attention from the gunman on the knoll, a diversionary shot from the Depository, and an omniscient goon squad to rough up awkward witnesses would be enough to provide anonymity and safe passage to assassins standing in broad daylight, in clear view?

There is a further reason to scoff at speculation of a shot from the knoll: the alleged gunman, one of the world's finest (according to Stone) or one of the Mafia's finest (in other versions), firing at point-blank range, missed the car and everyone in it with a bullet which was never recovered. The now decisively authenticated X-rays and photographs which were taken of the President's body the night of the assassination establish that no shots struck the President or Governor John Connally (who was with him in the motorcade) except shots fired from above and behind. There were no hits from the knoll.

Again, viewers of Stone's film will protest: what of the doctors at Dallas's Parkland Hospital, who for years after the shooting insisted that the small neat wound in Kennedy's throat was a wound of entry, inflicted from the front (hence, by another gunman)? What of their insistence, for years, that there was a massive wound of exit in the back, occipital region of his head, where the autopsy doctors had purported to find only a small wound of entry? And most memorably, what of the dramatic thrust of the President's body, backward and "to the left"— Kevin Costner, playing Stone's heroic protagonist, New Orleans District Attorney Jim Garrison, repeats the phrase "to the left" five times, while the gory Zapruder frames show the President, indeed, thrust backward and leftward — a movement consistent only with a hit from the right front?

It is true that several Dallas doctors once thought the throat wound was an entry wound, and said so at the time. And a few of them later recalled massive damage to the back of his head, not on the right side where the autopsy doctors placed the damage. The Dallas doctors agreed that there was no time for a proper "medical examination" of the President; all of their efforts were aimed at saving his life, not examining his wounds. So frenzied were their ministrations that they did not even notice at the time a small wound of entry in his back and a small wound of entry in the back of his head. Later, after the President was peremptorily removed from Dallas to the autopsy in Washington, to the considerable professional chagrin of the Dallas doctors, several of them came to insist that the wound in the throat "looked like" a wound of entry, and that there was a massive default in the rear, occipital, portion of the President's head, a glaring fact somehow missed by the official autopsy team.

Over and again, Stone and the conspiracists refer us to these incongruous comments by the Dallas doctors. What they do not tell us is that these doctors changed their minds when they reviewed the X-rays and the photos taken at the autopsy for a *Nova* documentary on public televison. The evidence in the X-rays and photos is of paramount importance. If the throat wound was an entry wound, that bullet, fired from the right front, would have torn into Kennedy's throat and probably out of the back or side of his neck. Or it would have lodged in the body, causing appropriate damage, all of which would be visible in X-rays and photos. Unless the photos and X-rays are fake, the throat wound is not a wound of entry. Every one of the by now more than twenty forensic pathologists who have examined those documents agrees there was no strike to the throat from the front.

Similarly with regard to the alleged massive wound of exit in the back of Kennedy's head — the result, according to Stone, of a bullet administered from the front right. The X-rays and photos clearly show that that massive wound of exit is on the right side of the head, not in the back, and was caused by a bullet entering in the rear of the skull where a small wound of entry was seen by the autopsy doctors.

Again, this is the conclusion of every one of the prominent forensic pathologists who have studied the photos and X-rays which show the location and nature of the wounds and the pattern of fracturing. Even Dr. Cyril Wecht, one of the stars of the A&E documentary, a frenetic critic of the official version, agreed on this point after examining the X-rays and photos over a two-day period. The Dallas doctors, too, examining these documents for the *Nova* program, agreed that their memory of the wound location had been erroneous.

Stone and the conspiracists, having spent hundreds of hours with the Zapruder film, examining it meticulously, frame by frame, must know all this. In frame 313, when Kennedy is struck in the head, and in subsequent frames, we see a large burst of pink — bone and brain matter — exploding out of the right side of his head, exactly where the X-rays and photos place it; the back of the head, clearly visible in these frames, is unruffled and completely intact. Where then is their theory of a massive rear exit? Robert Groden, one of Stone's technical advisers, has now taken to arguing that the Zapruder films too have been doctored, along with the X-rays and photos.

Well, are the X-rays and photos authentic? As to the photos, the analysis submitted to the House Assassinations Committee by a team of photographic experts found no evidence whatsoever of tampering. Far more important was the detailed report of the team of forensic anthropologists. Studying the photos of the President, fore and aft, the anthropologists meticulously measured the angle of his nasal septum, the lower third of the nose cavity, the nasal tip area, various features of his ear, the lip profile, facial creases, and the network of wrinkles across the back and side of his neck. All of them, when compared to previous, unquestionably valid photos, established that the wounded man in these photos was the dead President and no one else.

The authentication of the X-rays was equally decisive. X-rays are like fingerprints. Since every person has a unique bone structure, it is quite easy for forensic anthropologists to identify the mutilated remains of persons killed in combat or plane crashes. The only thing needed are previous X-rays for comparison; of course, many were available in this instance. Thus, the deviation in Kennedy's nasal septum was noted and compared with his other

JACOB COHEN   441

X-rays. The bony rims around his eyes, the honeycomb air cells of
the mastoid bone, the saddle-shaped depressions at the base of his
skull, the bony projections along the spine — all exactly matched
the comparison X-rays, as did features in the X-rays of Kennedy's
lower torso.

Furthermore, the damage in the photos matched the damage
found in the X-rays. Let us be clear about what this means: these
are X-rays and photos of the damaged President, taken the only
time in his life that he was damaged in that way. If they are phony,
whose body and face are in the fake X-rays and photos? The panel
of experts did not argue that the government was incapable of
contemplating forgery; they argued that such a forgery, even if
contemplated, would be next to impossible: "There can be no
doubt that they are the X-rays of John F. Kennedy, and no other
person."

Why did President Kennedy lurch backward and to the left if he
was struck from behind? Twice now, panels of experts examining
the question — once for the Rockefeller Commission in 1972, yet
again for the House Assassinations Committee — have concluded
that no bullet, by itself, could have caused that physical reaction.
Rather, the motion has been attributed to "a seizurelike neuro-
muscular reaction to major damage inflicted to nerve centers in
the brain." The House panel even assassinated some live goats to
demonstrate the effect.

Let us turn, finally, to the mother of all of Stone's and the other
conspiracists' canards, their account of the so-called magic bullet,
a term so deeply entrenched in discussions of the assassination
that routine newspaper accounts of the latest conspiracy allegations refer to it, without quotation marks, as if it were the God-
given name of the bullet. I have seen Stone's film three times, and
each time Kevin Costner's derisive account of the Warren Commission's supposed position on the subject has brought gasps of incredulous, mutinous laughter from the audience:

> The magic bullet enters the President's back headed downward at an
> angle of 17 degrees; it then moves upward in order to leave Kennedy's
> body from the front of his neck, wound number two, where it waits 1.6
> seconds, presumably in midair, where it turns right then left [right then
> left, Costner repeats] and continues into Connally's body at the rear of

his right armpit, wound number three. The bullet then heads downward at an angle of 27 degrees, shattering Connally's fifth rib, and exiting from the right side of his chest, wound number four. The bullet then turns right and reenters Connally's body at the right wrist, wound number five, shattering the radius bone. The bullet then exits Connally's wrist, wound number six, takes a dramatic U-turn and buries itself into Connally's left thigh, from which it later falls out and is found in almost pristine condition in a corridor of Parkland Hospital.

The Warren Commission, it should be unnecessary to say, argued no such thing. It contended that Kennedy and Connally were struck by the same bullet, somewhere between frames 207 and 223 of the Zapruder film. During that one-second period, the two men disappear behind a road sign. Just before Connally disappears behind the sign, and again a little less than a second — fifteen frames — later when he reappears, his right wrist is close to his lap, directly over his left thigh. He is holding the lid of a big Texas hat, knuckles up. His head has turned to the right — Connally has remembered doing this after hearing a shot (probably the first shot, the one that missed) — and in turning, his shoulders rotate rightward slightly, bringing his body into perfect alignment to receive all five of his wounds. It is only then, when the Commission held the two men were hit, that Connally could have been struck in a way to cause the scars which he indubitably has, to this day.

On three separate occasions in the last twenty years, panels of photographic experts analyzing the Zapruder frames and all the photographs have confirmed this analysis. Using the same evidence, and with the added help of wound locations established by X-rays and photographs, the panel of experts assembled by the House Committee showed that a line drawn through Connally and Kennedy's wounds leads right back, straight as an arrow, to the window from which someone fired Oswald's gun: no turns, no pauses.

Now consider Connally's position when Stone and other conspiracists say he was struck. (Costner: "Connally's turning here now, frame 238, the fourth shot, it misses Kennedy and takes Connally.") As I pointed out in *Commentary* seventeen years ago, in that frame Connally

has turned 90 degrees to the right and is facing out of the side of the car. A bullet striking Connally when the critics say he was hit would then have had to exit from the chest at a downward angle, to have taken two sharp turns upward, in midair — right and then left into the knuckle side of the wrist; and then, upon exiting on the palm side, further up in the air than the wound of entry, would have had to execute a very sharp U-turn into the thigh: plainly impossible.*

In other words, it is not the Warren Commission's account which requires these absurd zigs and zags, it is Stone's.

And the "amost pristine" bullet found "in a corridor" at Parkland Hospital? That bullet, unquestionably fired from Oswald's gun, was found next to Connally's stretcher in the basement of the hospital, exactly where it would be to support the single-bullet theory. It was not pristine; it lacked lead from its core in the amount found in Connally. It was also flattened at one end, and bent at its axis. In 1978, Professor Vincent Guinn, responding to a decade of demands by critics, employed recently improved neutron-activation techniques to compare the traces of antimony, silver, and copper in the lead from the "magic bullet" with the trace amounts of those metals in the lead recovered from Connally's wrist. He concluded that the wrist lead almost certainly came from lead missing from the "magic bullet."

Now, if the bullet found in the basement of Parkland Hospital next to Connally's stretcher, fired from Oswald's gun and missing the very lead found in Connally's wrist, is not the one which struck Connally, how did it get next to his stretcher? Stone suggests that someone from Assassination Central was sent over to drop a spare bullet somewhere in the hospital. Why the basement? Why Connally's stretcher and not Kennedy's? How could the Conspiracy have known where Connally's stretcher would be? How could it have known then that a bullet which had ended in the soft flesh of Connally's thigh needed to be placed with his stretcher in order to confirm a single-bullet theory which was not developed for another two months? And if this was not the bullet that hit Connally, what happened to the bullet that did?

In the film we see colonels and other gray eminences directing the autopsy like puppeteers, ordering doctors to lie about the damage to the President, to silence their curiosity about dangerous matters, and forever. But at that point the Conspiracy could

*"Conspiracy Fever," *Commentary*, October 1975.

not have known what directions to give. The single-bullet theory, to repeat, was not developed until months later, and only an omniscient demon could have figured out so soon what precise changes would be necessary in the autopsy report. When and how did the Conspiracy brief its agents in the autopsy room, and who did the briefing, and who briefed the briefers? It is a shame that Stone did not invent scenes dramatizing all this; they too would have been hilarious.

Similar objections may be raised to the theory developed by David Lifton in a best-selling book and reiterated in the A&E documentary. Kennedy's body, we are told, was taken to a secret laboratory after its arrival in Washington while an elaborate ruse — empty coffins, diversionary caravans — convinced the public that his body was being taken directly to the Bethesda Naval Hospital. With about forty minutes to do their work, the agents of the Conspiracy completely altered the President's wounds to make it look as if he had been hit by one assassin, firing from behind, disguising even the signs of their intervention from the X-rays and photos, although not from Lifton and A&E.

In this version, then, the autopsy itself is honest, only the doctors are working on an altered body. But how could the Conspiracy have known what alterations to make? How could its agents be sure forty minutes would be enough? Scores of people would need to be involved: those who prepared the alternate route, those who switched the body, those who performed the forty-minute surgical miracle, those who carefully brought the body to Bethesda through the back door, those who sent advance news of the nature of the wounds from the Parkland Hospital or the President's plane. And all have remained silent about the matter to this day.

There was, in sum, nothing magic about the "magic bullet." And there was no need to alter the body, no need to fabricate an autopsy. The overwhelming burden of the evidence indicates that one assassin shot the President, just as the Warren Commission said.

III

Was Lee Harvey Oswald that single assassin? Chief Justice Earl Warren, who according to Stone was a perjurer and either a willing or a moronic accomplice to a massive cover-up, said that in a lifetime as a lawyer and judge he had never seen such a clear case of guilt. Here I can only sketch the outline of the case, but even a sketch is sufficient to demonstrate the absurdity of ubiquitous charges that Oswald did not shoot the President, that he was a "patsy" set up to deflect attention from other assassins.

First, there is this pivotal fact: Oswald worked in the building from which the President was shot and obtained the job there, unsuspiciously, three weeks before unsuspicious decisions were made (by Kenneth O'Donnell, Kennedy's friend) which occasioned the President's appearance in front of that building.

Stone tells us in the film that on the day of the assassination the Conspiracy "sent" Oswald to the building. But it did not have to; he reported for work as usual. What Stone does not tell us is that Oswald carried a gun to work that morning. A co-worker who drove him in (Oswald could not drive) reported that Oswald had a long object wrapped in paper which he held from below, cupped in his palm, military style. ("Curtain rods," was Oswald's answer to the obvious question.)

Paper that had been fashioned as a gun carrier was later found on the sixth floor, near the murder window. Oswald's fingerprints were on it, as was his palm print at the base where he would have cupped it in the manner described. Also on the bag were strands of wool from the blanket in which Oswald's rifle had been wrapped. There were no curtain rods. The murder rifle, Oswald's, which fired all the bullets and shells later recovered,* was also found on the sixth floor. On it were strands of wool from Oswald's shirt and Oswald's palm print.† Oswald's finger and palm prints were also on the card boxes used as a gun prop and on the brown bag. (Stone mentions none of this.) In addition, two eyewitnesses who saw the gunman in the window identified Oswald as that gunman.

According to Stone and the conspiracists, the plotters went to extraordinary lengths to link Oswald to a rifle which they also claim was not used. But why not link him to the "real" gun? Viewers may

---

*One wonders how the conspirators recovered and disposed of the embarrassing bullets from the other alleged guns. They could not have known where they would end up. Scores of collaborators would have been needed, at the ready, in the plaza, in the car, in the hospital, to snatch away the damning missiles without being noticed.

†Conspiracists make a good deal of the charge that there were no other prints on the gun. The charge is untrue. The FBI report did not say there were no other prints, it said there were no other "identifiable" prints, which is not unusual. As experts testified, the rough wood stock and poor-quality metal of the gun tended to absorb moisture from the skin, making a clear print unlikely.

remember very brief shots of a photograph of Oswald being altered. These shots are spliced into *JFK*, out of context and narrative
sequence, in order to set the scene for Stone's later contention that
a photograph of Oswald holding the murder rifle and pistol in his
backyard was the crudest of forgeries. In that photo, the conspiracists say, two-thirds of Oswald's face has been pasted onto the chin
and body of a stand-in. A distinct line across the chin shows the intervention clearly, and anyway the shadows cast by the nose are in-
consistent with the shadows cast by the stand-in body.

What Stone does not tell us is that the photo was taken with Oswald's box camera, that his wife remembers taking it, that it is one
of several taken of him with gun and pistol at that time, and that
after exhaustive examination photographic experts employed by
the House Assassinations Committee found even the challenged
photo to be entirely unexceptionable, shadows and all. It also
should be noted that this photo, found among Oswald's effects
after the assassination, is superfluous to the proof that he possessed the gun: there are many other, superior, evidences of that.

Stone scoffs at the rifle, "the worst military weapon in the world."
But the laugh is on him, for the neutron-activation analysis and
ballistics findings prove that this supposedly defective rifle fired
the bullet which deposited lead in Connally's wrist and also the
bullet which hit Kennedy in the skull.* Someone used that rifle
very effectively, and if it was not Oswald, Stone needs to explain
why this brilliant Conspiracy, which used one world-class marksman, gave him the worst weapon in the world. He should also explain why, if the Conspiracy was framing Oswald, it would have
wanted to link him to such a ridiculous weapon.

Oswald left the building immediately after the shooting, retrieved a light-colored jacket and pistol from his rooming house,
and about forty-five minutes after the assassination was seen
shooting a Dallas policeman named Tippit. Twelve eyewitnesses
identify Oswald as Tippit's assailant — although, to be sure, a few
others, the ones presented by Stone and the A&E documentary,

*The traces of silver and antimony in the lead removed from Kennedy's brain were
compared to traces in the lead found in bullet fragments, fired from Oswald's gun,
which were recovered from the presidential limousine. Again, as was the case with
Connally's wrist, the match was perfect.

do not. The shells expended at the scene and the bullets in Tippit match the pistol found on Oswald when he was arrested. His jacket was found nearby. When the eyewitnesses reported the shooting to the police, using the radio in Tippit's car, police swarmed to the area. After a phoned report to them that a man had been seen ducking into a theater without paying, they rushed to the theater and arrested Oswald, who resisted, for the murder of Tippit. On him was the murder pistol; he had ordered it by mail, ten months earlier.

Astonishingly, Stone and many other conspiracists even question the contention that Oswald shot Tippit. Citing inconsistencies in eyewitness reports, which are to be expected in nearly all such reports, they imply that the bullets and shells were a plant, that the real ones were removed, that the jacket was a plant, and that the narrative by which the police traced Oswald to the theater was a contrived fiction.

What may have happened, according to Stone and the others, is that the Dallas police were expecting Oswald at the theater. They would murder someone in the neighbohood, a Dallas policeman murdered with the cooperation of Dallas policemen, and they would blame it on Oswald, presumably to prove that he was a murdering sort. The reader is invited to recapitulate the planning which would need to go into this part of the Conspiracy, involving now new bullet-snatchers and -replacers in the Dallas police, the elimination of anyone who could prove that Oswald was elsewhere than next to Tippit's car when the officer was shot, etc. Of course, all parties to this part of the Conspiracy have remained silent ever since.

It is often asked why Oswald denied having killed the President, as though guilty people do not deny things all the time. The fact is that Oswald denied everything. He himself was the first to insist that the backyard photo of him with the gun was a forgery. Shown it during his interrogation, he dismissed it at a glance. He denied having hunted in this country; he denied possessing the rifle, any rifle; he denied ever using the pseudonym Alec Hidell, which he had used to order the guns and on several identification documents; he made up an easily contradicted story that the manager of the Depository brought a rifle to the building; he denied the curtain rod tale, saying he carried only his lunch to work that morning; he denied killing Tippit; when asked his reason for visiting his estranged wife and children on Thursday, assassination eve, rather than his usual Friday, he made up a story about a birthday party; he denied using an alias at his rooming house. He also refused to take a polygraph test. The law familiarly says that lies of this sort indicate a "consciousness of guilt," especially if they are explicable only by the hypothesis that the accused knows he is guilty.

To sum up: Oswald (1) worked in the building which was the only source of shots; (2) owned and possessed the one and only murder rifle; (3) brought it to work with him the morning of the murder; (4) was at the murder window at the time the President was shot; (5) left the scene immediately after the shooting; (6) shot an officer who attempted to question him and then forcibly resisted arrest; (7) lied about crucial matters of fact when interrogated.

There is an eighth reason to believe he was the killer: this was not his first assassination attempt. Among the photographs in Oswald's effects were several of a house and adjoining driveway. Weeks after the assassination, the FBI discovered that the house in the photo was that of General Edwin Walker, a right-wing, anti-Castro, anti-civil rights fanatic. The G-men irrefutably established the exact date the photo was taken, which turned out to be just before someone unsuccessfully tried to assassinate Walker on April 10, 1963. The photo was taken with Oswald's camera; Oswald had a collection of news stories about the assassination attempt; bullets that had slammed into Walker's wall were consistent with Oswald's gun; a note written to his wife at the time, and her suspicions voiced then as well, indicate that he was Walker's would-be assassin. In the Marines he had twice been court-martialed, once for threatening a superior officer. Needless to say, Oliver Stone tells us nothing of this.

Why would Oswald try to kill a right-wing general? An obvious hypothesis, the one Stone and the critics feverishly try to silence, is that the attempt had something to do with Oswald's intense left-wing sympathies. Stone's campaign to transform him into a long-term right-winger, in league with Castro-hating activists, involves biographical surgery even more radical than the surgery which allegedly transformed the President's wounds the night of the assassination.

Oswald was already a left-winger at the age of thirteen when he distributed pro-Rosenberg material in New York. He defected to the Soviet Union and attempted to commit suicide when, notwithstanding his offer of radar data, the land of his dreams refused him citizenship. Disillusioned with the Soviet Union, he returned to the United States and transferred his fantasies to a new hero, Castro, whose picture he kept by his bed. He monitored radio broadcasts from Havana on his shortwave radio.

Oswald subscribed to the Communist *Daily Worker* and the Trotskyist *Militant;* these are the newspapers he holds in the authentic photos of him with gun and pistol taken in his backyard. He formed a one-person chapter of the pro–Castro Fair Play for Cuba Committee (FPCC), handed out FPCC leaflets, which he himself printed, and spoke on the radio in its behalf. Imagining himself a Castro operative, and acting alone, as always, he briefly attempted to infiltrate an anti-Castro group in New Orleans but then immediately revealed his pro-Castro sympathies, to the group's considerable dismay. He composed a schmaltzy and horrifically spelled "historic diary," as he called it, and several paeans to Marxism. He visited the Cuban and Russian embassies in Mexico City in October 1963, seeking a visa to Cuba, and reacted in fury when denied his request.

This recital only scratches the surface of Oswald's left-wing record and his unstable, lone-wolf personality. But it is enough to sustain at least the possibility that the sole assassin of John F. Kennedy was a left-wing fantasist who found himself working in a building in front of which would come the President of the United States, the man whom Castro had publicly named as responsible for assassination attempts on his, Castro's life. The same fantasist who went to the Soviet Union expecting to be accepted as a hero (and told his Russian wife that someday he would be "president of the world") now thought, incoherently, stupidly, that he would become a hero in Cuba as the assassin of Castro's enemies: General Walker and President Kennedy. Character, as the Greeks said, is fate.

IV

If there was only one assassin and he was Lee Harvey Oswald, if there was no massive frame-up or cover-up, then Stone's and every other conspiracy theory currently before the public are fatally wounded. The government's allegedly ubiquitous hand disappears. Absent that hand, what other grand conspirators — military industrialists, mafiosi — would use so unlikely a killer, stage so unlikely a killing?

For nearly thirty years, platoons of conspiracists have concertedly scavenged the record, floating their appalling and thrilling
might-have-beens, unfazed by the contradictions and absurdities
in their own wantonly selective accounts, often consciously, cunningly deceitful. They have refused to let go of any shred of their
earliest suspicions, even when these have been demolished by decisive scientific findings. And the media have patronized them, for
journalists love their thrilling insinuations and share many of their
philosophical and political assumptions; and with regard to the assassination, they remain stone ignorant. Small wonder that 85 percent of the American public thinks there was a conspiracy of some
sort.

Recently, thirteen thousand copies of a new study guide, sympathetic to *JFK*, were sent to American high school teachers. Our students know nothing about the case or the times. Their teachers
remember little, and many of them, especially the most "liberated," hold the view that to *question* any official version of anything
is important in and of itself, even if the questions are based on palpable falsehoods. I do not think we should rejoice that our children ask questions in this manner. I think we should weep; and
scold the scurrilous.

Reflections and Responses

1. Note that Cohen refers to Oliver Stone's *JFK* in his opening sentence as "notorious." What other terms might he have used? Why
did he not write "famous" or "controversial"?

2. According to Cohen, what does "nearly every conspiracy theory
extant" have in common? How important is this commonality to
Cohen's argument? Can you think of any theory of the assassination that would substantially differ from the commonly held theories?

3. Oliver Stone's film represents just one of a multitude of con-
spiracist theories. Why do you think Cohen devotes so much of his
attention to it? What elements of the film disturb him the most?

VICKI HEARNE

What's Wrong with Animal Rights

When people argue for the rights of animals, what exactly do they mean by "rights"? Does their definition of animal rights take into account the "certain unalienable rights" that Thomas Jefferson wrote into the Declaration of Independence—the right to "life, liberty and the pursuit of happiness"? In the following essay, Vicki Hearne skillfully combines personal and professional experience with philosophical reflections on happiness as she builds a case against the reductive view of animals that typifies the animal-rights movement. In Hearne's opinion, the problem with animal-rights advocates is not that they take their position too far; "it's that they've got it all wrong."

An active professional dog trainer and Yale University professor, Hearne is the author of two volumes of poetry, Nervous Horses *(1980) and* In the Absence of Horses *(1983), and two books of essays,* Adam's Task: Calling Animals by Name *(1986) and* Bandit: Dossier of a Dangerous Dog *(1992). A collection of prose,* Animal Happiness, *was published in 1994. "What's Wrong with Animal Rights" originally appeared in* Harper's Magazine *in 1991 and was selected by Susan Sontag for* The Best American Essays 1992.

Not all happy animals are alike. A Doberman going over a hurdle after a small wooden dumbbell is sleek, all arcs of harmonious power. A basset hound cheerfully performing the same exercise exhibits harmonies of a more lugubrious nature. There are chimpanzees who love precision the way musicians or fanatical housekeepers or accomplished hypochondriacs do; others for whom happiness is a matter of invention and variation — chimp vaudevil-

lians. There is a rhinoceros whose happiness, as near as I can make
out, is in needing to be trained every morning, all over again, or
else he "forgets" his circus routine, and in this you find a clue to
the slow, deep, quiet chuckle of his happiness and to the glory
of the beast. Happiness for Secretariat is in his ebullient bound,
that joyful length of stride. For the draft horse or the weight-pull
dog, happiness is of a different shape, more awesome and less obviously intelligent. When the pulling horse is at its most intense,
the animal goes into himself, allocating all of the educated power
that organizes his desire to dwell in fierce and delicate intimacy
with that power, leans into the harness, and MAKES THAT SUCKER
MOVE.

If we are speaking of human beings and use the phrase "animal
happiness," we tend to mean something like "creature comforts."
The emblems of this are the golden retriever rolling in the grass,
the horse with his nose deep in the oats, the kitty by the fire. Creature comforts are important to animals — "Grub first, then ethics"
is a motto that would describe many a wise Labrador retriever, and
I have a pit bull named Annie whose continual quest for the perfect pillow inspires her to awesome feats. But there is something
more to animals, a capacity for satisfactions that come from work
in the fullest sense — what is known in philosophy and in this
country's Declaration of Independence as "happiness." This is a
sense of personal achievement, like the satisfaction felt by a good
wood-carver or a dancer or a poet or an accomplished dressage
horse. It is a happiness that, like the artist's, must come from something within the animal, something trainers call "talent." Hence, it
cannot be imposed on the animal. But it is also something that
does not come *ex nihilo.** If it had not been a fairly ordinary thing,
in one part of the world, to teach young children to play the pi-
anoforte, it is doubtful that Mozart's music would exist.

Happiness is often misunderstood as a synonym for pleasure or
as an antonym for suffering. But Aristotle associated happiness
with ethics — codes of behavior that urge us toward the sensation
of getting it right, a kind of work that yields the "click" of satisfaction upon solving a problem or surmounting an obstacle. In his
Ethics, Aristotle wrote, "If happiness is activity in accordance with
excellence, it is reasonable that it should be in accordance with

*ex nihilo: Latin, "out of nothing."

the highest excellence." Thomas Jefferson identified the capacity for happiness as one of the three fundamental rights on which all others are based: "life, liberty, and the pursuit of happiness."

I bring up this idea of happiness as a form of work because I am an animal trainer, and work is the foundation of the happiness a trainer and an animal discover together. I bring up these words also because they cannot be found in the lexicon of the animal-rights movement. This absence accounts for the uneasiness toward the movement of most people, who sense that rights advocates have a point but take it too far when they liberate snails or charge that goldfish at the county fair are suffering. But the problem with the animal-rights advocates is not that they take it too far; it's that they've got it all wrong.

Animal rights are built upon a misconceived premise that rights were created to prevent us from unnecessary suffering. You can't find an animal-rights book, video, pamphlet, or rock concert in which someone doesn't mention the Great Sentence, written by Jeremy Bentham* in 1789. Arguing in favor of such rights, Bentham wrote: "The question is not, Can they *reason?* nor, can they *talk?* but, can they suffer?"

The logic of the animal-rights movement places suffering at the iconographic center of a skewed value system. The thinking of its proponents — given eerie expression in a virtually sadoporno-graphic sculpture of a tortured monkey that won a prize for its compassionate vision — has collapsed into a perverse conundrum. Today the loudest voices calling for — demanding — the destruc-tion of animals are the humane organizations. This is an inevitable consequence of the apotheosis of the drive to relieve suffering: death is the ultimate release. To compensate for their contradic-tions, the humane movement has demonized, in this century and the last, those who made animal happiness their business: veteri-narians, trainers, and the like. We think of Louis Pasteur as the man whose work saved you and me and your dog and cat from ra-bies, but antivivisectionists of the time claimed that rabies in-creased in areas where there were Pasteur Institutes.

An anti-rabies public relations campaign mounted in England in the 1880s by the Royal Society for the Prevention of Cruelty to

*Jeremy Bentham: British philosopher and social reformer (1748–1832) whose *In-troduction to the Principles of Morals and Legislation* appeared in 1789.

Animals and other organizations led to orders being issued to club any dog found not wearing a muzzle. England still has her cruel and unnecessary law that requires an animal to spend six months in quarantine before being allowed loose in the country. Most of the recent propaganda about pit bulls — the crazy claim that they "take hold with their front teeth while they chew away with their rear teeth" (which would imply, incorrectly, that they have double jaws) — can be traced to literature published by the Humane Society of the United States during the fall of 1987 and earlier. If your neighbors want your dog or horse impounded and destroyed because he is a nuisance — say the dog barks, or the horse attracts flies — it will be the local Humane Society to whom your neighbors turn for action.

In a way, everyone has the opportunity to know that the history of the humane movement is largely a history of miseries, arrests, prosecutions, and death. The Humane Society is the pound, the place with the decompression chamber or the lethal injections. You occasionally find worried letters about this in Ann Landers's column.

Animal-rights publications are illustrated largely with photographs of two kinds of animals — "Helpless Fluff" and "Agonized Fluff," the two conditions in which some people seem to prefer their animals, because any other version of an animal is too complicated for propaganda. In the introduction to his book *Animal Liberation,* Peter Singer says somewhat smugly that he and his wife have no animals and, in fact, don't much care for them. This is offered as evidence of his objectivity and ethical probity. But it strikes me as an odd, perhaps obscene underpinning for an ethical project that encourages university and high school students to cherish their ignorance of, say, great bird dogs as proof of their devotion to animals.

I would like to leave these philosophers behind, for they are inept connoisseurs of suffering who might revere my Airedale for his capacity to scream when subjected to a blowtorch but not for his wit and courage, not for his natural good manners that are a gentle rebuke to ours. I want to celebrate the moment not long ago when, at his first dog show, my Airedale, Drummer, learned that there can be a public place where his work is respected. I want to celebrate his meticulousness, his happiness upon realizing at the dog show that no one would swoop down upon him and swamp him with the goo-goo excesses known as the "teddy-bear complex" but that people actually got out of his way, gave him room to work. I want to say, "There can be a six-and-a-half-month-old puppy who can care about accuracy, who can be fastidious, and whose fastidiousness will be a foundation for courage later." I want to say, "Leave my puppy alone!"

I want to leave the philosophers behind, but I cannot, in part because the philosophical problems that plague academicians of the animal-rights movement are illuminating. They wonder, do animals have rights or do they have interests? Or, if these rightists lead particularly unexamined lives, they dismiss that question as obvious (yes, of course animals have rights, prima facie) and proceed to enumerate them, James Madison style. This leads to the issuance of bills of rights — the right to an environment, the right not to be used in medical experiments — and other forms of trivialization.

The calculus of suffering can be turned against the philosophers of festering flesh, even in the case of food animals, or exotic animals who perform in movies and circuses. It is true that it hurts to be slaughtered by man, but it doesn't hurt nearly as much as some of the cunningly cruel arrangements meted out by "Mother Nature." In Africa, 75 percent of the lions cubbed do not survive to the age of two. For those who make it to two, the average age at death is ten years. Asali, the movie and TV lioness, was still working at age twenty-one. There are fates worse than death, but twenty-one years of a close working relationship with Hubert Wells, Asali's trainer, is not one of them. Dorset sheep and polled Herefords would not exist at all were they not in a symbiotic relationship with human beings.

A human being living in the "wild"— somewhere, say, without the benefits of medicine and advanced social organization — would probably have a life expectancy of from thirty to thirty-five years. A human being living in "captivity"— in, say, a middle-class neighborhood of what the Centers for Disease Control call a Metropolitan Statistical Area — has a life expectancy of seventy or more years. For orangutans in the wild in Borneo and Malaysia, the life expectancy is thirty-five years; in captivity, fifty years. The wild is not a suffering-free zone or all that frolicsome a location.

The questions asked by animal-rights activists are flawed, because they are built on the concept that the origin of rights is in the avoidance of suffering rather than in the pursuit of happiness. The question that needs to be asked — and that will put us in closer proximity to the truth — is not, do they have rights? or, what are those rights? but rather, what is a right?

Rights originate in committed relationships and can be found, both intact and violated, wherever one finds such relationships — in social compacts, within families, between animals, and between people and nonhuman animals. This is as true when the nonhuman animals in question are lions or parakeets as when they are dogs. It is my Airedale whose excellencies have my attention at the moment, so it is with reference to him that I will consider the question, what is a right?

When I imagine situations in which it naturally arises that A defends or honors or respects B's rights, I imagine situations in which the relationship between A and B can be indicated with a possessive pronoun. I might say, "Leave her alone, she's my daughter" or "That's what she wants, and she is my daughter. I think I am bound to honor her wants." Similarly, "Leave her alone, she's my mother." I am more tender of the happiness of my mother, my father, my child, than I am of other people's family members; more tender of my friends' happinesses than your friends' happinesses, unless you and I have a mutual friend.

Possession of a being by another has come into more and more disrepute, so that the common understanding of one person possessing another is slavery. But the important detail about the kind of possessive pronoun that I have in mind is reciprocity: if I have a friend, she has a friend. If I have a daughter, she has a mother. The possessive does not bind one of us while freeing the other; it cannot do that. Moreover, should the mother reject the daughter, the word that applies is "disown." The form of disowning that most often appears in the news is domestic violence. Parents abuse children; husbands batter wives.

Some cases of reciprocal possessives have built-in limitations, such as "my patient/my doctor" or "my student/my teacher" or "my agent/my client." Other possessive relations are extremely limited but still remarkably binding: "my neighbor" and "my country" and "my president."

The responsibilities and the ties signaled by reciprocal possession typically are hard to dissolve. It can be as difficult to give up an enemy as to give up a friend, and often the one becomes the other, as though the logic of the possessive pronoun outlasts the forms it chanced to take at a given moment, as though we were stuck with one another. In these bindings, nearly inextricable, are found the origin of our rights. They imply a possessiveness but also recognize an acknowledgment by each side of the other's existence.

The idea of democracy is dependent on the citizens' having knowledge of the government; that is, realizing that the government exists and knowing how to claim rights against it. I know this much because I get mail from the government and see its "representatives" running about in uniforms. Whether I actually have any rights in relationship to the government is less clear, but the idea that I do is symbolized by the right to vote. I obey the government, and, in theory, it obeys me, by counting my ballot, reading the *Miranda* warning to me, agreeing to be bound by the Constitution. My friend obeys me as I obey her; the government "obeys" me to some extent, and, to a different extent, I obey it.

What kind of thing can my Airedale, Drummer, have knowledge of? He can know that I exist and through that knowledge can claim his happinesses, with varying degrees of success, both with me and against me. Drummer can also know about larger human or dog communities than the one that consists only of him and me. There is my household — the other dogs, the cats, my husband. I have had enough dogs on campuses to know that he can learn that Yale exists as a neighborhood or village. My older dog, Annie, not only knows that Yale exists but can tell Yalies from townies, as I learned while teaching there during labor troubles.

Dogs can have elaborate conceptions of human social structures, and even of something like their rights and responsibilities within them, but these conceptions are never elaborate enough to construct a rights relationship between a dog and the state, or a dog and the Humane Society. Both of these are concepts that depend on writing and memoranda, officers in uniform, plaques and seals of authority. All of these are literary constructs, and all of them are beyond a dog's ken, which is why the mail carrier who doesn't also happen to be a dog's friend is forever an intruder — this is why dogs bark at mailmen.

It is clear enough that natural rights relations can arise between people and animals. Drummer, for example, can insist, "Hey, let's go outside and do something!" if I have been at my computer several days on end. He can both refuse to accept various of my suggestions and tell me when he fears for his life — such as the time when the huge, white flapping flag appeared out of nowhere, as it seemed to him, on the town green one evening when we were working. I can (and do) say to him either, "Oh, you don't have to worry about that" or, "Uh oh, you're right, Drum, that guy looks dangerous." Just as the government and I — two different species of organism — have developed improvised ways of communicating, such as the vote, so Drummer and I have worked out a number of ways to make our expressions known. Largely through obedience, I have taught him a fair amount about how to get responses from me. Obedience is reciprocal; you cannot get responses from a dog to whom you do not respond accurately. I have enfranchised him in a relationship to me by educating him, creating the conditions by which he can achieve a certain happiness specific to a dog, maybe even specific to an Airedale, inasmuch as this same relationship has allowed me to plumb the happiness of being a trainer and writing this article.

Instructions in this happiness are given terms that are alien to a culture in which liver treats, fluffy windup toys, and miniature sweaters are confused with respect and work. Jack Knox, a sheepdog trainer originally from Scotland, will shake his crook at a novice handler who makes a promiscuous move to praise a dog, and will call out in his Scottish accent, "Eh! Eh! Get back, get BACK! Ye'll no be abusin' the dogs like that in my clinic." America is a nation of abused animals, Knox says, because we are always swooping at them with praise, "no gi'ing them their freedom." I am reminded of Rainer Maria Rilke's* account in which the Prodigal Son leaves — has to leave — because everyone loves him, even the dogs love him, and he has no path to the delicate and fierce truth of himself. Unconditional praise and love, in Rilke's story, disenfranchise us, distract us from what truly excites our interest.

In the minds of some trainers and handlers, praise is dishonesty. Paradoxically, it is a kind of contempt for animals that masquer-

---

*Rainer Maria Rilke: Austrian lyric poet (1875–1926).

ades as a reverence for helplessness and suffering. The idea of freedom means that you do not, at least not while Jack Knox is nearby, helpfully guide your dog through the motions of, say, herding over and over — what one trainer calls "explainy-wainy." This is rote learning. It works tolerably well on some handlers, because people have vast unconscious minds and can store complex preprogrammed behaviors. Dogs, on the other hand, have almost no unconscious minds, so they can learn only by thinking. Many children are like this until educated out of it.

If I tell my Airedale to sit and stay on the town green, and someone comes up and burbles, "What a pretty thing you are," he may break his stay to go for a caress. I pull him back and correct him for breaking. Now he holds his stay because I have blocked his way to movement but not because I have punished him. (A correction blocks one path as it opens another for desire to work; punishment blocks desire and opens nothing.) He holds his stay now, and — because the stay opens this possibility of work, new to a heedless young dog — he watches. If the person goes on talking, and isn't going to gush with praise, I may heel Drummer out of his stay and give him an "Okay" to make friends. Sometimes something about the person makes Drummer feel that reserve is in order. He responds to an insincere approach by sitting still, going down into himself, and thinking, "This person has no business pawing me. I'll sit very still, and he will go away." If the person doesn't take the hint from Drummer, I'll give the pup a little backup by saying, "Please don't pet him, he's working," even though he was not under any command.

The pup reads this, and there is a flicker of a working trust now stirring in the dog. Is the pup grateful? When the stranger leaves, does he lick my hand, full of submissive blandishments? This one doesn't. This one says nothing at all, and I say nothing much to him. This is a working trust we are developing, not a mutual congratulation society. My backup is praise enough for him; the use he makes of my support is praise enough for me.

Listening to a dog is often praise enough. Suppose it is just after dark and we are outside. Suddenly there is a shout from the house. The pup and I both look toward the shout and then toward each other: "What do you think?" I don't so much as cock my head, because Drummer is growing up, and I want to know what he thinks.

He takes a few steps toward the house, and I follow. He listens again and comprehends that it's just Holly, who at fourteen is much given to alarming cries and shouts. He shrugs at me and goes about his business. I say nothing. To praise him for this performance would make about as much sense as praising a human being for the same thing. Thus:

A. What's that?
B. I don't know. [Listens] Oh, it's just Holly.
A. What a gooooooood human being!
B. Huh?

    This is one small moment in a series of like moments that will culminate in an Airedale who on a Friday will have the discrimination and confidence required to take down a man who is attacking me with a knife and on Saturday clown and play with the children at the annual Orange Empire Dog Club Christmas party.

People who claim to speak for animal rights are increasingly devoted to the idea that the very keeping of a dog or a horse or a gerbil or a lion is in and of itself an offense. The more loudly they speak, the less likely they are to be in a rights relation to any given animal, because they are spending so much time in airplanes or transmitting fax announcements of the latest Sylvester Stallone anti-fur rally. In a 1988 *Harper's* forum, for example, Ingrid Newkirk, the national director of People for the Ethical Treatment of Animals, urged that domestic pets be spayed and neutered and ultimately phased out. She prefers, it appears, wolves — and wolves someplace else — to Airedales and, by a logic whose interior structure is both emotionally and intellectually forever closed to Drummer, claims thereby to be speaking for "animal rights."

    She is wrong. I am the only one who can own up to my Airedale's inalienable rights. Whether or not I do it perfectly at any given moment is no more refutation of this point than whether I am perfectly my husband's mate at any given moment refutes the fact of marriage. Only people who know Drummer, and whom he can know, are capable of this relationship. PETA and the Humane Society and the ASPCA and the Congress and NOW — as institutions — do have the power to affect my ability to grant rights to

Drummer but are otherwise incapable of creating conditions or laws or rights that would increase his happiness. Only Drummer's owner has the power to obey him — to obey who he is and what he is capable of — deeply enough to grant him his rights and open up the possibility of happiness.

Reflections and Responses

1. How does Hearne define happiness? What is its relation to work? Why, in her opinion, are the interrelated concepts of happiness and work not "in the lexicon of the animal-rights movement"?

2. Why does Hearne bring up the life-expectancy statistics of animals living "in the wild"? In what way do these statistics reinforce her argument? How might an animal-rights advocate respond to her use and interpretation of these statistics?

3. The Declaration of Independence reads: "We hold these truths to be self-evident, that all men are created equal, that they are endowed by their Creator with certain unalienable rights, that among these are life, liberty and the pursuit of happiness." Do you think Hearne legitimately or illegitimately extends Jefferson's words to apply to nonhumans? Explain your position.

Alternative Arrangements

Rhetorical Modes

Any distinguished essay will demonstrate a wide variety of rhetorical techniques. The essays in this volume are no exception. The following classification is designed for those who want to isolate a rhetorical strategy for observation and analysis. The five essays listed under each category were chosen because they distinctly and conveniently show a particular rhetorical mode in action.

ANALYZING CAUSES

CONSTRUCTING ARGUMENTS

Some Literary and Journalistic Techniques

As noted in the Introduction, the contemporary essay can be considered in terms of both literature and journalism. Some of the essays in this volume offer excellent models of the essay as a literary form, while others illustrate the art and craft of reportage. The following arrangement focuses on some of the most important features of both kinds of writing.

MOSAIC STRUCTURES

INTERVIEW AND QUOTATION

RESEARCH AND INFORMATION

Contemporary Issues

The essays in this volume are organized around seven primary themes. However, selections across the chapters share other thematic relationships as well. The following arrangement provides possibilities for linking these essays by their topics of contemporary interest.

CLASS VALUES

CULTURAL ANALYSIS

SPEECH AND SILENCE

RIGHTS AND REFORM

Index of Authors